Self-Determination and Secession in Africa

T0320190

This book provides a unique comparative study of the major secessionist and self-determination movements in post-colonial Africa, examining theory, international law, charters of the United Nations, and the Organisation of African Unity (OAU)/African Union's (AU) stance on the issue. The book explores whether self-determination and secessionism lead to peace, stability, development and democratisation in conflict-ridden societies, particularly looking at the outcomes in Eritrea and South Sudan.

The book covers all the major attempts at self-determination and secession on the continent, extensively analysing the geo-political, economic, security and ideological factors that determine the outcome of the quest for self-determination and secession. It reveals the lack of inherent clarity in international law, social science theories, the OAU/AU Charter, UN charters and international conventions concerning the topic.

This is a major contribution to the field and highly relevant for researchers and postgraduate students in African Studies, Development Studies, African Politics and History, and Anthropology.

Redie Bereketeab is Associate Professor of Sociology and a senior researcher at the Nordic Africa Institute, Uppsala, Sweden.

This is a seminal text on a theme often neglected and misunderstood in modernist discussions: the construction in Africa of viable states after the colonial era. A rich selection of chapters chart various paths towards self-determination, with a particular focus on secession and the reconfiguration of states. Here we see the roots of civil wars (as in Sudan and Nigeria), big power interventions (as in Somalia) and ongoing decolonisation (as in the Western Sahara). Broader themes emerge that will be of interest to students of post-colonial studies and human rights in development as well as African studies.'

Tim Anderson, University of Sydney, Australia

Self-Determination and Secession in Africa

The post-colonial state

Edited by
Redie Bereketeab

Routledge
Taylor & Francis Group

LONDON AND NEW YORK

First published 2015 by Routledge

2 Park Square, Milton Park, Abingdon, Oxon OX14 4RN

711 Third Avenue, New York, NY 10017, USA

First issued in paperback 2016

Routledge is an imprint of the Taylor & Francis Group, an informa business

British Library Cataloguing-in-Publication Data
A catalogue record for this book is available from the British Library

Library of Congress Cataloging-in-Publication Data
Self-determination and secession in Africa : the post-colonial state / [edited by] Redie Bereketeab.
    pages cm
    Includes bibliographical references.
    1. Self-determination, National–Africa. 2. Africa–politics and government–1960–
    3. Secession–Africa. 4. Africa–History–Autonomy and independence movements.
    5. Decolonization–Africa. I. Bereketeab, Redie, editor of compilation, author.
    DT30.5.S458 2014
    320.15096—dc23
    2014006843

ISBN-13: 978-1-138-79081-0 (hbk)

ISBN-13: 978-1-138-65973-5 (pbk)

Typeset in Goudy
by Swales & Willis, Exeter, Devon

Contents

Figures and tables

Figures

Tables

Contributors

Ladan Affi is a researcher at the Department of International Affairs at Qatar University, where she is working on a multi-year project on piracy in the Horn of Africa. She has taught and lectured at many universities in the US and in the Horn of Africa. She has a Ph.D. in political science from the University of Wisconsin-Madison.

Adam Haji-Ali Ahmed is an academic, practising lawyer and conflict resolution practitioner with a specialisation in international law and human rights (MA) from the UN-mandated University for Peace. He holds an LL B, BA, PGD-IPR (Postgraduate Diploma in Information Technology Law and Intellectual Property Rights) and EMBA (in human resource management). He is the Director of the Institute of Peace and Conflict Studies (IPCS), University of Hargeisa (UoH). Before he became the Director of IPCS, he was Assistant Dean of the Faculty of Law, University of Hargeisa, for about six years, and the Chairperson of Somaliland Non State Actors Forum (SONSAF) for two years. He has published several articles.

Redie Bereketeab is an associate professor of sociology. Currently he is working as a senior researcher at the Nordic Africa Institute, where he runs a research project on conflict and state building in the Horn of Africa. He is the author of several books, articles and book chapters. His latest publications include *The Horn of Africa: Intra-State and Inter-State Conflicts and Security* (ed.) (Pluto Books, 2013) and *Revisiting the Eritrean National Liberation Movement, 1961– 1991: Understanding, Interpretation and Critique* (Red Sea Press, 2014). His research interests include: political sociology, development sociology, nations, nationalism, identity, states, state building, governance and conflict.

Abdirahman Yusuf Duale (Bobe) was a lead figure in Somali politics for many years before retiring from his post as Minister of Information of Somaliland in 2012. Before that, he served a long tenure as the Deputy Executive Director of the Hargeisa-based think tank the Academy for Peace and Development. During the time of the Siyad Barre regime in Somalia, he served as the chief editor of the Somali Revolutionary Socialist Party's publication *The Struggle*, the Secretary of Information and a member of the Central Committee of the

Somali National Movement (SNM), later becoming Minister of State for Foreign Affairs of the newly liberated Republic of Somaliland. He has researched
and published numerous works on Somali culture, tradition, poetry, media and
politics.

Ole Martin Gaasholt is an independent researcher with a sustained interest
in Northern Mali and the Tuareg since the rebellion of the 1990s. His academic specialisation is in the field of politics and conflict, particularly as it
relates to this region and to the Tuareg and neighbouring Sahelian peoples.
He holds a Ph.D. in anthropology from the School of Oriental and African
Studies. During extensive fieldwork in the area he has studied democratisation and decentralisation, socio-political organisation, ethnicity and conflict resolution. In recent years he has been engaged in academic, policy and
popularising work regarding Northern Mali, particularly in the context of
the latest conflicts.

Belkacem Iratni is currently Dean of the Faculty of Political Sciences and International Relations, University of Algiers, where he has been teaching since
1989. He also taught at the Ecole Nationale d'Administration (ENA) in
Algiers in 1992–94 and the Institute of Diplomatic Studies and International
Relations (2003–05) and worked as a research associate at the National Institute of Strategic and Global Studies (INESG). He was a member of a team
of experts of the Peace and Security Council of the African Union in 2010.
He has conducted numerous research studies and published several articles on
Algeria's foreign policy and Maghreb politics, as well as on security aspects in
the Mediterranean and Sahel–Saharan region.

Dan Kuwali is a postdoctoral fellow at the Centre for Human Rights, Faculty
of Law, University of Pretoria and an associate professor of law, Centre for
Security Studies, Mzuzu University, Malawi. He is also a fellow at the Centre
for Human Rights Policy, Harvard Kennedy School of Government, Harvard
University and worked as a senior researcher, Centre for Conflict Resolution,
University of Cape Town and also as a division legal adviser in the then United
Nations Mission in the Democratic Republic of the Congo (MONUC).

Tukumbi Lumumba-Kasongo is Professor of Political Science (International
Relations, International Political Economy and Comparative Politics) at Wells
College. He is Chair of the Department of International Studies at Wells College. He is a visiting scholar in the Department of City and Regional Planning at Cornell University. Since 2006, he has been an adjunct professor of
government at Suffolk University. Previously, he has taught political science
at several universities and colleges. His research and teaching areas include
comparative politics, international political economy, international relations,
environmental issues, North–South and South–South relations, Asia, Europe,
South America and Africa. He has published many books, book chapters and
peer-reviewed articles. He is the editor-in-chief of *African and Asian Studies*,
published by Brill in the Netherlands, and co-editor of the *African Journal of*

International Affairs, published by the Council for the Development of Social Research in Africa (CODESRIA).

Francis A. S. T. Matambalya is Professor of International Trade and Marketing at the University of Dar es Salaam, where he has taught for over 15 years. His professional work centres largely on international trade and economic diplomacy, industrial development, and management. He is the author of nine books and editor of two. He is also the author of over 25 scholarly papers in professional journals, as well as many policy papers and reports, chapters in edited volumes, research reports, and discussion or working papers. Currently he works as a senior researcher at the Nordic Africa Institute.

Henning Melber is Director Emeritus of the Dag Hammarskjöld Foundation in Uppsala, Sweden and an extraordinary professor at the Department of Political Sciences, University of Pretoria and at the Centre for Africa Studies at the University of the Free State in Bloemfontein, South Africa.

Kidane Mengisteab is Professor of African Studies and Political Science and Director of the African Studies Program at the Pennsylvania State University. Among his current research interests are conflict resolution and democratisation in contemporary Africa, the relevance of African 'traditional' institutions of governance, and the socio-economic implications of the expansion of extractive industries and commercial farming in Africa. He is author or editor of several books on Africa. His most recent book is *The Horn of Africa: Hot Spot in the Global System* (Polity, 2014). He is currently editing a book on African traditional institutional systems and their implications for the continent's democratic transformation.

Leben Nelson Moro, D.Phil is Director of External Relations at the University of Juba, and teaches graduate courses in the areas of development, conflict, forced migration and humanitarian affairs at the University's Centre for Peace and Development Studies. He primarily conducts research on development-induced displacement and resettlement, focusing on oil, conflict and displacement in South Sudan. Some of the findings of his studies have appeared in the *Journal of Refugee Studies* (Oxford University), *St Anthony's International Review* (Oxford University), *Forced Migration Review* (Oxford University), *New Internationalist* and *Pambazuka News*.

Cyril Obi is a programme director at the Social Science Research Council (SSRC) and leads the African Peacebuilding Network (APN) programme. He is also a research associate of the Department of Political Sciences, University of Pretoria, South Africa and a visiting scholar to the Institute of African Studies (IAS), Columbia University, New York. He is widely published internationally. His publications include *The Rise of China and India in Africa: Challenges, Opportunities and Critical Interventions* (London and Uppsala, 2010, co-edited with Fantu Cheru) and *Oil and Insurgency in the Niger Delta: Managing the Complex Politics of Petro-Violence* (Zed Books, London, 2011, co-edited with Siri Aas Rustad).

Godwin Onuoha is an African research fellow at the Human Sciences Research Council, South Africa. His research interests are in nationalism, identity politics, and the interface between the state, resources and development. He is the author of *Challenging the State in Africa: MASSOB and the Crisis of Self-Determination in Nigeria* (2011), and his articles have appeared in *Nationalism and Ethnic Politics*, *African Studies*, *Ethnic and Racial Studies* and the *Review of African Political Economy*.

Sirisio L. Oromo is an assistant professor and Director of the Centre for Peace and Development Studies, University of Juba, South Sudan.

Samson Samuel Wassara is Professor of Political Science in the University of Juba. He is currently Dean of the College of Social and Economic Studies, and was appointed in 2010 as Vice-Chancellor of Western Equatoria Project University. He teaches political science subjects including international relations, conflict and peace at the university. His research interests include state building, the security sector, peace studies and hydro-politics. His most recent publications include 'Interests of Border Communities in Water and Pastures: Will They Influence Nile Water Policies of the Two Sudans?' in *UNISCI Journal/Discussion Papers* (33, October 2013) and 'Nation and State Building in South Sudan: Priorities for Research and Action' in *State Building and Development in South Sudan: Priorities for Development Policy Research* (ARRF, 2013).

Part I

Conceptions, international law and charters

1 Self-determination and secession

African challenges

Redie Bereketeab

Introduction

The recent secession of South Sudan raises a number of critical existential questions about the post-colonial state in Africa. In 1964, the Organisation of African Unity (OAU) declared colonially inherited borders sacrosanct and not to be changed. Consequently colonial boundaries were transformed into international borders, thereby acquiring international status and applicability in international law. The rationale for this approach to colonial boundaries was the fear that the colonially produced African state would not survive if identity groups were permitted to break away. It was feared that any secessionist assertion would open a Pandora's box. The OAU and its successor, the African Union (AU), have thus pursued strict policies against any attempted secession, and secessionism has been seen as an act of criminality.

The recognition of the secession of South Sudan, however, seems to have ushered in a new era in the history of self-determination and secession. It represents a watershed in the adherence to the regime of colonial borders. This is so because the independence of South Sudan represents a breach of the OAU/AU Charter, which has governed African border issues and statehood for over 50 years. Once breached, the sanctity of the colonial border principle may prove difficult to patch up again. The following crucial question comes to mind: is the AU aware of the gravity of its action? Further, does this recognition set a precedent when other quests for self-determination and secession on the continent have to be addressed? Has the Pandora's box already been prised open? Perhaps one should presume that the Pandora's box will remain largely intact in the near future, as is suggested by the way in which the AU is dealing with the issue of Somaliland's quest for sovereignty.

This double approach to affording recognition, as evidenced by the contrasting cases of South Sudan and Somaliland, perhaps illustrates how the AU is still bent on prioritising state integrity over people's rights. Preserving the territorial integrity of the existing state or colonially created state would mean denying people the right to exercise their self-determination. In the case of Somaliland, the AU is distinctly reluctant to recognise it as a separate state. That implies respecting the territorial integrity of the Republic of Somalia, which was created by the fusion of two colonial territories (British Somaliland and Italian Somaliland) in 1960 and subsequently became a member of the OAU. In this context, however, both theoretical and legal challenges to the sanctity of colonially inherited borders arise, as do questions about the ambiguity and paradoxicality of the behaviour of the AU. Somaliland and its borders are the creation of colonialism, which came to an end in 1960. Somaliland gained its independence on 26 June of that year, but opted to enter into a union with the former Italian Somaliland to found the Somali Republic following the independence of the latter on 1 July 1960 (Hansen and Bradbury 2007; Bradbury 2008; Jhazbhay 2009; Farley 2010). This should have facilitated its recognition, as in the aftermath of the Second World War European colonialism became the basis for the right of self-determination in international law. Nonetheless, it may be argued that, by voluntarily joining a union and rescinding its independence, Somaliland consummated its right of self-determination. Consequently, it cannot revoke that right of self-determination.

The discrepancy between the immediate recognition of South Sudan and Somaliland's quest for 20 years at the time of writing to gain recognition without success could be explained from both a theoretical and a legal point of view. From a theoretical perspective, the theory of suffering and remedial theory may serve as explanation (Anaya 1996: 80; Buchanan 1998: 231). These theories may also be reinforced by the theory of distance, which presumes that, where there is a great cultural distance between the superordinate and subordinate elements, secession may be warranted. From a legal perspective, international law stresses the importance of mutual consent between separatist entity and mother state. Nonetheless, self-determination is perceived as a fundamental human right of people in determining their political future (Whelan 2010).

Amid all the controversies and paradoxes surrounding the concepts of self-determination and secessionism, a critical question to be pondered is whether secession will bring peace, security, stability, democracy and development. The presumption underpinning the right to self-determination and secession is that it will lead to peace, security and development, or at least it will not perpetuate conflicts and wars. On the contrary, the rampant conflict that gave rise to the quest for self-determination and secession will abate subsequent to secession. Nonetheless, most empirical evidence shows that, at least initially, conflicts and wars continue even after secession. The question then becomes: if secession cannot resolve conflicts and wars, is it a goal worth pursuing? The opposite outcome, maintaining territorial integrity, has also proven to be problematic in sustaining peace, stability and development. The recent increase in secessionist movements is itself testimony to this problem. The predicament is rather an expression of the limits of self-determination (Burke 2010: 57).

This book aims to contribute to the debate on self-determination and secessionism in Africa. Both issues are perhaps the most neglected in academia and in policy circles related to Africa, even though several self-determination and secessionist movements are active on the continent. Indeed, new movements are frequently emerging. The objectives of the present book include: 1) generating serious academic debate on the challenges of self-determination and secession on the continent in the twenty-first century; 2) identifying various cases of self-determination and secession; 3) examining whether self-determination and secession spawn peace, security, stability and development; and 4) explaining how international law, as well as the UN and AU charters, deal with self-determination and secession.

In this introductory chapter, the next section presents a conceptual overview of the two concepts, while the third section discusses the OAU's principles of self-determination and secession. The fourth section explores whether self-determination leads to peace, security and stability, and the fifth examines the merits of regional integration following secession. The last section reviews the structure and themes of the book.

Conceptualising self-determination and secession

Self-determination

The attempts at reaching consensus within academia concerning the concept of self-determination have not led to consensus. Among the hurdles have been the varied approaches to and interpretations of the concept, but other obstacles have been the political, legal and international relations dimensions of the concept. The plethora of approaches to analysing, defining and understanding self-determination gives rise to serious challenges (Tesfagiorgis 1987; Etzioni 1992/93; Mayall 1999; Ferdous 2007).

The debate over self-determination can be divided into three broad categories: state-centric, society-centric and legalistic. This theoretical framework draws on all three categories. The concept of self-determination is intricately connected to the right of state formation. Nonetheless, the conceptualisation of the right of self-determination varies greatly depending on what is being discussed: the rights of the individual, group, ethnic entity or nation; economic, cultural or political rights; or the right to autonomy, independence or union.

The moral, legal and political foundations of the discourse also differ considerably depending on political and ideological persuasion, ranging from leftist (Marxist), to liberal, to conservative. In Marxist literature, particularly by Lenin (1974), Rosa Luxemburg and Stalin (1976), the right to self-determination (including secession) relates to oppressed nations and classes. The Marxist notion of self-determination (and secession), with its emphasis on class relations and materialism, contends that working-class interests should determine the exercise and outcome of self-determination. Notwithstanding all the divergences between the various schools of thought, the notion of self-determination seems to be grounded in a 'philosophical affirmation of the human drive to translate aspirations into reality, coupled with the postulates of inherent human equality' (Anaya 1996).

The criteria of statehood are invariably seen as 1) territory, 2) population, 3) government, and 4) independence (White 1981; Castellino 2008). Peoples who meet these criteria should in principle be accorded international recognition. In the culturalist perspective, there is greater emphasis on the congruence between the cultural and the political: the assumption tends to be that any culturally homogeneous community deserves to form its own state (Gellner 1983). In this conception of self-determination, the seceding nation should meet certain preconditions; notably it has to be culturally different from the entity from which it is seceding. The underlying logic is that multi-ethnic societies are inherently unstable and perhaps unable to sustain statehood: hence the perception that multi-ethnic states in Africa have failed or collapsed (Spears 2004, 2010).

There are a number of theoretical approaches that grapple with the issue of self-determination and secession. These include democratic theory, liberal theory (Beran 1998), communitarian theory (Raz 1986; Margalit and Raz 1990), realist theory (Buchanan 1991; Shehadi 1993) and territorial justice theory (Lehning 1998). Democratic theory stresses the democratic right of people to govern themselves and the right of free political association, while liberal theory advocates the right of the individual to determine her destiny and communitarian theory conversely seeks the right of self-determination for the collectivity, the nation. Realist theory focuses on the principle of the territorial integrity of states (Freeman 1999), while territorial justice theory advances the idea that people have the right to supremacy on their territory (Steiner 1998; Castellino 2008). Other less known theories of self-determination include the theory of suffering and remedial theory (White 1981; Freeman 1999).

Arguably, underlying these theoretical positions is the notion of the moral and political rights to secession (Lehning 1998). Not every act of self-determination, however, leads to secession. Indeed, self-determination may take the form of: 1) emergence of an independent state; 2) free association with an independent state; and 3) integration with an independent state (White 1981: 149; Anaya 1996: 84). Apparently, the controversy over the concept of self-determination relates to whether it has a universal value. The Wilsonian Doctrine limited the right of self-determination to only European nations (Hobsbawm 1990: 32, 102; Anaya 1996: 76; Karmis and Norman 2005: 12), while the post-Second World War debate on self-determination restricts it to societies subjected to European rule: the decolonisation debate (Burke 2010). In the post-colonial debate, self-determination has been deemed a closed chapter (Anaya 1996: 77), since peoples and nations subjected to alien European colonial rule have achieved independence.

The international regime governing the principle of self-determination is based on the traditional state-centred approach, according to which self-determination is viewed as stemming from the state as the legitimate unit (Castellino 2008: 501). A recent, humanitarian approach, however, sees the right of self-determination as a fundamental human right (Anaya 2000; Hannum 1996; Burke 2010). This is a profound shift from the familiar state-centred approach. However, the humanitarian approach has already been subjected to scathing criticism on the grounds that it has nothing to offer the project of nation-state building, which is widely perceived as the crucial problem in Africa (Zongwe 2010).

Colonial borders in Africa have long been accepted as sacrosanct and not to be tampered with. The principle of *uti possidetis* (Latin for 'as you possess') was enshrined in the charter of the OAU when the latter was launched in 1964. In the African context, *uti possidetis* thus entailed converting colonial borders into international boundaries (Farley 2010: 802). The leaders who gathered at the historic launching of the OAU declared that 'all Member States pledge themselves to respect the borders existing on their achievement of national independence' (Temin 2010), in other words to the principle of the inviolability of colonially inherited territorial integrity (Makinda 1982; Spears 2004; Lemay-Hebert 2009; Ndulo 2010). The conflation of *uti possidetis* and the principle of territorial integrity ensured the preservation of colonial territorial entities in Africa. The principle of *uti possidetis* could also be applied to secession provided it led to the restoring of a previous boundary (Farley 2010: 804–5). Chapter 3 explores in detail the OAU/AU Charter's treatment of self-determination.

The most challenging debate on self-determination relates to the tension between the territorial integrity of states and the aspirations of aggrieved nations (Lehning 1998; Freeman 1999: 365; Castellino 2008). Internationally, the principle of territorial integrity of states has produced a restrictive interpretation of the right to self-determination. This seems to stem from the perceived value of peace and stability in the international order (Caney 1998: 172–3; Freeman 1999: 357). Furthermore, 'the limited likelihood any secessionist movement would be internationally recognized considerably reduces the appeal of local separatist strategies of power in normal times' (Englebert and Hummel 2003: 31). How international law, conventions and the UN Charter deal with self-determination is further discussed in Chapter 2.

Secessionism

The political phenomenon known as secessionism has gained momentum worldwide following the collapse of the Soviet Union (Lehning 1998; Englebert and Hummel 2003; Weller and Metzger 2008). Secession is a concept intricately connected with the discourse on separate state formation. Separation is supposed to take place by the severing of relations with an existing state. It may also occur through the dissolution of a state (Farley 2010: 795). Political and economic factors play a significant role in secession. Geographical location either facilitates or hinders secession, but can also have a significant impact on the functioning of the new state if secession occurs (Trzcinski 2004).

Broadly speaking, secessionism is defined as political withdrawal from an established state (Trzcinski 2004; Tuttle 2004). In this definition, secessionism implies territorial disintegration through severance of part of an existing state territory. In this regard, it is stipulated that the consent of the state that loses territory as well as international recognition is needed (Lemay-Hebert 2009: 33). The political and legal implication of this is that, in the absence of such consent and recognition, separate statehood is not feasible. This is the situation Somaliland faces.

Whereas territorial secession signifies separation of part of a state from the rest of its territory accompanied by withdrawal by the separated territory from the state's political system – in short, the emergence of a new nation-state – cultural or ethnic secessionism can take the form of a drive by a group for far-reaching autonomy within the state (Trzcinski 2004: 208). In this sense, a distinction is made between territorial claims that lead to secession from an existing state and cultural claims where a cultural or ethnic group seeks recognition and respect for its uniqueness possibly through self-rule.

The factors underlying demands for secession may vary considerably. Ethnic or cultural distinctiveness may be invoked in support of a group's demands for secession. Past historical glories may also be evoked. Further reference may be made to subjugation. These drivers can be potent if the group occupies a unified territory (Trzcinski 2004: 208).

The conditions that invariably determine the outcome of secessionist movements in Africa include:

- interests of powerful states;
- attitude of the central government towards the secessionist movement;
- military balance between the secessionist movement and central government;
- strategic importance of the seceding region;
- external support for the secessionist movement or central government;
- recognition of the secession by the international community, particularly the UN;
- economic significance of the seceding region for the economy of the parent state.

(Trzcinski 2004)

All these factors, as we will observe in the empirical cases, play a decisive role in the outcomes of people's aspirations. Theoretically, at least, in order to exercise the right to secession, certain conditions must be met. The UN International Covenant of 1966 declares: 'All people have the right of self-determination, creating sovereign statehood. By virtue of that right they freely determine their political status and freely pursue their economic, social and cultural development' (Freeman 1999: 355). The earlier UN General Assembly Resolution 1541 (XV) concerning self-determination was adopted in reference to the decolonisation of peoples subjected to white domination (Castellino 2008: 511). Yet the UN based its conviction on contradictory principles of reconciling the territorial integrity of states (Article 2(4) of the UN Charter deals with territorial integrity of states) with the right to self-determination (secession) of peoples (Freeman 1999: 358).

The UN declaration on decolonisation and self-determination of 1960 followed more than a decade of bitter debates and contestations on the subject. Such fora of debates included the Universal Declaration on Human Rights of 1948 and the Bandung Conference of 1955 (Burke 2010; Whelan 2010). While African and Asian delegates to the UN General Assembly fora on human rights debates attempted to tie human rights to the right to self-determination and decolonisation, Western delegates strongly opposed the linkage between human rights and self-determination and decolonisation. Third World delegates presented 'self-determination as a fundamental precondition for all human rights. Anti-colonialism involved rights, and respects for rights necessitated decolonization' (Burke 2010: 35) was their argument. Colonisation was perceived as a violation of basic human rights. Therefore the debate on human rights served as a powerful instrument in dismantling colonisation. Finally the West came around and endorsed the linkage between human rights and self-determination and decolonisation. This coming around paved the way for the passing on 14 December 1960 of the Declaration on the Granting of Independence to Colonial Countries and Peoples, (Burke 2010: 55; Whelan 2010: 141). The Resolution was passed by an overwhelming majority; only nine Westerners abstained. 'With the official acceptance of the right to self-determination, the process of decolonization itself became a human right, and lent the moral legitimacy of human rights to anti-colonial struggles in Asia and Africa' (Burke 2010: 37).

The theory of suffering states that, if a people keep up guerrilla warfare for long enough, they will be rewarded with statehood (White 1981: 154). The severity of a state's treatment of its minorities becomes a matter of international concern in cases of remedial secession (White 1981: 160; Anaya 1996; Lehning 1998). Remedial theory and the theory of suffering are closely related. The former upholds the right to secession where serious and persistent violations of human rights exist, such as unjust conquest, exploitation or threat of extermination (Lehning 1998: 2–3), and no remedy other than self-determination can be envisaged (Freeman 1999: 360). This situation is epitomised in the case of South Sudan. The theories of suffering and remedy are further buttressed by the theory of cultural distance. Cultural distance postulates that, if the cultural gap between the subordinate and superordinate sections of the population is very wide, and if this gap is coupled with theories of suffering and remedy, it constitutes a compelling moral and political imperative to legitimately pursue secession. The voluntarist theory differs from remedial theory in postulating that human rights violations are neither necessary nor sufficient conditions for the right to secede. It holds that nations have the fundamental right of self-determination (and secession) (Freeman 1999: 360).

Self-determination and secession encounter formidable challenges in the form of the notion of state sovereignty. States enjoy sovereignty: this is the basis of equality of states and the inviolability of their territorial integrity and political independence. Secession thus assails the sanctity of the state as the basic unit of the international system (White 1981: 162) and the associated Westphalian system that until recently dominated the regime governing interstate relations. Overall, sovereignty deals with the relations of a state with other states (Mamdani 2011). In this sense, it could be argued that statehood is externally oriented, particularly in terms of its legitimacy.

Cosmopolitan theorists such as Buchanan (1991) and Barry (1991) (cf. Freeman 1999) view secession as conditional. The new state that emerges from secession must be able to provide peace, security and respect for human rights not only to the people within its geopolitical borders but also to those beyond. In other words, the exercise of secession is premised upon whether it leads to peace, security, stability, respect for human rights and development. The presumption is that, if these objectives will not be achieved through secession, recognition may be withheld.

This is related to another notion, people's well-being. In this line of argument (Caney 1998), secession is endorsed on the grounds that it promotes the well-being of people, an outcome multinational entities supposedly cannot achieve. In both an instrumentalist and an intrinsic sense, the well-being argument justifies the presumption of secession (Caney 1998: 169): instrumentally, secession is presumed to bring autonomy and self-governance, while intrinsically it is presumed to effect self-fulfilment (Anaya 1996: 107–9).

In conclusion, self-determination that leads to secession is required to meet certain conditions. First, it should bring peace, security, stability and development to the secessionists (Anaya 1996; Crawford 2006) and, second, it should, at a minimum, not be a cause of instability and insecurity for neighbouring people and beyond (Caney 1998; Lehning 1998). There are those who argue, however, that secession will not reduce violence (Horowitz 2003; Mayall 2008; Spears 2010). Rather, the argument goes, it has been shown in many cases that those seceding open new doors for minority claims to self-determination and secession, thereby perpetuating conflict and violence (Etzioni 1992/93).

The OAU and the principle of self-determination and secession

At the Cairo summit, 1964, the OAU adopted a clause that prioritised state integrity. It was agreed that the integrity of emerging post-colonial states should reign supreme. To ensure this, colonially inherited borders were declared sacrosanct. Accordingly any act that threatens the integrity of member states was virtually declared to be criminal. Identity movements that aspired to secede from an existing state and form their own state were condemned, whatever the legitimacy of their demands.

The OAU's decision to preserve colonial boundaries transformed them into recognised international borders with international legal status. The UN and other international bodies and conventions immediately acknowledged the legality of the colonial borders, and the concomitant states were recognised as legal entities and became members of the international state system. Secessionist movements were therefore condemned not only by the OAU, but also by the UN and international conventions. The consent of the mother state thus became a prerequisite for regional and international recognition of secession.

The sanctity afforded to colonial borders and state integrity at the expense of people's rights was rationalised by the trepidation at the prospective chaos, conflicts and wars that awaited Africa if existing borders were open to redefinition and reconstruction. This fear arose from the fact that colonial states were brought together in a way that paid no attention whatever to prior cultural, language, ethnic, topographical, religious, livelihood or climatic differences. Referring to this reality, Lewis (1983: 73) notes:

It is a remarkable irony that the European powers who partitioned Africa in the late 19th century when the idea of the nation-state was paramount, should have created in Africa a whole series of Habsburg-style states, comprising a medley of people and ethnic groups lumped together within frontiers which paid no respect to traditional cultural contours.

This poly-ethnic, poly-religious, poly-linguistic and poly-cultural composition, it was argued, rendered post-colonial states fragile, precarious, weak and amenable to any sort of pathology. One significant outcome of the colonially engineered creation of African states was its negative influence on the process of nation building and state building. Thus, the post-colonial state had to be shored up against secession and self-determination through the declaration of colonially inherited borders as sacrosanct. The priority for post-colonial nationalist leaders became building functional and sustainable nation-states, a project that overshadowed all else. The neglect of the other issues, however, came at a high price. It led to ethnic domination, marginalisation of minorities (sometime even majority groups), one-party systems, military dictatorship, economic stagnation and so on (Olikoshi and Laakso 1996; Mkandawire 2003). All this in turn prompted identity groups to seek redemption by employing coercive means through what is commonly known as liberation movements to achieve the right of self-determination (Mkandawire 2002).

The crucial question then is: has the sanctity afforded to colonial borders saved Africa from festering conflict and war? A categorical answer may be impossible, since the record from the last five decades is mixed. On one hand, conflicts directly related to the quest for self-determination and secession have not been many, although they are gaining momentum. The first few secessionist movements were brutally crushed by the mother state, with moral, diplomatic and legal backing from the OAU. This may have served as a deterrent, for those who would dare to challenge the murderous machinery of the post-colonial state?

On the other hand, throughout the post-colonial period, Africa has been plagued by rampant conflict and war. Slowly, these wars seem to have given rise to a paradigm shift whereby people's rights are gradually beginning to assume priority over the rights of the state. Both within academia and policy circles and among activists there is a growing tendency to support the rights of peoples in all their forms. This development could give rise to a radical reconfiguration of post-colonial states. This compels us to raise a crucial question: what will this paradigm shift mean to the existence of the post-colonial African state? This anthology endeavours to tackle this predicament facing Africa in the twenty-first century.

Self-determination, peace, security and stability

The moral philosophy and political economy behind recognition of self-determination and secession are the quest for peace, security and stability. The dynamics behind the possible paradigm shift prioritising people's rights over state rights seem to arise from the perception that peace, security, stability and development might thus arise. The logic seems to be that, by containing aggrieved identity groups within its internationally acclaimed borders, the post-colonial state has not spawned peace, security and stability: rather it has produced rampant conflict and suffering. The solution then should be letting the aggrieved group establish its own statehood. This line of reasoning raises two crucial questions. The first is: how possible is it to allow all ethnic groups so seeking to exercise self-determination and secession? The second is: would self-determination and secession lead to peace, security, stability and development? Pragmatically, it would be extremely difficult to allow all ethnic groups to exercise the right of self-determination, with the resultant possibility of secession. Indeed, the continent would be plunged into unimaginable chaos and turmoil. As to the second question, although experience of self-determination and secession is very limited and it would be premature to draw conclusive lessons, the few examples there are have not yet proven promising. A few years after Eritrea exercised its right to self-determination, Ethiopia and Eritrea were plunged into bloody war between 1998 and 2000. South Sudan seceded from Sudan in July 2011, yet the two countries are locked in bloody conflict. South Sudan is also suffering from chronic internal maladies.

This less promising outcome as regards peace, security, stability and development then compels us to pose another crucial question, namely whether secession is a worthwhile route to follow. If neither the sacrosanct post-colonial state nor the right of peoples can secure peace, security and stability, what then is the way forward? The emergent people's rights paradigm raises more questions than answers. Indeed it could with great confidence be asserted that self-determination displays serious limitations. These limitations are of multiple natures. One perhaps concerns the international legal system, which is widely perceived as ambiguous and sometimes contradictory in its dealing with self-determination. The second concerns the inconsistencies and partiality of regional and global actors with regard to application of the right of self-determination. As Burke (2010: 37) notes, the behaviours of many actors are characterised by double standards that make the principle of self-determination highly controversial. Why are some allowed to exercise the right of self-determination while others are denied? There is also the phenomenon of unguided employment of violence in the name of self-determination that leads to grave violation of human rights.

Can we rightly claim that sacrosanct colonial borders have served Africa well in bringing peace, security and stability or have they only served to imprison a state's peoples, as many argue? The experience of the last five decades has been mixed. On one hand, it could be claimed that identity-based conflicts bedevilled Africa, while on the other, when one considers the ethnic plurality of the post-colonial state, the level of identity-based conflict should not be exaggerated. Nevertheless, the continent has been plagued by war and conflict. It is high time that concerted efforts were made to find more functional and sustainable solutions to the challenge of conflict. This anthology seeks to grapple with this crucial problem.

There is an expectation that those allowed to achieve statehood through self-determination and secession will provide peace, stability, security and development to their own people, their region and the continent as a whole. It is a not unreasonable expectation that, after all the carnage, suffering and destruction associated with their struggle, the people concerned will demand that their efforts be rewarded with peace, security, stability, harmony, respect for all sorts of rights, and development. But complexities of demography, ethnicity, topography and socio-economic modes of life, not to mention culture, history, genealogy, contested identity formation and territorial claims and counter-claims, seem to preclude clean separation.

A former UN Secretary-General, Boutros Boutros-Ghali, was apprehensive about the unfettered exercise of the right of self-determination, and expressed his fears thus: 'If every ethnic, religious or linguistic group claimed statehood, there would be no limit to fragmentation, and peace, security and economic well-being for all would become even more difficult to achieve' (quoted in Mayall 1999: 475). Endless fragmentation and disintegration may lead to endless tension, conflict and war, resulting in insecurity, instability and underdevelopment.

The moral, political, economic, human and philosophical dilemma this prospect poses, coupled with the practical difficulties of delineating and demarcating lines between the legal, territorial and political entities that emerge from the exercise of self-determination and secession, necessitates the engineering of an alternative politico-organisational mechanism and body.

Post-self-determination and secession: regional integration and cooperation

The endeavour to find a solution to the predicament posed by the conflict between the principle of state integrity and people's rights is at the centre of this anthology. Following self-determination and possible secession, relations between the parties of the erstwhile united state may remain locked in conflict on account of unresolved or contested issues that preclude or delay lasting solutions. This situation makes it imperative that the units born of the split earnestly try to foster regional integration and cooperation. Immediate post-divorce relations may be amicable, as they were between Eritrea and Ethiopia, until those states went to war again in 1998. They may also be characterised by unsettled issues and conflicts, as with Sudan and South Sudan.

The few successful cases of self-determination and secession testify that, although the final divorce took place through amicable agreements and popular plebiscites, what followed the divorce was anything but peace, security and good neighbourliness. Three factors perhaps explain post-divorce bloody conflict: 1) consent to separation being not entirely free-will; 2) unresolved issues flowing from separation; and 3) management of post-separation. It was military victory that produced separation in the case of Eritrea and diplomatic pressure in the case of South Sudan. This forced divorce-generated grievances among citizens of the 'mother state' that served as the seeds of conflict. Any opportunity is then exploited to reverse or undermine the divorce.

In such cases, it may help if the parties are involved in an overarching regional political and territorial body. Regional integration may be able to address several levels of grievance. Quite often contested territories, divided identity groups and contested strategic resources (oil in the case of the two Sudans, and port facilities in the case of Ethiopia and Eritrea) constitute the grievance that perpetuates conflicts. Through supranational, regional political forums, the parties may be able to mitigate these tensions.

More specifically, small units may face insurmountable challenges in addressing the daunting socio-economic, security, infrastructural, integration and capacity-building challenges that often follow conflict and secession. The aggregation of resources, capacities and know-how may be needed to tackle these problems. 'There is a general consensus in the literature that, properly designed and implemented, regional integration has the potential to promote socio-economic development of member countries, to foster both regional and internal peace and to enhance the collective capabilities of members' (Mengisteab 2012: 4).

Regional integration, with open borders that allow free movements of goods and people, would have a number of benefits. As Kidane Mengisteab (2012: 15) notes, divided communities, particularly pastoralists, would benefit from a variety of ecosystems stretching across political borders. Furthermore, in cultural terms, divided identities could achieve greater integration that would not only reduce conflicts, but also empower them economically, culturally and politically.

> Such improvements, if they take place, are also likely to reduce the grievances of fragmented identities against the state. It is also conceivable that improved management of fragmented identities, including policies of decentralization, would also have an impact in addressing the grievances of non-fragmented marginalized groups. . . . Progress in dealing with the problems of both groups of identities (fragmented and non-fragmented marginalized) is likely to reduce both state-identity and inter-state conflicts.
>
> (Mengisteab 2012: 15)

Fostering regional integration would therefore bring benefits at two levels: intra-state and interstate. At the interstate level, the benefit would be that peaceful neighbourliness could be cultivated between recently divorced states. At the intra-state level, intra-communal, intercommunal/ethnic, rebel-state conflicts might find resolution. Proxy wars that emanate from divided ethnic groups may also be resolved or forestalled.

A regional integration that promotes regional peace, security and stability would ensure dividends in areas such as democratisation, nation building and economic development and would prevent destructive interstate conflicts. Transnational trade, common markets, common tariffs, transboundary infrastructure, transnational investment, common agricultural projects and proper utilisation of resource complementarities are some of the measures that would enhance the integration process. All these enable the supra-state organisation to devise, foster and develop mechanisms and institutions that enable it to better manage the various pathologies ravaging the region.

Themes and structure of the book

The main thread running through the chapters and tying the book together is the notions of self-determination and secession. The point of departure for the chapters is that self-determination and secession are a primary challenge to the post-colonial state in Africa in the twenty-first century. Another central theme the chapters confront is whether the independence of South Sudan has ushered in a paradigm shift from state-centred rights, dominant since the Westphalian Convention of 1648, to people-centred rights. While the former celebrates the primacy of territorial integrity of the state, people-centred rights give primacy to the right of a people to freely determine their political future, including constituting sovereign statehood. The two rights are usually placed in binary opposition. Another theme in the anthology is not only examination and analysis of the two bodies of rights, but also exploration of ways and mechanisms to reconcile these rights.

The contributors also consider whether self-determination and secession lead to peace, security and stability in post-colonial Africa. It is widely understood that holding colonialism's inherited borders as sacrosanct may have contributed to ravaging conflicts and wars on the continent by institutionalising the so-called artificiality of African states and perpetuating the colonial engineering that forcibly brought together heterogeneous societies. Advocates of this strand of thought have diligently advocated the dismantling of colonially inherited borders. The anthology therefore examines the merits of this prescription for addressing the problem of the post-colonial state in Africa.

With the recent breaching of the principle of the sacrosanctity of colonial borders, the book tries to assess whether this represents a paradigm shift and considers whether this change will lead to peace, security, stability and development. Another issue the anthology explores is why some quests for self-determination and secession succeed while others fail.

In exploring self-determination and secession in Africa, the book examines some of the prominent quests to this end across the continent since 1960. There appear to be four categories of such quests, which are distinguished by whether they have colonial origins or not and their degree of success. The four categories are: 1) a case that was not a colonial creation involving the right to self-determination and the achievement of independence; 2) cases that were created by colonialism but where there was forcible annexation by neighbouring countries following the end of colonialism; 3) cases of non-colonial creation involving secession from the post-colonial state; 4) cases created by colonialism whereby states voluntarily join a union, but later wish to rescind the union.

Overall the book is structured in five parts. Part I consists of three chapters that deal with general issues. Chapter 2 takes further the notion of self-determination and secession and looks into international law conventions and the UN Charter with regard to the right of self-determination leading to sovereign statehood. The chapter notes that, while territorial integrity is closely connected to the principle of *uti possidetis juris* where the right of self-determination must not violate existing frontiers at the time of independence, secession involves violation of territorial integrity and takes place unilaterally, without the consent of the existing state. The last chapter of Part I, Chapter 3, examines the OAU's treatment of self-determination and secession. The OAU's acceptance of the sacrosanctity of colonial borders, thereby upholding the territorial integrity of the post-colonial state, denied aggrieved peoples and nations the right to determine their political future and led to conflict and war.

Part II consists of three chapters dealing with South Sudan, a case that was not a colonial creation, yet was successful in achieving state sovereignty. All the chapters analyse the formation of the new state, its struggle for self-determination and the conditions that contributed to its independence. Chapter 4 provides a political history of South Sudan before the independence of Sudan. Chapter 5 examines the first civil war for self-determination, while Chapter 6 discusses the second civil war, whose aim was the creation of a united 'New Sudan'.

Part III deals with colonially created states that initially got independence but voluntarily joined a union, later however seeking to rescind the union. The first three chapters deal with Somaliland, Chapter 7 with the history of Somaliland pre-1960 and Chapter 8 with the period between 1960 and 1991. The latter chapter analyses the intricate factors that contributed to the failure of the merger and the tragic quest for 'Greater Somalia'. Chapter 9 then explores the reasons for Somaliland's failure to gain international recognition. Chapter 10 examines the case of Zanzibar, specifically the union with Tanganyika and why the quest for secession is becoming louder.

Part IV deals with cases of non-colonial origin involving secession from the post-colonial state. It relates to three cases, notably Katanga in Congo, Biafra in Nigeria and the Tuareg in Mali. Chapter 11 discusses the quest for and failure of secession in Katanga. Its conclusion is that the quest for self-determination failed because it was perceived to reflect the rights of only a segment of society and the white settlers. Chapter 12 examines Biafra's secession, which failed when the rebels suffered defeat at the hands of federal forces in 1970. Chapter 13 examines the Tuareg secessionist movement in Northern Mali in pursuit of a separate territory called Azawad. The conclusion drawn is that the main driving motive for secession is the improper incorporation of the Tuareg into the Malian state.

Part V deals with states that were created by colonialism but were forcibly annexed by neighbouring countries after the end of colonialism. These include Namibia, Eritrea and Western Sahara. Chapter 14 analyses the colonial history of Namibia, specifically how it became a protectorate of South Africa by decision of the League of Nations following the defeat of Germany in the First World War. The territory was then annexed by South Africa. The chapter analyses how Namibia eventually gained its independence following complicated negotiations. Chapter 15 explores the colonial past of Eritrea, including the British rule that followed the demise of Italian colonialism. It analyses how the territory was tied to Ethiopia through a UN-sponsored federation that was abrogated by Ethiopia when it annexed Eritrea. After 30 years of liberation struggle, Eritrea won its independence in 1991. Chapter 16, the last in the book, discusses the colonial history of Western Sahara, the country's annexation by Morocco following the withdrawal of Spain, and the struggle of the Saharawi people, led by Polisario, for self-determination. The chapter shows how powerful Western interests in Morocco have obstructed resolution of the Saharawi problem.

As a last note, there are two reasons for the fact that there are three chapters each on South Sudan and Somaliland. First, South Sudan and Somaliland were the main subject of the Juba conference in August 2012, where the idea for this book originated. Second, the two cases span the whole problematic of self-determination and secession, including international recognition and the ambiguities in and differences among the theories, international laws, conventions and policies relating to self-determination and secession.

References

Anaya, S. James. 1996. *Indigenous Peoples in International Law*. New York: Oxford University Press.

Anaya, S. James. 2000. 'Self-Determination as a Collective Human Right under Contemporary International Law', in Pekka Aikio and Martin Scheinin (eds), *Operationalizing the Right of Indigenous Peoples to Self-Determination*. Turku/Åbo: Institute of Human Rights, Åbo Akademi University.

Barry, Brian. 1991. *Liberty and Justice: Essays in Political Theory 2*. Oxford: Oxford University Press.

Beran, Harry. 1998. 'A Democratic Theory of Political Self-Determination for a New World Order', in Percy B. Lehning (ed.), *Theories of Secession*. London: Routledge.

Bradbury, Mark. 2008. *Becoming Somaliland*. Oxford: James Currey.

Buchanan, Allen. 1991. *Secession: The Morality of Political Divorce from Fort Sumter to Lithuania and Quebec*. Boulder, CO: Westview Press.

Buchanan, Allen. 1998. 'The International Institutional Dimension of Secession', in Percy B. Lehning (ed.), *Theories of Secession*. London: Routledge.

Burke, Roland. 2010. *Decolonization and the Evolution of International Human Rights*. Philadelphia: University of Pennsylvania Press.

Caney, Simon. 1998. 'National Self-Determination and National Secession: Individual and Communitarian Approaches', in Percy B. Lehning (ed.), *Theories of Secession*. London: Routledge.

Castellino, Joshua. 2008. 'Territorial Integrity and the "Right" to Self-Determination: An Examination of the Conceptual Tools', *Brooklyn Journal of International Law*, vol. 33, no. 2, pp. 499–564.

Crawford, James. 2006. *The Creation of States in International Law*. Oxford: Clarendon Press.

Englebert, Pierre and Hummel, Rebecca. 2003. 'Let's Stick Together: Understanding Africa's Secessionist Deficit', First draft, prepared for African Studies Association 46th Annual Meeting, Boston, MA, 30 October – 2 November.

Etzioni, Amitai. 1992/93. 'The Evils of Self-Determination', *Foreign Policy*, no. 89, pp. 21–35.

Farley, Benjamin R. 2010. 'Calling a State a State: Somaliland and International Recognition', *Emory International Law Review*, vol. 24, no. 2, pp. 777–820.

Ferdous, Syed Robayet. 2007. 'Self-Determination: Idea and Pragmatism', *Asian Affairs*, vol. 29, no. 3, pp. 29–43.

Freeman, Michael. 1999. 'The Right to Self-Determination in International Politics: Six Theories in Search of Policy', *Review of International Studies*, vol. 24, pp. 355–70.

Gellner, Ernest. 1983. *Nations and Nationalism*. Oxford: Blackwell.

Hannum, Hurst. 1996. *Autonomy, Sovereignty, and Self-Determination: The Accommodation of Conflicting Rights*, rev. edn. Philadelphia: University of Pennsylvania Press.

Hansen, Stig Jarle and Bradbury, Mark. 2007. 'Somaliland: A New Democracy in the Horn of Africa?', *Review of African Political Economy*, vol. 34, no. 113, pp. 461–76.

Hobsbawm, Eric L. 1990. *Nations and Nationalism since 1780: Programme, Myth, Reality*. New York: Cambridge University Press.

Horowitz, Donald L. 2003. 'The Cracked Foundations of the Right to Secede', *Journal of Democracy*, vol. 14, no. 2, pp. 5–17.

Jhazbhay, Iqbal D. 2009. *Somaliland: An African Struggle for Nationhood and International Recognition*. Johannesburg: Institute for Global Dialogue and South African Institute of International Affairs.

Karmis, Dimitrios and Norman, Wayne. 2005. *Theories of Federalism: A Reader*. New York: Palgrave Macmillan.

Lehning, Percy B. (ed.). 1998. *Theories of Secession*. London: Routledge.

Lemay-Hebert, Nicolas. 2009. 'Statebuilding without Nation-Building? Legitimacy, State Failure and the Limits of the Institutionalist Approach', *Journal of Intervention and Statebuilding*, vol. 3, no. 1, pp. 21–45.

Lenin, Vladimir I. 1974. *Om Nationers Självbestämmanderätt*. Stockholm: Arbetarkultur.

Lewis, I. M. (ed.). 1983. *Nationalism and Self-Determination in the Horn of Africa*. London: Ithaca Press.

Makinda, Samuel M. 1982. 'Conflict and the Superpowers in the Horn of Africa', *Third World Quarterly*, vol. 4, no. 1, pp. 93–103.

Mamdani, Mahmood. 2011. 'South Sudan: Rethinking Citizenship, Sovereignty and Self-Determination', *Pambazuka News*, http://pambazuka.org/en//category/features/72924 (accessed 17 May 2011).

Margalit, Avishai and Raz, Joseph. 1990. 'National Self-Determination', *Journal of Philosophy*, vol. 87, no. 9, pp. 439–61.

Mayall, James. 1999. 'Sovereignty, Nationalism, and Self-Determination', *Political Studies*, vol. 47, no. 3, pp. 474–502.

Mayall, James. 2008. 'Nationalism, Self-Determination, and the Doctrine of Territorial Unity', in Marc Weller and Barbara Metzger (eds), *Settling Self-Determination Disputes: Complex Power-Sharing in Theory and Practice*. Leiden: Martinus Nijhoff.

Mengisteab, Kidane. 2012. 'Relevance of Regional Integration in the Greater Horn Region', in Kidane Mengisteab and Redie Bereketeab (eds), *Regional Integration, Identity and Citizenship in the Greater Horn of Africa*. Oxford: James Currey.

Mkandawire, Thandika. 2002. 'The Terrible Toll of Post-Colonial "Rebel Movements" in Africa: Towards an Explanation of the Violence against the Peasantry', *Journal of Modern African Studies*, vol. 40, no. 2, pp. 181–215.

Mkandawire, Thandika. 2003. 'Institutions and Development in Africa', Paper submitted to the *Cambridge Journal of Economics* Conference on Economics for the Future, 17–19 September.

Ndulo, Muna. 2010. 'Ethnic Diversity: A Challenge to African Democratic Governance', in Francis M. Deng (ed.), *Self-Determination and National Unity: A Challenge for Africa*. Trenton, NJ: Africa World Press.

Olikoshi, Adebayo and Laakso, Liisa. 1996. *Challenges to the Nation-State in Africa*. Uppsala: Nordic Africa Institute.

Raz, Joseph. 1986. *The Morality of Freedom*. Oxford: Oxford University Press.

Shehadi, Kamal. 1993. *Ethnic Self-Determination and the Break-Up of States*, Adelphi Papers 283. London: Brassey's for the International Institute for Strategic Studies.

Spears, Ian S. 2004. 'Debating Secession and the Recognition of New States in Africa', *African Security Review*, vol. 13, no. 2, pp. 35–48.

Spears, Ian S. 2010. *Civil Wars in African States: The Search for Security*. Boulder, CO: First Forum Press.

Stalin, Joseph. 1976. *Marxism and the National-Colonial Question*. San Francisco: Proletarian Publishers.

Steiner, Hillel. 1998. 'Territorial Justice', in Percy B. Lehning (ed.), *Theories of Secession*. London: Routledge.

Temin, Jon. 2010. *Secession and Precedent in Sudan and Africa*, Peace Brief no. 68, 17 November. Washington, DC: United States Institute of Peace.

Tesfagiorgis, Gebre Hiwet. 1987. 'Self-Determination: Its Evolution and Practice by the United Nations and Its Application to the Case of Eritrea', *Wisconsin International Law Journal*, vol. 6, no. 1, pp. 75–128.

Trzcinski, Krzysztof. 2004. 'The Significance of Geographic Location for the Success of Territorial Secession: African Example', *Miscellanea Geographica* (Warsaw), vol. 11, pp. 207–17.

Tuttle, Andrew. 2004. 'Secessionist Behaviour and International Organisation: Participation or Pragmatism', Final analytical research paper IAFF 005-10.

Weller, Marc and Metzger, Barbara. 2008. *Settling Self-Determination Disputes: Complex Power-Sharing in Theory and Practice*. Leiden: Martinus Nijhoff.

Whelan, Daniel J. 2010. *Indivisible Human Rights: A History*. Philadelphia: University of Pennsylvania Press.

White, Robin. 1981. 'Self-Determination: Time for a Re-assessment?', *Netherlands International Law Review*, vol. 28, no. 2, pp. 147–70.

Zongwe, Dunia P. 2010. 'The Effectiveness of the International Community's Response to the Humanitarian Crisis in Darfur: A Legal Assessment', in Muna Ndulo and Margaret Grieco (eds), *Failed and Failing States: The Challenges to African Reconstruction*. Newcastle upon Tyne: Cambridge Scholars Publishing.

2 Acquisition of autonomy
Application of the right of self-determination in Africa

Dan Kuwali

Introduction

The principle of territorial integrity is contingent on the principle of non-interference in the internal affairs of states. Establishing respect for state sovereignty as the status quo crucially serves for the maintenance of stability and peace in relations between and among states (Musgrave 1997: 181; Gudeleviciute 2005: 48). The principle of *uti possidetis juris* – that colonial borders shall be sacrosanct – is one of the guiding principles of the African Union (AU), which served to ensure the stability of the territorial status quo of African states after independence. The principle of self-determination of peoples prevails over the principle of territorial integrity in international law (UN 1945; Cassese 1995). In matters of territorial changes for non-self-governing territories, the international community recognises a limited scope of external self-determination. The principle of self-determination prevails only under the condition that the term 'a people' means the entire population of a non-self-governing territory (Gudeleviciute 2005: 49, 58). The fulfilment of the right of self-determination is impossible without the expression of free will. Thus self-determination entails the right of peoples to freely determine their political status and freely pursue their economic, social and cultural development.[1]

The right to self-determination is conferred on peoples by international law itself and not by states. Self-determination is not an event or outcome, but rather a continuous process belonging to peoples and not to states or governments. The right to self-determination does not dictate how the decision to exercise the right is to be made or what the outcome should be. Self-determination lies in the right of choice, so that the outcome of a people's choice should not affect the existence of the right to make a choice. For some, the goal is a degree of political, cultural and economic autonomy, sometimes in the form of a federal relationship. For others, the right to live on and manage a people's traditional lands free from external interference and incursion is the essential aim of a struggle for self-determination.[2]

Since the unilateral declaration of independence of the Republic of Somaliland in 1991, the perennial question for the international community has been whether or not to recognise Somaliland as a state independent of Somalia. Although the Republic of Somaliland has been a relatively stable and democratic state, the international community has been indifferent to the question of recognition of the Republic of Somaliland. Since the people of Somaliland unilaterally decided to pursue peace, the region has enjoyed a period of relative stability. Nonetheless, Somaliland has not enjoyed corresponding economic prosperity, partly because it is unable to form meaningful relationships with other nations, which refuse to recognise the government of Somaliland as being independent from that of Somalia (Kreuter 2011: 364). The people of Somaliland have expressed their wish to secede from Somalia, but no government currently recognises their right to independence (Farley 2010: 777; Kreuter 2011: 364). This chapter, therefore, assesses the implementation of the right of self-determination in the context of South Sudan and the long-standing quest of Somaliland for recognition as an independent state and its implication for the principle of *uti possidetis juris*. Specifically, it assesses whether Somaliland can be recognised as an independent state. If so, how? If not, why not?

The right to self-determination in international law

The right of self-determination (or the right to self-determination) 'is a right that protects a group as a group entity in regard to their political participation, as well as their control over their economic, social, and cultural activity as a group' (McCorquodale 2010: 366). The principle of self-determination entails that nations have the right to freely choose their sovereignty and international political status with no external compulsion or external interference. The Charter of the United Nations (UN Charter) places the right of self-determination into the framework of international law and diplomacy. Indeed, Article 1(2) of the UN Charter outlines that one of the purposes of the UN is to 'develop friendly relations among nations based on respect for the principle of equal rights and self-determination of peoples, and to take other appropriate measures to strengthen universal peace' (Dersso 2012: 8).

The principle of self-determination has been converted into a legal right by Article 15 of the Universal Declaration of Human Rights (UDHR), which guarantees that everyone has the right to a nationality, which one should not be arbitrarily deprived of or denied the ability to change (Universal Declaration of Human Rights 1948). The right to self-determination has also been elaborated in, and buttressed by, common Article 1 in both the International Covenant on Civil and Political Rights (ICCPR) and the International Covenant on Economic, Social and Cultural Rights (ICESCR). Both conventions provide that '[a]ll peoples have the right of self-determination. By virtue of that right they freely determine their political status and freely pursue their economic, social and cultural development' (Gudeleviciute 2005: 49). The right of self-determination is crucial 'because its realization is an essential condition for the effective guarantee and observance of individual human rights and for strengthening of those rights' (McCorquodale 2010: 367).

Article 8 of the African Charter on Human and Peoples' Rights (Banjul) elaborates that all peoples have the right to existence and that they have the unquestionable and inalienable right to self-determination, to freely determine their political status and to pursue their economic and social development according to the policy they have freely chosen. The African Charter goes further to say that colonised or oppressed peoples have the right to free themselves from the bonds of domination by resorting to any means recognised by the international community.

Under existing legal norms, there is a difference between a right to self-determination and a broad right to independence (Bunick 2009: 1013–14). Although the right to self-determination is entrenched in law and practice, the principle does not state how the decision is to be made, or what the outcome should be, whether it be independence, federation, protection, some form of autonomy or even full assimilation. The right of self-determination does not specify what the delimitation between states should be or what constitutes a state. In fact, there are conflicting definitions and legal criteria for determining which groups may legitimately claim the right to self-determination. Self-determination is just one of many principles applied to determining international borders (Anstis 2010). It should also be noted that the UN Charter and other resolutions do not insist on full independence as the best way of obtaining self-government, nor do they include an enforcement mechanism. In any case, new states are usually recognised by the legal doctrine of *uti possidetis juris*, meaning that old administrative boundaries become international boundaries upon independence even if they have little relevance to linguistic, ethnic and cultural boundaries. The full realisation of self-determination requires the provision of the necessary legal, institutional and political guarantees that enable peoples to elect freely a government of their choice, which should protect their personal security, consolidate peace and stability, and duly account for its activities and decisions.

The clearest understanding of the right to self-determination is related to: the decolonisation process in relation to the liberation of African peoples from former colonialism; liberation of peoples under military occupation to have the right to self-determination as separate peoples recognised by international law; and the pursuit by unrepresented or oppressed peoples, that is, definable groups that are denied meaningful access to government, of their political, economic, social and cultural development.[3] In this case, the exercise of the right to self-determination is envisaged to take place within the previously defined boundaries or territories. McCorquodale (2010: 340 n. 8) points out that:

> The right of self-determination applies to any peoples in any territory (including non-colonial territories) who are subjected to 'alien subjugation, domination and exploitation'. Indeed, it would be contrary to the concept of a human right if the right of self-determination could only be exercised once (such as by a colonial territory) and then not again. So, all peoples in all states have the right of self-determination.

In this sense, the people in question are entitled to exercise the right to external self-determination because they have been denied the ability to exercise internally their right to self-determination.[4] In the case of Somaliland, the fact that Somaliland declared independence unilaterally, without a Somalia-wide referendum approving its separation from the rest of Somalia, raises questions as to compliance with the principle of self-determination.

The procedure for exercising the right of self-determination – of peoples, not states

The exercise of the right of self-determination must be by the people themselves. The generally accepted conception of self-determination is the reference to the freedom of the population of a sovereign state to determine its internal political order without external interference. This view derives from the Declaration on the Granting of Independence to Colonial Countries and Peoples, which guarantees that '[a]ll peoples have the right to self-determination; by virtue of that right they freely determine their political status and freely pursue their economic, social, and cultural development' (UNGA 1961). It is clear from this construction that the right to self-determination is vested in the 'peoples' and not states. Considering that the right of self-determination is guaranteed to the entire population of the state, then any case for exercising the right to self-determination requires the decision of the population.

In the *Western Sahara* case, the International Court of Justice (ICJ) confirmed that 'the application of the right of self-determination requires a free and genuine expression of the will of the peoples concerned'.[5] The question is how to determine the will of the peoples concerned as a whole. The most straightforward way is through popular consultation such as a plebiscite or referendum. This explains why the Badinter Commission decided that the will of the peoples had to be ascertained by a referendum held under international supervision (Badinter Commission 1992). The same is the case with the January 2011 referendum as regards the question of the independence of South Sudan (*BBC News* 2011). Where the position of the peoples concerned is clear there may not be the need for consultations.

Therefore, in determining the exercise of the right of self-determination, to prevent discrimination between different groups of peoples it is necessary to view 'a people' as the entire population of a particular territorial unit (Gudeleviciute 2005: 53). In this case, 'a people' means: 1) the entire population of an independent state, governed in a way that represents the whole population; 2) the entire population of a non-self-governing territory; 3) the entire population of a particular occupied territorial unit living under foreign military occupation; 4) the entire unrepresented or oppressed part of a population of a particular territorial unit. This interpretation shows the primary connection between peoples and territory. Generally, for independent states, the principle of self-determination of peoples prevails over the principle of territorial integrity but only under the condition that the term 'a people' means the entire population of a state (Gudeleviciute 2005: 54, 66). According to McCorquodale:

Consistent oppressive action by those in power over another group may also indicate an acceptance of the group as a 'people', not least because it may be a catalyst for the self-identification of the group as a people with the right of self-determination. External recognition by a state or group of states can be very useful for the group (such as the recognition by many states of the Palestinian people) but it is not conclusive of the group being a people for the purposes of the right of self-determination.

(McCorquodale 2010: 371)

It is necessary that there is some territorial nexus for a 'people' with a right of self-determination (McCorquodale 2010: 370). As confirmed by the ICJ in the *Namibia* advisory opinion, the right of self-determination applies to all peoples in colonial territories.[6] Thus, the right of self-determination applies to 'peoples' in all states and can be exercised in many ways. Contemporary manifestations of the right of self-determination are within the boundaries of a state (McCorquodale 2010: 365). Dissolution, like secession, is a non-consensual separation of territory and population giving rise to new states. However, unlike secession generally, dissolution is characterised by the extinction of the parent state and its replacement by two or more newly created states. It is not clear whether the approval of the entire population is required in instances of dissolution.

The exercise of the right of self-determination

To determine whether the people of Somaliland can exercise the right to self-determination, the starting point is to ascertain whether the people of Somaliland constitute 'a people' in the sense of Article 2 of the Declaration on the Granting of Independence to Colonial Countries and Peoples, which classifies the methods as to how the right of self-determination can be exercised: 'The establishment of a sovereign and independent State, the free association or integration with an independent State or the emergence into any other political status freely determined by a people constitute modes of implementing the right of self-determination' (UNGA 1970).

To this end, some of the methods of exercising the right to self-determination include independence (common among former colonial territories), merger (for example British and the Italian Somaliland colonies) and free association (for example Bougainville and Papua New Guinea). Some states have attained independence after a period of international territorial administration (such as Kosovo in 2008) or independence after protracted armed conflicts (in the case of Eritrea from Ethiopia) (McCorquodale 2010: 375).

The foregoing examples reflect the exercise of 'external self-determination', where there is a change in the international relationships between the people exercising their right of self-determination and the original state or colonial power as well as other states and international actors. In this case, 'internal self-determination' relates to a situation where there is a shift towards autonomy in internal relationships and administrations within a State without a change in the external relationships. Autonomy and governance are some of the examples of internal self-determination where there is an agreement with the government for significant autonomy within a State. It is, thus, clear that while the principle of self-determination is generally broad, it is theoretically divided into internal and external self-determination.

Firstly, international custom recognises a right to internal self-determination, that is, where dissatisfied constituents have the right to use existing political processes as a tool for self-determination.[7] As a process of participatory democracy, internal self-determination is implemented inside the boundaries of the existing state and, therefore, it does not affect the territorial integrity of the state (Gudeleviciute 2005: 49). The Declaration on Principles of International Law outlines internal self-determination as being where 'government [is] representing the whole people belonging to the territory without distinction as to race, creed or colour'. Internal self-determination enables the people to 'freely make political choices and pursue economic, social and cultural development within' their territory and beyond.[8]

Secondly, there is external self-determination, meaning separation from the existing state of which the group concerned is a part, and the setting up of a new independent state. Thus, external self-determination is the right to decide on the political status of a people and its place in the international community in relation to other states, particularly secession and claims for independence from the parent state (Cassese 1995: 144; Dersso 2012: 9). The case of the independence of Somaliland relates to external self-determination.

Limitation of the right of self-determination

As with most – if not all – human rights, there are limitations on the exercise of the right to self-determination. The limitation on the exercise of the right to self-determination relates to the restriction not to 'engage in any activity or perform any act aimed at the destruction of any of the rights and freedoms' of others.[9] The other limitation on the exercise of the external right of self-determination relates to prohibition of action that 'would dismember or impair, totally or in part, the territorial integrity or political unity of sovereign and independent States'.[10]

The other limitation on the exercise of the right of self-determination is the international principle of *uti possidetis juris*, meaning that territorial boundaries at the time of independence shall remain sacrosanct (McCorquodale 2010: 381–2). The other potential limitation is that of competing claims, in cases where more than one state asserts sovereignty over a territory involving people possessing a right of self-determination.[11]

External self-determination: the need for justification for secession

Secession is the 'creation of a State by the use or threat of force and without the consent of the former sovereign' (Crawford 1979: 247). Secession is characterised by the 'separation of part of the territory and population of an existing State' (Kohen 2006: 3). Secession, when successful, results in the emergence of one or more new states recognised by the international community and the continued existence of the parent state from which those states seceded (Bederman 2006: 60–62). The secessionist entity's independence must also either not be disputed or be 'manifestly indisputable' (Crawford 1979: 266). Secessionist entities must be, in fact, independent and effective. Secession, because it results in the 'dismemberment of a previously unified, independent State', necessarily threatens the state-centred order (Buchheit 1978: 97–9). It is for this reason that secessionist entities are usually described as illegitimate when they attempt to secede. However, secession is not prohibited under international law (Dugard 1987: 91). While there is no express right of secession in international law, likewise there is no explicit prohibition against secession (Lauterpacht 1948: 6; Farley 2010: 797, 815). International law does not specifically grant component parts of sovereign states the legal right to secede unilaterally from their 'parent' state.[12]

Categories of secession

There are three legal theories of secession – bilateral, unilateral ('remedial') and de facto (Kreuter 2011: 385). Groups claiming a right to self-determination have frequently pursued secession, but self-determination and secession are not necessarily coextensive. Even a group that does not qualify as a people, and is therefore not vested with the right to self-determination, may pursue secession. When a putative secession does not implicate self-determination, however, the critical criterion of statehood is the 'maintenance of a stable and effective government' to the exclusion of the metropolitan state (Crawford 1979: 266).

Firstly, the use of domestic law to secure secession and independence is termed 'bilateral' secession. In practice, two things can together justify bilateral secession: 'a clear expression of democratic will' by those wishing to secede, and negotiations between the secessionists and the parent country (Deng 1973: 19). In conducting negotiations, the government must consider the rule of law, democracy, federalism, and the protection of minority rights.[13] In this way, the parent country grants independence in response to democratic pressure, effectively justifying secession. On the basis of bilateral secession, Somaliland could exercise the right to self-determination through internal self-determination, by using Somalia's established political procedures and mechanisms of self-rule to realise its policy goals. The recent gains made in state building in Somalia may make it easier for Somaliland to petition the official government of Somalia in its furtherance of self-determination.

Secondly, as regards the 'unilateral' or 'remedial' method of secession, the requirements for justifiable secession pertaining when the parent state opposes it are that: 1) those wishing to secede are 'a people'; 2) they are subject to serious violations of human rights at the hands of the parent state; and 3) the state authorities have denied the population free exercise of internal self-determination and no other remedies are available to them (Kreuter 2011: 370).[14] The concept of remedial secession is primarily focused on the right of a people to participate in the decision-making processes of the state (Raic 2002: 237). The unilateral right to secede – the right to secede without agreement of the whole population or without constitutional authorisation – should be understood as remedial in the sense of a last-resort response to serious injustices (Sterio 2010).[15] A secessionist entity is valid once its parent state accedes to its independence (Akehurst 1997: 78; Musgrave 1997: 210).

Thirdly, the secessionists may attempt to secede by simply declaring themselves independent from a parent state, that is, de facto secession (Vidmar 2009: 817–18). This occurs without a blessing from the parent state or justification under the unilateral standard. Such de facto secession is the most difficult to justify and may in fact be unjustifiable.[16] The only possibility for justification in the case of de facto secession occurs through recognition of the secessionists' independence by other nations. De facto secession is exactly what has happened in the Somaliland scenario, where Somaliland declared independence from the parent state of Somalia.

In practice, however, the application of the legal theories of secession is not so straightforward. This is because political considerations often play a more significant role than legal theories in motivating states to recognise seceding territories as independent states. The influence of politics on the legal issue of self-determination makes the successful exercise of this right more difficult, and possibly arbitrary, for less influential nations. Usually, apart from meeting the legal requirements of secession, secessionist states must also gain the recognition of influential states in order to attain legitimacy. In this case, approval or recognition largely relies on the will and motives of the powerful states, as opposed to the legal persuasion of the secessionists' claims to self-determination. This practice makes the sovereignty of less powerful states slightly less important than that of more powerful states.

Given the sanctity of state sovereignty, international law has set a high threshold for aspiring secessionists to overcome to justify their actions. Secession is valid so long as the seceding territory is a distinct, cohesive and recognisable unit.[17] However, going by the theories of secession, Somaliland probably lacks the justification to secede. The absence of an effective government in Somalia to accede to the secession or approve independence prevented the people of Somaliland from exercising their right to self-determination. This attests to a need to broaden the law of secession, to fill the analytical void pertaining to secession in the case of a failed state (Eggers 2007: 217).

The *uti possidetis* rule

Uti possidetis is a principle that governs the international frontiers of a newly emergent state.[18] The inviolability of colonial borders has been the cardinal principle on which African international relations has been premised. African states committed themselves to the principle of *uti possidetis* or *uti possidetis de jure*, that old administrative boundaries will become international boundaries when a political subdivision achieves independence.[19] Although African states have been committed to the sanctity of the colonially defined borders, the permanence of Africa's post-colonial borders has not been absolute. This is because several states, such as the Republic of Somalia, are amalgamations of former colonial possessions that achieved independence separately. The principle of *uti possidetis* has since evolved into a limitation on the validity of secession.

The Badinter Commission extended the principle of *uti possidetis* from decolonisation scenarios to dissolution, stating that, in defining territorial units that emerge after the dissolution of a state, 'the former boundaries become frontiers protected by international law'.[20] In the case of secession or dissolution of states, pre-existing administrative boundaries must be maintained to become the borders of the new states and cannot be altered by the threat or use of force, be it on the part of the seceding entity or the state from which it breaks off. In this sense, the concept of 'dissolving secession' mirrors that of remedial secession. Dissolving secession occurs where a state is created without the consent of the former sovereign owing to its collapse and lack of effective central government (Worster 2009). Therefore remedial or dissolving secession provides a minority region with the right to petition for the right to secede in the event of state dissolution.

Distinguishing Katanga and Biafra from Somaliland

A distinction should be made between the attempted secession in Katanga and Biafra, where the purported secessionist did not exist initially, on the one hand, and Somaliland and Eritrea, which existed as separate colonial territories. Somaliland's independence, therefore, conforms to *uti possidetis*. In fact, Somaliland has an even better claim to satisfaction of *uti possidetis* than its neighbour Eritrea (Farley 2010: 804–5). Unlike Eritrea, Somaliland underwent the process of decolonisation before losing its international personality to a larger entity (Farley 2010: 818). In this case, the parent state dissolved and the constituent states re-emerged within their colonial boundaries, satisfying *uti possidetis*. Somaliland's adherence to its colonial boundaries, then, satisfies the doctrine of *uti possidetis* as it has been applied in Africa in post-colonial secessions. Therefore an independent state of Somaliland would not infringe upon the principle of *uti possidetis* and Somali sovereignty.

The principle of *uti possidetis* provides that states emerging from colonial administrative control must accept the pre-existing colonial boundaries. The key reason is to achieve stability of territorial boundaries and to maintain international peace and security. This was pointed out by the ICJ in the *Frontier Dispute* case: 'The essential requirement of stability in order to survive, to develop and gradually to consolidate their independence in all fields, induced African states judiciously to consent to the respecting of colonial frontiers.'[21]

Although the principle of *uti possidetis juris* sought to preserve international peace and security at the time of independence, it has not prevented many boundary disputes given that these boundaries were mostly created to preserve the interests of the colonial states and not the natural or cultural boundaries set by the peoples themselves (McCorquodale 2010: 381). Given its flawed genesis, the principle of *uti possidetis* is of questionable legitimacy as a limitation to the right of self-determination, which can only reasonably apply in situations of decolonisation. The independence of South Sudan suggests that 'there may be a relaxation of the firmly held view in Africa that colonial borders are non-negotiable' (Dersso 2012: 7).

The requirements of statehood

The 1933 Montevideo Convention on the Rights and Duties of States provides that a state 'shall constitute a sole person in the eyes of international law' (Montevideo Convention 1933). For this reason, 'States are juridically equal, enjoy the same rights, and have equal capacity in their exercise' (Montevideo Convention 1933). The Montevideo Convention prescribes the classical criteria for statehood: 'The state as a person of international law should possess the following qualifications: a) a permanent population; b) a defined territory; c) government; and d) capacity to enter into relations with the other states' (Montevideo Convention 1933). Apart from this, the 'political existence of the state is independent of recognition by the other states' (Montevideo Convention 1933; see also Gudeleviciute 2005: 68). This is where the legal concept of recognition by other states is derived (Akehurst 1997: 79).

It can be contended that the Republic of Somaliland meets the statehood criteria set out in the Montevideo Convention. It has a permanent population, a defined territory, a government, and the capacity to enter into relations with other states. Somaliland claims a population of close to 3.5 million people (Worster 2009: 166). The Republic of Somaliland meets the objective criteria of statehood, and its emergence through the dissolution of the Republic of Somalia conforms to international norms (Farley 2010: 805). Somaliland has fixed and clearly determined borders, satisfying the territory criterion of statehood. At secession, the Republic of Somaliland explicitly declared its territory as that comprising the British protectorate of Somaliland (Farley 2010: 806). Somaliland possesses an 'organized political authority', satisfying the government criterion of statehood.

Somaliland is responsible for national defence. It maintains law and order. It even engages in those auxiliary activities of government such as the printing of currency, operating a central bank and issuing passports (Walls 2009: 379; Farley 2010: 788). Somaliland's central government is so effective that several Western nations refuse to grant Somalilanders asylum because Somaliland is 'safe and secure' (Farley 2010: 806). Somaliland's government has even managed to demilitarise its population without outside support or funding. Additional indicators of the effectiveness of Somaliland's government are found in its dealings with pirates and Islamist militants. In stark contrast to rump Somalia, where pirates operate with impunity, Somaliland's government operates a coastguard that actively pursues pirates. Somaliland qualifies for statehood even if the measure is effectiveness rather than the Montevideo Convention criteria (Farley 2010: 809).

The requirement of recognition of a state

The fact that secession is the 'outcome of the struggle' has repercussions for state sovereignty and territorial integrity (Akehurst 1997: 76). It is unlikely that a part of a state's population, which is usually struggling against a superior force, will be able to secede without foreign assistance (Gudeleviciute 2005: 67). The principle of territorial integrity applies to relations between states and requires respect from other states to the sovereign state's territorial integrity and its opposite respect to other states (Cassese 1995: 108; Gudeleviciute 2005: 64). The UN Charter prohibits the world body from intervening 'in matters which are essentially within the domestic jurisdiction of any state' (UN 1945). Therefore, recognition of a new seceding state can be viewed as an intervention into the domestic jurisdiction of the existing state. However, if recognition is not a requirement for the formation of a new state which emerges prior to recognition, the parent state cannot claim intervention any longer (Gudeleviciute 2005: 68).

International law gives great deference to state sovereignty. If other nations, through the act of recognition, hold the power to give or to withhold the right to secession, the parent state's right to sovereignty becomes subject to the willingness or unwillingness of recognising states. Although the parent state has an option to declare secession illegal under domestic law, that may not be effective if other states recognise a seceding state. However, the principles of territorial integrity, state sovereignty and *uti possidetis* may be infringed upon in the case of recognition of an illegal secession. It can be argued, however, that Somaliland has already gained independence since 1991 through de facto secession. De facto secession on its own, however, is legally insufficient. Somaliland might have a better argument for legal de facto secession if foreign nations recognised its independence, but no state has done so. Such de facto secession might be acceptable if influential or enough nations recognise the seceding state (Kreuter 2011: 390).

Generally, there are two schools of thought regarding the legal impact of recognition on a putative state (Lauterpacht 1948: 38–42). On the one hand, the constitutive school holds that recognition is a fundamental criterion of statehood, implying that an entity becomes a state only once it has been recognised. The declaratory school, on the other hand, holds that recognition has no legal effect; recognition merely announces what is already fact, meaning that the entity in question is a state (Farley 2010: 792). Under the declarative theory of statehood, a region attains statehood by declaring itself a state, by satisfying the Montevideo criteria of having a permanent population, by having a defined territory, by having a government, and by having the capacity to enter into relations with other states (Montevideo Convention 1933). Thus, statehood does not depend on recognition or acknowledgement by other nations. Another perspective that goes beyond the traditional constitutive–declaratory dichotomy is the 'perception school', which does not focus on 'when a state is a state, but rather to whom is a state a state' (Farley 2010: 792). From this perspective, it means that a state may be a state internally but not externally.

Scholars submit that existing states have an obligation to recognise or not to recognise an emerging state (Lauterpacht 1948: 6; Farley 2010: 797). In this sense, existing states have an obligation not to recognise putative states whose creation violated a peremptory norm of international law in the form of aggression, a racist regime, disrupting existing frontiers or violating norms of self-determination (Farley 2010: 794). In this case, it is difficult to understand why Somaliland cannot be recognised, since it was created peacefully without flouting the rules of international law.

Recognition under the declarative school

The declaratory theory is premised on the objective criteria outlined under the Montevideo Convention. Under the declaratory theory, statehood is recognised when the four conditions of the Montevideo Convention criteria are met, regardless of international consent. Going by the Montevideo Convention criteria, it can be argued that Somaliland meets the theoretical requirements of statehood. Somaliland's population is relatively stable, unlike in the south, which has suffered a steady exodus of refugees since the civil war began. Somaliland's borders from its days as a British colony still serve as a hypothetical line of demarcation, albeit informally and without legal effect because of its unification with Somalia in 1960. Somaliland can point to the relative success of several peaceful local elections as evidence of the existence of government. Although no nation recognises Somaliland, it still maintains some informal contacts with other nations, such as Ethiopia and Yemen (Kreuter 2011: 382). On these bases, Somaliland appears to have a strong claim to statehood (Eggers 2007; Kreuter 2011: 382).

Recognition under the constitutive school

Under the constitutive theory, statehood is not automatic but rather is dependent on recognition by the international community (Worster 2009: 120). Proponents of the constitutive theory do not claim that recognition creates the state but that 'existing states merely act as the gatekeepers to ensure that *de facto* States meet the criteria outlined under the Montevideo Convention' (Raic 2002: 29–31). Recognition occurs when a nation publicly accepts the existence of the state (Worster 2009: 120). Nevertheless, critics argue that this approach leads to uncertainty, especially when some nations choose to recognise a state but others do not (Kreuter 2011: 366). They also contend that it hinders the exercise of the right of self-determination because it places more importance upon the judgment of the recognising nation than upon the rights of the state exercising self-determination. Under the constitutive theory of statehood, Somaliland could meet the requirements of statehood upon recognition of independence by other nations or international bodies (Kreuter 2011: 379). As the case is today, however, Somaliland is still unable to engage in official relations with other nations, which are concerned about the political ramifications of recognising a breakaway state.

To recognise or not to recognise a state

In light of the political nature of recognition, states may choose recognition when it serves their interests. It is possible to contend that, since Somaliland meets the requirements of statehood, it is therefore already independent of Somalia. The legality of such a claim depends upon an evaluation of the legal status of Somaliland using the declarative or constitutive theory of statehood. The constitutive theory of statehood requires recognition by other states and the international community, whereas the applicability of the declarative theory is contingent upon several social, geographical and political factors (Kreuter 2011: 379–80). Somaliland's independence and statehood are not recognised by any other state.

The dominant reason advanced for not recognising Somaliland has been that the peace process in rump Somalia must take precedence over recognition of Somaliland, thereby opting for the preservation of a unitary Somali state (Farley 2010: 810). Thus, the reasons underlying Somaliland's non-recognition are political rather than legal. Another reason for not recognising Somaliland is driven partly by fears of opening a 'Pandora's box' by encouraging ethnic conflict and irredentism across the continent (Eggers 2007: 220–22). Since decolonisation, Africa has been preoccupied with the fragility of its inherited borders; most African states are ethnically heterogeneous, and tribal and ethnic groups straddle many of Africa's borders. The other argument is that recognition of Somaliland will inevitably legitimise an entity like al-Shabaab, which exercises de facto control over rump Somalia (Farley 2010: 819).

It is, however, questionable how recognising Somaliland can open a Pandora's box leading to widespread disruption of African borders, since the secession is not motivated by ethnic concerns and cannot provide justification for ethnic separatist movements.[22] Somalia is one of the most ethnically homogeneous states in Africa, with the vast majority of the populations in both Somaliland and rump Somalia being Somali, sharing a similar adherence to Sunni Islam and nomadic pastoralism. Further, Somaliland's independence is unlikely to encourage the forcible alteration of post-colonial borders, because Somaliland conforms to the borders it inherited at decolonisation (Farley 2010: 811).

In weighing the *pro et contra* of recognising Somaliland, on the one hand, the obvious downside is that it may exacerbate the instability in the Horn of Africa. For example, the pirates who are currently kept at bay by Somaliland's coastguard would be able to expand their base of operation around the Horn of Africa. The same is true with al-Shabaab, whose terrorist activities might flourish in a more lawless territory where they can hide, train, prepare and eventually launch transnational terrorist acts. On the other hand, recognising Somaliland would afford it access to bilateral aid and development assistance, thereby making it able to sustain the security measures it provides towards international security as a bulwark against piracy and al-Qaeda-affiliated militants (Eggers 2007: 211, 221).

Further, the secession of Somaliland does not impinge upon the four peremptory norms that impose an obligation on the international community to decline to recognise a state, namely aggression, a racist regime, disrupting existing frontiers or violating norms of self-determination. In any case, going by the precedent set by the dissolution of the former Yugoslavia and the United Arab Republic, no such recognition is needed for Somaliland for its independence to be valid (Crawford 1979: 256–7).[23] If this is the case, then the Republic of Somaliland can be regarded as an independent state, the reason being that Somaliland has re-emerged as an independent state following the dissolution of the Republic of Somalia. Somaliland has attempted to repel the 'failed state' fate of Somalia.

Conclusion

The territorial integrity and political unity of a sovereign state are sacred. The exception is when a state does not conduct itself in compliance with the principle of equal rights and self-determination of peoples because its government does not represent the whole population without distinction. The *raison d'être* of the right of self-determination is to enable the rights holders to determine their political, economic, social and cultural destiny as they wish, while not overriding the legitimate interests of others affected. The main interrelation between the principle of self-determination of peoples and the principle of territorial integrity is that a claim to external self-determination covers a claim to territory. Related to the issue of territorial integrity is the principle of *uti possidetis juris*, which dictates that the right to self-determination must not involve changes to existing frontiers at the time of independence. However, the independence of South Sudan suggests that respect for the territorial integrity of African states and the principle of *uti possidetis* is no longer absolute.

The question of secession is most closely related to the principle of territorial integrity. Secession is a territorial change, which occurs when part of an independent state or non-self-governing territory separates itself to become a new independent state. The principle of self-determination is usually invoked in connection with unilateral secession, that is, secession undertaken without the consent of the existing state and without constitutional sanction. Since all land area is claimed by some state and use of force is prohibited, 'secession is the only real method of new state formation, and a prohibition of secession is equivalent to a veto on new States' (OAU 1981).

It is correct to contend that, under the current international standards for secession, Somaliland lacks a sufficient legal basis to secede and become an independent, sovereign nation. The people of Somaliland may not exercise the right of self-determination, as they may not qualify as a 'people' according to the accepted definition, in terms of an ethnic or cultural minority. They have arguably not faced the types of human rights violations that can justify secession. Secession may not be a last resort, as they may have other possible remedies short of secession. International law provides a minority region with the right to petition for secession. However, the law envisions that the parent state and the minority region will negotiate the terms of secession. It is thus not clear what happens when a central government is unable (as opposed to unwilling) to negotiate, as is the case with Somaliland. In such circumstances, the Republic of Somaliland faces an unproductive choice between attempting reconciliation with Somalia and continued non-recognition by the international community.

Nonetheless, it is reasonable to argue that Somaliland qualifies to be a de facto state given that it satisfies the four Montevideo Convention criteria of statehood. Further, it can also be argued that Somaliland gained its independence through dissolution, that is, implosion of a parent state leading to the creation of new states; and its secession conforms to the limiting principle of *uti possidetis*, requiring territorial adherence to colonial boundaries. Somaliland is a state that merely lacks recognition. Recognition, however, is a political act, and its validity turns on whether the creation of the state to be recognised satisfies the norms of international law. This means that, until international 'personality' is granted, Somaliland may not be attributed any of the rights or duties of states. As indicated earlier, recognising Somaliland would not violate any norm of international law that precludes secession.

Furthermore, given that Somaliland regained its independence in the context of dissolution and in adherence with the principle of *uti possidetis*, its recognition would neither set a new precedent nor open the feared Pandora's box of tribal fragmentation of African states. Rather, the greatest impact it could have would be to return Africa to its status at the outset of decolonisation. Nonetheless, Somalia still needs to be recognised by the international community as an independent state able to take part in international relations. In the absence of such recognition, Somaliland may need to resort to domestic remedies before seceding. Such remedies include advocating independence through a national referendum similar to the one of 1960, or suggesting a form of federalism and decentralisation to gain at least an element of autonomy from the Somali federal government in Mogadishu. However, it is unlikely that such remedies are available under the current circumstances in rump Somalia.

A case can be made that Somaliland, which has had a functional government since it declared independence in 1991, should be recognised as such by the international community. The lack of an effective central government in Somalia created an impasse, making it impossible for Somaliland to apply for secession. It should be remembered that, shortly after undertaking the union of the two states, the people of Somaliland voted against the union in a unification referendum. The reasons for non-recognition of Somaliland as an independent state border more on politics than just law. There is a lacuna in the law as to the secession of a people from a parent state that has collapsed, as was the case in Somalia. There is a need to balance the interests of states in preserving state sovereignty and the right of people to exercise self-determination where the state has failed. In the absence of internal self-determination and the right to negotiate for secession, remedial secession theory offers an avenue for the people within a failed state to justifiably secede.

Notes

1 See 'The Implementation of the Right to Self-Determination as a Contribution to Conflict Prevention', Report of the international conference of experts organised by the United Nations Educational, Scientific and Cultural Organization (UNESCO)

Division of Human Rights, Democracy and Peace and the UNESCO Centre of Catalonia, 21–27 November 1998, Barcelona, http://www.unpo.org/print.php? arg=01&par=446 (accessed 5 November 2012).

2 For example, South Sudan actually seceded from (northern) Sudan following a 2005 peace agreement with Sudan which contained a referendum for self-determination – as part of a deal to end years of civil war.

3 *Reference in re Secession of Quebec* (SCR) 2(1998), 217, para. 138; see also *International Legal Materials*, 1998, 1340 and 1373, http://scc.lexum.umontreal.ca/en/1998/1998rcs2- 217/1998rcs2-217.pdf (accessed 15 September 2012), para. 6; see also Cassese (1995: 108).

4 *Reference in re Secession of Quebec*, para. 138.

5 *Western Sahara* case [1975] ICJ Rep 12, para. 55.

6 *Namibia* opinion [1971] ICJ Rep 16, para. 52.

7 *Reference in re Secession of Quebec*; see also Kreuter (2011: 367).

8 *Reference in re Secession of Quebec*, para. 136.

9 International Covenant on Economic, Social and Cultural Rights (ICESCR) and International Covenant on Civil and Political Rights (ICCPR), Art. 5(1).

10 Declaration on Principles of International Law (UNGA 1970).

11 This was the issue in the *East Timor* case, where the ICJ accepted that Portugal, as the colonial power, and Indonesia, as the occupying power, had forms of sovereignty over the same territory, as did the people of East Timor, who had the right of self-determination. See *East Timor* case (*Portugal* v. *Australia*) [1995] ICJ Rep. 90, para. 32.

12 *Reference in re Secession of Quebec*, para. 111.

13 *Reference in re Secession of Quebec*, para. 85.

14 As above, paras 264–5, 281–6; Kreuter (2011: 370); see also *Report Presented by Commission of Rapporteurs on the Aaland Islands Question*, League of Nations Doc. B7.21/68/106, (1921), para. 21.

15 See also the *Congrès du peuple katangais* v. *Zaire* (*Katanga* case), African Commission on Human and Peoples' Rights, Communication 75/92, 8th Annual Activity Report (1994–95).

16 *Reference in re Secession of Quebec*, para. 296.

17 See *the Aaland Islands Question*, n. 14 above.

18 See the *Frontier Dispute* case (*Burkina Faso* v. *Mali*), ICJ 554, 565 (22 Dec.).

19 See 1964 OAU Resolution on Border Disputes among African States, OAU document AHG/Res. 16(I).

20 See *Conference on Yugoslavia, Arbitration Commission*, Opinion No. 3, 92 I.L.R. 170 (1993) [Badinter Opinion 3].

21 *Frontier Dispute* case, n. 18 above, para. 25.

22 Unlike the case of Somaliland, Eritrea's secession was ethnically driven and, therefore, more likely to inspire the dissolution of Africa's ethnically heterogeneous states (Farley 2010: 811).

23 In contrast, Eritrea seceded from Ethiopia – Ethiopia did not dissolve – and it was only with Ethiopia's accession that Eritrea became independent (Crawford 1979: 256–7).

References

Akehurst, Peter Malanczuk. 1997. *Modern Introduction to International Law*, 7th edn. London: Routledge.

Anstis, Sebastian. 2010. 'The Normative Bases of the Global Territorial Order', *Diplomacy and Statecraft*, vol. 12, no. 2, pp. 306–23.

Badinter Commission. 1992. The Arbitration Commission of the Peace Conference on Yugoslavia, Opinion 4, (1992) 31 ILM 1495 (Badinter Commission), para. 4.

BBC News. 2011. 'South Sudan Backs Independence – Results', 7 February, http://www.bbc.co.uk/news/world-africa-12379431 (accessed 12 December 2012).

Bederman, David J. 2006. *International Law Frameworks*, Concepts and Insights Series. New York: Foundation Press.

Buchheit, Lee C. 1978. *Secession: The Legitimacy of Self-Determination*. New Haven, CT: Yale University Press.

Bunick, Nicola. 2009. 'Chechnya: Access Denied', *Georgetown Journal of International Law*, vol. 40, pp. 985–1025.

Cassese, Antonio. 1995. *Self-Determination of Peoples: A Legal Reappraisal*. Cambridge: Cambridge University Press.

Crawford, James. 1979. *The Creation of States in International Law*. Oxford: Oxford University Press.

Deng, Francis M. 1973. *Dynamics of Identification: A Basis for National Integration in the Sudan*. Khartoum: Khartoum University Press.

Dersso, Solomon. 2012. *International Law and the Self-Determination of South Sudan*, Paper no. 231, February. Addis Ababa: Institute for Security Studies.

Dugard, John. 1987. *Recognition and the United Nations*. Cambridge: Cambridge University Press.

Eggers, Alison K. 2007. 'When Is a State a State? The Case for Recognition of Somaliland', *Boston College International and Comparative Law Review*, vol. 30, pp. 211–22.

Farley, Benjamin R. 2010. 'Calling a State a State: Somaliland and International Recognition', *Emory International Law Review*, vol. 24, pp. 777–820.

Gudeleviciute, Vita. 2005. 'Does the Principle of Self-Determination Prevail over the Principle of Territorial Integrity?', *International Journal of Baltic Law*, vol. 2, no. 2, pp. 48–74.

International Covenant on Economic, Social and Cultural Rights (ICESCR) and International Covenant on Civil and Political Rights (ICCPR), Art. 5(1).

Kohen, Marcelo G. 2006. 'Introduction', in Marcelo G. Kohen (ed.), *Secession: International Law Perspectives*. Cambridge: Cambridge University Press.

Kreuter, Aaron. 2011. 'Self-Determination, Sovereignty, and the Failure of States: Somaliland and the Case for Justified Secession', *Minnesota Journal of International Law*, vol. 19, no. 2, pp. 363–97.

Lauterpacht, Hersch. 1948. *Recognition in International Law*. Cambridge: Cambridge University Press.

McCorquodale, Robert. 2010. 'Rights of Peoples and Minorities', in Daniel Moeckli, Sangeeta Shah and Sandesh Sivakumara (eds), *International Human Rights Law* (pp. 365–90). Oxford: Oxford University Press.

Montevideo Convention. 1933. *Montevideo Convention on the Rights and Duties of States*, entered into force on 26 December 1934, Art. 2.

Musgrave, Thomas D. 1997. *Self-Determination and National Minorities*. Oxford: Clarendon Press.

OAU. 1981. African [Banjul] Charter on Human and Peoples' Rights, adopted 27 June 1981, OAU Doc. CAB/LEG/67/3 rev.5, 21 I.L.M. 58(1982), entered into force 21 October 1986.

Raic, David. 2002. *Statehood and the Law of Self-Determination*. Leiden: Martinus Nijhoff.

Sterio, Milena. 2010. 'On the Right to External Self-Determination: "Selfistans", Secession and the Great Powers' Rule', *Minnesota Journal of International Law*, vol. 19, pp. 137–76.

Universal Declaration of Human Rights. 1948. G.A. Res. 271A (III), U.N. Doc A/810 at 71 (1948).

UN. 1945. Article 2(7) of the Charter of the United Nations, 26 June 1945, 59 Stat. 1031, T.S. 993, 3 Bevans 1153, entered into force 24 October 1945.

UNGA. 1961. The Declaration on the Granting of Independence to Colonial Countries and Peoples, G.A. Res. 1514 (XV), 15 UN GAOR Supp. (No. 16) at 66, U.N. Doc. A/4684(1961).

UNGA. 1970. Declaration on Principles of International Law Concerning Friendly Relations and Cooperation among States in Accordance with the Charter of the United Nations, G.A. Res. 2625, Annex, 25 UN GAOR, Supp. (No. 28), UN Doc. A/5217 at 121 (1970).

Vidmar, Jure. 2009. 'International Legal Responses to Kosovo's Declaration of Independence', *Vanderbilt Journal of Transnational Law*, vol. 42, pp. 779–851.

Walls, Michael. 2009. 'The Emergence of a Somali State: Building Peace from Civil War in Somaliland', *African Affairs*, vol. 108, no. 432, pp. 371–89.

Worster, William Thomas. 2009. 'Law, Politics, and the Conception of the State in State Recognition Theory', *Boston University International Law Journal*, vol. 27, no. 1, pp. 115–71.

3   The OAU doctrine on colonial boundaries and conflicts of separation in the Horn of Africa

Kidane Mengisteab

Considering that border problems constitute a grave and permanent factor of dissention . . .

Considering further that the borders of African States, on the day of their independence, constitute a tangible reality;

SOLEMNLY DECLARES that all Member States pledge themselves to respect the borders existing on their achievement of national independence.
(AHG/Res. 16(I), Assembly of Heads of State and Government
Meeting in Its First Ordinary Session in Cairo, UAR, 17–21 July 1964)

Introduction

The Organisation of African Unity (OAU) in its first ordinary session of the Assembly of Heads of State and Government, held in Cairo between 17 and 21 July 1964, passed a resolution "that all Member States pledge themselves to respect the borders existing on their achievement of national independence." Confronted with Somalia's conflicts against Ethiopia and Kenya over its claims to the Somali-inhabited Ogaden of Ethiopia and the North Eastern Province of Kenya, the founders of the organization saw the writing on the wall that the colonial boundaries, which partitioned many ethnic groups into several states, would be challenged by many states and ethnic identities alike. Understandably, they were concerned that attempts to bring about territorial readjustments by post-colonial states or other political actors would lead to a plethora of conflicts that would tear up the continent's young countries. Preserving the colonial boundaries thus became a landmark doctrine of the new continental body.

There are claims that the doctrine, as intended by the founders of the OAU, has contributed to reducing wars of secession and conflicts related to territorial claims and border disputes (Touval 1967; Keller 2007). Undoubtedly, the number of secessionist wars in the continent has been rather small relative to the large number of ethnic groups partitioned by the colonial boundaries. However, conflicts over demands for socioeconomic rights by identities who perceive themselves to be marginalized have made the continent the host of the largest number of civil wars and civil conflicts in the post-1960s global system. The number of successful secessions has also been very small. Yet it is not clear how much of the credit belongs to the OAU's boundary doctrine. The failure of Africa's most notable wars of secession, such as those of Katanga, Biafra, and the Ogaden, were essentially due to military defeats rather than due to the influence of the continental body's doctrine, although the OAU provided political support to states fighting secessionist forces. The Western Sahara war of self-determination, which received political support from the continental body, has also not succeeded, although there have not been other such cases.

The doctrine's most apparent failures in deterring secessions and in mitigating territorial conflicts have occurred in the Horn of Africa. The successes of Eritrea and South Sudan in winning their independence after bitterly fought long wars are the most notable examples. Somaliland's declaration of independence and the Ogaden's long and still on-going war are other cases that manifest the doctrine's weak influence in the Horn of Africa. This chapter grapples with the question of why the OAU's doctrine has not succeeded in deterring secessions and territorial wars in the Horn of Africa. Without delving into detailed historical accounts, the chapter examines the secessions in the Horn of Africa, including Eritrea, South Sudan, and Somaliland, as well as the Ogaden's intractable conflicts, in an attempt to explain why the OAU doctrine has neither deterred wars nor prevented breakups of countries in the region.[1] The chapter is organized as follows. First there is an outline of some general propositions that help explain why the OAU doctrine has been rather ineffective in the Horn of Africa. Then there is a brief examination of the specific factors behind the doctrine's failure in each of the identified four cases. Finally there are some policy-relevant lessons learned from the four cases.

General factors

A number of factors related to the region's specific historical context seem to have contributed to the failure of the OAU doctrine in the Horn of Africa. One aspect of the context revolves around the legacies of the region's expansionist pre-colonial empires. These empires left behind, on the one hand, marginalized identity groups who resisted their subjugation and continued to struggle against their incorporation and marginalization. On the other hand, the empires left behind successor states, which attempted to maintain the territories the empires left behind and to reclaim those lost during colonization but often did little to address the grievances of marginalized identities. Another aspect of the historical context relates to intervention by global powers, which engaged in territorial readjustments during the period of decolonization in a manner that suited their strategic interests. The following four propositions attempt to capture the most important contextual factors that undermined the OAU doctrine in the region:

- *Proposition 1:* All of the four cases in this study had separate (or quasi-separate) colonial existence from the countries they were incorporated into at the time of decolonization. The secessionist wars waged by the four entities can thus be viewed as an attempt to reverse their involuntary incorporation

(Somaliland is an exception in this regard) and to reaffirm the separate (or quasi-separate) political identity they obtained under colonialism.

- *Proposition 2*: Another factor that produced resistance to the OAU doctrine in the region relates to the conflict between the doctrine and the historical struggle for self-determination by groups who were forcibly incorporated by expansionist pre-colonial empires. The territorial composition of modern-day Ethiopia is, for example, largely a product of robust expansion carried out by the Abyssinian Empire during the time of European colonization of many parts of the Horn, roughly between 1875 and 1910. Some of the identities incorporated by the Abyssinian Empire, including the Somali inhabitants of the Ogaden, waged lingering resistance against their subjugation by the Abyssinian Empire. They resisted their incorporation into Ethiopia during the era of decolonization after they were severed from Ethiopia by colonialism, and they continue to battle for secession from Ethiopia. Obviously, the various rebel groups of the Ogaden view their resistance against the empire and its successor state as a legitimate struggle for self-determination and against marginalization. The OAU doctrine offers little to such groups, as it does not accept self-determination as justification for secession and provides little recourse against persistent marginalization.[2]
- *Proposition 3*: Another complicating factor is that some of the colonial powers in the region engaged in territorial changes and governance rearrangements on the eve of their departure from their colonies, in large part to accommodate the strategic interests of global powers. Some of these changes provoked resistance and conflicts well before decolonization. Eritrea, South Sudan, and the Ogaden experienced such changes. The OAU doctrine, which largely affirmed such contested administrative and territorial rearrangements made in the waning years of colonialism, could not serve as an effective means of transforming the region's conflicts.
- *Proposition 4*: Poor management of diversity by the post-colonial states in the region exacerbated the grievances of identities that were merged into states they did not choose to be part of and triggered various chronic conflicts. In some cases the struggle against poor governance also became intertwined with the secessionist conflicts or at least reinforced the secessionist conflicts undermining the OAU doctrine.

We now examine how a combination of the identified propositions explains the Eritrean, Ogaden, and South Sudan conflicts. We also briefly examine the Somaliland case, which differs from the other three cases in some notable respects, although it too had a separate colonial experience. It is, however, a secession that has not received recognition by the African Union or other countries in the global system.

Eritrea's war of independence

All the identified propositions apply to Eritrea's 30-year war of independence. Ethiopia's claim over Eritrea at the time of the latter's decolonization was made on the basis that Eritrea allegedly was an integral part of the Abyssinian Empire before its colonization. Eritrea's claim for independence, on the other hand, was grounded in its political identity formed by colonialism. Eritrea was a colony created by Italy in the late 1890s and did not exist as a unified political entity before its colonization by Italy. After the defeat of Italy's East African empire in 1941 by British forces, Eritrea came to be administered by the United Kingdom, which acted as a U.N. trustee. Following a ten-year British administration, the disposal of Eritrea was brought to the U.N. for debate, and a number of conflicting positions were expressed at the U.N. General Assembly. One position was expressed by Ethiopia, which, as noted already, laid a claim to Eritrea, primarily contending that Eritrea was part of the Abyssinian Empire before it was severed by colonialism. The claim that Eritrea was a part of the empire is rather dubious, however. Eritrea did not exist as a political entity and, while some parts of it were subjugated by the Abyssinian Empire at different times, other parts were essentially beyond the reach of the modern Abyssinian Empire, which arose in the second half of the nineteenth century. More importantly, Ethiopia signed several treaties with Italy, conceding any claim on Eritrea and delineating its boundaries with the new colony. Its case, which rested on uncertain pre-colonial relations with what emerged to become Eritrea, thus was rather untenable. Nonetheless, one political party in Eritrea, the Unionist Party, supported union with Ethiopia, in part because Ethiopia represented a symbol of independence from European colonization.

Another position, expressed by the governments of the U.K. and Italy, was to dismember Eritrea, adjoining the western parts of the country with the Anglo-Egyptian Sudan and giving the eastern portion to Ethiopia.[3] This proposal was strongly opposed by all political parties in Eritrea except the Unionist Party. All other political parties in the country formed a bloc in opposing the country's dismemberment and demanded immediate independence. Despite the vocal opposition by the Eritrean political parties and the backing of several Arab and Moslem countries, as well as the Soviet bloc countries, the British–Italian proposal was only narrowly defeated at the U.N. The demand for independence also failed to secure enough support at the U.N. General Assembly.

A dominant position with regard to Eritrea's disposal was expressed by the U.S., which enjoyed a large backing at the U.N. This position strongly opposed Eritrea's independence in favor of linking it with Ethiopia. The U.S. took this position largely for two reasons. One was the concern that, owing to its large Muslim population, Eritrea would ally itself with the Arab world, turn the Red Sea into an "Arab lake," and threaten American as well as Israeli interests in the region (Yohannes 1991). Ethiopia, on the other hand, was viewed as a country with a strong Christian heritage that would be inclined to be favorable to Western interests. The Ethiopian monarch, Haile Selassie, was also viewed as a staunch anti-communist. Another reason was its interest in maintaining its access to the strategic naval radio station, Radio Marina, which was left behind by Italian rule in Asmara, Eritrea's capital city. The station was handed over to the U.S. by the British military administration of Eritrea in 1943. Located on nearly the same longitude as the Soviet deep space command center in the Crimea, the station, which was renamed Kagnew, was a Cold War listening station later furnished with large dishes used to monitor telemetry from a variety of Soviet spacecraft. The base was considered at the time "one of the most valuable U.S. telecommunications centers in Africa, Asia, and the Middle East" (Schraeder 1992: 590). Given the importance of the base and the suspicion that an independent Eritrea would ally itself with the Arab world, the U.S. did not want to risk losing the base by allowing Eritrea's independence. Adjoining Eritrea with Ethiopia thus became a strategy of securing its continued access to the base. Like the U.S., Israel also adhered to a policy that strongly opposed Eritrean independence. Like their American counterparts, Israeli policy makers believed that an independent Eritrea would be an "Arab-oriented" (and anti-Israel) state that would turn the Red Sea into an "Arab lake" (Schraeder 1992: 579–80).[4]

Despite its strategic interests, the U.S. government gave some consideration to Eritrea's right to self-determination. To bridge the gap between its own strategic interests and Eritrea's right to self-determination, the U.S. proposed a federal arrangement between Eritrea and Ethiopia, which at the time appeared to be a compromise solution. This compromise was candidly expressed by the leader of the U.S. delegation to the U.N., John Foster Dulles, who served as secretary of state between 1953 and 1959. Dulles stated that:

> From the point of view of justice, the opinions of the Eritrean people must receive consideration. Nevertheless, the strategic interests of the United States in the Red Sea Basin and considerations of security and world peace make it necessary that the country [Eritrea] has to be linked with our ally, Ethiopia.
>
> (Yohannes 1991)

The United Nations finally approved the U.S.-proposed compromise of federating Eritrea with Ethiopia. The Ethio-Eritrean federation, which was established in 1952, lasted only ten years, as Ethiopia unilaterally annexed Eritrea in 1962. The annexation was of little surprise to those who expressed serious reservations about the federal arrangement on the grounds that such an arrangement between two unequal countries would not work. This group, which was led by the Soviet Union and included many Arab countries, had warned that the federal arrangement gave Ethiopia a blank check to annex Eritrea. In reality, the U.N. settlement of the Eritrean case ultimately proved to be an accommodation of the geostrategic interests of the U.S. and the interests of its ally, Ethiopia, in securing a sea outlet at the expense of the right to self-determination of the Eritrean people.

Poor governance

The federal experience with Ethiopia proved to be ruinous for Eritrea, in large part owing to poor governance. The Ethiopian government restricted various political rights, including the press and political organization. The vibrant press that existed in Eritrea under the British trusteeship was silenced with the banning of various newspapers. The right of political organization was also trampled, with leaders opposed to union with Ethiopia facing persecution and assassination. Eritrea's economy was crippled by the closure of a number of factories, which were made to relocate to Addis Ababa (Habte Selassie, 1989). The Ethiopian government also attempted to reorient Eritrea's educational system into Amharic, Ethiopia's official language. In 1957 the policy went to the extent of burning educational texts in Tigrigna and Arabic, the official languages in Eritrea. The Ethiopian government also attacked one of the symbols of Eritrean nationalism by lowering the Eritrean flag in November 1958. With these measures, which were perceived in Eritrea as an all-out assault on Eritrean identity and a prelude to annexation of the country, an armed struggle for independence was waged in 1961, one year before the official annexation of the country and some three years before the formulation of the OAU doctrine of non-violability of colonial boundaries. Eritrean nationalists initiated armed struggle as they realized that Ethiopia's annexation of Eritrea was imminent.

It is hard to say if good governance would have averted Eritrea's armed struggle for self-determination. However, poor governance undoubtedly enhanced popular support for the struggle. In any case, a combination of post-Second World War manipulations by global powers, which deprived Eritrea of self-determination, and repressive rule by Ethiopia explains the Eritrean war. Moreover, from the point of view of Eritrean nationalists the Eritrean war hardly represents a violation of the OAU boundary doctrine. Eritrean nationalists saw their cause as consistent with the doctrine, since their country's boundaries were established by the colonial state and they were struggling against Ethiopia's unilateral abrogation of the U.N.-instituted federal arrangement. For them Ethiopia's illegal annexation of their country was clearly in contravention of the OAU doctrine. The OAU, however, never questioned Ethiopia's annexation, nor did it conduct any investigation into the plight of the Eritrean people during the 30-year war. Instead, it saw the conflict as Ethiopia's internal affair, in which it could not interfere, owing to its principle of non-interference in the internal affairs of member states. The fact that Ethiopia hosted the continental body and Ethiopia's Emperor Haile Selassie was a key figure in the founding of the organization may have prevented the organization from at least conducting an investigation into the case. In any case, from the Eritrean perspective the OAU simply failed to adhere to its own doctrine in the Eritrean case.

The South Sudan case

Unlike the Eritrean case, South Sudan's secession appears to contravene the OAU boundary doctrine, at least technically, since at the time of Sudan's independence South Sudan was an integral part of Sudan. However, the British colonial administration, for all practical purposes, had administratively separated South Sudan from the rest of the country, creating a separate political and cultural entity for roughly half a century. During the last decade of colonial rule, the British colonial administration changed its policy and merged South Sudan with Sudan and at independence in 1956 left a divided but one Sudan. The policy change in the waning years of colonial rule, however, could not reverse the separate identity of South Sudan that the British helped erect for half a century. Proposition 1 thus seems to apply to South Sudan, if not nominally at least in substance. Another highly relevant proposition for South Sudan is Proposition 4, since South Sudan was a politically, economically, and culturally marginalized entity within Sudan. For much of its duration the South Sudan war of liberation was also fought with the stated goal of socioeconomic rights and equality rather than for independence. This section of the chapter attempts to explain why South Sudan in the end opted for secession and what the implications of the secession are to the OAU boundary doctrine.

South Sudan was part of the Turkiya (Ottoman) Empire, which ravaged the whole of Sudan with heavy taxation and, more importantly, with slave raids, especially from the South. The South was also part of Sudan's Mahdiya state (1885–98), which professed Arab identity, culturally marginalizing various identities in the country, especially those in the South. The Mahdiya state was also supported by slave-raiding communities. The rule of the Mahdiya state was rather short, but it left behind complex scars in inter-identity relations, particularly between the Northern and Southern regions of the country (Deng 2010).

With the defeat of the Mahdiya state by British forces, South Sudan became part of the Anglo-Egyptian condominium of Sudan, which was proclaimed in 1899. However, South Sudan was essentially kept separate from the rest of Sudan by the British colonial administration. In 1902, three years after the colonization of Sudan, the colonial administration formulated a policy of keeping South Sudan separate from the rest of the country. Two tenuous and self-serving reasons were the basis for the policy. One was that the populations of the South were racially and culturally distinct from the Northern Arab Sudanese.[5] The second premise, which is based on the first, was that the South was eventually either to develop into a separate political entity or to be integrated into British East Africa (Wai 1980). On the grounds of these two suppositions, South Sudan was racially, culturally, politically, and economically segregated from the North.

In 1922 the administration tightened the separation of the two regions of the country by enacting the Passports and Permits Ordinance, which made the South "offlimits [sic] to all non-African Sudanese" (Wai 1980: 377). The ordinance also made Sudan inaccessible to Southerners. In addition, the policy attempted to replace any cultural influence of the North on the South, such as Islam and the Arabic language, by Western culture, including Christianity and English. Yet the Southern policy did little to promote socioeconomic development in the South and left the region economically deprived relative to the North.

During the second half of the 1940s the colonial administration reversed its Southern policy in favor of integrating the South with the North and leaving behind a single Sudan. A number of factors accounted for this policy shift. Realization that colonialism had become unsustainable rendered integrating the South with British East Africa moot. Egyptian influence was also a factor in not separating the South from Sudan. There were also concerns that South Sudan would not be economically viable as an independent state. In any case, despite reservations expressed by British administrators in the South, integrating the South with the North became the new policy of the colonial administration, and Sudan obtained its independence as a single country with deep divisions.

As independence approached, it became clear that integrating North and South was going to become a huge challenge to the new country. The Anyanya insurgency of the South was already in full swing in 1955 before the country's independence. Memories of pre-colonial slave raids under the Turkiya and Mahdiya states and the separate socioeconomic identity the colonial administration instituted were certain to require capable governance with effective institutions of diversity management. However, these were all in short supply in the new country. Poor governance, manifested in the desire on the part of the government to undo the cultural and political separation of the South by the colonial state through induced assimilation, reinforced the South's fears of domination by the North. Under such circumstances, the country descended into a chronic civil war, which ultimately resulted in the secession of the South in what appears to be a contravention of the OAU doctrine of boundaries.

Integrating the two entities through effective processes of diversity management and nation building was no doubt possible, even if challenging. The ten-year peace following the 1972 Addis Ababa Agreement, which gave the South some autonomy, was indicative that a united Sudan could have been forged with good governance that addressed the grievances of the marginalized South.

Unfortunately, the Addis Ababa Agreement was abandoned by the government in 1983, reigniting a second round of bitter civil war that lasted until the signing of the Comprehensive Peace Agreement in 2005. The second civil war was even more destructive than the first. Casualty figures from the first civil war (1955–72) are estimated at 500,000.[6] The second civil war (1983–2005) is said to have produced some 2 million dead, 420,000 refugees and over 4 million displaced. The Sudan People's Liberation Movement (SPLM), which led the second civil war, finally brought about the independence of South Sudan in July 2011. While not inevitable, the secession of South Sudan was made likely by the colonial policy of socioeconomic and administrative separation of the two regions. Poor governance, which not only failed to rectify the scars left by pre-colonial and colonial administrations but also continued economic and political marginalization and cultural degradation of the South, compounded the indignation of the South. The OAU doctrine was, thus, not sufficient to prevent the country's breakup.

Given the long history of discrimination and marginalization under the Turkiya and Mahdiya states, the separate governance under the British administration, and the failure of the post-colonial Sudanese state to implement constructive policies to remedy the problem of the South, the OAU doctrine could not be upheld. However, the Sudanese state's agreement for the settlement of the South Sudan case through a referendum has served as legal justification for the independence of the new country, as was the case with Eritrea in 1993.

The Ogaden case

The Ogaden war, which was of significant influence in the formation of the OAU boundary doctrine, remains active half a century after the start of the war and the formation of the doctrine. This war, like that of South Sudan, contravenes the OAU doctrine. Like the South Sudan case, it also has pre-colonial, colonial, and post-colonial contexts that engendered chronic conflicts. While South Sudan experienced a separate colonial administrative arrangement, the Ogaden was transferred from one power to another several times before it was handed over by global powers to Ethiopia, which laid claim to it on the basis that the Ogaden was part of the pre-colonial Abyssinian Empire. All four propositions are useful in explaining the Ogaden case.

The Somali-inhabited territories in the Horn of Africa fell under British, Italian, and French colonial rule in the late 1880s. The Ogaden, another Somali-inhabited territory, fell under the rule of the expansionist Abyssinian Empire in the late 1890s, despite some fierce resistance. The Ogaden, however, was passed from the rule of one power to another several times between the late 1890s and the late 1940s. With Italian occupation of Abyssinia in 1936, the Ogaden was severed from Ethiopia and integrated with Italian Somalia. When the British took control of the territories under Italy's empire in the Horn of Africa and liberated Ethiopia from Italian rule in 1941, the Ogaden yet again came under a new power. This time the British kept the Somali-inhabited Ogaden region and the border regions with French Somaliland under their control (Anglo-Ethiopian Agreement of 1944). The British were in favor of unifying the Somali-inhabited areas, including Italian Somaliland, British Somaliland, the Ogaden, and Kenya's Northern Frontier District, to create Greater Somalia.

With U.N. deliberations about the disposal of Italian colonies in the Horn of Africa in the aftermath of the Second World War, Ethiopia leveled a claim to the Ogaden on the basis of an 1897 Anglo-Ethiopian Treaty, which affirmed Abyssinia's claim to the Ogaden following the territory's occupation by the expanding Abyssinian Empire. Reversing the policy of creating Greater Somalia, the United Kingdom handed over the Ogaden to Ethiopia in 1948 under U.S. influence. Italy also regained control of its former colony, Italian Somaliland, as a U.N. trustee to administer the territory for ten years. The U.K. kept British Somaliland.

The British also reversed their plan with respect to Kenya's Northern Frontier District (now North Eastern Province) and decided to keep it as part of Kenya instead of adjoining it with Greater Somalia, which did not materialize. When British Somaliland and Italian Somaliland gained independence in 1960, they quickly formed a union to establish the Republic of Somalia. The new republic also aimed to create Greater Somalia by bringing under its control the Ogaden and Kenya's North Eastern Province.[7]

The Ogaden conflict is thus a struggle against incorporation by the Abyssinian Empire and its successor state, Ethiopia. However, since Ethiopia's claim over the Ogaden was affirmed by global powers, the U.K. and the U.S., in 1948, the struggle against incorporation into Ethiopia also became entangled with the struggle against colonial boundaries. From the point of view of the Ogaden Somalis and the Republic of Somalia, the Ogaden problem was an issue of self-determination, since the struggle was against forced incorporation on the basis of pre-colonial boundaries. From Ethiopia's perspective, however, self-determination only applied to populations under European colonization and not to territorial disputes among African countries (Touval 1967). For Ethiopia, thus, the Ogaden issue is governed by the OAU boundary doctrine. In any case, problems of poor governance and continued marginalization also afflict the Ogaden. The chronic conflict contributes to the marginalization, creating a vicious cycle. Moreover, the Ogaden continues to face gross human rights violations, which intensify the bitterness of the territory's population.

The case of Somaliland

Somaliland declared its independence from Somalia in 1991 and has since remained a de facto independent state without international recognition. Somaliland's secession is rather different from those of Eritrea and South Sudan. It is also different from the Ogaden problem in a number of respects. Claims of poor governance and mismanagement of diversity, which allegedly disadvantaged Somaliland, as well as the seemingly endless civil war in Somalia, are the key factors for Somaliland's declaration of independence. Unlike in the other three cases, only Proposition 4, which relates to poor governance, applies in explaining the Somaliland case. However, not unlike the Eritrean case, the OAU boundary doctrine does not seem to apply to the Somaliland case. As noted already, Somaliland was a British colony, while the rest of the Republic of Somalia was an Italian colony. The two regions experienced a separate colonial history and formed separate political entities, made up of a partitioned ethnic group. As the two regions gained their independence in 1960, they voluntarily formed a union to create the Republic of Somalia. Thirty-one years after their union, during the country's civil war, where a number of armed groups fought to oust the regime of Siad Barre, Somaliland declared its independence, unilaterally nullifying the union.

From the legal point of view, thus, Somaliland's secession does not contravene the OAU doctrine of non-violability of colonial boundaries. Rather, like the Eritrean case, it represents a return to the colonial boundary. Unlike the case of Eritrea, however, Somaliland's union with Somalia was voluntary, and Somaliland was a key player in bringing about the union. Under the circumstances the secession raises different kinds of legal and political questions. One central question is whether a union of two political entities brought about by mutual consent can be abrogated unilaterally by one of the parties without the agreement of the other. A related question is what kind of international law governs such cases of separation. These are questions beyond the scope of this chapter. Suffice to point out that the Somaliland case raises new legal questions, which are best resolved through negotiated agreements by the two sides when Somalia's political situation stabilizes.

Lessons learned

Of the four cases we examined the secessions of Eritrea and Somaliland do not seem to contravene the OAU boundary doctrine. Rather these two cases represent a return to the colonial boundaries, which were changed after decolonization, involuntarily in Eritrea's case and voluntarily in Somaliland's case. In the Eritrean case the war of independence was to reverse the country's annexation by Ethiopia. In the Somaliland case, the secession represents unilateral abrogation of a union in reaction to poor governance by the post-colonial Somali state as well as to dissociate itself from Somalia's endless civil war. By contrast, the South Sudan case represents the only secession in Africa which succeeded, despite the fact that it contravened the OAU doctrine of non-violability of colonial boundaries. However, even in this case, the secession came though the Comprehensive Peace Agreement of 2005, which paved the way for legal secession.

The Ogaden case, on the other hand, represents one of several unsuccessful secession attempts which were launched in various parts of Africa in contravention of the OAU boundary doctrine. Both the South Sudan and Ogaden cases, however, reveal that those two territories incurred changes in the colonial powers or colonial administrative policies, which played major roles in unsettling the two regions. Additionally, the challenges to the colonial boundaries in these two cases overlapped with resistance to incorporation by expansionist pre-colonial African empires. In other words, the right of self-determination against forced incorporation by pre-colonial African empires and their handover to successor states of empires during decolonization have been aspects of the struggles in the secession struggle in those two cases. The challenge to the OAU doctrine in these two cases thus rests on mitigating historical circumstances, which the doctrine fails to consider.

One important lesson learned from all four cases is that the OAU doctrine, while useful at the time of its formation, was deficient, since it failed to create a commission that would adjudicate special cases that do not easily fit into the doctrine. Poor governance and abuses of human rights were also critical reasons why secessionist movements managed to mobilize popular support. Poor governance keeps alive historical memories of oppression and abuse, making nation building a daunting endeavor.

Despite its shortcomings and failures in preventing secessions and secessionist wars in the Horn of Africa, the doctrine still remains vital in the settlement of boundary disputes throughout the continent. It is particularly vital in settling boundary problems in the countries that have been formed through secessions. The colonial boundaries have, for example, become the basis for addressing the boundary problems between Eritrea and Ethiopia following the 1998–2000 border war between the two countries. The Ethiopia–Eritrea Boundary Commission, which was established to demarcate the border between the two countries, based its ruling on the colonial boundaries, although Ethiopia has yet to allow the physical demarcation of the boundary. Settlements of the boundary dispute between Sudan and South Sudan, as well as those between several other countries in the region, are also likely to be on the basis of the colonial boundaries in line with the OAU doctrine.

Another critical lesson is that secession, which is intended to bring about liberation by removing oppressive governance, does not, in itself, bring about liberation and good governance. Neither Eritrea nor South Sudan has distinguished itself in bringing about good governance. In other words, secession is not a cure to poor governance, although poor governance is a leading factor in initiating wars of secession. It is also conceivable, at least theoretically, that good governance can materialize without secession. Unfortunately, we do not yet have empirical support for this theoretical possibility in the Horn of Africa.

Notes

1 Somaliland declared its independence from the rest of Somalia in 1991 and has existed as a de facto independent state since, but it has not obtained any international recognition. Unlike the other three cases, the Ogaden has not seceded. It is, however, included because there has been a major conflict in the region for about half a century.
2 The legacy of pre-colonial empires also applies to the Mahdiya state of Sudan, which was expansionist like the Abyssinian Empire and had left behind animosities among some of its subjects. Unlike the Abyssinian Empire, however, the Mahdiya state fell victim to colonization, and some of its legacies were changed by the colonial state.
3 Italy's support for this position was in exchange for British support of its efforts to obtain trusteeship of the Tripolitania portion of Libya. Britain, on the other hand, wanted to incorporate western Eritrea into its colony of Sudan.
4 Despite the U.S.–Israeli perceptions, however, the ratio of the Muslim to the Christian population in Eritrea and Ethiopia is not markedly different.
5 There is little doubt that there is Arab and African culture in Sudan, but drawing a line of demarcation between these two cultures is not feasible. The same African–Arab divide has become a discourse in the conflicts in Darfur, as well as South Kordofan, two regions that were classified with the Arab North under the colonial administration.
6 The estimates for casualty figures are extracted from the various estimates compiled in the *Twentieth Century Atlas: Death Tolls and Casualty Statistics for Secondary Wars and Atrocities*, http://necrometrics.com/20c300k.htm#Sudan.
7 Mussolini is said to have boasted of nearly uniting all Somali people under one state when Italy annexed British Somaliland as well as Juba land and other Kenyan areas from the British in 1940. Between 1897 and 1908, Italy made agreements with the Ethiopians and the British that marked out the boundaries of Italian Somaliland. Italy also took the Ogaden area from Ethiopia by the late 1920s.

References

Deng, Francis Mading. 2010. *Self-Determination and National Unity: A Challenge for Africa*. Lawrenceville, NJ: Africa World Press.
Habte Selassie, Bereket. 1989. *Eritrea and the United Nations and Other Essays*. Trenton, NJ: Red Sea Press.
Keller, Edmond. 2007. "Secession in Africa," *Journal of African Policy Studies*, vol. 13, no. 1, pp. 1–26.
Schraeder, Peter J. 1992. "The Horn of Africa: U.S. Foreign Policy in an Altered Cold War," *Middle East Journal*, vol. 46, no. 4, pp. 571–93.

Touval, Saadia. 1967. "The Organization of African Unity and African Borders," *International Organization*, vol. 21, no. 1, pp. 102–27.

Wai, Dunstan M. 1980. "Pax Britannica and the Southern Sudan: The View from the Theatre," *African Affairs*, vol. 79, no. 316, pp. 375–95.

Yohannes, Okbazghi. 1991. *Eritrea: A Pawn in World Politics*. Gainesville: University of Florida Press.

Part II

Non-colonial creation successful secession case: South Sudan

4 Political history of Southern Sudan before independence of the Sudan

Samson Samuel Wassara

Introduction

Different historical legacies combined to distinguish the identity of South Sudan from that of the Sudan. The political history of Southern Sudan was characterised by resistance against foreign forces during different historical periods. This territory began to be exposed gradually to foreign powers, such as the Turco-Egyptian expeditions in 1820s under Mohamed Ali Pasha. The southward expansion of this regime led to unfriendly contacts with the Nilotic tribes, notably the Shilluk, the Nuer and the Dinka. The Turco-Egyptian regime, during its early years, engaged in raiding the Shilluk Kingdom and other Nilotic tribes for slaves. The opening of the Nile waterway through the Sudd wetland in the 1840s expanded contacts with Nilotics and the Nilo-hamites in the Upper Nile south of the Sudd. Turco-Egyptian rule in the Sudan extended substantially to the South. Interests of the invaders in the nineteenth century were trade in ivory and slaves. This was followed by the Mahdist revolt against the Turco-Egyptian regime in 1881. The Mahdist movement forcibly conscripted its fighting forces from the tribes of Southern Sudan. The first two historical periods of foreign invasions witnessed the fragmented resistance of the different peoples of Southern Sudan. The slave trade became one of the historical grievances that entered into oral literature among inhabitants of the territory. It remained a factor of differentiation between the people of Southern Sudan and those of Northern Sudan before and after independence of the Sudan.

The European scramble for Africa also made Southern Sudan a battleground for spheres of influence. Belgian and French intrusions from the South and the British pursuit of remnants of Mahdists in the North made Southern Sudan a contested area. In the process of European advances from the Atlantic Ocean towards Southern Sudan, the Azande became a shield, like the Shilluk, Dinka and Nuer in the North. The Fashoda Crisis of 1898 marked the end of the scramble for Southern Sudan, which became part of the Sudan in 1899 under the condominium authority in which Britain and Egypt were rulers until independence in January 1956. Aggressive competition between Britain and Egypt for political influence in the Sudan during the condominium rule left its mark on the history and political consciousness of Southern Sudan. The condominium period shaped decisively the history of Southern Sudan and people's political consciousness before independence of the Sudan in January 1956.

Hence, the purpose of this chapter is to demonstrate how historical and political phenomena contributed to the construction of a space that claims a distinct identity today as South Sudan. This chapter treats historical developments whose legacies have left marks of differentiation on Southern Sudan since the nineteenth and twentieth centuries. There are five guiding questions of the study as follows:

1   To what extent did the antagonistic scramble for territory in the Nile basin contribute to shaping the future destiny of South Sudan?
2   How did major tribal groups react to the invasions of foreign powers?
3   Who were the main actors in political events of Southern Sudan before the independence of the Sudan in 1956?
4   How did they contribute to construction of a separate identity?
5   What factors contributed to forming a sense of consciousness and subsequent nationalism in Southern Sudan?

Answers to these questions require an exploration of the dynamics of history during the Turco-Egyptian period, the Anglo-Egyptian condominium regime, and the period leading to the independence of the Sudan in 1956. The main method of study is historiography, where two important tools of analysis are employed. They are Events Data Research (EDR) and World Events Interaction Survey (WEIS). Both EDR and WEIS refer to actions and declarations of policy makers, demonstration of cooperative behaviour or manifestations of hostilities, and many other reactions to events which paved the way for claims of a separate political entity in Southern Sudan (Morgan 1975: 172–3; Ray 1979: 158–60). These tools of analysis enable us to explain patterns of interaction, and the political autonomy that subsequently led to the emergence of South Sudan.

Contacts with uninvited guests from the North

Territories of Southern Sudan were influenced in varying stages by political forces originating from the North. Much of the early southward expansion was marked by the brutality of the invading forces. Consecutive invasions from the North were checked by the Nilotic tribes for centuries. Hostile contacts between the inhabitants of Southern Sudan and the North are, nevertheless, documented after the occupation of the Sudan in 1821 by the Turco-Egyptian army of Mohamed Ali Pasha. During this period, history records the beginning of hostile contacts with the people of Southern Sudan under the administration of Ali Khurshid Agha. In 1827, he led the first expedition from al-Rusayris in the former Funj Sultanate into the territories of the Upper Nile up to the confluence of the Sobat River and the White Nile in the search for slaves. It is recorded that Kurshuk's expedition took about 500 slaves. Kurshuk organised a second expedition in 1830 using river boats. His boats sailed up the White Nile as far as the Sobat River for the second time. The Shilluk Kingdom attacked Khurshid's troops but later opened the way for his expedition to proceed towards the confluence of the Sobat River with the White Nile. On the return journey, the expedition came under heavy attack by the Shilluk. They recovered the booty and freed most of the slaves Khurshid's expedition had taken. The expedition was forced to retreat northwards with only 200 captives (Holt and Daly 2011: 46). Indeed, the Shilluk-sustained resistance hindered the progress of the Turco-Egyptian expeditions into the heart of Southern Sudan. The failure of Khurshid to subdue the tribes of the Upper Nile region frustrated his main goal of taking many slaves. After the failure, Kurshid redirected his attention to Eastern Sudan.

The resistance of the peoples of Southern Sudan to external forces from the North was sustained over centuries. Thus the Shilluk and the other Nilotic groups developed a culture of resistance. They never doubted that the invaders were determined to displace them. They remembered how their ancestors were gradually pushed southwards by waves of invasion by the people of the North. This assumption is justified by scholars such as Sanderson, who confirmed that the Dinka and Nuer had a tradition of resistance to external influence of any kind (Sanderson and Sanderson 1981: 4–8).

The most decisive action of the Turco-Egyptian regime that exposed Southern Sudan to the outside world was Mohamed Ali's drive to discover the source of the Nile. To this end, Mohamed Ali sent expeditions under the command of Salim Gupdan to reach the regions of the Nile south of the Sudd. After fighting his way through the great swamp during the period 1839–41, Salim managed to reach Gondokoro in 1841. This adventure revealed the riches of Southern Sudan in ivory and other exotic commodities such as crocodile skins and ostrich feathers among others. This discovery of the world beyond the Sudd marked the first important contact between other communities south of the Sudd and the ivory traders. Southern Sudan experienced interactions with the Turco-Egyptian administrators, ivory traders and later slave traders (Collins 1971: 328). The immediate goal of the Turco-Egyptian government was to acquire ivory to meet the cost of administration. Officials strove to acquire wealth quickly. Thus the ivory trade was monopolised by the administration and officials of the Turco-Egyptian government. European traders broke the government monopoly in 1848 when they entered the market after putting the Turco-Egyptian authorities under tremendous pressure.

European traders purchased boats and firearms; they recruited servants and enlisted soldiers from the detribalised communities along the main Nile for their business ventures in Southern Sudan. Prominent among them were individuals like the Frenchman Alphonse de Malzac, the British vice-consul John Patherick, the Maltese A. Debono and the Savoyard (French) Antoine Brun-Rollet. Soon, Arab traders, such as the Syrian Ibrahim Abbas, and Egyptians, such as Mohamed Ahmed al-Aqad, Ghattas and Mohamed Abu Sudd, were engaging in business competition with the Europeans (Elbashir 1974: 51–7). The intensification of the ivory trade led to frequent conflicts with the natives along the White Nile beyond the Sudd. With all their skills and experience combined, the ivory traders depleted supplies of ivory along the White Nile. This led them to explore other areas where ivory was expected to be abundant. Tribes south of the Sudd resisted the newcomers, but were consumed by fragmentation. They lacked the tradition of centralised authority of their Shilluk counterparts north of the Sudd. The principle of centralised authority was unfamiliar in the area. This did not mean that the people south of the Sudd were docile to the invaders. For example, the British administrators in the Latuka territory described the people as 'pig-headed and exceedingly stubborn'. This expression of frustration demonstrated that the foreign invaders had a difficult time in suppressing the Latuka (Collins 1971: 82).

In the meantime, Arab traders from Northern Sudan penetrated the Bahr al-Ghazal River and established business centres known as 'zaribas'. This type of business was on a small scale. John Patherick nevertheless discovered the waterway up the Bahr al-Ghazal River from the White Nile in the mid-1850s (Evans-Pritchard 1971: 294). This new discovery enabled European ivory traders with their Arab agents to establish zaribas deep inside Southern Sudan (Smith 1972: 5). Records show that over 80 zaribas mushroomed in the Bahr al-Ghazal River basin in the territories lying between the Dinka and the Azande. For example, the Frenchman Alphonse de Malzac was the first European to establish trading posts at Rumbek in 1856. He conducted raids for cattle, which were used for food and to barter for ivory. Unlike Alphonse de Malzac, the British trader John Patherick made peaceful contacts with the Azande in 1858. Arab agents of European traders swarmed over the territories of current Southern Sudan and beyond. In the competition for ivory, Arab traders exhausted the stocks of ivory in the Bahr al-Ghazal basin and travelled deep into the Uele in the Congo basin. However, the Azande chiefs controlled the routes that led to the other unexploited territories further south that later fell under Belgian rule (Gray 1961: 61–2). Europeans, including John Patherick, recruited many Northern Sudanese, such as Zubeir Rahma Mansur and his son Suleiman al-Zubeir Rahma, Ghattas, Biselli, Ali Abu Amri and Mohamed Abd el Samad among many others. These Arab intermediaries conducted a ruthless trade in slaves after the departure of their European bosses (Santandrea 1964: 24–30). Their European patrons were busy visiting the zaribas throughout Southern Sudan. For example, Patherick, Piaggia, Georg Schweinfurth and many others spent years at the courts of friendly Avongara rulers in Zandeland. Patherick and Schweinfurth published details of their experiences in dealing with the people during the period of the ivory business (Schweinfurth 1873: 417–68).

Trade and slavery under the Turco-Egyptian administration

The weakness of the Turco-Egyptian administration in the new-found territories of Southern Sudan was that it gave the upper hand to the ivory traders on the White Nile. The unregulated trade led to the exhaustion of stocks of ivory on the White Nile, and trade in the commodity shifted to the Bahr al-Ghazal basin. Slave traders invaded the area and easily subjugated the weak tribes living between the Dinka and the Azande. Stocks of ivory were exhausted, and traders shifted to taking slaves. The Bahr al-Ghazal region was seriously exposed to a predatory slave trade at an extraordinarily high rate and much higher than that recorded in the Upper Nile. The exit of the European bosses of the slave traders from Southern Sudan under pressure from international anti-slave campaigners enhanced the increase in human trade. Powerful slave traders such as Zubeir Rahma Mansur formed their slave armies to venture deep into areas across the Nile–Congo water divide for the business of ivory and slaves. During the period 1850–60 the trade in slaves overtook that of ivory. The proliferation of zaribas depended on the size of the slave armies established by the Arab traders. The situation was described as follows:

> As on the White Nile, however, the zariba system necessitated slave establishments of some size. A special feature of the trader communities of the Bahr al-Ghazal were bodies of slave troops, known as 'bazingers', which ultimately amounted to half of the armed forces of the traders. Many Azande voluntarily joined their ranks. The Jallaba, who had previously paid tribute to the tribal chiefs, now found protection and opportunities for trade in zaribas.
>
> (Holt and Daly 2011: 52)

Concentrations of zaribas in the Bahr al-Ghazal basin meant the continual arrival of large numbers of petty Arab slave traders in the region from Darfur and Kordofan. They brought with them more of the commodities needed by the slave agents who raided the people. It was estimated that 80,000 slaves were taken from Bahr al-Ghazal alone. Most of the victims were from the Bongo, the Jur and the Fertit. The most prominent slave traders included Abu Gurun at Tonj, Ghattas at Rumbek and Tonj, Ali Kurshid at Wau and the famous Zubeir Rahma Mansur at Daim Zubeir (Santandrea 1964: 29–30). Besides weak people like the Bongo and the Fertit, the northernmost Azande became victims of the slave raids. However, powerful Azande kings along the Nile–Congo divide vowed to confront the slave traders (Schweinfurth 1873: 417–18). Despite the arms superiority of the slave traders, the Azande organised well-developed armies to mount resistance (Evans-Pritchard 1971: 263). The Azande, under the courageous leadership of the Avongara, fought numerous battles and wars with the slave traders from the 1870s. They inflicted heavy casualties on the Arab slave traders, to the extent that these traders sought alliances and trade agreements with the Avongara kings.

The Azande destroyed tiny merchant and slave trade stations (zaribas) located on their frontiers with the tribes of Western Bahr al-Ghazal. However, it is imperative to mention two decisive wars fought against the Arab slave traders. The first major war was in December 1870, when the Azande, under Prince Ndoromo, annihilated the united slave caravan commanded by Abu Gurun. The caravan was called united because Abu Gurun, Hassaballa and Ali Kurshid pooled their forces to subdue the Azande. Secondly, Gbudwe took decisive action against Mohamed Abd el Samad's zariba. It was stationed in the territory of his cousin Ngangi. The latter had allowed the slave traders to establish a large zariba north of the present Ibba. Many subjects of Ngangi were unhappy about the disappearance of their young people, who were taken away but never came back. So Gbudwe decided to dislodge Mohamed Abd el Samad's zariba in the battle of Baambu, which was fought on 14 November 1874. Mohamed Abd el Samad's zariba was destroyed, and he was killed in the attack. These major victories sent a shock message to the slave traders, their intermediaries in Bahr al-Ghazal and their bosses in Khartoum. Some zariba leaders were compelled to seek new relations with the Azande to ensure the flow of ivory they were looking for in Zandeland and beyond.

While the slave trade was ravaging communities in the Bahr al-Ghazal basin, international pressure was building on the Turco-Egyptian rulers. On his accession to power in 1854, Mohamed Said prohibited the transportation of slaves to Egypt. He closed the slave market in Omdurman, although the slave traders transferred the market to Kaka in Shilluk Kingdom. Mohamed Said took the action of sending an expeditionary force against the slave traders in Southern Sudan. He was able to establish a post called Tafukia at the mouth of the Sobat in 1855. Soldiers stationed at the post inspected all boats travelling to the North for slaves. The post was withdrawn in 1857 because of the resistance of the slave traders. Anarchy reigned, and protests by missionaries kept up Austrian and British pressure on the viceroy to step up action against the slave traders. As a result, Mohamed Said instructed the hukumdar, Musa Hamdi, to take action against the slave trade. In October 1862, Musa Hamdi notified the traders that only boats with ivory would be allowed to sail from the South to Khartoum (Holt and Daly 2011: 52–5). All the actions taken during the regime of Mohamed Said were a failure, and the slave trade flourished.

A strong anti-slave policy was maintained during the period of Khedive Ismail (1863–81). The khedive appointed more Europeans in the administration of Southern Sudan than all his predecessors. In order to check the rampant slave trade, Khedive Ismail sought to control the areas of the Upper Nile and Bahr al-Ghazal. In April 1869 he appointed the British explorer Samuel Baker to lead an expedition with the goal of annexing all the territories in the Nile basin, suppressing the slave trade and establishing a chain of posts in the acquired territories. Samuel Baker performed exceptionally well; he was able to conquer the White Nile basin south of the Sudd, with the support of Southern Sudanese soldiers enlisted into his army. He extended the khedival authority into Uganda (Holt and Daly 2011: 55–6). The Turco-Egyptian regime built on the success of Baker to take Bahr al-Ghazal from the slave traders. Khedive Ismail appointed Mohamed al-Hilali to suppress the slave trade. The slave traders forged an alliance of zariba rulers under the leadership of Zubeir Rahma Mansur that attacked and killed al-Hilali. The Turco-Egyptian regime then recognised Zubeir as the governor of Bahr al-Ghazal. Khedive Ismail appointed Charles Gordon in 1874 as the governor of Equatoria. Lado became the provincial headquarters. Gordon organised garrison stations in Equatoria and engaged in the suppression of the slave trade in the areas under his control. Like, his predecessor, Gordon faced resistance from the slave traders. This led him to resign as governor in 1876, but he was appointed the following year as the governor-general of the Sudan. As governor-general, Gordon appointed Romolo Gessi, an Italian, as governor of

Bahr al-Ghazal. Gessi's mission was to suppress Suleiman al-Zubeir Rahma, who intensified the slave trade after the death of his father. The new governor built anti-slave fronts that were interrupted by the Mahdist revolt in 1881 (Holt and Daly 2011: 56–8).

In short, the actions of the slave traders and the resistance of the inhabitants of Southern Sudan are a factor in the contested identity of the Sudanese people. The reference to people of Southern Sudan by Northerners as slaves or *abd* remained an insult for more than a century. This label was a constant source of scorn towards the Southern Sudanese, which nurtured hostility before and after the independence of the Sudan. The search for a separate identity in Southern Sudan is definitely attributed to the discomfort of the inhabitants of Southern Sudan when they read their past history.

Southern Sudan towards the end of the nineteenth century

Two related events shaped the history of Southern Sudan during this period: the Mahdist expansion into parts of Southern Sudan and the European scramble for Africa. Both events tell stories of the humiliation of the indigenous people. The behaviour of invaders from the South (the Belgians and the French) and from the North (the Mahdists and the British) is a source of injury to national pride for the populations of Southern Sudan. The scramble for Southern Sudan and the Nile by foreign powers wreaked havoc in the form of pacification and consequent resistance of the people. The fall of Khartoum to the Mahdist rebellion on 26 January 1885 meant that the new regime had to expand into Southern Sudan. The Mahdists established their control over the White Nile and Bahr al-Ghazal, with Mohamed Dafalla and Karmalla as governors of Equatoria and Bahr al-Ghazal respectively. This event interfered with the designs of the European powers for sharing the African territories as stipulated by the Berlin Conference of 1885. Southern Sudan was at the centre of competition between the British, the Belgians and the French. The Mahdist presence in Southern Sudan threatened the national interests of the European powers that were competing for the Upper Nile basin.

All protagonists in the scramble for Africa had designs for occupying the Nile basin. The strategic importance of the Nile brought Britain, Belgium and France into competition. Charles Gordon, the governor-general of the Sudan, urged King Leopold of Belgium as early as 1880 to check the slave trade in Bahr al-Ghazal. After the Berlin Congress of 1885, Leopold urged his troops, *La Force Publique*, to acquire as much territory as was possible from his rivals in the Congo and the Nile basins. In the process of doing this, the Belgians came into contact with the Azande. They arrived during the period when the Mahdists had antagonised the Zande kingdoms that had established trading partnerships with Arab merchants in Bahr al-Ghazal under the Turco-Egyptian regime. Some kings such as Zemio, who detested the Mahdists, saw the Belgians as the right allies. The Belgian colonial forces had forged an alliance with King Zemio in the Mbomu basin against the Mahdists in Bahr al-Ghazal under Karamalla. The alliance was short lived when the Azande discovered the real intentions of the Belgians. The Azande fought Lieutenant Jules Miltz until he defeated them in1896.

King Gbudwe launched another decisive war against the Belgian military expedition into his territory in what is known among the Azande as the battle of Mayawa. Previous victories of the Azande over Belgian military expeditions overwhelmed King Leopold in his quest to supersede his other European competitors in the scramble for the Nile basin. Leopold entered into a military pact with the Italian government. Italy sent 64 officers to serve for three years in the Belgian Congo. Many of these officers, such as Alfredo Cardelli, Alessandro Platone, Amedeo Couture, Ugo Pasquinelli and Sergeant Pareys, took part in the great battle against Gbudwe in August 1904. They were part of the expedition commanded by the Belgian officer Leon Colin. The Azande, under Gbudwe, fought the battle of Mayawa with determination and fierceness. This battle was Gbudwe's last major military action against Europeans, but the human cost was tremendous. A writer on the Azande (Gero n.d.: 164) cited the Italian officer Ugo Pasquinelli, who fought the battle, as follows: 'After a month Mbio [Gbudwe] suddenly faced us with five to six thousand spearmen and about 200 riflemen. He had organised a supply service with women and old men in the nearby village, who carried provisions to the encamped warriors.'

The French emerged as another European power to bid for the Upper Nile basin. The French interest in the Sudan was dictated by their principle of West–East expansion across Africa and the bid for Egypt. The principle of expansion contradicted the British policy of linking Cairo and Cape Town. French interests in Southern Sudan lay in the occupation of the territory between the Atlantic Ocean and the Red Sea. The reference point on the White Nile was Fashoda. The French hydrologist Victor Prompt had explained the strategic importance of the place to the French government in a series of lectures in January 1893. Carnot, the French president, proposed an expedition to occupy a space in the Egyptian territory (Shibeika 1952: 391–2), but this was forestalled by the Anglo-Belgian agreement of 24 May 1894 in which the British ceded the Lado Enclave to the Congo Free State. In August the same year the Congo Free State signed an agreement with France, which enabled subsequent French penetration into Bahr al-Ghazal.

Thus in November 1895 Leon Bourgeois, the French foreign minister, granted permission for the Nile expedition under Captain Jean-Baptiste Marchand. In July 1896, Marchand led the expedition across the Congo–Nile watershed. The expedition faced many logistical challenges, such as moving a steamer from the Congo River system to the Nile basin. With the help of Tambura, the Azande were able to carry pieces of the steamer, which was later assembled at Rafili on the Bahr al-Ghazal River. From there the steamer sailed to Fashoda. Marchand reached Fashoda on 10 July 1898. He hoisted the French flag, established a camp and made peace with the reth, the Shilluk king. The French occupation of Fashoda provoked a deep crisis with Britain.

In the meantime, the British were striving to regain control of the Sudan from the Mahdists. General Kitchener was aware of the French presence at Fashoda in January 1898. On 2 September 1898, the Anglo-Egyptian troops overran the forces of Khalifa Abdullahi at the battle of Karari. This victory paved the way for Kitchener to move against the French in Fashoda. After taking orders from Lord Cromer, Kitchener moved his troops to Fashoda and sent Marchand an ultimatum dated 18 September 1898. It was countered with defiance by Marchand in a letter of the following day. This exchange provoked a serious crisis that almost led to a declaration of war between Britain and France over Southern Sudan. The French were in a weaker position, so they capitulated, and the Anglo-French Declaration was signed in March 1899. This marked the end of French activities in the Nile Valley. The British proclaimed the rights of the khedive and the Anglo-Egyptian condominium over the White Nile Valley and Bahr al-Ghazal (Holt and Daly 2011: 85–7).

There were two important forces left to deal with: the Azande resistance under their king Gbudwe and the Belgians in the Lado Enclave. First, the Azande had decisively resisted British military expeditions from Khartoum before the Belgians broke their military power from the South in 1904 during the battle of Mayawa. The Azande faced British expeditions on the orders of Gbudwe. The British sent a 'friendly mission' to the king in 1903. Prince Mange attacked the mission on 9 March in the same year when it crossed the Sue River. The mission was compelled to withdraw. In February 1904, Prince Rikita repulsed another British force of three companies dispatched in order to establish friendly relations with the Azande. The force had to retreat to Shambe (Santandrea 1989: 39–40).

Colonel W. A. Bulnois commanded the final expedition against Gbudwe. Momentum began to build when recruitment for Sudanese battalions started in Wau and Rumbek respectively. This was followed by the visit to Wau by the governor-general in December 1904. This visit was intended to test the degree of allegiance of the tribal chiefs in Wau and to inspect the military that moved against Gbudwe in early 1905. When these preparations were being made by the British to invade decisively the territory of Gbudwe, Tambura took the initiative in good faith to alert him, as a cousin, of the danger that was waiting in the foreseeable future. Tambura sent an emissary persuading Gbudwe to cooperate with the British forces to avoid the damage that would be incurred in the event of military confrontation.

Gbudwe reverted to tradition in expressing his disapproval of the proposal of his ruling cousin. Traditionally, a Zande king sent his emissary with a symbol of the declaration of war in the form of a spear for the other king to accept or reject the offer. In the case of acceptance, the king in question will retain the spear and send back the emissary with a message of alliance or friendship. If the king disagrees the spear is broken and sent back with the same emissary, and war will be declared (Lelon 1946: 79). In the situation of the message of Tambura, Gbudwe took an exceptional measure and mutilated the emissary as a message of disapproval. Here is what a missionary (Santandrea 1964: 43) wrote about the anger of Gbudwe concerning Tambura's message: 'Tambura, knowing that the two armed expeditions had already met with fierce opposition, sent Yambio [Gbudwe] a message advising him to take the same unavoidable step he had taken: to surrender. Yambio sent the man back with his ears and hands cut off.'

Against this background, the British expeditionary force arrived in the compound of Gbudwe on 7 February 1905. The warrior commanders who survived the battle of Mayawa deserted the king. Gbudwe was fatally wounded when he resisted the armed delegation sent to talk to him. He was taken prisoner (Santandrea 1989: 40). Records confirm that Gbudwe died of his wounds on 10 February 1905. This day marked the end of the sustained resistance of the Azande to Europeans in the history of Southern Sudan.

Britain was left with one European power, Belgium, to get rid of in the Nile basin. Lado Enclave was leased to the Congo Free State under the Anglo-Egyptian Treaty of August 1894. King Leopold had the ambition not only to occupy the Lado Enclave but to make it a springboard from which to occupy the Nile basin. The achievement of the king's goal was to be determined by the success of the military expedition of 1896 commanded by Baron Dhanis to occupy Lado Enclave. The military expedition gained control of Rejaf from the Mahdists after defeating the Mahdists in the enclave. By 1900, Leopold's claims on the Lado Enclave were so strong that the British agreed to negotiate the issue of territorial acquisition for three years. As Leopold grew old, he consolidated his position in the Lado Enclave by amassing troops, arms and ammunitions in the territory. This angered the British, who displayed their military might, forcing the Belgians to retreat further south. The British threat forced Leopold to accept the Anglo-Congolese Treaty of 1906. The treaty stipulated that Leopold was to possess Lado Enclave until the time of his death. The territory reverted to the Anglo-Egyptian authority after the Leopold's death on 17 December 1909. This marked the end of the European scramble for territories in Southern Sudan.

However, the subjugation of the Azande after the declaration of condominium rule in 1899 and the expulsion of the Belgians from Lado Enclave were not the end of resistance in many parts of the White Nile and Bahr al-Ghazal basins in Southern Sudan. The British had to engage in expeditions to pacify the tribes that continued to resist their rule in Southern Sudan. Records indicate that it took the British about three decades, sending military expeditions to pacify tribes like the Nuer, Atwot and Alliab Dinka, and the Latuka and Toposa in Equatoria (Beshir 1968: 18–20).

British protective policy and the identity of Southern Sudan

The dispute between Britain and Egypt over administration of the Sudan was the driving force in forging an identity for Southern Sudan. The idea of forming a separate identity for the territory was first introduced in 1910 by R. C. Owen, the governor of Equatoria and the Lado Enclave. This started with the creation of the Equatoria Corps in 1917. Its composition was exclusively Southern Sudanese. The creation of this military institution in Southern Sudan was the first demonstration of a crack in the ranks of the condominium rulers of the Sudan. It was a way of counterbalancing the Egyptian influences in the Sudanese army. In the 1920s, nationalist forces emerged in the North that worked in collaboration with Egypt. This was the case for the League of Sudanese Union in 1920. This

Egyptian-sponsored organisation was decidedly anti-British. Ali Abdel Latif, an ex-officer of Southern Sudanese origin, was imprisoned for his leadership in the White Flag League in 1923. This political development encouraged the British administration to launch the Southern Policy. The policy was aimed at curbing Arab and Islamic influences in Southern Sudan. It was also a strategy to undermine Egyptian influence in the Sudan. To this effect, the Milner Report provided a number of measures to construct two identities for the Sudan based on the principle of decentralisation. The four key features of the Southern Policy were the following:

1 In 1921, governors in Southern Sudan were no longer required to attend meetings of governors held annually in Khartoum. They held their own meeting in Southern Sudan.
2 The Passports and Permits Ordinance of 1922 empowered the governor-general to declare any part of the Sudan a 'closed district'. In the same year Southern Sudan was declared a closed area.
3 The Permits to Trade Order of 1925 provided that no person other than a native would be allowed to trade without a permit in South Sudan.
4 A language policy culminated in the 1928 Rejaf Conference.

These elements of the Southern Policy were aimed at excluding Egyptians, Northern Sudanese and other Muslims from Southern Sudan. The markets in Southern Sudan were left for Christian Copts, Syrians, Armenians and other acceptable trading partners of the condominium regime (Beshir 1968: 40–42). The implementation of the Southern Policy fostered cooperation in the ranks of the Northern Sudanese, who established the Graduates' Congress in 1938. This organisation criticised the Southern Policy, and its voice was echoed both in Cairo and in Khartoum, so the Northern Sudanese and Egyptians persuaded the governor-general to reverse the policy. For example, the Graduates' Congress submitted a memorandum in 1942 which called for the abolition of the Closed Areas Ordinance. In 1944, the civil secretary, Sir Douglas Newbold, informed the Governor-General Council that there was a need to abandon the Southern Policy because it was taking Southern Sudan backwards compared with the North. This situation led the governor-general to make a proposal concerning the future of Southern Sudan on 4 August 1945. The proposal contained three options:

1 integration of the South into the North;
2 integration of the South into East Africa; and
3 integration of parts of South Sudan with the North and other parts with East Africa.

Given the pressure from Northern Sudan and Egypt, the British administration opted for the integration of the South into the North. A new Southern Policy was formulated despite initial objections from governors and senior administrators of the Southern provinces. Newbold's note led to the organisation of the 1946

Administrative Conference, which transformed the Governor-General Council into the Executive Council and a proposed Legislative Assembly. The conference recommended that Southern Sudan should be represented in the Legislative Assembly. Thus, the Southern Policy was abandoned. Although the British administrators in the Southern Sudan showed their dissatisfaction with the recommendations of the 1946 conference, the civil secretary, Sir James Robertson, went ahead to organise the Juba Conference on 12–15 June 1947. According to the proceedings of the conference, the three governors of the Southern provinces, 17 chiefs and people of some level of education from the South, six well-educated Northerners and the director of establishment attended this conference (Beshir 1968: 136). Whatever the outcome of the conference, it was certain that Southern Sudan was integrated into a united Sudan.

As a turning point in the history of Southern Sudan, it meant that Southern Sudan had to play a role in the Sudan as determined by the 1946 Administrative Conference. The process of the implementation of the new policy was taking the Sudan towards self-determination without adequate preparation of the Southerners for the political tasks in the immediate future. There were no elections organised for representation in the Legislative Assembly in 1948. Thirteen Southern representatives were nominated to the Legislative Assembly. They were not members of any political party, so they had no political programme except a request for special status for Southern Sudan in the so-called 'United Sudan'. They all agreed to support the case for a federation in accordance with fears expressed by the participants of the Juba Conference. The British, through the Juba Conference, had the Southern Sudanese engage in a de facto situation of imposed unity. The years they spent in the Parliament could be considered as a learning process of politics. Their counterparts from the North were guided by party principles that were designed from the time of the establishment of the Graduates' Congress in 1938 and refined when the congress transformed into political parties. The political consciousness of Southern members of Parliament began to crystallise during their interactions with the Northern representatives of the Legislative Assembly.

The politics leading to Sudan's independence

The political dissatisfaction of the inhabitants of Southern Sudan with the hasty unity arrangements and their cumulative grievances translated into anxiety about an uncertain future for Sudan's self-government processes. The immediate preparation by Southerners for electoral politics began in 1953 after they were denied participation in the Cairo Conference of 1951. The Southern Sudanese were not invited by the Egyptian government on the ground that they did not have a political party. This situation led Southern politicians to launch a political party known as the Liberal Party. It was officially launched under the patronage of Stanslaus Paysama, Buth Diu and Abdel Rahman Sule. The chairmanship went to Benjamin Lwoki, and Paysama became the deputy chairman. The secretary-general was Buth Diu, and Abdel Rahman Sule became the patron of the Juba branch of

the Liberal Party. The overall goal of the party was to secure self-government status for Southern Sudan. This goal was vigorously pursued by the Liberal Party in
pre-independence politics (Bob and Wassara 1989: 297–9). The establishment of
the Liberal Party and its role in politics during the self-government period before
formal independence created a forum for the participation of Southern Sudanese
in the political developments of the Sudan. The elections of 1953 resulted in the
participation of 22 Southerners in Parliament.

Two key events in the politics of the transitional period left their mark on the
political system. The first event related to the division of Southerners between
the Liberal Party and the National Unionist Party (NUP). The latter was the
ruling party, to which a number of Southerners crossed. The NUP unveiled
its Sudanisation programme for the civil service, which brought serious disappointment to Southern Sudan. Southern MPs, including those who were in the
NUP, were disappointed by the action of the government. This development was
regarded by Southern politicians and intellectuals as a process of recolonisation
of Southern Sudan by the Arabised elites in Khartoum. When they complained,
the then prime minister, Ismail al-Azhari, responded with the threat of the use of
force. The Southern NUP members met in October 1954 and submitted a political demand requesting the government to appoint more Southerners to senior
administrative positions. This demand fell on deaf ears in the NUP government.
The Liberal Party took advantage of this situation to organise a conference in
Juba in November 1954. The conference demanded federal status for Southern
Sudan. Recommendations of the conference were ignored by the NUP government in Khartoum. This was the first wave of political mobilisation, which was
launched in 1954 right after the realities of the Sudanisation programme were felt
(Bob and Wassara 1989: 300–01).

The second event consisted of the reaction of Southern MPs against the policies of the NUP government, especially the threat issued by Ismail al-Azhari
regarding the political demands of the first Juba Conference. There was another
political mobilisation in May 1955 when NUP ministers resigned their posts
from the NUP government and joined the Liberal Party to form a single political bloc that was known as the 'Southern Bloc'. The bloc was composed of
all Southern MPs irrespective of the political party to which they belonged.
Members of the bloc called for a second conference in Juba, with the motive of
discussing a constitution that would embody federal status for Southern Sudan.
The prime minister issued a stern warning on 13 May against holding such a
conference. He stated that he would dismiss any government official who participated in the conference (Albino 1970: 30–32; Sanderson and Sanderson
1981: 340). However, Southerners went ahead, and the conference took place
on 5–6 July 1955. The conference made a number of recommendations, which
included among others unity among Southerners, special political status for
Southern Sudan and the demand for federation. A ten-person delegation was
constituted to disseminate the recommendations of the conference in Khartoum and to lobby other Northern political parties for support for the demand
for federation.

The district commissioner (DC) of Yambio provoked a situation where some chiefs were summoned to endorse a document condemning the Juba Conference. The Southern Bloc MPs requested Elia Kuzee, the MP for Zande East constituency, to travel immediately to address the problem in Yambio. He organised a public rally in his capacity as MP for Zande East constituency on 25 July 1955 without the approval of the DC. The rally challenged the DC and passed resolutions condemning his actions, protesting against Northern rule as a new form of colonialism, and demanding the resignation of the chiefs who signed the document. Elia Kuzee was apprehended and charged with criminal intimidation. News of the arrest of Elia Kuzee and labour unrest in Nzara factory precipitated riots on 26 July 1955 that targeted Northerners and their properties. Six Zande individuals lost their lives during the riots. The event also marked the transfer of political heroism from politicians to the military. The baton was passed on to the military, which resulted in the Torit Mutiny in the Southern Corps on 18 August 1955. The central government used force and excessive violence to put a temporary halt to the mutiny. It is in this context that the British and Egyptian governments hurriedly gave independence to the Sudan after the bloodshed. They avoided being embroiled in the bloody confrontations of the South and the North on the territory of Southern Sudan.

Concluding remarks

This discourse on the history of Southern Sudan serves as not only a description of events but a revelation of historical legacies that shaped political consciousness. Despite the heterogeneity of the peoples of the region, the humiliations suffered at the hands of different actors in the slave trade, the scramble for Southern Sudan, the Southern Policy and the forced unity of the South and the North constructed a different culture, identity, language and economic system. Geography also revealed glaring differences between the North and the South. This development was accompanied by a parallel consciousness that led the Southern Sudanese to demand a form of autonomy from the North during the Juba Conference of 1947. The complexity of historical and political development forced the condominium rulers to relinquish power and to grant independence to the country in 1956 after the bloodshed of 1955.

History cuts across knowledge about society, thus making it a wide discipline. In this chapter, history is narrowed to the analysis of the political events that shaped the territory and political destiny of Southern Sudan. This territory was a contested area for nearly two centuries from the invasion of the Sudan by the Turco-Egyptian expedition in 1821. The area is the cradle of resistance against invading forces in the North and the South. Unfortunately, the tribes of Southern Sudan lacked a common heritage to provide them with social cohesion.

There are lessons learned from this study. One of them is the forging of a separate identity for Southern Sudan. It can be safely inferred that, in Southern Sudan, oral traditions and forces of history contributed directly or indirectly to the independence of South Sudan five decades later. We have seen how Egyptians and the educated elites in the North diverted the attention of the British administration from pursuing the Southern Policy. It is certain that Northern elites managed to achieve their independence in 1956 at the expense of the aspirations of the Southern Sudanese people. The methods used to achieve independence for the Sudan and the tricks played by the Sudanese rulers who claimed independence resulted in the shedding of the blood of innocent workers at Nzara who were demanding their rights to better salary and working conditions. The Nzara incident invited the retaliation of the military from their base in Torit in August 1955. The action of the Equatoria Corps set the foundation for the long struggle for national liberation and increased people's consciousness about their destiny after the independence of the Sudan.

Therefore, Southern Sudan's history paved the way for the pursuit of a separate identity in the decades that ensued. The half-century liberation movements created their own history that could be examined by scholars from different disciplines. Experts in the history of Southern Sudan are challenged to examine the roles of South Sudan's nationalities in the struggle for liberation rights from 1955 to 2005, when the Comprehensive Peace Agreement (CPA) was signed. The political achievements realised today are the outcome of sustained resistance by the Southern Sudanese against the various forces of Arab and European imperialism at the regional and international levels. Therefore, historical heritage and legacy contributed in many ways to the emergence of an independent South Sudan.

References

Albino, Oliver. 1970. *The Sudan: A Southern Viewpoint*. Oxford: Oxford University Press.

Beshir, Mohamed Omer. 1968. *The Southern Sudan: Background to Conflict*. London: C. Hurst & Co.

Bob, Ali and Wassara, Samson S. 1989. 'The Emergence of the Organized Political Movement in Southern Sudan 1946–1972', in Mahasin Abdel Gadir Hag Al Safi (ed.), *The Nationalist Movement in the Sudan*. Khartoum: Institute of Afro-Asian Studies (IAAS), University of Khartoum.

Collins, Robert O. 1971. *Land beyond the Rivers: The Southern Sudan, 1898–1918*. New Haven, CT: Yale University Press.

Elbashir, Ahmed E. 1974. 'Confrontation across the Sudd: The Southern Sudan's Struggle for Freedom 1839–1957', Ph.D. thesis, Howard University, Washington, DC.

Evans-Pritchard, E. E. 1971. *The Azande: History and Political Institutions*. Oxford: Clarendon Press.

Gero, F. (n.d.). *Cannibalism in Zandeland: Truth and Falsehood*. Bologna: Editrice Missionaria Italiana.

Gray, Richard. 1961. *A History of Southern Sudan, 1839–1889*. London: Oxford University Press.

Holt, P. M. and Daly, M. W. 2011. *A History of the Sudan: From the Coming of Islam to the Present Day*, 6th edn. Harlow: Longman.

Lelon, M.-H. 1946. *Mes frères du Congo*, vol. II. Algiers: Baconnier.

Morgan, Patrick M. 1975. *Theories and Approaches to International Relations*, 2nd edn. New Brunswick, NJ: Transaction Books.

Ray, James Lee. 1979. *Global Politics*. Boston, MA: Houghton Mifflin.

Sanderson, Lilian Passmore and Sanderson, Neville. 1981. *Education, Religion and Politics in Southern Sudan, 1899–1964*. London: Ithaca Press.

Santandrea, Stefano. 1964. *A Tribal History of the Western Bahr al Ghazal*. Bologna: Editrice Nigrizia.

Santandrea, Stefano. 1989. *A Popular History of Wau: From Its Foundation to about 1940*. Khartoum: Encounter.

Schweinfurth, Georg. 1873. *The Heart of Africa: Three Years' Travel and Adventures in the Unexplored Regions of Central Africa from 1868 to 1871*, vol. II. London: Sampson Low.

Shibeika, Mekki. 1952. *British Policy in the Sudan, 1882–1902*. London: Oxford University Press.

Smith, Iain R. 1972. *Emin Pasha Relief Expedition, 1886–1890*. Oxford: Clarendon Press.

5   Sudan's first civil war for self-determination

Sirisio L. Oromo

Historical background

Sudan's post-independence history has been dominated by long, recurring, and bloody civil wars. The first civil war in the Sudan was characterised as a conflict between the North and the South. The Northerners were presented as Muslims and the Southerners were presented as Christians (Idris 2013: 3). The North was presented as Arabs and the South as Christians and Africans. Presumably religion, ethnicity, and region were the key factors that shaped relations of the two sides in the early days of the conflict.

The origin of the first civil war in the South dates back to the 1950s. On 18 August 1955, the Equatoria Corps, a military unit composed of Southerners, mutinied at Torit. Rather than surrender to the Sudanese government authorities, many mutineers later went into hiding with their weapons, marking the beginning of the first civil war in Southern Sudan (Johnson 2003; Rolandsen 2005: 24; LeRiche and Arnold 2012: 16).

Many factors had exacerbated the first civil war, making settlement impossible. Unfair distribution of resources, coupled with the denial to grant South Sudan federal status in the Juba Conference of 1947, sparked the first civil war. Equitable resource distribution and federalism, on which the Southern grievances were based, would have avoided the first civil war. The Northern political elite however demonstrated that they were incapable of striking a compromise.

Most commentators have attributed the country's political and civil strife either to an age-old racial and ethnic divide between Arabs and Africans or to colonially constructed inequalities (Abbas 1952; Abd al-Rahim 1969). In order to understand the root causes and trajectories of Sudan's civil wars we need to understand the underpinning historical, political, economic, and social factors. Douglas Johnson in his book *The Root Causes of Sudan's Civil Wars* (2003) depicts the essential differences between the first (1955–72) and the second (1983–2005) civil wars and the other minor conflicts in modern Sudan. Johnson, further, cites factors such as regional and international humanitarian aid, oil revenue, and terrorist organisations that exacerbated the violence.

The Khartoum governments recurrently reneged on their promises to Southerners to create a federal system. Southerners felt disenfranchised and cheated and therefore were compelled to pursue the war option in order to realise their wish for self-determination. This war lasted for 17 years, from 1955 to 1972, and only ended with the signing of the Addis Ababa Accord. The Addis Ababa Accord gave self-rule to the South. The violation of the Addis Ababa Accord however sparked a second civil war.

This chapter examines the developments that led to the outbreak of the first civil war in Sudan. It provides brief analyses of the civil war, the accord that brought its end, and the violation of the accord. It argues that the violation of the Addis Ababa Accord in 1983 that sparked the second civil war and the recurrent abrogation of subsequent promises and agreements by the Northern ruling elite spawned the final division of Sudan.

The Juba Conference of 1947: prelude to the end of British rule

The Juba Conference held between 12 and 13 June 1947 was attended by British and Sudanese delegates in Juba (Akol 2007: 35–6), then regional capital of Equatoria Province in South Sudan (and today the national capital of South Sudan). The aim of the conference was to explore the participation of Southerners in the proposed Legislative Assembly in Khartoum. The discussion also entailed whether the North and the South should constitute a united country. Further discussions about the establishment of the Southern Advisory Council and provincial councils took place. The Southerners expressed their fear that they would be dominated by Northerners. Strong resistance to participation in the proposed Legislative Assembly was also expressed. The resistance was due to the contention that the Southerners lacked the experience and education that would enable them to function as legislators and thus they would be easily manipulated by the Northerners (Marwood 1947).

The British ruled the South and the North as two separate entities for nearly 20 years (Abd al-Rahim 1973; Johnson 2003: 25). They even entertained the idea of joining the South with their East African colony of Kenya and Uganda. This separate rule was to have serious implications for the unity of Sudan. The British exerted little effort with regard to development in the South.

The South was left to maintain tribal structures, and no attempt was made to introduce infrastructure or a modern education system. By the time Sudan got its independence, South Sudan was one of the most backward regions. The British encouraged missionaries to go into the South to convert the native tribes that followed traditional African religions. As a result, many Southerners were converted to Christianity, while others followed their traditional beliefs.

On the other hand almost the entire Arab-Muslim North was left alone and remains until today a Muslim stronghold. The British however carried out pervasive development projects and activities in the North. The North experienced considerable investment in industry, agriculture, and education. This generated a large gap in development between the North and the South that was employed by the British for its divide-and-rule scheme (Johnson 2003: 17–19). The condominium government created in the South an entirely separate system of administration from that in the North, leaving the administration of the South almost entirely to the chiefs of small villages and ethnic groups. This should have been a positive move, but in fact caused an even greater sense of the separateness of the North and the South. Along the way the South Sudanese grew increasingly suspicious of the condominium's policies and intentions. Indeed they increasingly felt that the condominium government was favouring the North.

The apprehension of Southerners was realised when 800 administrative posts were vacated by the British in preparation for the Sudanisation of 'self-rule', and only four of the government posts went to Southerners (Akol 2007: 52–3). In discussions to determine the future of the post-colonial state of Sudan, the Southern provinces were largely excluded from the political process.

In February 1953, the United Kingdom and Egypt concluded an agreement providing for Sudanese self-government and self-determination. The transitional period toward independence began with the inauguration of the first Parliament in 1954 in Khartoum (El Mahdi 1965: 147–8), with the consent of the British and Egyptian governments, and Sudan achieved its independence on 1 January 1956 under a provisional constitution. The United States was among the first foreign powers to recognise the new state.

The federal question in the run-up to Sudan's independence

The calls for federalism were principally driven by the Southerners' fear of Northern domination that had already begun manifesting itself in the numerical disparity between the South and the North in the Legislative Assembly (Albino 1970; Alier 1973). In the run-up to the grant of independence, a 12-person commission was appointed to recommend *inter alia* the way to advance towards self-government in Sudan. The commission produced a draft constitution, which provided for certain safeguards for the South, including the appointment of a minister for Southern affairs. The minister was to be responsible for promoting and introducing measures for the economic and social betterment of the peoples of South Sudan in the Council and Parliament. But these recommendations were rejected by the majority of Northern representatives during the ensuing debate in the Legislative Assembly in January 1952 (Johnson 2003: 26). Later in the same year, Southerners were excluded from crucial constitutional talks that took place in Cairo between the Northern political parties and the condominium powers.

These events increased Southern apprehension about the Northerners' intentions towards the South. To most Southern Sudanese, this was clear proof that the Northerners wanted to include the Southerners in the new constitution and the new Sudan on their own terms and not on the terms that the Southern Sudanese wanted. This increasingly tense situation was further aggravated by the policy of 'Sudanisation', through which the working force in the country was to be transformed to a Sudanese one as opposed to a foreign one. Of the 1,222 jobs which were to be Sudanised, 1,069 of which were held by Britons and 153 by Egyptians, only four were given to Southerners. This more than anything else at the time demonstrated to the Southerners that the Northerners were simply new colonisers. In the heat of the moment, though federalism continued to be their main demand, some of the more radical Southerners of the time began to call for the complete separation of the South from the North. Others called for a referendum under the auspices of the United Nations (UN) to determine the future of the South. The Southerners were therefore determined that either there should be a federal dispensation or they should go their separate way.

The federal question after Sudan's independence

No sooner had independence been declared than the term 'federalism' became a taboo, tantamount to subversion, in the political language of the Northern elite, who on the eve of independence were assuring their Southern compatriots that they sympathised with their cause. In 1957, a parliamentary committee set up to look into the federal question rejected the idea on the ground that it was unsuitable for the Sudan (O'Ballance 1977: 46; Johnson 2003: 30). It then came to the fore that the clause had been inserted as a political manoeuvre rather than as a genuine promise on the part of the North. The then leader of the opposition, Mohammed Ahmed Mahgoub, explained that they had canvassed all the parties to secure unanimity but failed. They also encountered some difficulty in convincing the Southerners, so they inserted a special resolution to please them pledging that the constituent Assembly would give full consideration to the claims of Southern members of Parliament for a federal government for the three Southern provinces. This pledge was however later voted down by the National Union Party (O'Ballance 1977: 46). In November 1958, the Sudanese government was overthrown in a military coup led by General Ibrahim Abboud, and the new military regime set about dealing forcefully with dissent in the South. It became official government policy that Islam and Arabic would be introduced throughout the country. This was taken up with all speed in order to integrate the South Sudanese in the emergent Sudan with the hope that this would stifle calls for federalism. African traditional religions practised mainly in the South were discouraged, and in February 1962 all foreign Christian missionaries in the South were expelled (Fluehr-Lobban 2012: 33). As unrest in the South mounted, Northern forces attacked Southern villages, with as many as half a million Southerners fleeing into exile. The government of Abboud declared a state of emergency and warned that any talks of federalism would be considered treason (O'Ballance 1977: 49; Assegais 1987).

However, in the run-up to the granting of Sudan's independence, the civil service and administration were placed increasingly in Northern Sudanese hands, largely excising the Southern Sudanese from the government. The British failure to ensure equity for both the North and the South had created lasting effects. The Arab-led Khartoum government reneged on its promises to Southerners to create a federal system, which led to a mutiny by Southern troops in the Equatoria Province in Torit (known as the Torit mutiny). Feeling disenfranchised and cheated, the Southerners began an initially low-intensity civil war aimed at establishing an independent South.

Outbreak of the first civil war

The origin of the civil war in the Sudan dates back to the 1950s. On 18 August 1955, the Equatoria Corps, a military unit composed of Southerners, mutinied at Torit. Rather than surrender to the Sudanese government authorities, many mutineers went into hiding with their weapons and subsequently were involved in guerrilla warfare. This marked the beginning of the first war in Southern Sudan.

The immediate causes of the mutiny were a trial of a Southern member of the National Assembly and an allegedly false telegram urging Northern administrators in the South to oppress Southerners. The rumours spread quickly, sparking the mutiny. The action from the Sudanese army was swift and harsh. The mutinies were suppressed, though survivors fled the towns and began an uncoordinated insurgency in rural areas. Poorly armed and ill organised, they were little threat to the outgoing colonial power or the newly formed Sudanese government.

According to O'Ballance (1977) the government was unable to take advantage of rebel weaknesses because of its own factionalism and instability. The first independent government of Sudan, led by prime minister Ismail al-Azhari, was quickly replaced by a stalemated coalition of various conservative forces, which was in turn overthrown in the coup d'état of chief of staff Lieutenant-General Ibrahim Abboud in 1958. Resentment at the military government paved the way for a wave of popular protests that led to the creation of an interim government in October 1964. However, the insurgents gradually developed into a secessionist movement composed of the 1955 mutineers and Southern students. These groups formed the Anyanya guerrilla army. Starting from Equatoria, between 1963 and 1969 Anyanya spread throughout the other two Southern provinces: Upper Nile and Bahr al Ghazal. However, the separatist movement was crippled by internal ethnic divisions. O'Ballance (1977: 62) writes that one of the Sudanese army's four infantry brigades had been stationed in Equatoria Province since 1955, being periodically reinforced as required, and had to engage the badly organised rebels.

By 1969 the rebels had developed foreign contacts to obtain weapons and supplies. Israel, for example, trained Anyanya recruits and shipped weapons via Ethiopia and Uganda to the rebels (Johnson 2003: 36–7). Anyanya also purchased arms from Congolese rebels and international arms dealers with monies collected in the South and from among Southern Sudanese exile communities in the Middle East, Western Europe, and North America. The rebels also captured arms, equipment, and supplies from government troops.

In 1971 Joseph Lagu, who had become the leader of the Southern forces opposed to Khartoum, proclaimed the creation of the Southern Sudan Liberation Movement (SSLM). Anyanya leaders united behind him, and nearly all exiled Southern politicians supported the SSLM (O'Ballance 1977: 135; Holt and Daly 2011: 132–3). Although the SSLM created a governing infrastructure throughout many areas of Southern Sudan, real power remained with Anyanya, with Lagu at its head (O'Ballance 2000: 78).

It was indicative of the nature of relations between the North and South that the civil war began even before the Sudan officially got its independence in 1956.

Just as the transfer of power from the British to the mostly Northern administrators was in progress and just as the garrison in Torit in the South was being transferred to Northern control, the mutiny broke out that sparked off the Anyanya separatist movement and showed how precarious was the North–South integration. The civil war continued until 1972, when the Addis Ababa Accord that gave regional autonomy to the South created an uneasy peace that lasted until 1983.

The 1965 Round Table Conference

Among the significant aspects of this conference were the divisions amongst Southerners as to whether the South should remain a single political unit and if so whether its independence was a viable option. Three factions, namely Sudan Africa Nationalist Union (SANU) (I), SANU (O) and Southern Front (SF), represented the South. They came to the Round Table with different views. The Northern parties consisted of the Umma Party, the National Union Party (NUP), the People's Democratic Party (PDP), the Islamic Charter Front (ICF), and the Communist Party (Akol 2007: 90–96). The Northern politicians were prepared to concede only limited regional autonomy to the South in areas such as primary education, health, and roads, leaving control over economic planning, financial policy, state security, armed forces, foreign affairs, and other areas of national policy to the central government.

The Southerners, on the other hand, insisted that a federation was necessary to ensure that they would exert control over their own affairs and resources. However, although there was general agreement amongst the Southerners on their right to self-determination, there was a divergence of views amongst them on how it was to be asserted. SANU (I) insisted that federation was necessary in order for the Southerners to exert control over their affairs and resources. The division within the ranks of Southerners certainly undermined their negotiating position vis-à-vis the Northerners.

Ultimately, the conference appointed a 12-person committee to draw up a working paper on North–South relations. The committee, made up of an equal number of Southern and Northern members, deliberated for a year before submitting a report (Akol 2007: 97). Although the committee finally agreed that the South should be separate from the North, it was still unable to agree on several key issues, particularly the most vital question of whether the South should be one region, as most Northerners wanted, or three regions, as advocated by the Southerners. There were also fundamental differences over what relationship would exist between Southern and Northern troops and on the fiscal aspects of the proposed federal arrangement.

By the time the committee's report was submitted, the civil war in the South had degenerated. The then president Ibrahim Abboud resigned as head of state, and a transitional government was appointed to serve under a provisional constitution of 1956 (Khalid 2003: 89). The coalition government that came to power after April 1965 reneged on the question of reconvening the conference to discuss the federal question. At the same time the civil war was gathering momentum. The coalition was in turn ousted from power by the military, led by Colonel Ja'afar Nimeiri, on 25 May 1969 (Johnson 2003: 36).

Despite his political problems, Nimeiri remained committed to ending the Southern insurgency. He believed he could end the fighting and stabilise the region by granting regional self-government and undertaking economic development in the South. By October 1971, Khartoum had established contact with the SSLM. After considerable consultation, a conference between SSLM and Sudanese government delegations convened in Addis Ababa, Ethiopia, in February 1972 (Johnson 2003: 39). Initially, the two sides were far apart, the Southerners demanding a federal state with a separate Southern government and an army that would come under the federal president's command only in response to an external threat to Sudan. Eventually, however, the two sides, with the help of Ethiopia's emperor Haile Selassie, reached an agreement.

The Addis Ababa Accord

The Addis Ababa Accord was mediated by Haile Selassie of Ethiopia. The accord guaranteed autonomy for the Southern region, composed of the three provinces of Equatoria, Bahr al Ghazal, and Upper Nile, under a regional president appointed by the national president on the recommendation of an elected Southern Regional Assembly. It was stipulated that the accord would bring not only peace and stability but also development to the war-ridden region. It was promised that development investment as a means of integrating and stabilising the region would be forthcoming (Rolandsen 2005: 25; Fluehr-Lobban 2012: 34). The characterising features of the accord were creation of regional autonomy for the South, a single entity, a people's Regional Assembly, and a High Executive Council (HEC). It also included the integration of the Anyanya combatants into the national army, police, security forces, and civil service, and repatriation of South Sudanese refugees (Tvedt 1994: 71–2). According to the accord the Southern problem was to be settled within a federal system. A federal state dispensation whereby South Sudan would constitute an autonomous state would curb the quest for secession.

The High Executive Council or cabinet named by the regional president would be responsible for all aspects of government in the region except such areas as defence, foreign affairs, currency and finance, economic and social planning, and interregional concerns, authority over which would be retained by the national government, in which Southerners would be represented. Southerners, including qualified Anyanya veterans, would be incorporated into a 12,000-person Southern command of the Sudanese army under equal numbers of Northern and Southern officers. The accord also recognised Arabic as Sudan's official language, and English as the South's principal language, which would be used in administration and would be taught in schools.

This autonomy was therefore accepted by the South Sudanese as a second-best and practical solution. Initially great hope was placed in it, and it was thought that peace, stability, democracy, and development would reign in the troubled South.

Executive power under the Addis Ababa Accord

Regional executive authority was vested in the HEC, headed by a president with a mandate to act in the South on behalf of the national president. According to Article 18, the HEC was charged with specifying the duties of the various government departments in the Southern region. The national president appointed the president of the HEC on the recommendation of the People's Regional Assembly. The HEC president in turn proposed its members to the national president for appointment, the process being the same for removing appointees from office. As a chief executive, the president of the HEC had the constitutional mandate to promulgate administrative regulations, enforcement of which was the responsibility of Council members. Abel Alier became the first president of the HEC (LeRiche and Arnold 2012: 29). Joseph Lagu, who later replaced Alier as president of the HEC, joined the Sudan Armed Forces (SAF) as senior commander (Alier 1973).The national president's constitutional power to regulate the relationship between the Southern administration and the central ministries was also problematic. The Addis Ababa Accord was not clear on how the regional departments should relate to the central ministries, and the role of provincial commissioners exacerbated the confusion. Provincial commissioners were nominated by the HEC president and appointed by the national president. Although their work directly concerned matters assigned by the Act to the regional government, these commissioners reported to the central government authorities in Khartoum. This not only posed practical and political problems but also caused a lack of constitutional clarity and confrontations that eventually led to the end of the Addis Ababa Accord.

The demise of the Addis Ababa Accord

The Addis Ababa Accord collapsed when President Nimeiri failed to abide by its commitments. From the very outset Nimeiri reneged on his commitments and began undermining the accord by violating its core tenets (LeRiche and Arnold 2012: 30). Most of the provisions were either ignored or poorly implemented.

To begin with, the Anyanya fighters were not happy with the accord; they had not fought for independence in order to join their enemies in the Sudan Armed Forces. In addition, the poor implementation of the provisions further angered them; therefore they decided to remain in the bush, occasionally engaging the SAF. There also emerged differences among the Southern leadership, particularly between Alier and Lagu, which opened an opportunity for Nimeiri to exploit.

Owing to the fact that the Southern government was entitled to revenues received from natural resources in the South under the Addis Ababa Accord, it was enthusiastic in wooing oil companies to explore the region. This could not have been appreciated by the Khartoum government, which was bent on thwarting the self-rule of the South (Adar et al. 2004).

Finally the Nimeiri regime, in June 1983, in violation of the accord, decided to divide South Sudan into three provinces (O'Ballance 2000: 130; LeRiche and

Arnold 2012: 30). The boundary between the North and South was shifted in such a way that Bentiu and other areas of the South, rich in agriculture and minerals, were incorporated into the North. Yet, in delivering another blow to the accord, in September 1983, under the influence of Hassan Al Turabi, the then leader of the National Islamic Front, Nimeiri introduced Sharia rule throughout the country, commonly known as the September Laws (Ahanotu 1992). All this virtually dismantled the self-rule of South Sudan. The introduction of Sharia law, division of the South into three provinces, and the overall dismantling of the provisions of the Addis Ababa Accord turned the clock back to 1955, sparking a mutiny of South Sudanese soldiers. In the same way as the Torit mutiny was believed to have induced the first civil war, the Bor mutiny was believed to have spurred the second civil war. What sparked the munity of South Sudanese soldiers in Bor however was the decision by the Nimeiri regime, in an effort to undermine the accord, to move the ex-Anyanya soldiers incorporated in the SAF from their base in the South to the North. The munity is generally accepted as being the marking point for the second civil war, which was to last for another 22 years.

Conclusion

Sudan has been afflicted by a civil war mainly between the 'Arab North' and the 'African Animist Christian South' for nearly four decades. The first civil war began in 1955 when a South Sudanese unit in the Sudanese army stationed in Torit mutinied. The main factor that sparked the mutiny was fear of domination by the North in the imminent independent Sudan. The independence of Sudan proved that fear. General Abboud, who came to power through a military coup, embarked on an intensive Islamisation and Arabisation campaign in the South. This aggravated the civil war. The civilian government that replaced Abboud did not behave better either. The civilian government was itself overthrown by the military, headed by General Ja'afar Nimeiri. Nimeiri struck a deal with the SSLM, mediated by Ethiopia, in 1972 that gave the South self-rule. The self-rule was abrogated by Nimeiri, and the second civil war began in 1983.

Two factors could be identified as the chief contributing causal factors to the first civil war. The first factor relates to colonialism. The condominium government, for most of the time, ruled the Sudan as two separate entities. It was only when it became clear that the independence of Sudan was inevitable that an attempt at integrating the two entities received serious consideration. Therefore, at independence, there was not any meaningful integration between the North and the South. Indeed the two entities were worlds apart from each other. The second factor related to the behaviour of the ruling political elite in the North. The Northern ruling elite, military as well as civilian, located in Khartoum, pursued politics of domination that completely marginalised and excluded Southerners. The nation-state-building project of the post-colonial state of Sudan increasingly proved to be brutal, exclusionary, marginalising, humiliating, and dehumanising to the South Sudanese. This convinced Southerners that the solution could only be found in the quest for independence. The quest for self-determination however collided with the sacrosanctity of colonial borders, which impeded the realisation of the wish of the people of South Sudan until 2011.

Alternatively, one option would have been to push for peace and democracy driven by political integration along lines of coexistence within a framework that accommodated diversity within unity. In essence this would have meant resorting to federalism. Unfortunately this was not the road taken by the Northern ruling elite.

Contrary to the customary conception of federalism in the conventional sense of a federation, federalism in the case of Sudan would have meant a normative approach conducive to various forms of applications. This renders federal political systems such as federations, autonomous arrangements, and decentralised or devolved arrangements simply varied applications of the federal principle. Indeed, the federal principle has proved critical as a tool of political integration in pluralistic societies. It has served as a tool of democratisation. In discharging this function of integration, the constitution proves to be a vital avenue through which it finds expression. The incorporation of the federal principle in the constitutional framework can create federal arrangements that manage to deal with the challenges of multiculturalism. The failure to find a political formula that accommodated multiculturalism necessitated the continuation of the civil war and brought about the second civil war, which ended with the implementation of self-determination in the South and culminated in the independence of the country in July 2011.

References

Abbas, M. 1952. *The Sudan Question*. London: Faber and Faber.

Abd al-Rahim, M. 1969. *Imperialism and Nationalism in the Sudan: A Study in Constitutional and Political Development 1899–1956*. Oxford: Clarendon Press.

Abd al-Rahim, M. 1973. 'Arabism, Africanism and Self-Identification in the Sudan', in D. Wai (ed.), *The Southern Sudan: The Problem of National Integration*. London: Frank Cass.

Adar, K., Yoh, J. and Maloka, E. 2004. *Sudan Peace Process: Challenges and Future Prospects*. Pretoria: Africa Institute of South Africa.

Ahanotu, A. 1992. *Religion, State and Society in Contemporary Africa: Nigeria, Sudan, South Africa, Zaire and Mozambique*. New York: Peter Lang Publishing.

Akol, Lam. 2007. *Southern Sudan: Colonialism, Resistance and Autonomy*. Trenton, NJ: Red Sea Press.

Albino, O. 1970. *The Sudan: A Southern Viewpoint*. London: Oxford University Press.

Alier, A. 1973. 'The Southern Sudan Question', in D. Wai (ed.), *The Southern Sudan: The Problem of National Integration*. London: Frank Cass.

Assegais, H. 1987. *Mediation of Civil Wars: Approaches and Strategies – The Sudan Conflict*. Boulder, CO: Westview Press.

El Mahdi, Mandour. 1965. *A Short History of the Sudan*. London: Oxford University Press.

Fluehr-Lobban, Carolyn. 2012. *Shar'a and Islam in Sudan: Conflict, Law and Social Transformation*. London: I. B. Tauris.

Holt, P. M. and Daly, M. M. 2011. *A Short History of the Sudan: From the Coming of Islam to the Present Day*, 6th edn. Harlow: Pearson Education.

Idris, Amir. 2013. *Identity, Citizenship, and Violence in Two Sudans: Reimagining a Common Future*. New York: Palgrave Macmillan.

Johnson, Douglas. 2003. *The Root Causes of Sudan's Civil Wars*. Oxford, Bloomington and Kampala: James Currey, Indiana University Press and Fountain Publishers.

Khalid, Mansour. 2003. *War and Peace in Sudan: A Tale of Two Countries*. London: Kegan Paul.

LeRiche, Matthew and Arnold, Matthew. 2012. *South Sudan: From Revolution to Independence*. London: Hurst & Company.

Marwood, B. V. 1947. Juba Conference 1947. EP/SCR/1.A.5/1.

O'Ballance, Edgar. 1977. *The Secret War in the Sudan: 1955–1972*. London: Faber and Faber.

O'Ballance, Edgar. 2000. *Sudan, Civil War and Terrorism, 1956–99*. London: Macmillan.

Rolandsen, Oystein H. 2005. *Guerrilla Government: Political Challenges in the Southern Sudan during the 1990s*. Uppsala: Nordic Africa Institute.

Tvedt, Terje. 1994. 'The Collapse of the State in Southern Sudan after the Addis Ababa Agreement: A Study of Internal Causes and the Role of the IGOs', in Sharif Harir and Terje Tvedt (eds), *Short-Cut to Decay: The Case of the Sudan*. Uppsala: Scandinavian Institute of African Studies.

6   Second civil war

Creation of the united 'New Sudan'

Leben Nelson Moro

Introduction

The war in the old Sudan resumed in 1983 after a short period of shaky peace between 1972 and 1982. In contrast to the armed rebels who waged the first war against the central government between 1955 and 1972, the leader of the second rebellion, Dr John Garang de Mabior, said that his group would struggle not for a separate state in the Southern region of the country but for a united 'New Sudan', in which equality, democracy, and secular governance would prevail (Garang de Mabior 1996). It is argued that the idea of a united 'New Sudan' proved elusive because it became too difficult and costly to achieve, particularly after the military coup of 1989 that brought to power Islamists bent on imposing Islamic or *Shari'a* law over the country.

The rise of Islamists in the old Sudan was connected to the resurgence of the Islamist movement in Arab and Muslim countries in North Africa and the Middle East, which gained momentum during the so-called 'Arab Spring' sweeping the region. This development, however, has deepened fear among non-Muslims and other people who are opposed to a big role for Islam in public affairs. In the old Sudan, in which the role of religion in politics was intensely contested, the increasing fortunes of the Islamists widened the political fault lines in the country. Dr Barnaba Marial Benjamin quoted Garang as saying that:

> the Sudanese post independent state is essentially an alien political system with an institutional framework that excludes the vast majority of its citizens. How can there be peace? And after the 1989 National Islamic Front (NIF) coup, the system further excluded non-fundamentalist Moslems, while women have always been excluded at all times. We call this Old Sudan based on religion (Islam) and race (Arabism).
>
> (Benjamin 2004: 47)

As a result of the determined efforts by the NIF to impose Islam over the country, the secession of Southern Sudan became a more feasible and acceptable option to the major power brokers in the North and South of the country as well as some powerful countries around the world.

After the death of Garang, the brain and force behind the notion of a united 'New Sudan', in a helicopter crash in June 2005 shortly after the formal end of fighting in January, the split of the country became more likely. When Southerners got the chance to vote in a referendum in January 2011, it was not surprising that they overwhelmingly opted for independence and not unity under the notion of a united 'New Sudan'. Nonetheless, the idea continued to fuel agitation for fundamental change among marginalized groups in Northern Sudan, which retained the name Sudan after Southern Sudan broke away.

This chapter investigates the failure of the people of old Sudan to realize Garang's cherished dream to maintain the unity of the country under a new political dispensation or united 'New Sudan'. The next section discusses the long and futile dream of elites from the Northern part of the old Sudan, both civilian and military, to mould a united country under the banner of Arabism and Islam. The chapter then analyses the idea of a united 'New Sudan', before examining the rejection of the notion of a united 'New Sudan' by a group of rebel leaders after the split of the Sudan People's Liberation Movement/Army (SPLM/A) in 1991, which almost provided the Sudanese army with the opportunity to crush the rebellion. The chapter then discusses the Comprehensive Peace Agreement (CPA) and acceptance of self-determination for the people of Southern Sudan. It then tackles the birth of the Republic of South Sudan, which marked the death of the notion of a united 'New Sudan' in Southern Sudan. The last section concludes the chapter.

Forced unity under Arabism and Islamism

The independence of Southern Sudan was, to a great extent, a logical outcome of the intransigence of elites from the Northern part of the old Sudan, especially Islamists, who were averse to unity in diversity and instead sought to forge a nation based on Arabism and Islamism. This set the country on a perilous path of war, which in turn led to the split of the country.

The real ambition of the elites from the Northern part of the old Sudan, who hailed from a small number of 'Arab' and Muslim tribes, was retention of power. So greed for power was their motive, and talk of the unity of the country under the banner of Islam and Arabism was mainly the cover. Unity was unfortunately the casualty of the actions of the politically dominant 'Arab' and Muslim tribes. As Jok Madut Jok has tellingly pointed out, the politically dominant old Sudanese groups, who self-identified as Arabs, had sought 'to forge the Sudanese national identity as "Arab" and "Islamic" while the majority of the population increasingly preferred to identify themselves by specific ethnic/tribal names or simply "African" or "Black"' (Jok 2008: 2). Accordingly, Francis Deng perceived the problems of the old Sudan as 'conflict of identities' (F. M. Deng 1995). He explained the forms of the identity crises as follows:

> One has to do with the gap between the definition of the country as Arab and Islamic, when the majority of Sudanese, even in the North are not Arabs.

The second has to do with the fact that even those who claim to be Arab are in fact a hybrid of African–Arab elements, which implies a gap between what people think they are and what they really are, judged by objective physical or visible indicators.

(F. M. Deng 2000: 134)

While it was true that many old Sudanese felt frustrated because of lack of recognition of their identities, it was also the case that many people did not fully share in the national cake. The economy was totally dominated by the elites from the politically powerful 'Arab' and Muslim tribes. The majority of old Sudanese, particularly in the South, West and East, felt excluded. They were marginalized economically because they were excluded from the political establishment, which made decisions on resource allocations.

The domination of the country by minority Muslim and 'Arab' tribes in the Northern part of the old Sudan spawned violent conflicts, with Southern Sudanese being at the forefront. A few months before the old Sudan's independence in 1956, Southerners took to the bush to wage war against the central government. The old Sudanese who led the nationalist struggle against the British and Egyptian colonialists 'appealed to ideas and passions primarily associated with Arabization and Islamization', which were detested in the South (Collins 1999). This was partly to do with the fact that some of the intruders or invaders of the Southern region, in particular slave traders, were followers of Islam and claimed Arab descent.

The first round of fighting lasted for 17 years and ended with a peace accord, the Addis Ababa Agreement, between the government of President Jaafar Nimeiri (1969–85) and the Anyanya rebels. Shockingly, President Nimeiri abrogated this agreement ten years later, in 1982, and subsequently imposed *Shari'a* law over the whole country. Southerners overcame their usual tribal and historical differences to confront this law (Collins 2005).

The collapse of the agreement not only angered many Southerners but also deepened the feeling that 'Arab' and Muslim elites were deceptive and not worth trusting. In his *Southern Sudan: Too Many Agreements Dishonoured*, Abel Alier, a veteran Southern Sudanese politician, dealt with this behaviour of the 'Arab' and Muslim elites and the erosion of trust in them among marginalized Sudanese (Alier 1992). Again Southerners headed for the bush to resume the struggle against the regimes in Khartoum.

SPLM/A and the idea of 'New Sudan'

In 1983, Southern rebels gathered in Ethiopia to agree on how to prosecute the war against the regime in Khartoum. Without doubt, the disastrous end of the Addis Ababa Agreement shaped their views about the new round of the struggle. For some of them, particularly Dr John Garang, nothing good would come out of separation, and the solution was a revolution paving the way to the emergence of a united 'New Sudan', in which the interests of all regions and peoples would be guaranteed.

The new insurgents were determined to remove from power President Nimeiri as well as his supporters in the Southern region who helped him dishonour the agreement. They were particularly frustrated by Southern leaders who conspired with Nimeiri against the interests of their own region and people so as to further their own individual greed for power and wealth. As Dr Lam Akol, a compatriot of Garang at the time, pointed out, 'Nimeiri felt at liberty of overlooking some articles of the Self-Government Act 1972 at the acquiescence, if not connivance, of those in charge of the regional government in Juba' (Akol 2001: 1). As a result, 'Nimeiri was condemned for reneging on the Agreement while Southern politicians in Juba were despised for having allowed themselves for self-interest to be used by Nimeiri in his destructive machinations against the South' (Akol 2001: 2).

It was not surprising that Garang dismissed the Addis Ababa Agreement 'as an arrangement about jobs reached between elites' (Johnson 2003: 64). For him, the problem of the Sudan was not 'problems of Southern Sudan', as had been conceptualized by Northern elites as well as many other people, but a problem of the whole old Sudan, whose remedy was total reform of the old Sudanese system. As pointed out by Dr Luka Biong Deng, Garang perceived the 'problem of Sudan as problem of the centre and not the problem of the peripheries' (L. B. Deng 2012: 33).

Therefore, contrary to the case in the first rebellion, which fought for independence of the Southern region from the 'Muslim' and 'Arab' North, Garang and his compatriots struggled for a united 'New Sudan'. The interests of the South were better defended in Khartoum and not in Juba (Johnson 2003). The idea of 'New Sudan' was elaborated in a manifesto produced by the SPLM/A in 1983, and found significant support from peoples in Northern Sudan who felt marginalized by the regime in Khartoum. It is no wonder that one of the staunchest Northern members of the SPLM/A, Yasir Arman, reportedly described 'Dr John Garang as a gift to humanity and the most influential Sudanese leader in the twentieth Century' (L. B. Deng 2012: 33). Together with other Northern leaders who followed Garang, he is still fighting for the same dream of 'New Sudan' in what remained of the old Sudan after the breakaway of the Southern region.

The 'New Sudan' idea made sense not only in other marginalized parts of the country but also in some African countries, particularly Ethiopia, and in the OAU, which supported the maintenance of the borders inherited from the colonialists. President Mengistu of Ethiopia, who was locked in a bitter armed struggle against secessionist Eritrean rebels, became Garang's key supporter. This would probably not have happened if the SPLM/A had adopted a separatist agenda for Southern Sudan. Some countries, such as Nigeria and former Zaire, were naturally opposed to separatism because some of their regions had taken up arms so as to break away.

Within the SPLM/A, however, the idea was not accepted by all. It 'was at variance with the will and aspirations of many of its members who believed that South Sudan should secede from the rest of the Sudan to enable a South Sudanese national identity to evolve and develop' (Nyaba 2000: 7). Many of the Southerners who joined Garang entertained the thought that the idea was merely a clever strategy to win support among some Northern groups and outside Sudan, and hence would be revised in time. For example, Dr Lam Akol explained his reasons for joining the SPLM/A as follows: 'As alluded to already, what made me join the SPLA was not so much the socialism it espoused or the unity of Sudan it set itself to preserve but basically the idea of the Southerners getting organized politically to wage a revolutionary armed struggle' (Akol 2001: 15).

Accordingly, the idea did not serve as a strong basis for unity among Southern rebels and hence was easily used against the rebellion, particularly its leader, Garang, by opponents of the SPLM/A. In fact, it fuelled serious disunity and internal fighting right from the beginning of the rebellion, which was readily exploited by the government in Khartoum. The first battles for the 'New Sudan' were therefore fought not against the old Sudanese army but against Southerners who did not believe in it or were suspected of harbouring ambitions to wrest the leadership of the movement. According to Akol:

> Then followed a period of bitter infighting among Southerners (between the Anya-nya 2 and the SPLA) which was to continue for four years. The lives lost in the process were more than the number lost in fighting the enemy over the same period. Naturally the enemy exploited the split and supplied the Anya-nya with arms and ammos to fight the SPLA.
>
> (Akol 2001: 203)

Moreover, Akol argued that the deaths should be blamed on competition over power among Southern rebel leaders rather than conflicts over the future of the Southern region. He explained this as follows: 'Therefore, the SPLA started off with interfighting among the Southerners. Contrary to Garang's later propaganda, the first bullet was not shot at the separatists but at competitors over power and the top position in the movement' (Akol 2001: 203).

In the future, the struggles for power deepened and claimed more lives. Akol was to play a big role in the intensification of disunity and violence in Southern Sudan, mainly because of who was to lead the rebellion. Naturally, the idea of 'New Sudan' was manipulated by opponents of Garang so as to depose him.

The 1991 rebellion against Dr John Garang

The fall from power in 1991 of President Mengistu, the most loyal of Garang's backers, had a dramatic impact on the SPLM/A. Simmering differences within the movement gave way to open revolt and infighting that turned tribal. Expectedly, the government exploited the divisions, which almost led to the demise of the movement.

Just after the exit of Mengistu from power, the SPLM/A suffered a major split in August 1991. Three key commanders claimed the takeover of the movement from Garang, a Dinka from Jonglei. Led by Dr Riek Machar (Dok Nuer), Dr Lam Akol (Shilluk) and Gordon Kong Chuol (Jikany Nuer), the coup was allegedly staged because Garang was a dictator and abuser of human rights. Indeed, many lost their lives on flimsy charges of being against his leadership (Nyaba 2000: 69). Partly because of this, opponents of the idea of the united 'New Sudan' within the movement could not come out openly and forcibly.

The fall of Mengistu created the environment in which Garang's leadership and ideas could be challenged. Besides announcing Garang's overthrow, the three commanders said the idea of a united 'New Sudan' was abandoned and independence of the Southern region would be the goal of the struggle. This struck a chord with many people, as independence was the dream of the majority of Southerners. So separation was easily exploited by Garang's opponents to wrest power. Followers of the united 'New Sudan' idea from the North did not know what to do. Some of the rebels from Darfur began to mobilize for a rebellion that fought for their interests.

The attempt to wrest power from Garang did not succeed, however. Instead it deepened tribal differences and violence along tribal lines. The main victims of the violence were the communities from which the key rebel leaders engaged in the bitter power struggle hailed. They all became embroiled in bitter infighting, whose main victims were women, children, and other civilians.

To the surprise of many, Garang's opponents, the three commanders, began receiving arms from Khartoum, which was totally opposed to the separation of the South from the other parts of the country. With these arms, they launched devastating assaults against civilians in Garang's home area. The forces loyal to Garang responded in kind.

Clearly, the war in the South had degenerated into a bloody tribal confrontation, mainly pitting Dinka against Nuer fighters, with most victims being civilians (Jok and Hutchinson 1999). Consequently, more people lost their lives in inter-factional fighting amongst Southerners than in armed encounters with government forces (Amnesty International 2000). These deaths were neither for achievement of a united 'New Sudan' nor for attainment of a separate state in the South. They were the result of greed for power.

The unity of the three commanders was short-lived, though. In 1994, Machar parted company from Akol, who formed a new group composed mainly of his tribesmen. His group operated in his home area, the Shilluk heartland, with support from the government army.

What remained of Machar's group later disintegrated into rapacious groups which preyed on Nuer civilians. Over time intra-ethnic violence among Nuer came to dominate the fighting in the Upper Nile. Violence became endemic and localized. It benefited the government enormously.

Ironically, this suffering of the Southern Sudanese was caused by the greed for power of the most educated leaders of Southern Sudan. Garang was a highly educated man, with a Ph.D. from an American university. Machar held a doctoral degree in mechanical engineering from Bradford University in the United Kingdom; and Akol has a Ph.D. in petrochemical engineering from the University of London. These highly educated sons of the South played into the hands of the enemy in Khartoum and forgot, at least temporarily, the very reason for taking up arms against Khartoum.

The bloody infighting allowed the government army to recover lost territory. Garang's fighters, the real opponents of the government, were rapidly driven towards the Ugandan and Kenyan borders. By '1993 and 1994 the military situation in the Southern Sudan was effectively altered and tilted in favour of the Sudan Government' (Madut 2006: 313). It was only several years later that they began to confront the government effectively. In the second half of the 1990s, Garang's forces succeeded in halting the government army push and began positioning themselves for major counter-attacks (Johnson 2003: 100).

As the forces loyal to Garang were suffering defeats, the government in Khartoum began building closer ties with Southern militia leaders, particularly Machar. This was not difficult, as they were already receiving arms and logistical support from the government army. To formalize the collaboration, the government entered into a fake peace agreement, called the Khartoum Peace Agreement, with the militia leaders in 1997. It included a promise of self-determination for the people of Southern Sudan.

In reality, the government had no intention of carrying out the terms of the agreement but was mainly interested in its military benefits. The militias managed to coordinate their attacks against Garang's forces and subsequently secured the oil areas for companies to operate in (Human Rights Watch 2003). With revenues from oil, the government bolstered its military position. By this time, the militias had 'cavalierly abandoned any thoughts of an independent Southern Sudan in return for survival as petty warlords and bandits' (Collins 2005).

Control over the oil areas, however, proved problematic. Machar interpreted the Khartoum Peace Agreement to mean the forces he commanded would be responsible for security in the South. However, the government intended to control the oilfields directly or through more loyal local proxies. It mobilized other more trusted militias against Machar's group, further escalating local conflicts. The escalation of violence caused the collapse of the peace agreement in 1999 (ICG 2002: 135). In 2000, Machar left the government, and two years later made peace with Garang and rejoined the SPLM/A. Nonetheless, a lot of his forces were left at the mercy of the government.

Many of the militia leaders or commanders were mostly autonomous, and ruled their small fiefdoms in the South as they pleased. They protected and exploited communities under their control, while plundering neighbouring communities. As a result, violence became localized and endemic; often battles were waged over issues or grievances that were local, with no or little bearing on national issues.

After several years of collaborating with the Sudanese government army, Akol switched sides and rejoined Garang, a blow to government resolve to end the fighting on the battleground. Perhaps realizing that the SPLM/A was not going to surrender, the government began paying more attention to peaceful resolution of the war.

Garang also learned lessons from the bitter experience which nearly brought down the movement he led in an authoritarian manner. The split of the movement 'clearly pushed Garang and the SPLM to accept self-determination, at least ostensibly, for the Southern Sudan despite its danger of separatism which would vitiate Garang's vision of united Sudan' (Collins 2005). It also appeared that, after long years of fighting and continued intransigence on the part of the Islamists in Khartoum, the dream of a united 'New Sudan' became even more far-fetched. Accordingly, self-determination was firmly inserted into negotiations with the government.

The CPA and self-determination

In 2005, the old Sudanese government and the SPLM/A concluded the CPA. The Intergovernmental Authority on Development, with the support of US and other Western countries, brokered this deal. In contrast to the agreements reached in the past, especially the Addis Ababa Agreement of 1972 and the Khartoum Peace Agreement of 1997, the CPA took a long time to negotiate and offered detailed and broad-ranging solutions to the conflict between Southern Sudan and the central government.

The Machakos Protocol of the CPA, which was signed on 20 July 2002, dealt with the disagreement over national unity as well as the role of Islam in politics. It guaranteed Southerners the right to vote in a referendum on whether to remain part of old Sudan or to form a separate state after a six-year interim period. It also exempted the South from *Shari'a*, which continued to be imposed on the North. The other three protocols which formed part of the CPA resolved disputes over power sharing, Southern Kordofan and Blue Nile, and the Abyei area. The CPA also contained agreements on security arrangements and wealth sharing, especially oil revenues.

The CPA was welcomed by both signatories as a good document that took into account their key concerns. Indeed, Garang told the people who gathered to witness the signing of the agreement that the CPA signalled the beginning of a united 'New Sudan', in which justice, honour, and dignity would be respected, and that if the country failed to move away from the old Sudan to the united 'New Sudan' then the union would be dissolved through the right of self-determination.

The leaders from Khartoum were also upbeat about the agreement. While visiting Juba after the agreement was signed, President Omer al Bashir 'hailed the peace agreement as a new beginning for the people of Sudan' (Mbugua 2005: 30). He seemed to be particularly happy with the retention of *Shari'a* in the North, a crucial aspect of the 'civilizational project' which aimed to transform the country into an Islamic state (El-Affendi 2008: 61). Even more importantly, the agreement removed the security threat posed by the SPLA to oil production, a key to the economic survival of the regime. Sally Healy rightly observed that the 'growing importance of oil revenues in the Southern conflict areas introduced a business case for ending the war' (Healy 2008: 31). Moreover, the Islamists in Khartoum hoped that the agreement would lead to a thaw in relations with the US and other Western countries.

Unfortunately, the CPA did not meet the aspirations of the marginalized people in the North who were worried about the South breaking away and leaving them to face the enemy in Khartoum alone. It is no wonder that the people of

Darfur took up arms against the regime in Khartoum, sparking a huge catastrophe. It can be argued that the attainment of the CPA caused the insurgency in Darfur, whose people felt that their interests were not covered. The same feeling was evident in Southern Kordofan, Blue Nile, and Eastern Sudan, which had long complained about exclusion from the old Sudanese state.

It is worth pointing out that the agreement was not readily accepted by all South Sudanese. Some groups, among them militia groups allied to the regime, found themselves on the wrong side and hence were bent on spoiling the peace. These militias were supposed to be demobilized, but the government was slow to do this and instead wanted to maintain them for future use if necessary. Indeed some of these groups sparked deadly conflicts which threatened to unravel the agreement and a return to wider fighting.

The SPLM/A complained many times about the activities of the militias, and accused the government of trying to evade responsibility for full implementation of the CPA. Indeed, it appeared that after Garang's death in July 2005 the government was more confident about ignoring implementation of key aspects of the CPA. Even though Garang's successor, Salva Kiir, was a respected and popular military commander, he did not have the political stature of his predecessor. It was also not certain that he totally agreed with Garang's united 'New Sudan' idea, which must have worried the marginalized peoples in the Northern part of old Sudan who had faith in Garang's vision.

The fear that the government was dragging its feet on the implementation of the CPA deepened as international engagement seemed to slow because of the unfolding humanitarian crises in Darfur. Without full engagement of the world powers, especially the US, the implementation of the CPA could have stalled. In the first place, the agreement itself came about because of the intense involvement of Western countries, especially the US (Malwal 2005). The US involvement in peacemaking in Sudan, which hosted Osama bin Laden from 1991 to 1996, was part of the so-called 'war on terror' (Miller and Meyer 2007). Therefore, it was possible that the implementation of the agreement would have suffered if US interests had shifted somewhere else. The long history of many agreements dishonoured was still fresh in the minds of the Southern Sudanese, especially the leaders who made the agreement.

Indeed some leaders in Khartoum had sent our frightening signals. For example, the deputy chairman of the ruling National Congress Party (NCP) threatened to cancel the agreement 'if the UN troops intervened in the war-torn Darfur region with the SPLM support' ('SPLM Warns' 2006: 1). The reckless outburst triggered alarm bells in SPLM circles, as implementation of key aspects of the agreement had fallen behind schedule. Some of the key complaints of the SPLM were stated by President Salva Kiir before the Southern Sudan Legislative Assembly in September 2006 as follows: first, the Abyei Boundaries Commission (ABC); second, the National Petroleum Commission (NPC); third, the North–South Border Commission; and, fourth, the Civil Service Commission ('Kiir Defines' 2006: 19).

The ABC, which consisted of five international experts and five representatives each from the government and the SPLM/A, prepared the ABC report that charted the way out of the contest over Abyei between the local Ngok Dinka and Arab groups. It was rejected by President Omer al Bashir. Later the matter was referred for arbitration at the international Court in The Hague, whose ruling was accepted by Southern leaders and dismissed by al Bashir. Thus, Abyei remained a flash point. On the oil issue, the NPC was not an effective institution and therefore disputes over oil were not effectively dealt with. Oil issues continue to divide Khartoum and Juba. Likewise, the North–South Border Commission did not make any meaningful progress in demarcating the border between the South and North, and hence the border has been a source of conflict. These are matters that should have been resolved but were not. Consequently, they continue to generate conflict. In fact, they played a big part in convincing Southerners that the notion of a united 'New Sudan' was unattainable.

Birth of the Republic of South Sudan

On 9 January 2011, the South Sudanese overwhelmingly voted in a referendum to form a separate state in their region of the old Sudan. Six months later, on 9 July, a huge crowd gathered at Garang's mausoleum to hear the declaration of the birth of the new Republic of South Sudan. This was not the outcome Garang had advocated, but the dream of the majority of the Southern Sudanese, which was pointed out by a journalist as follows:

> The rebel leader had fought for a united 'New Sudan', but his vision died with him in a helicopter crash in 2005. Today few people visit the area. The concept of a 'New Sudan' for the marginalized peripheries has been taken up, instead, by insurgents in the new South of the North.
>
> (*The Niles* 2012: 6)

It is true that Garang's dream of a united 'New Sudan' predicated on democracy, equality, and secularism ended in the South, which went its way. But in the North, now the Sudan, the situation is different. The dream lives on among some of the marginalized peoples who are still struggling under difficult circumstances for a united 'New Sudan' in what remains of the old Sudan in the North.

The people of Darfur took up arms in 2003 before the CPA was signed. It was quite clear that the negotiations that led to the CPA ignored their interest in an equitable sharing of power and resources in the country. Essentially, the CPA dealt with the main concerns of the Southern region and provided the way to a future that Southerners always dreamt of, independence. However, the break-up of the country was totally at odds with the aspirations of the people of Darfur. It would not only neglect the quest of the people of Darfur for justice but also expose them to the full weight of misrule by Khartoum leaders and their aggressive policies.

The people of Southern Kordofan and Blue Nile also found themselves in a more vulnerable position. They would probably have been in a better situation compared to the marginalized people in Darfur and Eastern Sudan if the CPA had been fully carried out. The agreement gave them the right to conduct popular consultations on the type of political system that would suit them even though not independence. Unfortunately, the consultations did not take place. This was another dishonoured agreement. The government in Khartoum ordered forced disarmament, which was ignored by the former SPLA soldiers from that region. Fighting broke out, sending thousands of refugees into South Sudan. The fighters in this region still hope to establish a 'New Sudan' in the new country in which the interests of all the marginalized regions are respected.

Conclusion

The SPLM/A was founded in 1983 to struggle for a united 'New Sudan', but that dream did not materialize. Instead the Southern Sudan broke away to form a new state in July 2011. It seemed the case that the struggle to maintain a united Sudan under a new political dispensation, predicated on democracy, secularism, and equality, had proved too difficult and costly to achieve, as the regime which usurped power in 1989, and has since retained power, was determined to reshape Sudan as an Arab and Islamic country.

Following the secession of Southern Sudan, the dream of a 'New Sudan' ended in the South. However, it did not end in what remained of the old Sudan, which continued to face armed struggle by groups that felt left out. Many of the armed opponents of the present Sudan were part of the SPLA, the present army of the independent state in the South. They are fighting for a better deal from the intransigent elites in Khartoum. For them, the idea of 'New Sudan' remains alive and achievable despite the high price being paid. Already the humanitarian and other consequences of the new war are appalling. Many people have been killed or displaced. Some of the refugees have found their way to South Sudan, whose abandonment of the idea of 'New Sudan' is probably construed by them as a betrayal. Nonetheless, their suffering must be blamed on the dogged pursuit of the exclusionary ideology of the 'Muslim' and 'Arab' elites in Khartoum, against which the SPLM/A took up arms.

References

Akol, L. 2001. *SPLM/SPLA: Inside an African Revolution*. Khartoum: Khartoum University Press.
Alier, A. 1992. *Southern Sudan: Too Many Agreements Dishonoured*, 2nd edn. Reading: Ithaca Press.
Amnesty International. 2000. *Sudan: Oil in Sudan: Deteriorating Human Rights*. London: Amnesty International Publications.
Benjamin, B. M. 2004. 'The Sudan People's Liberation Movement/Army (SPLM/A) and the Peace Process', in K. G. Adar, J. G. Nyuot and E. Maloka (eds), *Sudan Peace Process: Challenges and Future Prospects* (pp. 35–58). Pretoria: Africa Institute of South Africa.
Collins, R. O. (1999) 'Africans, Arabs and Islamists: From Conference Tables to the Battlefields in the Sudan', *African Studies Review*, vol. 42, no. 2, pp. 105–23.

Collins, R. O. 2005. *Civil Wars and Revolutions in the Sudan*. Los Angeles: Tsehai Publishers.

Deng, F. M. 1995. *War of Visions: Conflict of Identities in the Sudan*. Washington, DC: Brookings Institution.

Deng, F. M. 2000. 'Abyei: A Bridge or a Gulf? The Ngok Dinka of Sudan's North–South Border', in J. Spaulding and S. Beswick (eds), *White Nile, Black Blood: War, Leadership, and Ethnicity from Khartoum to Kampala* (pp. 133–66). Lawrenceville, NJ: Red Sea Press.

Deng, L. B. 2012. 'Dr. John Garang: African Icon of Visionary Leader', *New Nation*, no. 012, 23 July – 5 August.

El-Affendi, A. W. 2008. 'Sudanese Futures: One Country or Many', Contemporary Arab Affairs, vol. 1, no. 1, pp. 61–70.

Garang de Mabior, J. 1996. 'The Shaping of a New Sudan', *Mediterranean Quarterly*, vol. 7, no. 4, pp. 6–16.

Healy, S. 2008. *Lost Opportunities in the Horn of Africa: How Conflicts Connect and Peace Agreements Unravel – A Horn of Africa Group Report*. London: Chatham House.

Human Rights Watch. 2003. *Sudan, Oil and Human Rights*. New York: Human Rights Watch.

ICG (International Crisis Group). 2002. 'God, Oil and Country: Changing the Logic of War in Sudan', *Africa Report*, no. 39.

Johnson, D. H. 2003. *The Root Causes of Sudan's Civil Wars*. Oxford, Bloomington and Kampala: James Currey, Indiana University Press and Fountain Publishers.

Jok, J. M. 2008. *Sudan: Race, Religion, and Violence*. Oxford: Oneworld.

Jok, J. M. and Hutchinson, S. E. 1999. 'Sudan's Prolonged Second Civil War and the Militarization of Nuer and Dinka Ethnic Identities', *African Studies Review*, vol. 43, no. 2, pp. 125–45.

'Kiir Defines the Four Obstacles to Peace'. 2006. *Juba Post*, vol. 3, no. 36, 14–21 September.

Madut, A. 2006. *Sudan's Painful Road to Peace: A Full Story of the Founding and Development of the SPLM/SPL*. Rochester, NY: BookSurge.

Malwal, B. 2005. *Sudan's Latest Peace Agreement: An Accord That Is neither Fair nor Comprehensive: A Critique*. Omdurman: Abdel Karim Mirghani Cultural Centre.

Mbugua, K. 2005. 'Armed Militias and Second Tier Conflicts: An Impediment to the Sudan Peace Process', ACCORD Conflict Trends, no. 2, http://www.trainingforpeace. org/pubs/accord/ct2_2005_pgs30_37.pdf (accessed 30 June 2008).

Miller, G. and Meyer, J. 2007. 'U.S. Relies on Sudan despite Condemning It', *Los Angeles Times*, 11 June.

Nyaba, P. A. 2000. *The Politics of Liberation in South Sudan: An Insider's View*. Kampala: Fountain Publishers.

'SPLM Warns against Sabotage of CPA'. 2006. *Khartoum Monitor*, vol. 6, no. 1024, 4 October.

The Niles. 2012. Panorama, 9 July, www.theniles.org.

Part III

Colonial creation unsuccessful cases of self-determination: Somaliland and Zanzibar

7   Guests in our own houses
Somaliland and British colonialism

Ladan Affi

Introduction

Michael Mariano, the well-known Somali politician, on a visit to Britain to argue for the return of lost Somali territories to Ethiopia, described the actions of the British as making the Somalis guests in their own houses. This chapter seeks to examine the history, politics and society of this territory. What were the ways in which British colonialism shaped and transformed Somali culture, institutions and society? How did Somali society respond to colonialism? How did the dismemberment of Somali territories drive Somali nationalism and the call for the unification of all Somali territories? This chapter finds that the different colonial experiences of the Somali territories influenced post-colonial Somalia in ways that it continues to grapple with today.

The majority of Somalis are to be found in the Horn of Africa, living as far north as the Awash Valley and as far south as the Tana River (Bradbury 2008: 9). Somalis are ethnically homogeneous, sharing one culture, language (Somali) and religion (Islam), but the Somalis are members of different clans, with the Isaaq, the Samaroon and the Harti clans as well as smaller communities living together in Somaliland. The population of this region is estimated at 3 million, with about 55 percent of the population practicing pastoralism, making the Somalis a group with the highest rates of pastoralism (Bradbury 2008: 160).

One of the defining characteristics of Somali culture is the Somalis' love of literature, particularly of poetry, and as Richard Burton, the British traveler, noted, "the country teems with poets" (Burton 1854). Oral poetry is part of the daily life of Somalis, and well-known poets like Mohamed Ibrahim Hadrawi transmit their poetry through live performances and audio-material, which still attracts thousands of listeners. Oral poetry also "plays a significant role in traditional courts and in tribal and political affairs" (Jama 1994: 185). Other ways of popular communication include proverbs and riddles, used not only as a primary form of communication but as an educational tool for children.

Social structure

Somali society is primarily defined by a shared culture and religion. Some scholars (Lewis 1994) consider the primary identity of a Somali to be that of the clan, but the basic building block of Somali society, like other societies, is the family, which may include parents, children, grandparents, aunts, uncles, and relatives in need of protection or assistance, who constitute a *qoys*. In the nomadic environment, a few related families, called the *reer*, will set up compounds around water wells, and this constitutes the next building block of Somali society. A group of *reer* living in the same area constitute *qolo* or *laf* or sub-clan. All the sub-clans claiming descent from a single ancestor constitute a *qabiil* or a clan. Somali society is patriarchal, and descent is traced through a male ancestor.

At all levels of society, men hold the decision-making power, with the husband being the head of the family. The elders, who can be any male adults, might form a council to resolve conflicts between clans and decide on issues related to marriage, migration and divorce (Sheikh-Abdi 1993: 18). The elders meet only as needed and for as long as it takes to resolve communal issues. Thus politically Somali society is highly decentralized, and decisions are consensual and egalitarian, although inequalities exist between men and women and between generations (Bradbury 2008: 17).

Somali society practices the division of labor whereby men are responsible for large livestock such as camels, the water wells, conflict resolution, defending the family and their property and taking part in communal meetings. Women are in charge of building and dismantling the Somali *aqal* or house, preparing meals, taking care of smaller animals like goats and raising the children (van Notten 2006: 25).

Colonialism

Britain arrived in the Somali territories as early as 1827, when it signed treaties with some coastal Somali clans, but it was not until the opening of the Suez Canal in 1869 that British and French interest in this region grew, resulting in the establishment of colonies, precipitating the departure of Egyptian and Turkish forces from the Somali territories (Sheikh-Abdi 1977: 657). Britain's interest in the Somali territories was driven by its need for food provisions for its garrison in Aden. The Somalis had a long history of trading with other continents, including the Middle East and Asia, and the British believed that they would be more welcoming in trade than the Yemenis, who were trying to forcibly dislodge the British. The northern Somali coastal areas became a British protectorate in 1885, while other Somali territories were occupied by the French and the Italians (Sheikh-Abdi 1977: 657).

As in other parts of Muslim lands that were occupied by Europeans, colonialism generated an Islamic revival. The resistance to Britain in the Somali territories was led by Sayyid Mohamed Abdulle Hassan, who came into conflict with the British on his arrival from Yemen in Berbera in 1895. When asked by a British colonial official to pay tax on his merchandise, the Sayyid responded with "Who collected tax from you when you arrived? Does this land belong to you? Why are you asking tax from me?" (Ciise 2005: 36). The Sayyid, who belonged to the Salahiyya brotherhood, married and settled in Berbera, while trying to get Somalis to leave the older brotherhoods, including the Qaadiriya and Ahmadiya (Beachey

1990: 37). Several events took place that would initiate the Sayyid's 20-year war against the British and those whom he perceived as their supporters.

The first encounter between the Sayyid and the British was due to the opening in 1891 of a Catholic mission in Berbera, Dhaymoole and Maja-Aseeye. The missionaries opened a school, which began to recruit and convert young Somali children. For several years, the Sayyid unsuccessfully sought to cause an uprising against the British by describing Europeans' efforts to make "our children their children" (Ciise 2005: 44). Thus, throughout his 20-year opposition to white and black colonialism, the Sayyid's primary grievance was the attempted Christianization of Somalis.

The Sayyid began to preach against the colonizers and to warn the Somalis and, owing to his charismatic speaking skills, he was able to convince people to listen to him. The second event, which in a way confirmed the Sayyid's warnings against the British, occurred when a colonial officer who lived next door to a mosque, disturbed by the daily calls to prayer, shot the imam of the mosque. This created an uproar in Berbera and validated the warnings against the colonizers by the Sayyid (Ciise 2005: 37–8). But, finding that many in Berbera were still not very receptive to the austere Salahiyya doctrine, the Sayyid moved inland.

The Sayyid was born in 1856 near Buhoodle, part of British Somaliland, to an Ogadeni father and a Dhulbahante mother, and his parents' clans would form the backbone of his resistance movement throughout his 20-year (1899–1920) war against British, Italian and Ethiopian colonization of Somali territories and people (Bemath 1992: 37).

From 1899 until his death in 1920, the Sayyid sought to expel foreign Christian rule over Somali territories. He left Berbera and sought to find a secure enclave where his religious-military movement, called the *Daraawiish* or Dervishes, could base itself. The Sayyid used Islam and poetry to appeal to Somalis to rise up against colonialism, and forced Britain to try to counter "the formidable barrage of propaganda unleashed against it by the Sayyid." The Sayyid utilized his powerful poems, which spread "like wildfire" and proved to be a formidable weapon against the British (Sheikh-Abdi 1977: 660). The Sayyid made alliances with different clans, appealing to their shared cultural and religious values, and so threatened colonial interests that Britain, Italy and Ethiopia mobilized forces to defeat him in 1900 (Sheikh-Abdi 1977: 660; Geshekter 1985: 17). In a letter addressed to the British, the Sayyid sought to encourage the departure of the colonizers from Somali territories:

> I wish to rule my own country and protect my own religion. We have both suffered considerably in battle with one another. I have with me camels and goats and sheep in plenty. I will not take your country. I have no forts, no houses, no cultivated fields, no silver or gold for you to take. If the country was cultivated or contained houses or property, it would be worth your while to fight. If you want wood and stone you can get them in plenty. There are also many antelopes. The sun is very hot. All you can get from me is war, nothing else. If you wish peace I am also content. But if you wish peace, go away from my country to your own.
>
> (Cited in Geshekter 1985: 17)

Having just defeated the Mahdist uprising in Sudan, the British were not willing to tolerate another revolution within their empire. The British were fearful that the Sayyid provided "an independent entity organized to provide Somalis with an alternative political identification" (Geshekter 1985: 17). Somalis were attracted to the Sayyid's call for jihad, because they did not want Christians on their land, but importantly they responded to him because of the Sayyid's powerful poetry. Much more important was their opposition to the dismemberment of Somali territories, which disrupted their nomadic life and their access to grazing areas and water wells. The Sayyid received a boost when the British made the Anglo-Ethiopian Treaty in 1897 with Menelik of Ethiopia, giving away one-third of British Somaliland, in contravention of treaties that Britain had earlier signed with Somali clans (Mohamed 2002: 1179). The Haud was particularly important to the Somali nomads, who moved there during the rainy season to access the grazing lands and temporary waterholes. The movement of the nomadic lifestyle was intended to protect the land from over-grazing, soil erosion and ecological degradation, and for the Somalis the loss of the Haud was a "mortal blow" because of its vital importance to their daily lives and to the economy of Somaliland (Mohamed 2002: 1181).

Despite the devastating impact of the conflict between the Sayyid and the British on the Somalis, most of whom wanted neither to support the Sayyid nor to side with the British, Britain sought to mobilize Somali pastoralists against the Sayyid, particularly among the Dhulbahante and the Isaaq, by arming them and using them as a buffer (Slight 2010: 30). At the same time, the Sayyid decided that persuasion was not sufficient to dislodge the colonizers and began to target any clans whom he suspected of allying with them (Mohamed 1999: 510). The conflict between the Sayyid and the British eventually spread to the Somalis, igniting "a massive civil war of cruel inter-clan reprisals among northern clans" (Geshekter 1985: 17). After years of failing to oust the Sayyid, the British launched an unprecedented assault operation and, for the first time in the history of British imperialism, attacked using "airplanes to coordinate a combined aerial, naval, and ground attack in one of the earliest applications of the doctrine of air power" (Geshekter 1985: 17).

The Sayyid, regarded as the first Somali nationalist leader, died in 1920 from natural causes, resulting in the end of the Dervish movement but not the Somali opposition to colonialism. That a Somali without external assistance took on the British, the Italians and the Ethiopians and resisted for two decades continued to live in the memory of the Somalis. The Sayyid's resistance to European and African colonialism continued and, within a decade, urban-based political associations appeared, although they did not take up arms. The British colonizers were more receptive to their appeals on how to govern the protectorate. Chief among them was Haji Farah Omar's Somali-Islamic Association (Sheikh-Abdi 1977: 659).

Colonial legacy

The consequences of the 20-year conflict between the Sayyid and the colonizers was devastating to the Somalis and their territories. First, the division of Somali territories as well as the giving away of one-third of British Somaliland deeply affected the livelihood of Somalis by disrupting their migratory movement, which was based on an "elaborate and rational system of herding" intended to manage and protect their use of the land (Mohamed 2004: 535). Although the best use of Somali territory was for livestock production, the reduced amount of land available for herding pushed some Somalis into cultivation, which led to soil erosion, as land was overused and trees cut. The British were also interested in making the Somalis into a settled and sedentary population, because that would make them easier to control and govern.

The disruption of the migratory patterns of the Somalis undermined long-established coping mechanisms against droughts which then developed into famines (Mohamed 2004: 548). From 1920 until independence, Somaliland experienced 11 droughts, with some lasting for multiple years. For example, in the 1943 drought about 60 percent of sheep, goats and cattle and 10 percent of camels died (Mohamed 2004: 549). During each drought which became a famine, the Somalis were forced to seek assistance from the British, who opened feeding centers. Thus, a people who had devised the best way to live in their environment in a manner that preserved it and supported their needs found themselves dependent on foreign assistance, with this reliance only increasing over time.

Another fallout of British colonialism was the frequent epidemics that affected the people of the region. Previous to their arrival, various European travelers noted no epidemics among the Somalis. In fact, Richard Burton, who was no friend to the Somalis, since they had tried to kill him, commented that the Somali people suffered from no serious diseases and that even their old people "were hale and strong, preserving their powers . . . in spite of eighty or ninety years" (quoted in Mohamed 1999: 509). From the 1890s to the 1930s, British Somaliland was affected by epidemics including smallpox, influenza, cholera, relapsing fever, tuberculosis and venereal diseases. Some of these diseases, such as cholera and relapsing fevers, were new to Somalis; for example, the 1892 cholera epidemic and the 1899 smallpox epidemic were caused by Ethiopian expeditionary forces raiding Somali pastoralists and transmitting the disease to the Somalis, resulting in the death of hundreds of Somalis. Other epidemics such as malaria and venereal disease were due to the arrival of imperial forces brought by the British from India, Arabia and Central Africa (Mohamed 1999: 509).

Another consequence of the Sayyid and his Dervish movement was that in effect the British "civilizing mission" was defeated, as the British forbade Christian missionary activity. Henceforth, the British would rule Somaliland with a light touch and through indirect rule. In fact, as I. M. Lewis notes, "the expatriate administration subsequently received stern admonitions from London that nothing was ever to be done again that could possibly provoke the Somalis." The fear of another "Mad Mullah" preoccupied the British; they were very responsive in not upsetting the Somalis, and thus no taxes were imposed on the Somalis (Lewis 1977: 229).

Post-Sayyid Somaliland

Despite this hands-off rule in the form of a very small colonial administration, the British remained apprehensive about another uprising; at least a third of the budget went towards military expenditures in Somaliland, and Britain barely expended any effort to develop the region (Bradbury 2008: 30). The British used traditional leaders to help them govern, paying the salaries of some and exiling those who resisted their authority. It is for this reason that the administration in Somaliland was one of the smallest in the British empire, with a staff numbering around 50 officers and civil servants. The Somalis labeled it "a deaf government," whose only policy was "to have no ideas and spend no money" (Geshekter 1985: 19). Throughout British control of Somaliland, the British practiced retrench-ment and stern frugality, and even into the 1950s Somalis complained to the British that "for seventy-five years you have been in this land and there is not a chimney or a rail to show for it . . . the British really did nothing for our country . . . except to give portions of it away" (Geshekter 1977: 19).

Aside from clearing a few roads, establishing some agricultural projects and sending a few students, financially supported by their families, to Sudan, Somali-land's slow pace of development was interrupted by World War II, when Soma-liland was briefly occupied by Italy in 1941. Despite this indifference to the development of Somaliland, a small urbanized class of bureaucrats, civil servants and traders appeared. As in other parts of the world, these elites were swept up in the anti-colonial sentiments growing in Africa, and they were the main support-ers of the Somali nationalist parties that emerged throughout the Somali-inhab-ited lands (Bradbury 2008: 30–31).

Somali nationalism and the call for Greater Somalia

After the end of World War II, the United Nations placed southern Somalia under an Italian trusteeship, which was scheduled to become independent in 1960. Thus Italy began a process of Somalization of state institutions. Meanwhile, Somaliland remained a British protectorate, and even as late as 1954 Britain believed that Somaliland "must remain for the foreseeable future under British rule." It was only in 1958 that Britain decided to give Somaliland independence (Mohamed 2002: 1177). However, the Somaliland that would become independ-ent was much smaller than the territory seized by Britain 75 years earlier. In a series of treaties beginning in 1897, the British gave in to Ethiopian demands for the Haud, Ogaden and the Reserved Area, culminating in the 1954 Anglo-Ethiopian Agreement, which recognized Ethiopian control over these lands. The Somalis were unaware of these agreements between Britain and Ethiopia, and demonstrations took place all over the country once they became public (Bulhan 2008). The result of this betrayal resulted in the nationalist parties receiving a boost in membership when many Somalis joined, seeing independence as the only way to regain Somali territories from Ethiopian control (Mohamed 2002: 1178).

The Somalis' determination to reunite Somali-inhabited lands was partially due to their shared culture and religion, but it was driven by economic and ecological necessity as the Somalis sought to maintain their livelihood. Their experience with the Ethiopians, which fluctuated from sheer intimidation, raids, killings and looting to indifference, made them violently resist being placed under the Ethiopians. "For Somalis dealing with Ethiopians, there was only a sense of cultural disparagement, deep anger over patronizing attitudes, and contempt for their would-be conquerors. Scarcely integrated into the Ethiopian empire-state, never considered equals by their Amhara colonizers, Somalis developed no loyalty whatsoever towards Ethiopia" (Geshekter 1977: 12). That the Ethiopians were Christians deepened Somalis' aversion to Ethiopian rule.

Aside from the general desire to be independent and to govern their own future, the push for Somali independence was primarily driven by political and economic considerations. Despite the presence of Somali political parties in Somaliland, the push for independence was greater in southern Somalia, which faced political and economic oppression under the Italian trusteeship. The Somali Youth League (SYL), a Mogadishu-based political party, had established branches in Somaliland. There was also the Somali National League (SNL), created in 1944, which was a major political party headed by Mohamed Haji Ibrahim Egal, who would go on to become the prime minister of the Somali Republic from 1967 to 1969 and the second president of Somaliland from 1993 to 2002. Both the SYL and the SNL suffered from little grassroots support. This changed once the handover of the Haud and Reserved Area became public knowledge to the Somalis (Ghalib 1995: 25). In response to the giving away of Somali territories in 1954–55, political parties emerged – the National United Front for Retaining the Reserved Area and the Haud (NUFRRH) and the United Somali Party (USP). Additionally, the SYL and the SNL both received a boost in support and increased membership. The NUFRRH was headed by Michael Mariano. As its name indicates, the NUFRRH's primary goal was the recovery of lost Somali territories. Since this was an issue that was of concern to all Somalis, the NUFRRH received a great deal of popular support (Mohamed 2002: 1184). All these political parties were founded by and led by educated, urban Somalis (Bradbury 2008: 31).

Somalis came together and donated to send a Somaliland delegation to argue for the retrieval of the lost Somali territories. Led by Mariano, the delegation left first for Mogadishu to secure support from other Somali parties and then on to London and New York. In London, the delegation met with the secretary of state for the colonies to unsuccessfully attempt to persuade the British government to honor its 1885 Anglo-Somali treaties, which preceded the agreements made with Ethiopia. Mariano reminded the British government that that agreement stated that the British undertook "never to cede, sell, mortgage or otherwise give for occupation, save to the British Government, any portion of the territory inhabited by them or being under their control" (Mohamed 2002: 1185).

Having been unsuccessful in their attempts to have the British rescind their agreement with the Ethiopians, the Somali delegation turned their attention to the United Nations General Assembly and to have their case heard and referred to the International Court, but they were unsuccessful in this also, as no country would sponsor their case (Mohamed 2002: 1188).

After 76 years of British rule, Somaliland became an independent nation on 26 June 1960 and joined with Italian Somaliland on 1 July 1960.

Concluding remarks: the impact of colonialism

The impact of colonialism disrupted all aspects of Somali society. For example, the British tendency to pay the salaries of elders for their loyalty and replace or exile those who opposed them undermined their independence and legitimacy. Before colonialism, the process of leadership selection and qualification was established, but the arrival of colonizers who disregarded these processes created "competition among the lineages, thereby damaging the integrity of the clan and with it the office of the clan leaders" (Issa-Salwe 1996: 5). The colonizers obliterated the personal nature of politics, where warring clans would sit together until a solution could be reached, replacing it with politics that was "faceless, anonymous and remote" (Laitin and Samatar 1987: 27).

In addition, the introduction of state institutions which were centralized and violent and disregarded the needs of the people contradicted the Somali way of governing, which was open, egalitarian and consensual. The creation of a small, urban elite and an administration with coercive institutions – the military and security services – damaged Somali politics in a way from which it has yet to fully recover. For the colonizers, the urban elites assisted them in evading and undermining shared traditional Somali cultural norms and law through the introduction of Western culture and ways of governing, while the coercive institutions taught Somalis that only those who control the institutions can benefit from them (Bryden 1998: 12). That the Somali elite adopted this model partially explains the problems encountered by Somalis after independence. Economically, the Somali economy, which was based on subsistence, was disrupted when first it was forcibly integrated into the world economy and secondly Somalis lost access to grazing lands (Issa-Salwe 1996: 5).

The Somali campaign for independence was driven by several factors. First, Somalis experienced violence and brutality under multiple colonizers, and the division of Somali-inhabited lands also disrupted the daily lives of pastoralists. This life demanded the integrity of the Somali-inhabited lands to be maintained, and it was the division of Somali-inhabited lands that drove unification and the call for Greater Somalia. Some scholars have explained the collapse of the Somali state as originating from this push for the unification of Somali territories. The collapse of the Somali state is attributed to colonial policies, which dismembered previously cohesive territories, communities and livelihoods. The different colonial experiences of the two territories that would form the Somali Republic also contributed to the collapse of the state. As can be seen now, one of the reasons that Somaliland puts forward today for its claim to separate from the rest of Somalia is that it was an independent country first, with a different political and economic system (Mohamud and Kusow 2006: 15).

References

Beachey, Ray. 1990. *The Warrior Mullah: The Horn Aflame 1892–1920*. London: Bellew Publishing.

Bemath, Abdul S. 1992. "The Sayyid and Saalihiya Tariga: Reformist, Anticolonial Hero in Somalia," in Said S. Samatar (ed.), *In the Shadow of Conquest: Islam in Colonial Northeast Africa*. Trenton, NJ: Red Sea Press.

Bradbury, Mark. 2008. *Becoming Somaliland*. Bloomington: Indiana University Press.

Bryden, Matt. 1998. *Somalia between Peace and War: Somali Women on the Eve of the 21st Century*. Nairobi: UNIFEM.

Bulhan, Hussein Abdillahi. 2008. *Politics of Cain: One Hundred Years of Crises in Somali Politics and Society*. Bethesda, MD: Tayosan International Publishing.

Burton, Richard. 1854. *First Footsteps in East Africa: An Exploration of Harar*. London: Longman, Brown, Green and Longmans.

Ciise, Aw Jaamac Cumar. 2005. *Taariikhdii Daraawishta iyo Sayid Maxamed Cabdulle Xasan 1895–1920*. Djibouti: CERD.

Geshekter, Charles. 1985. "Anti-Colonialism and Class Formation: The Eastern Horn of Africa before 1950," *International Journal of African Historical Studies*, vol. 18, no. 1, pp. 1–32.

Ghalib, Jama Mohamed. 1995. *The Cost of Dictatorship: The Somali Experience*. New York: Lilian Barber Press.

Issa-Salwe, Abdisalam. 1996. *The Collapse of the Somali State: The Impact of the Colonial Legacy*. London: Haan Publishing.

Jama, Zainab Mohamed. 1994. "Silent Voices: The Role of Somali Women's Poetry in Social and Political Life," *Oral Traditions*, vol. 9, no. 1, pp. 185–202.

Laitin, David and Samatar, Said S. 1987. *Somalia: A Nation in Search of a State*. Boulder, CO: Westview Press.

Lewis, I. M. 1977. "Confessions of a 'Government' Anthropologist," *Anthropological Forum*, vol. IV, no. 2, pp. 226–38.

Lewis, I. M. 1994. *Blood and Bone: The Call of Kinship in Somali Society*. Lawrenceville, NJ: Red Sea Press.

Mohamed, Jama. 1999. "Epidemics and Public Health in Early Colonial Somaliland," *Social Science and Medicine*, vol. 48, no. 4, pp. 507–21.

Mohamed, Jama. 2002. "Imperial Policies and Nationalism in the Decolonization of Somaliland 1954–1960," *English Historical Review*, vol. 117, no. 474, pp. 1177–1203.

Mohamed, Jama. 2004. "The Political Ecology of Colonial Somaliland," *Africa*, vol. 74, no. 4, pp. 534–66.

Mohamud, Abdinur S. and Kusow, Abdi M. 2006. "Why Somalia Continues to Remain a Failed State," *African Renaissance*, vol. 3, no. 5, pp. 13–23.

Notten, Michael van. 2006. *The Law of the Somalis: A Stable Foundation for Economic Development in the Horn of Africa*. Trenton, NJ: Red Sea Press.

Sheikh-Abdi, Abdi. 1977. "Somali Nationalism: Its Origins and Future," *Journal of Modern African Studies*, vol. 15, no. 4, pp. 657–65.

Sheikh-Abdi, Abdi. 1993. *Divine Madness: Mohammed Abdulle Hassan of Somalia (1856–1920)*. London: Zed Books.

Slight, John P. 2010. "British and Somali Views of Muhammad Abdullah Hassan's Jihad (1899–1920)," *Bildhaan: An International Journal of Somali Studies*, vol. 10, pp. 16–35.

8 Less and more than the sum of its parts

The failed merger of Somaliland and Somalia and the tragic quest for 'Greater Somalia'

Abdirahman Yusuf Duale (Bobe)

Introduction

The merger of the two Somali independent territories came as a result of a widely accepted vision of the amalgamation of all the Somali territories, which consisted of British Somaliland, Italian Somalia, the Somali French Coast (modern-day Djibouti[1]), the Ethiopian Somali territory and the Northern Frontier District of Kenya. This vision most vividly manifested itself in the work of the Somali composers and playwrights of that era, who depicted the union of the two regions as a she-camel (named *Mandeeq*) who delivered the two calves of modern-day Somaliland and southern Somalia. An endless number of songs and poems were composed in honour of *Mandeeq*, the entirety of which have remained an indelible fixture in the minds of the Somali people to this day.

This chapter will be composed of three main parts, each representing a major epoch in Somaliland's failed experiment as part of the Somali Republic. At each stage, an argument will be presented that will call into question the widespread legitimacy or deep-rootedness of the 1960 union between present-day Somaliland and Somalia that most policy makers involved in the current state-building project in the Horn of Africa seem to believe is of paramount truth.

The section on the period between 1960 and 1969 will challenge the notion that the merger was ever the culmination of a complete ideological process or the achievement of a natural matching of ethnic identity and territorial governance that provides the basis for state creation in the modern state system. The Act of Union was always part of a larger quest to unite all the Somali peoples, of which those making up the two merging regions were a large but not complete part. Without the inclusion of the Somalis of the Ogaden region of Ethiopia, the north of Kenya and Djibouti into the fold of a single state, the entire concept of a Somali state collapses, and with it the entire idea that there is anything sacred and necessarily worth saving in the Somali state as it existed from 1960 to 1991.

The section on the period between 1969 and 1981, the early years of military dictatorship, will demonstrate the fact that the concept of unity never manifested itself on the ground in the form of unified governance and administration. Despite some early evidence of commitment to the development of the Somali state as a whole, the competing forces of centralisation and region-based clan affiliations meant that the south and the north were never treated as equal partners.

In the last ten years of the Somali Republic, the incompatibility of the two political communities reached its apex once the Barre regime's project of 'Greater Somalia' failed in a highly devastating manner (the 1977–78 Ogaden war) and degenerated into a system of open patronage and clan favouritism. The vast majority of the north was left out of this arrangement, and it was as a result of this shared experience of marginalisation and abuse that a new political community was founded with the goal of resisting the rule of Siad Barre. This movement, the Somali National Movement (SNM), in turn provoked a counter-insurgency of such brutality and devastation that its effect on the attitudes of Somalilanders to their southern brothers continues to reverberate to this day. This period went to show both that the contours of the British colonial boundaries provide a much more legitimate and pragmatic basis for establishing a political community, and that the shared Somali ethnic identity of the north and the south was no guarantee of nationhood or against repressive acts of genocidal proportions.

1960–69

The Act of Union reached between the former British Somaliland protectorate and the Italian Somalia on 1 July 1960 has become the point of departure from which any idea of Somalia is to be conceived of by many within the international community and within Somalia itself. What was then merely a contingent and pragmatic agreement based upon a larger goal has morphed in the eyes of many into a kind of natural joining of two halves of the same nation that had been temporarily separated by foreign rule. A more detailed historical account, which I intend to provide below, will show just how tenuous this agreement was, and how its 30-year preservation was less a result of a national or politically shared project by all, but instead a result of internal and external political manipulation in which the early scepticism, dissent and resistance to such a project were erased from the narrative of state building.

In order to get to the heart of the matter, it is important to understand the reasons that formed the basis of Somaliland and Italian Somalia's decision to join together, as it was upon this contingent and hastily arrived-at moment that current arguments for the 'territorial integrity' of this unified region are today based. It is also necessary to understand how the nation-building experiment shifted from intellectual genesis to administrative practice, as it was within this transition that the first complications regarding the union began to take hold.

Somaliland–Somalia unity as a means, not an end

As explained above, the merger of Somaliland and the Italian Trusteeship of Somalia was predicated on the promise not of a bilateral treaty, but rather of a multilateral one in which the three remaining Somali territories would also ultimately be incorporated (Geshekter 1997: 71–3). The five-point star that has adorned Somalia's flag from independence up until this day is the symbolic manifestation of the 'Greater Somalia' idea. As well documented by Touval (1963), the period immediately following decolonisation of the British and Italian Somali territories was one in which elites from both sides worked furiously to incorporate the other three territories into the Somali state – above and beyond many of the other programmatic considerations of governance.[2] In sum, the decision to join together Somaliland and Italian Somalia into the Somali Republic was never a goal in its own right, but a strategic decision meant to pave the way for the inclusion of the other three Somali territories in the fold.

So when the British decided in 1963 to award the mainly Somali-inhabited Northern Frontier District (NFD) to the newly independent Kenya – thus disregarding their pledge to respect the findings of an independent commission that an overwhelming majority of the people in the NFD sought unity with Somalia – the foundation of 'Greater Somalia' on which the initial act of unity was built was dealt a major blow. With the legitimacy of the Somaliland–Italian Somalia union hinging on the creation of a 'Greater Somalia', this decision by the colonial powers had an enduring impact on the relations between the only two members of the 'Greater Somalia' project at the time.

Although full recognition of the impossibility of 'Somali unity' would not be evident just yet, early signs began to surface during this period. As early as August 1960, when the prime minister of Somalia, Dr Abdirashid Ali Sharmarke, embarked on his first tour of the northern regions of what was then the Somali Republic, deep scepticism over the form that the integration process was taking was palpable. The prime minister was ceremoniously received by a cheering crowd in the small village of Kalabayd in the Gebilay district, but the mood was in no way one of unconditional admiration for the newly formed government. Among the cheering crowd was the famous nationalist poet Abdillahi Suldan 'Timacadde', who had no hesitation in highlighting the ways in which the original objectives of the merger decision were already in danger of being betrayed. The poem which he recited in front of the prime minister's delegation, 'Socdaal' [The travel], captures the moods of both possibility and concern which were widely felt at the time:

Maalintii dabku qiiqayeen,	The day the spark of liberation
Isticmaarki is-diidnay,	Against the oppressors was ignited,
Nimankii danta sheegtayee,	We are those who expressed their wish,
Dariiqooda ka leexanee,	We are those who have not lost their way,
Dacwaddooda dhammaystayee,	We are those who clearly presented their case,

Dalkan caawa an joogno,	We are those who liberated this country
Dulligii isticmaarkiyo,	From the yoke of colonialism and its misery,
Dahaadhkiiba ka siibayee,	We are the ones who forced Carl to quit
Karal daaqad ka saarayee,	We are not eleventh hour arrivals,
Duddaanu ahayne	Our interest is not to remain divided,
Dawlad soo gashay mayhine,	We discard the statements we have been
Danteennaa laba diiddaye,	hearing,
Dabuub aanu maqlaynay,	That our Parliamentarians will be seated in
Dareen baan ka qabnaayoo,	Mogadishu,
Dugsigii Barlamaankiyo,	That the favoring of the sea port in Mogadishu
Dekeddii Xamar baa leh,	Will mean Berbera being swallowed up by
Berbera daadku ha qaado,	the sea waters,
Doonniyi yaanay ku leexan,	With no dhow to anchor at its port,
Duqeydii Barlamaankaay,	Oh! Parliamentarians,
Labadaa kala daaya oo,	Divided we will never succeed,
Yaan loo daymo la'aan.	And this has to be observed with diligence.

(Duale 2012: 46–8)

From the outset, elites from the former Italian colony held the vast major-ity of top governmental positions, including the presidency, prime ministership, commanders of the armed forces and police, and ministers of the most politi-cally significant sectors of government, including foreign affairs, the interior and finance among others. For its part, the former British Somaliland was given the positions of the speaker of the House of Parliament and the minister of defence, with the latter, Mohamed Haji Ibrahim Egal, later also serving two years as prime minister at the end of the period of civilian rule. This marked an imbalance in representation that characterised the early days of the power-sharing formula, unreflective of either the demographics or the political importance of the two regions, and led to northern discontent and disappointment that proved to be well founded in terms of the uneven and unjust effects, especially in terms of wealth distribution according to region (Farah 1999: 239). Furthermore, as John Drysdale (1994: 132) notes, the plot to skew representation in favour of the south was hidden from British Somaliland leaders at the moment of merger, meaning that misinformation and deception lay at the heart of its decision to join with Italian Somaliland.

Although Somalia is currently claiming to be the heart of Greater Somali nationalism, the reverse was the case at the time of the merger. During the fate-ful year of 1960, Somaliland was the hub and the heart of the Somali nationalist movement. The south, and especially its capital Mogadishu, had plunged into complete clan-based competition and fragmentation following the introduction of the Trusted Italian Administration of Somalia (AFIS) in 1950, a development that distracted from the larger task of nation building.

As General Liqliqato (2000: 131) noted at the time in his book *Taariikhda Soomaalida* [The history of the Somalis]:

> The Somali Youth League (SYL) has diverted from its mission of independence and the unification of the Somali territories that it has been pursuing for the last fifteen years. Among the ranks of the SYL a clan controversy that has divided its membership has started. The unity in the search for independence has been undermined and the people have lost confidence in the leadership of the SYL.

The different colonial legacies experienced by north and south were always going to be an obstacle to the full integration of the two entities, with different administrative lingua francas, legal frameworks, tax regimes, levels of development and degrees of external intervention during the period of empire (Bradbury 2008: 32). But what took the Somalilanders by surprise was the extent to which politicians in the south were able to exploit these differences to their own advantage. Thus the union was realised with Somalia taking the lion's share of principal positions within government, leading to accusations by the major northern poets and intellectuals of the era that those in power were merely cheap impersonators of their former colonial masters (Duale 2005: 139). A 2006 International Crisis Group report captures the situation aptly when it writes: 'By embracing the merger unconditionally, Somaliland entered the union at a distinct disadvantage: Somalia retained the capital city and obtained two-thirds of the seats in parliament, while Southern leaders (including the president and prime minister) dominated the first unitary cabinet.'

It did not take long before the northern citizens of the Somali Republic became aware that the terms under which they had entered the union had been betrayed by politicians with agendas different from their own. Less than a year after the initial Act came into effect, a referendum was held on a unitary constitution in which Somaliland voters, irrespective of their location within the former British colony, chose overwhelmingly to reject its authority.[3] Six months later, a coterie of officers from the north staged a popular but ultimately unsuccessful coup in Hargeisa with the aim of reclaiming Somaliland's independence, and in October 1962 northern ministers and deputies resigned from their respective posts out of frustration that their inclusion in the country's political affairs was premised on a position of inferiority and marginalisation (Drysdale 1994: 133–4). It was therefore not only after 30 years of abuse and eventual state collapse that the people of Somaliland sought to piece together some semblance of an organised and functioning state; from the beginning, it became clear that the union had been based on false suppositions.

The incongruity of the merger is also evidenced by the fact that no harmonisation of the Act of Union was ever agreed upon or put into effect by the separate governments during the integration process. While both sides drafted and approved their own legal documents in support of the merger (the Union of Somaliland and Somalia Law in the north and the Somalia Act of Union in the south), the

> legal validity of the legislative instruments establishing the Union were questionable because:

(a) The Union of Somaliland and Somalia Law, and the Somalia Act of Union were both drafted in the form of bilateral agreements, but neither of them was signed by the representatives of the two territories.
(b) The Union of Somaliland and Somalia Law purported to derogate in some respects from the Constitution of the Somali Republic.
(c) The Somalia Act of Union was approved 'in principle' but never enacted into law.
(d) The decree-law of July 1, 1960, did not come into effect since it was not converted into law in accordance with Article 68 of the Constitution.

Cotran 1968: 1010–11

And, although another Act of Union was later put into effect that was supposed to supersede previous laws and give final (retroactive) authority to the union, this was only ratified through the constitutional process, which was overwhelmingly rejected by the north, and even this Act was not effective as a legally binding agreement in many later Somali Supreme Court cases (Carroll and Rajagopal 1993: 663–4).

These legal complications, combined with growing frustration over the unequal distribution of power first voiced by those like Timacadde and later manifested among the majority of northerners, caused a crisis of legitimacy for the nascent Somali Republic that quickly led to difficulties at home. The first major act of resistance to the state's existence came little more than a year after the merger, when senior military officers from the north staged an unsuccessful coup meant to nullify the union.[4] Over the course of the short nine-year period of parliamentary civilian rule (1960–69), the country's experiment with a centralised form of externally crafted Western democracy proved poorly adapted to the clan-based nature of Somali politics and was soon corrupted. With popular discontent growing all over the country, the president of the country was shot on 15 October 1969 by one of his bodyguards in Laas-Caanood. On 21 October 1969 General Maxamed Siad Barre, the commander-in-chief of the army, seized power through a bloodless coup.

Before turning to the period of escalated marginalisation and abuse experienced by those living in the north of the Somali Republic, as well as the bloody self-destruction of the concept of 'Greater Somalia', which characterised the years of military dictatorship, it is important to note the significance of these early years of the Somali Republic.

The union was based on shaky ground and of questionable legitimacy from the beginning, and its basis for existence rested on foundations that, as history would retroactively make clear, were necessarily unsustainable. The union faced serious contestation at every phase of its enacting, and, although the momentum for the union originated from former British Somaliland, the political terms by which the union would occur derived from the former Italian colony. With Somaliland never sufficiently incorporated into the power structure of the newly created state, its people refused to give the state their blessing whenever given the chance to voice their opinion, be it the constitutional referendum or the unsuccessful coup of officers. The lack of overwhelming support for the union forced its legality to be pieced together from a patchwork of different court rulings and political pacts. Therefore, although the union of both territories may have eventually become accepted as fact, the political struggle over the creation of a workable state was still being fought at the end of the 1960s, and in fact would never be resolved.

This idea is well summarised by the distinguished academic Ali Mazrui (1997: 6), who comments:

> When independence came, it took the form of unifying Italian Somaliland and British Somaliland. Somali nationalism made the two halves want to unite, but was there enough national identity to keep them united? Nationalism is a form of infatuation which may be enough to make two halves propose marriage, even want marriage, even go into the ceremony of marriage. But nationalism on its own is not enough to keep the two halves married.

1969–81

Siad Barre and his Supreme Revolutionary Council received a warm welcome by the Somali people at large on their ascension to the leadership positions of the country, especially by those frustrated by the parochial and predatory nature of the civilian government. Barre's inaugural few years of rule produced a few notable successes, including the establishment of the written Somali language and concerted attempts to curtail poverty, disease, illiteracy, clanism and other policies that matched the aspirations of the Somali people (Lewis 2008: 38–42).

But this initial popularity was not long-lived, thanks to the championing of both an internal and an external foreign policy that revolved around ideologies that were out of step with the realities on the ground and therefore were destined to fail. In the domestic sphere, Siad Barre's dictatorial military regime introduced 'Scientific Socialism' as the banner for its crash modernisation programme as a means for winning the backing of the Soviet Union and also to justify the building up of a formidable army. Unfortunately, the economic programme's focus on rapid mechanisation, nationalisation of key industries, large-scale agriculture and a move away from 'backward' pastoralism could not be implemented successfully given the structure of the Somali socio-economy. Instead, its failure led to heavy dependence on foreign aid, and the use of development projects as forms of clan-based patronage (in fact, close relatives of the regime's inner circle were appointed as the managers or directors of almost every major institution), as well as the establishment of informal and parallel economies that undermined the legitimacy of the Somali state (Ahmed and Green 1999: 116–18). The north bore the brunt of the negative effects of these policies, as most of the Barre regime's aid and trade policies were concentrated in the south, something evidenced by the fact that the 1974–75 drought and famine that plagued the country hit the northerners much harder (Lewis 2007: 177–8).

This centralised form of rule brought with it the establishment of many other oppressive institutions, including the National Security Service (NSS) and the Security Court. As a means for solidifying total control over the entire country, the regime did not spare any aspect of Somali private or public identity, be it culture, family life, traditional authority, social organisations or religious beliefs – these were all denounced as anachronistic or subversive and targeted for reform. At first subtle and behind the scenes, but later the sole basis for the regime's legitimacy, were the pervasive exercises of corruption and clan politics as a means for enhancing the power of the central government in the face of these economic failures and political crimes (Lewis 2007: 154–72).

Despite all the shortcomings of the Barre regime's internal policy, an even bigger threat to the existing Somali state was found in the government's attempt to actualise the idea of 'Greater Somalia' through the external projection of military might. Despite Djibouti's declaration in 1977 of its status as an independent nation and the blow it caused to the idea that the French-ruled Somalis would ever join the Somali state, the Barre regime decided that same year to launch an offensive into Ethiopia in order to absorb the Ethiopian Somalis of the Ogaden region. Trying to capitalise on regime change in its neighbour, the Barre regime found its hubris no match for the changing geopolitical situation in which the Soviet Union's shifting alliances meant that it and its allies' armies decided to come to the aid of the Ethiopian forces, leading to the resounding defeat of a Somali military that had up until that point been considered one of the strongest in Africa.

The undertaking of the Somali–Ethiopian war of 1977–78 marked a watershed moment for the regime, both politically and ideologically. With regard to the former, the massive human influx of refugees into the country, which by 1981 constituted 40 per cent of the national population (a disproportionate number of whom were resettled in the north), represented a huge burden for the regime in terms of service provision and population control. Furthermore, owing to clan affiliations between the Ogadeni refugees and the Barre regime, as well as generous international aid packages bestowed upon these forced migrants, the new citizens of Somalia were seen by the northern clans, whose territory now had to be shared with these alien communities, as being given preferential treatment, thereby denigrating the latter's status and creating unresolved conflict and tension (Ahmed 1999: 241–2).

More importantly, this defeat all but signalled the death of the idea of 'Greater Somalia' that had laid the foundation for the 1960 Act of Union in the first place. Once this dream died, with it went the narrative that held together the original union, thus retroactively nullifying the entire political edifice on which subsequent attempts to justify the rule of Mogadishu over the northern Somali peoples were based. Furthermore, after years of repressive tendencies and marginalisation of the north, combined with the unequal burden of the costs of war placed on the north, the idea of 'Greater Somalia' as it had been appropriated by the Barre regime was exposed as more of a tool of governmentality and legitimisation than a heartfelt project as had been championed by the early unionists of the immediate post-independence period.

1981–91

This takes us to the final decade of the 30-year experiment of the Somali Republic (Somaliland and Somalia). It was during this period that any pretence of a state was abandoned, replaced by clan-based patronage networks and military oppression – funded almost entirely by international aid – that were used by the regime as a means for state survival. It was in these final years of Barre's rule that the union's nature was fully exposed as something that survived only on paper and in the minds of international supporters of the regime. The atrocities committed by Barre's government against the people of the north gave evidence of the fact that the people of Somaliland were seen not as equal partners in a national project but instead as obstacles to the continued predatory rule of a few.

For the ten years between 1981 and 1991, the northern regions of Somalia (Somaliland) became a military camp run by despotic and ruthless generals like the infamous Morgan and Ganni.[5] People lived under a constant and merciless order of curfews, systematic searches and other violations of their basic human rights. Rampage, robbery, theft and rape were state-sanctioned practices. The oppressive army, reinforced by militias from refugee camps recruited and armed by the government, were given licence to do as they pleased with the civilian population in the northern regions, a policy which led to abuse and rapaciousness conducted in an environment of impunity. Cities were levelled to the ground, with Hargeisa coming out of the civil war with almost 100 per cent of its infrastructure destroyed. Nearly half a million Somalilanders fled the country and sought refuge in Ethiopia. Ironically, the ultimate aim of the regime's aggressive policy towards the north was to completely cut off the land and its people from the other regions of the country, something that imposed a kind of de facto disunion orchestrated by Mogadishu itself. None of these atrocities were ever mentioned at the time of their occurrence, and Somalia was seen as peaceful by both the regime and the majority of the Somali people. Instead the attention of the population was being diverted to regional football tournaments and other government-sponsored circus-like spectacles.[6]

Although the Somaliland region in many ways bore the brunt of the military onslaught, many other clans making up the population of current-day Somalia had also suffered greatly at the hands of the Barre regime, and opposition movements summarily sprang up throughout the country in response. To this effect, the Somali National Movement (SNM) was founded in London on 6 April 1981 after an endless chain of consultations among the northern people of Somalia, Saudi Arabia and Britain.

After its inception, the SNM not only launched a protracted resistance movement against the regime that lasted a decade, but also sought the establishment of a democratic regime. The SNM leadership's practice of collective decision making and its dependence on popular participation in mobilising the war effort (as it garnered little support from outside backers) put in place certain institutional foundations and procedures of governance that would create a legacy for post-civil war politics in Somaliland.[7] Shedding light on the formidable role the

SNM's operation had on the later formation of the Somaliland state, Ibraahim Meygaag Samatar (1997: 30), a leading figure in the SNM hierarchy, had this to say in his essay entitled 'Light at the End of the Tunnel': 'If self-reliance, internal democracy and resolution of problems through dialogue and compromise are the characteristics that today differentiate Somaliland from Somalia, it is because these qualities were learned and practiced by the SNM in the heat of the struggle for liberation.'

Thus, the effectiveness of the SNM's guerrilla war came from its ability to combine military discipline with a political project that not only spoke to the grievances of the people it was claiming to represent, but also directly acted to put in place a system of governance both within the organisation and between the organisation and the people that reflected an alternative and more just form of rule.

As the SNM's rebellion escalated into an all-out liberation war at the end of the 1980s and nascent anti-regime armed movements began mushrooming all over Somalia, the SNM began seriously preparing for life after the regime. It was obvious to the SNM that a top priority for ensuring a stable post-Barre society would be to undertake reconciliation and peace building between clans that had taken opposite sides during the decade-long civil war, so as to prevent a different kind of civil war over the vacated helm of the government. Drawing from this conclusion, the SNM initiated a series of reconciliatory efforts on both its eastern and western fronts during the tail end of its rebellion. It was in these regions of Somaliland that clans other than the Isaaq, the SNM's main support base, were concentrated, and these groups had been integrated through clan politics into the regime's loose coalition of militia in order to fight against the SNM.

To avoid a bloody aftermath to the rebellion, the SNM, through its sub-clan supporters, arranged reconciliatory meetings with the regime-allied eastern clans. Spearheaded by traditional leaders from two major Isaaq sub-clans, these successive attempts at negotiation ended with the signing of a ceasefire and peace agreement with their adversaries, concluded at the SNM headquarters in Balligubadle. Representatives from both the Central Committee and the Executive Committee signed a peace and cooperation agreement with the delegation led by Garaad Cabdiqani Garad Jaamac, one of the most distinguished traditional chiefs of the Dhulbahante clan, in the first week of September 1990. These successive peace agreements would have a tremendous impact on the course of events of the war, as a political solution to the animosity between the Isaaq and the non-Isaaq clans on their borders removed the need for military intervention by SNM forces, which would have cost many lives. Instead, this peaceful endeavour sowed the seeds of mutual respect and brotherhood between two fraternal clans.

The SNM also did not spare any effort in carrying out the same reconciliatory initiatives on its western front. These endeavours continued up until the late hours of the war of liberation, when a delegation from the SNM-affiliated Council of Elders engaged in a chain of talks with prominent leaders from the western region's capital city of Boroma. The main objective of this dialogue was to reach an agreement with the community there before the SNM's military offensive built on its previous gains in Berbera and spread west. The reconciliatory efforts of both the SNM and the Council of Elders, although unable to prevent military confrontation, were decisive in minimising both the human and the material costs of such conflict.

What was the collective impact of both the increased illegitimacy of the state and the rise of the SNM as a political and military force on the legitimacy of the idea of 'Greater Somalia', in terms of both its relevance for future state-building endeavours and its ability to justify past decisions?

The political maturity and legitimacy of the SNM can first and foremost be seen in the way it structured its internal governance and administration – something which more resembled a government-in-waiting than a rebel group. Between its inception on 6 April 1981 and the date of the total liberation of the northern regions in early February 1991, the SNM held six nationwide congresses and succeeded in changing its leadership six times through a peaceful transfer of power. Among the fundamental documents guiding the SNM were its political programme and constitution. These were operationalised by the SNM's complex, extensive bureaucratic institutional structure, made up of various organs with their own guiding principles. These included the SNM penal code, financial regulations, administrative regulations, and set of institution-specific internal regulations for the Central Committee, Standing Committee, Executive Committee, external branches, Security Office and Auditing Department.[8]

These institutional mechanisms were employed with the purpose of meeting the SNM's short- and long-term objectives. At the most basic and immediate level, the plan was to overthrow the dictatorial regime of Siad Barre by means of armed revolt, and in its place set up a democratic interim administration that would be dedicated to the spread of local political inclusion through decentralisation. As noted above, democratic governance would not follow from victory in armed struggle, but would be included as an integral part of the overall strategy of armed struggle from the outset, as a way to win the hearts and minds of the people – the movement's only supporters in the absence of any substantial external backing. Thus part and parcel of the SNM's activities during its ten-year campaign were efforts to develop the northern economy (especially the agriculture and livestock sectors), provide social services to the areas under its control, reintegrate refugees and internally displaced persons back into society, facilitate reconciliation amongst combating clans, and protecting the democratic rights of the people in a way consistent with cultural norms and Islamic values.

The SNM's long-term objectives followed from its realisation that only through the toppling of the Barre regime could a sustainable future for the Somali people be built. Thus it included the creation of a new administration and system of rule based on the consensus and shared guidance of legitimate resistance movements, the establishment of a society governed by democratic norms and practices as well as respect for human rights, the reinstatement of law and order, the separation of the civil and military spheres, and the enacting of compensational and restorative justice measures against the upper echelons of the previous regime for the war crimes and embezzlement perpetrated under their rule.[9]

The unique character which separated the SNM from other insurgent movements in Somalia and its effect on Somaliland's post-civil war trajectory have been noted by Mark Bradbury (2008: 61), who writes in his book-length study of Somaliland that:

> Although [the SNM] was a clan-based response to the autocratic regime in Mogadishu and the consequences of the Ogaden war, its political objectives, internal organisation and source of financing distinguished it from the opportunistic and predatory armed factions that emerged in southern Somalia in the late 1980s. Furthermore, the practice of 'participatory democracy' in the SNM . . . influenced the form of government that emerged in Somaliland.

Conclusion

What the historical record of the two Somali territories' experiment with unified statehood shows is a story of ideological social engineering gone astray. From the outset, poets, politicians, military officials and the majority of the general public in the former British Somaliland expressed their concerns once it became clear how power was to be distributed between the different regions. The period of civilian rule offered some promise in terms of the development of democratic institutions, but ultimately failed to overcome the temptations of clan favouritism and corruption. The post-coup military regime also made some early achievements in the fields of education and agricultural industrialisation, but the limitations of its nation-building project soon surfaced in the form of a devastating interstate war in pursuit of the dream of 'Greater Somalia' and in the regime's inability to govern the state through the endorsement of society alone. Instead it relied on a combination of external support, military coercion and the manipulation of clan identities as a form of 'divide and rule'.

In the midst of all this, a different form of government sprang up in response to the needs of a marginalised people. Whether a result of the integrity of its leaders or a reliance on the population for support, the SNM engaged in a ten-year military and political campaign aimed at liberating the Somali Republic from tyrannical rule while, at the same time, laying the foundations for an experimental form of governance. Although a self-governing state of Somaliland was just as new an endeavour in 1991 as the Somali Republic was in 1960, its origins were much more organic. Not only did a political community germinate and come together through the shared struggle against oppression and marginalisation, and not only did the governing entity (the SNM) realise early on that the inclusion of all clans into its structure was necessary for its success, but the eventual catalyst for Somaliland's declaration of statehood came not from an elite-led intellectual project but from a popular upsurge of support from below.

Therefore, in addition to satisfying all the international requirements for statehood, Somaliland also transcends them. The evidence of this in terms of democratisation, peace building and the revitalisation of key industries and trade sectors has been well documented, but its origins and implications must be understood. As this chapter shows, Somaliland's success is not the result of a fluke or some enigmatic cultural trait, but a result of a hard-fought popular political struggle based on a desire for prosperity and security and a realisation that this desire could not be achieved through either 'Greater Somalia' or even a unified north and south.

These lessons, learned first-hand by Somalis throughout the Horn of Africa and heeded by the many willing to give their lives in pursuit of change, must inform current debates surrounding the future statuses of Somalia and Somaliland. As was realised by those who dreamt of a 'Greater Somalia', Somalis, whatever their location, share (to a greater degree than most peoples) the bonds of ethnic identity, language, culture, religion, history and economic exchange. Somaliland and Somalia's current leaders studied and worked alongside each other; businesspeople in Hargeisa continue to have one foot in Mogadishu (and vice versa); and the two countries share the same concerns in terms of drought, piracy, terrorism, regional security and negative international perceptions. It is thus imperative that cooperation between all Somali territories be promoted in the areas of economic relations, social and cultural exchange, the free movement of people and goods, and security.

But, as post-civil war Somali history has shown, this type of coordination in no way entails a return to political integration. Somalis have utilised information technology, personal relationships and business exchange as means for substantial interaction and collaboration for a long time, something which centralised governmental authority has only served to stifle. Recognition on the parts of Somaliland and Somalia of the other as a brotherly sovereign entity would allow for divisive politics to be overcome, thus paving the way for cooperation in an environment of shared trust. For the Somaliland people to maintain the democratic and security safeguards that independent autonomy allows in no way precludes the integration of Somali communities and territories into the greater institutional mechanisms governing the Horn. Instead, the fear of a return to the injustices of the past can be avoided while at the same time building on the collective efforts of all Somali people.

What does this account of the history of Somaliland's temporary acquiescence of sovereignty mean for self-determination, specifically on the African continent? Plenty of commentators have argued that Somaliland's success in bringing democracy, peace, stability and development to a region where these values are in relatively short supply is reason enough to justify independence. This line of argument is one that seeks to redefine the self-determination process to include measures of moral weight and justice. Other commentators have taken a very strict international legal line of reasoning and have argued that Somaliland's colonial past and the invalidity of the Act of Union give Somaliland the political right to self-determination. Although there are some parallels and shared sympathies with these approaches, this chapter takes a more political approach to arguing for self-determination.

Whereas morality and international legal norms most certainly will play a part in Somaliland's quest for self-determination, the major obstacle at this point is political. There are assumptions amongst those in the international community either that a unified Somali Republic (Somalia and Somaliland) is the best way to create peace and stability or at least that any reconstitution of the Somali state is incomplete without Somaliland. As this analysis has shown, a legitimate and tenable version of Somalia–Somaliland unity never existed and was in fact one of the major obstacles to stability in the region. Therefore, just as the splitting up of Sudan and South Sudan was for the most part predicated on the idea that both states could not live together as part of the same government without violence and marginalisation, this exploration wanted to show that a similar situation presents itself in the case of Somalia and Somaliland.

Notes

1 Before the referendum of 19 March 1967, Djibouti was called the Somali French Coast. From 1967 to 1977 it was called the Afar Essa Territory, and in 1977, when it gained its independence, it got its current name of the Republic of Djibouti.

2 It should be noted that the fact that the current national identity of Somalia continues to incorporate the five regions into its notion of Somalia provides sufficient proof that no nation-building project can be conceived of without reference to this unification of all Somali peoples.

3 As Drysdale (1994) points out, over 60 per cent of the 100,000 northern voters opposed the constitution, including 72 per cent in Hargeisa, 69 per cent in Berbera, 66 per cent in Burao and 69 per cent in Erigavo. The Somali National League, 'the principal political party in the north', also chose to boycott the referendum.

4 It is important to note that the treason charges brought against the coup leaders by a Mogadishu court were eventually dropped owing to a decision that the court had no jurisdiction over Somaliland, as the Act of Union had never been successfully ratified.

5 Generals Mohamed Said Hersi Morgan and Mohammed Ganni commanded Siad Barre's armed forces in Hargeisa and its surrounding areas (what was then known as the 26th Sector) between 1982 and 1988. General Morgan was the husband of one of Siad Barre's daughters and one-time minister of defence, and Ganni was also a close relative of the dictator. While the other regions of Somalia were governed by civilian governors and party secretaries, the north-western region remained under the military emergency rule of these figures. They were responsible for some of the most egregious instances of war crimes and violations of human rights of the entire civil war period, both in Somaliland and in other regions of Somalia.

6 In southern Somalia in the late 1980s, the cognitive dissonance on display was brilliantly satirised by famous singer and composer Abdi Muhummed Amin, who produced a set of highly sarcastic and critical songs which quickly became popular with disillusioned Somalis. Among the most famous were 'Landcruiser', sung by Sado Ali Warsame, and 'Juba', sung by Abdi Muhummed Amin and Sado Ali Warsame, which parodied the discrepancies in wealth between the ruling class and the famished populace, as well as the decaying state of the country.

7 This is not to romanticise the SNM, as its governance structure did have a variety of limitations, many of which have been well documented by Compagnon (1998). The struggle to establish stability and democratic norms in Somaliland went on well beyond the end of the civil war, and included a whole variety of other segments of society, including women, youth and the business community.

8 This information was taken from official documents resolved by the SNM congresses and Central Committee meetings.

9 This information was gathered from the unpublished Political Programme of the SNM approved by the 6th Congress in 1990.

References

Ahmed, I. 1999. 'Understanding Conflict in Somalia and Somaliland', in A. Adebayo (ed.), *Comprehending and Mastering African Conflicts: The Search for Sustainable Peace and Good Governance* (pp. 236–56). London: Zed Books.

Ahmed, I. A. and R. H. Green. 1999. 'The Heritage of War and State Collapse in Somalia and Somaliland: Local-Level Effects, External Interventions and Reconstruction', *Third World Quarterly*, vol. 20, no. 1, pp. 113–27.

Bradbury, M. 2008. *Becoming Somaliland*. London: Progressio.

Carroll, A. J. and Rajagopal, B. 1993. 'The Case for the Independent Statehood of Somaliland', *American University Journal of International Law and Politics*, no. 8, pp. 653–82.

Compagnon, D. 1998. 'Somali Armed Units: The Interplay of Political Entrepreneurship and Clan-Based Factions', in C. Clapham (ed.), *African Guerrillas* (pp. 73–90). Oxford: James Currey.

Cotran, E. 1968. 'Legal Problems Arising out of the Formation of the Somali Republic', *International and Comparative Law Quarterly*, July, pp. 1010–26.

Drysdale, J. 1994. *Whatever Happened to Somalia?* London: HAAN Associates.

Duale, B. Y. 2005. 'The Role of the Media in Political Reconstruction', in WSP International (eds), *Rebuilding Somaliland: Issues and Possibilities* (pp. 123–88). Lawrenceville, NJ: Red Sea Press.

Duale, B. Y. 2012. *Cabdillahi Suldaan Maxamed (Timacadde): Poetry and Life History*. Addis Ababa: Flamingo Printing Press.

Farah, A. Y. 1999. 'Political Actors in Somalia's Emerging De Facto Entities: Civil–Military Relations in Somaliland and Northeast Somalia', in *Conference on Civil–Military Relations*, Nairobi, Kenya, April, http://www.somaliawatch.org/archivefeb01/010414202.htm.

Geshekter, C. 1997. 'The Death of Somalia in Historical Perspective', in H. M. Adam and R. Ford (eds), *Mending Rips in the Sky: Options for Somali Communities in the 21st Century* (pp. 65–98). Lawrenceville, NJ: Red Sea Press.

International Crisis Group. 2006. *Somaliland: Time for African Union Leadership*, Africa Report no. 110. Addis Ababa: International Crisis Group.

Lewis, I. M. 2007. *Blood and Bone: The Call of Kinship in Somali Society*. Lawrenceville, NJ: Red Sea Press.

Lewis, I. M. 2008. *Understanding Somalia and Somaliland: Culture, History, Society*. New York: Columbia University Press.

Liqliqato, M. I. M. 2000. *Taariikhda Soomaalida*. Mogadishu.

Mazrui, A. A. 1997. 'Crisis in Somalia: From Tyranny to Anarchy', in H. M. Adam and R. Ford (eds), *Mending Rips in the Sky: Options for Somali Communities in the 21st Century* (pp. 5–11). Lawrenceville, NJ: Red Sea Press.

Samater, I. M. 1997. 'Light at the End of the Tunnel: Some Reflections on the Struggle of the Somali National Movement', in H. M. Adam and R. Ford (eds), *Mending Rips in the Sky: Options for Somali Communities in the 21st Century* (pp. 21–48). Lawrenceville, NJ: Red Sea Press.

Touval, S. 1963. *Somali Nationalism: International Politics and the Drive for Unity in the Horn of Africa*. Cambridge, MA: Harvard University Press.

9 Identifying challenges to winning international recognition and its prospects in Somaliland

Adam Haji-Ali Ahmed

Introduction

Somaliland, which is located at the northern tip of the Horn of Africa, is bordered by Djibouti in the northwest, Ethiopia in the west, Puntland in the northeast, Somalia in the south and Yemen across the Red Sea. The people of Somaliland are ethnic Somali, sharing with other Somalis a common language, religion (Sunni Islam), and traditional livelihood system based on nomadic pastoralism. Most come from three main "clan families" – the Isaaq, Dir (Gadabursi and Iise) and Harti (Warsengeli and Dulbahante) of the Darod clan federation (Walls and Kibble 2010). But there are also other small clans which are scattered across the country.

After being a British protectorate since 1884, Somaliland became an independent country on June 26, 1960. The rest of present-day Somalia, then administered by Italy, became independent a few days later. Within days, the two colonies decided to merge. But Somalilanders felt humiliated and betrayed for their patriotism in seeking a greater Somalia (which was the objective of the union) almost from the start, since most of the power went to the South of the country. Somalilanders rejected a referendum on a unitary constitution in June 1961 and, later that year, military officers in Hargeisa began an unsuccessful rebellion to reassert Somaliland's independence (Walls and Kibble 2010).

There was a coup to seize state power in 1969, led by General Mohamed Siad Barre. The new military junta led by Siad Barre instituted a Marxist regime, and became a close ally of the Soviet Union (Ibrahim and Terlinden 2008). Although the North of Somalia was initially enthusiastic about forming a union with Italian Somaliland, the euphoria quickly changed to disenchantment as many in the North felt increasingly marginalized in government and other sectors of society (Schoiswohl 2004). While the authoritarian government of Siad Barre was becoming increasingly unpopular with Somalis, nowhere was the regime more resented than in the North (Lewis 2002).

Historically and culturally, Somaliland was certainly a separate region from the rest of Somalia before it hastily and voluntarily united with the Italian part of Somalia (Khadiagala 2008). The first formal treaties between the sovereign leaders of the people of Somaliland and the British were signed in the nineteenth century. Somali leaders in the North sought political protection from the British government as a "quid pro quo for the export of their livestock, which Britain needed at its coaling station in Aden" (Schoiswohl 2004). The British Somaliland protectorate was officially founded in July 1887, after the signing of the so-called "protection treaties" with various Northern Somali clans. However, it was briefly independent for five days in 1960 after the British withdrawal before throwing in its lot with the formerly Italian South, a decision which its people have regretted ever since. In this brief period, over 34 countries, including Egypt, Israel and the five permanent members of the Security Council, recognized "Somaliland" diplomatically, and interestingly Israel was the first to do so (Tannock 2009).

Somaliland contends that it is a legal entity or state whose recognition would set no precedent relevant to the rest of Africa. Somaliland did exist as an independent state in 1960, albeit only for a matter of days, before voluntarily merging with the rest of Somalia. Since Somaliland currently exists within the old colonial boundaries of British Somaliland (Nasir 2011), it argues that it is simply returning to its previous status as an independent state and that its existence in no way threatens the inviolability of inherited colonial boundaries (Somaliland Ministry of Foreign Affairs 2002). One of the most commonly articulated concerns about the idea of Somaliland's independence is that it would set a dangerous precedent by sanctioning a redrawing of the African map.

African states and some Western governments have treated the inviolability of Africa's colonial boundaries as a core principle for the sake of preserving stability. Similarly, proponents of Somaliland independence must also confront the objections of many Somalis who definitely reject the prospect of formally dismantling the larger Somali state, regarding Somaliland as a secessionist state (Nasir 2011). However, pro-independence Somalilanders often rely on moral and historical grounds and believe that this case is exceptional and is not secession. They argue that Somaliland emerged from the ashes of a failed union and a bigger project that failed and as a consequence of that union it suffered more than it ever did at the hands of Britain (HRW 2009).

This chapter examines Somaliland's quest for international recognition. Hence it examines actors, dynamics, challenges and prospects influencing international recognition. The chapter also attempts to understand why the world imagines that Somaliland does not exist and interrogates the faults of the international politics of recognition. The chapter unveils why both regional and international bodies failed to respond to Somaliland's demand for recognition by taking the opportunity to engage as a neutral third party, without prejudice to the final determination of Somaliland's sovereign status. In a nutshell it endeavors to examine the quest for self-determination of Somaliland and the obstacles it faces.

Recognition and statehood under international law

Concept of recognition

Recognition is a process whereby certain facts are accepted and endowed with a certain legal status, such as statehood, sovereignty over newly acquired territory, or the international effects of the grant of nationality. The process of recognizing a state as a new entity that conforms to the criteria of statehood is a political one, each country deciding for itself whether to extend such acknowledgment. Normal sovereign and diplomatic immunities are generally extended only after a state's executive authority has formally recognized another state (Shaw 2004). Recognition in international law is a method of accepting certain factual situations and endowing them with legal significance, but this relationship is a complicated one (Shaw 2004). Recognition basically is a unilateral political act, with domestic and international legal consequences, whereby a state acknowledges an act or status of another state or government. Recognition can be accorded either *de facto* or *de jure*, and most often recognition is in the form of a special official act whereby states declare that they have decided to recognize a new entity as an independent state (Kaczorowska 2002; Müllerson 2004).

Recognition of states in international law

When a new state comes into existence, other states are confronted with a dilemma as to whether or not to recognize the new state (Schoiswohl 2004). Recognition of a new state acknowledges that the entity fulfills the criteria of statehood. Recognition means a willingness to deal with the new state as a member of the international community. No state is obliged to recognize other states. However, for purposes of determining the complicated relationship between statehood and recognition, it is vital to distinguish recognition of states from recognition of governments (Schoiswohl 2004). While the former refers to the issue of an entity's legal personality (statehood), the latter concerns the international legal capacity of actors who are assuming functions of governance to act on its behalf (Nasir 2011).

Criteria for statehood

Historically, states were considered to be the only subjects of international law. Since the end of World War I, this view has become increasingly indefensible, although independent states continue to remain the most important subjects (Hillier 1999). The legal criteria for statehood are generally accepted to be those set out in Article 1 of the Montevideo Convention: "the state as a person of international law should possess the following qualifications: (a) a permanent population; (b) a defined territory; (c) government; and (d) capacity to enter into relations with the other states" (Kaczorowska 2002; Crawford 2006).

Statehood and recognition

Before examining state practice on the matter, it is necessary to refer to the underlying conflict over the nature of recognition. A further effect of nineteenth-century practice has been to focus attention more or less exclusively on the act of recognition itself, and its legal implications, rather than on the problem of the elaboration of rules determining the status, competence and so on of the various territorial governmental units (Nasir 2011). To some extent, this was inevitable as long as the constitutive position retained its influence, for a corollary of that position was that there could be no such rules (Crawford 2006). Examination of the constitutive theory is, therefore, first of all necessary. In addition, the declaratory position suggests that the formation of a new subject of international law is a matter of fact not law. A new state can, therefore, come into existence irrespective of whether it has been recognized by existing states (Müllerson 2004).

Therefore, while declaratory of an existing fact, the coming into existence of a new state is constitutive in its nature, at least as far as concerns relations with the recognizing state. According to the declaratory theory, recognition of a new state is a political act, which is, in principle, independent of the existence of the new state as the subject of international law. As is so often the case with international law, discussion of recognition has led to the development of two competing theories. The principal question which the two theories attempt to answer is whether recognition is a necessary requirement for, or merely a consequence of, international personality (Hillier 1999).

Secession, self-determination and recognition

Secession can generally be defined as the "separation of part of the territory of a state carried out by the resident population with the aim of creating a new independent state or acceding to another existing state and which originally takes place in the absence of consent of the previous sovereign" (Schoiswohl 2004). Yet the lack of consent distinguishes secession from devolution or grant of independence.

As history has proven, states are not never-ending entities, but are subject to constant changes in shape and character. States have come and gone throughout the last 350 years or so, since the "birth" of statehood in Westphalia in 1648 (Schoiswohl 2004). But even a glance back into more recent history reveals substantive changes in the scenery of international relations. However, numerous states have emerged following the fall of the Berlin Wall and the collapse of the Soviet Union. Since 1945, the number of states has almost quadrupled, with 191 members of the United Nations in 2003 (Schoiswohl 2004). In general, international law does not interfere with the political processes of state emergence and extinction, but leaves these matters to the people and the facts on the ground. The means by which a state emerges is accordingly not a matter of international law. It remains rather confined to the acknowledgment of the factual emergence of a new entity and to the evaluation of its legal status, according to the specific criteria necessary for statehood: population, territory, effective governance and eventually – depending on the contextual circumstances – international recognition (Lowe 2007).

It is necessary to distinguish between secession in pursuance of and in violation of self-determination. If the territory in question secedes unilaterally, it may be presumed that the secessionist government possesses the general support of the people. On the other hand, it is possible for a seceding government manifestly to lack the general support of the people concerned (Müller-son 2004). However, revolution and self-determination are not mutually exclusive. On the contrary, the former may be an extreme form of the latter, and it seems that not only revolution but secession similarly is an extreme form of self-determination and that they both should have equal status under international law.

State practice since 1945 in relation to secession of this type has not been entirely consistent. However, in three of the earlier cases of seceding territories, at least some degree of international recognition was extended at a relatively early stage. The Indonesian situation was the first of these. Indonesian nationalist leaders declared the Republic of Indonesia on August 17, 1945. There followed a protracted conflict, military and diplomatic, with the Netherlands before sovereignty was formally transferred on December 27, 1949 (Crawford 2006). The events of this period have been described elsewhere. What is of interest here is that, although Indonesia was probably not a fully independent state before December 1949, it was accorded a certain – even considerable – legal status during the conflict. It was recognized as a *de facto* government by the Netherlands itself and by a number of other states; in addition, several states accorded it *de jure* recognition.

Similarly, the status of the Democratic Republic of Vietnam (DRVN), after the declaration of independence in 1945, was complicated by the conflicting grants of authority by France to various local governments, and by the claims of both governments to represent Vietnam as a whole (Crawford 2006). As in the Indonesian case, various states recognized the DRVN. France also extended a somewhat equivocal *de facto* recognition. On the other hand, these complicating features were not present in the case of Algeria. The Algerian Republic was proclaimed on September 19, 1958 and after protracted hostilities was granted formal independence by France on July 3, 1962 (Crawford 2006). After some hesitation, the General Assembly took the matter up in 1960 and 1961, calling upon the parties to negotiate "with a view to implementing the right of the Algerian people to self-determination and independence respecting the unity and territorial integrity of Algeria" (Crawford 2006). Algeria had also been recognized before July 3, 1960 by a certain number of states.

The case of Somaliland is quite different from the thesis discussed above (Nasir 2011). Somaliland was a British protectorate and gained its independence from the United Kingdom on June 26, 1960. Four days later, it unilaterally united with its Italian Southern counterpart of Somalia. Over 34 countries, including the five permanent members of the UN Security Council, Egypt and Israel, recognized the State of Somaliland (Tannock 2009). Nevertheless, Somaliland argues that it is not seceding from its parent state, but that it regained its independence and suspended only the dysfunctional unity with its counterpart, while asserting and maintaining the territory and boundaries left by the British government in 1960.

Challenges and obstacles to recognition

Actors and dynamics

Social structure is subject to social dynamic changes. Social change means any observable difference of social phenomena that appears to us over any period of time. In other words social change is the alteration in patterns of social structure, social institutions and social behavior over time. All societies on this globe are subject to continuous change (Chauhan 2007). Somaliland as part and parcel of the international community has simply reasserted its separate existence as a British colony before independence and abrogated its 1960 union with the former Italian Somalia. By doing so, it has avoided the devastation of war that has afflicted the rest of Somalia through compromise politics between clan elders (Kinfe 2002). However, its *de facto* statehood since 1991 has not received international recognition of the kind accorded to Eritrea in 1993.

On the other hand, there are many actors adding to the dynamics of domestic, regional and international dimensions of the recognition of Somaliland. Since society is a harmonious organization of human relationships, moving away from expected behavior norms can cause social disorganization. The major factor or dynamic element which has been disruptive in Somaliland society is the clan system, which mainly causes social disorganization. This factor led the society to remain in general unrest, communal tension, unemployment and mutual distrust, at the expense of collective interest. This directs the society at large to the lack of education, violation of social rules, natural catastrophes, aggression and war, violence and hatred, backwardness and selfish attitudes.

On the contrary, the biggest indicators of the troubled situation and the anxiety of the international community stem from such factors as fear of being involved in the legal breakup of the Somali state. The worry is about setting a precedent outside the African Union (AU) belief in keeping boundaries sacred, and about Somaliland leading the way for other parts of Somalia to follow suit. The other factor is the reluctance of the international community, particularly the donors and the United Nations, to reward Somaliland with project support for it to put its house in order and to strengthen peace and stability. Moreover, there are external factors affecting the affairs of the subregion, specifically Italy, which is not in favor of Somaliland as an independent state. It is trying to persuade its trading partners not to buy Berbera's products and suggesting that international travel permission should be denied to the officials and citizens of Somaliland.

But the Somaliland authorities have rejected this on many occasions, on the basis that the Somaliland claim for separation had begun long before the overthrow of the Siad Barre regime. They strongly argue that the desire to keep sacred colonial boundaries does not apply to Somaliland, on the ground that it was a separate entity as a British colony and that its union with the former Italian colony was based on an impulse rather than the will of the majority (Kinfe 2002). Furthermore, the Somaliland authorities argue for independence by drawing a parallel with the similar motives of the Sahrawis and Eritrea before independence.

Legal challenges

The Somaliland case: is it a unilateral secession or dissolution with legal
self-determination under international law?

One of the most important challenges facing Somaliland's quest for recognition is
to clarify the status of Somaliland since 1991 after it declared the regaining of its
independence from the ashes of collapse of the Somali state in 1991. The question
is: does Somaliland's declaration of independence amount to unilateral secession,
or is it dissolution from a failed state? How will the case of Somaliland have legitimacy without the consent of the parent state? The above questions need to be
answered and amount to challenges for Somaliland's quest for recognition.

The act of secession has different aspects in international law, such as unilateral
declaration of independence without the consent of the parent state (Schoiswohl
2004). In this regard, new states may arise from the partition or unification of
old states. England and Scotland became the state of Great Britain. The United
Kingdom was again partitioned when the Irish Free State was formed. Norway
and Sweden became separated, Belgium and Holland were separated, while the
states of Germany were united (Maciver 2006).

Similarly, dissolution is quite different from secession. However, in international law, dissolution is when a state has broken up into several entities and no
longer has power over those entities. An example of this is the case of the former
USSR dissolving into different republics (Nasir 2011).

By the same token, Senegal emerged from the dissolution of the Mali Federation – a federal arrangement formed between it and Sudan[1] under the French
constitution of 1958. The former colonies of Senegal and Sudan became "autonomous states" within the French Community (Crawford 2006). Subsequently,
it was agreed that the Mali Federation would be established, and Senegal
and Sudan agreed to join it. Under the constitution of the Mali Federation
of January 17, 1959, its constituent units were regarded as "sovereign," as was
the Federation itself. Shortly after the Federation was inaugurated, serious difficulties arose between Senegal and Sudan, and on August 20, 1960 Senegal
purported to withdraw. This was initially opposed by Sudan but was accepted
on September 22, 1960 when Sudan asserted its independence outside the
French Community under the name of Mali (Crawford 2006). The situation
was described in different terms by different members of the Security Council
when it considered the applications for United Nations membership by Senegal
and Mali on September 28, 1960 (Crawford 2006). However, it was on common
ground that the two entities resolved their differences, that each had achieved
separate independence, and that the Mali Federation had thereby ceased to
exist.

So the issue of the status of Somaliland has not been addressed, and it is important that it is discussed between Somaliland and the rest of Somalia in order to
resolve it. Otherwise it will remain a challenge for "Somaliland" to get statehood
recognition.

Does Somaliland have the right to exercise self-determination?

A broad claim to self-determination may be made by Somaliland. The *first* justification that Somaliland may claim lies in its history as a British colony. A colony has a legal right to exercise self-determination for independence from its colonizer; some argue that Somaliland, as a former colony, may exercise its right to self-determination because it has not yet done so, since the invalidation of its union with South Somalia was not based on a national referendum or popular vote on the matter. If there was no union, Somaliland still exists as an independent entity, and discussions pertaining to secession are moot (Kreuter 2010).

This argument may be nullified by the fact of the union; even though there was no national vote on the issue, democratically elected leaders of each former colony oversaw the unification process (Kreuter 2010). These leaders did not act contrary to the will of the people. So Somaliland legal experts, government and other supporters must prepare a legal answer to the above critique for a Somaliland argument.

The *second* option by which Somaliland could legally exercise its right to self-determination is through internal self-determination, by using Somalia's established political procedures and mechanisms of self-rule to realize its policy goals. The circumstances in Somalia, however, make it difficult for Somaliland to exercise internal self-determination (Kreuter 2010). However, self-determination has become possible since the start of talks between Somaliland and Somalia at the London conference, and the dynamics and geopolitics of the region are dramatically changing. In fact any region within a failed state may have little or no opportunity to petition against its government in the furtherance of self-determination, simply because the state lacks a functioning government. Some scholars argue that Somaliland's inability to exercise internal self-determination is strong enough and therefore a lot has to be done about this issue by talking with Somalia and achieving internal self-determination by Somalilanders (Kreuter 2010).

Does Somaliland have a legal basis for self-determination?

Perhaps Somaliland's best legal argument for independence in the furtherance of self-determination arises from one of the three legal theories of self-determination – bilateral, unilateral or *de facto*. Let us examine the pros and cons of each theory for the Somaliland case.

BILATERAL SELF-DETERMINATION

Under this theory, the primary aim is cooperation between the party seeking independence and the parent state. It has two requirements. First, Somalia's domestic law would need to make some provisions for secession. Second, Somaliland would need to engage in "principled negotiations" with the Somali government on the issue of secession. To meet these requirements there are two insurmountable barriers to any efforts at bilateral secession. First, the current state of lawlessness in the South precludes such political action; and, second, even if that were not the case, the Somali government is not favorable to the idea of a breakup of the country (Kreuter 2010).

But now, since the opening of a channel of communication between the warring parties, Somaliland and Somalia, it is possible for Somaliland to attain bilateral self-determination through talks and convincing its counterpart that the interests of both sides are to split into two states which will live side by side as brother states.

UNILATERAL SELF-DETERMINATION

This theory requires three elements: that the Somalilanders are a "people," that the Somali government subjected them to serious human rights violations and that no other viable options exist (Kreuter 2010). These conditions are no easy matters to prove, because there needs to be viable reasonable evidence that a genocide really did happen in Somaliland during Siad Barre's regime. Thus Somaliland must prepare and build a strong case to submit to international forums which proves beyond reasonable doubt that massacres and mass killing amounting to serious human rights violations really happened and that there is no viable option apart from self-determination.

If Somaliland cannot succeed in proving that serious human rights violations happened during Siad Barre's regime and that Somalilanders were victims of atrocities at the hands of the Somali government, then it will be difficult to argue for unilateral self-determination in the international law arena.

Despite the human rights abuses perpetrated against the people of Somaliland, it is unclear whether they are sufficiently significant to support an argument in favor of justified unilateral secession. If any other remedies exist, Somaliland must resort to such remedies before seceding (Kreuter 2010).

DE FACTO SELF-DETERMINATION

On the other hand it may be argued that, since 1991, Somaliland has already gained independence through *de facto* secession. *De facto* secession on its own, however, is legally insufficient. Arguing *de facto* secession is better if there are some nations that have already given recognition. In the case of Somaliland no country has done so (Kreuter 2010). Somaliland has seceded *de facto*, but this is not enough, and Somaliland has to double its diplomatic efforts to secure the *de jure* recognition which is suitable for its nation and statehood ambitions.

Local challenges

As has been discussed, Somaliland has fulfilled the criteria of statehood; however, there are challenges which undermine the efforts of Somaliland to obtain international recognition. These include the abuse of the principles of democracy,[2] bad governance or in a broader sense absence of good governance, and corruption, which remain the major factors challenging Somaliland's acquisition of *de jure* recognition. In addition, there are scholars who argue that the recognition comes from the way of governance of the "state" striving to obtain an international personality in the international system. In their view, there are factors which cripple a state's goal to reach that target, such as widespread corruption, maladministration and so on. As one of the interviewees argued, "There is no society on this globe claiming to have an independent state and at the same time aspiring to attain international recognition and working less than three hours daily in the public offices" (Nasir 2011).

On the other hand, the international organizations working in Somaliland came to Somaliland in the name of Somalia, putting aside the name of Somaliland. Some argue that, when the leaders of Somaliland do not question that, it implies that Somaliland is not serious about acquiring international recognition. Similarly, the public servants are not getting sufficient payments, while senior officials are using an extensive amount of money for their own interests. These incurred costs cast shadows over the existence of Somaliland as a "state."

It is important to note that the successive authorities in Somaliland failed to extend their authority over the whole state territory,[3] particularly the remote eastern regions of Somaliland. Consequently, out of the six regions which Somaliland comprises, two of them use the currency of the former Somalia state. Therefore, by looking into these factors, some argue that Somaliland does not deserve to acquire international recognition, as such domestic issues do not encourage the international community.

However, it is possible to argue that the failure of the Somaliland people and government to talk to the Somalia government over the last 20 or more years has been one of the main obstacles to Somaliland acquiring *de jure* recognition from the international community. Therefore, dealing with matters from a practical point of view, it is possible to argue that the contradictory and confusing aspects of the issue of recognition make it difficult to reach a sustainable agreement among the concerned Somali parties.

Regional challenges

After the collapse of the Somali state in 1991, Somaliland unilaterally proclaimed its separation from the rest of Somalia. However, the major regional challenge facing Somaliland's dream comes from the Southern part of Somalia, the parent state of Somaliland, which has remained in a difficult and warring situation since 1991. In this regard, the authorities in Somalia have consistently opposed any formal dismantling of the larger Somali state (HRW 2009). Despite this, there are divisions among Somalis regarding clan factors among others. Moreover, Somalia has been poorly positioned to engage in talks regarding either independence or significant autonomy for Somaliland, as it lacked any form of authority that might control the territory of Southern Somalia (ICG 2006). For the attainment of international *de jure* recognition, Somalia remains the major challenge to Somaliland, as it claims that Somaliland is part and parcel of its territory, disregarding all historical realities that Somaliland was a separate British protectorate that willingly joined the Italian South in 1960, in pursue of greater Somalia, which is now doomed.

Likewise, the Arab states and the Muslim countries are not interested in seeing a divided and disintegrated Somalia. Rather they want to see a united Somalia to counterbalance Ethiopia's claim as the state aspiring to be the regional power. Generally speaking, Arab countries' approach is aimed at creating a strong central government in Somalia with an anti-Ethiopian stance (Tadesse 2002). In this regard, some dominant Arab states, in particular Egypt and Saudi Arabia, are reluctant to empower Somaliland with recognition, because they see it as an Ethiopian ally and do not wish to strengthen Ethiopia's regional position (HRW 2009).

Moreover, as some sources indicate, the key regional obstacle to Somaliland's recognition is Saudi Arabia, which not only objects to the secular, democratic model promoted by Somaliland, but is a strong ally of Somalia, which is a member of the League of Arab States and the Organization of the Islamic Conference (OIC). As part of its agenda instrument, Saudi Arabia supports the Transitional Federal Government (TFG) financially and politically to enhance its interest (Tannock 2009). Therefore many Somaliland scholars argue that Arabs are supporting a united Somalia and are against the case of Somaliland. These scholars advocate that people work hard to convince other states to support Somaliland's right to remain a separate state.

Correspondingly, the African Union appreciated Somaliland's achievements and progress, but hesitated to recognize it, fearing that it could encourage other secessionist waves which might hit all over the continent if Somaliland were allowed to join the international community. In addition, the Charter of the Organisation of African Unity (OAU) mentions respect for the sovereignty and territorial integrity of each state and for its inalienable right to independent existence (Adam 1994). Therefore, the African Union has maintained many features of its predecessor (the OAU), including its commitment to the unity and territorial integrity of member states such as Somalia, which is a member of the African Union. In this regard, Professor Ali Mazrui argues that the African Union should serve as a kind of court, providing Somaliland with an opportunity for a fair hearing of its case (ICG 2006: 12).

International challenges

As well as local and regional challenges to Somaliland's quest to acquire international recognition, there are also international challenges which deserve to be mentioned. At the international level, both law and state interests confer a powerful advantage to existing states. The recent collapse of communism has allowed Western states to break the state sovereignty taboo in an enthusiastic rush to recognize the dismemberment of the USSR, Yugoslavia and Czechoslovakia. Other parts of the world, especially Africa where the OAU code continues to exert its influence, have not been treated by the same standards. Prior to recent events,

Bangladesh provided a rare case of a secession that won international recognition. This was due to geography – East Pakistan (Bangladesh) was separated by Indian territory from West Pakistan – as well as the decisive intervention of the Indian army and India's diplomatic offensive (Adam 1994: 36).

Contrary to the above-indicated situations, there are numerous resolutions against Somaliland, issued by global and regional bodies such as the UN, AU and Arab League, which emphasize the sovereignty and unity of Somalia. These bodies attempt to persuade the parties particularly concerned (Somalia and Somaliland) to discuss and resolve their differences. So far, there are no signs showing the restoration of the Somali state (Nasir 2011). Despite this, the United Nations has an inbuilt hostility toward dismemberment of states which are full members (Adam 1994). Thus the UN has been reluctant to provide Somaliland with the assistance its problems deserve.

The above-mentioned regional and international actors' interests and influences could be a possible explanation as to why the international community has failed to recognize Somaliland. However, many people attribute it to a different cause. Some scholars argue that it is the failure of the international community to accept the independence of Somaliland. Others argue that the collapse of the Berlin Wall, which ended the Cold War, undermined Somalia's strategic location including Somaliland.

Nevertheless, international reluctance to come to terms with Somaliland begins in Africa. The UN and various Western donors have indicated at one time or another that Somaliland's broader prospects for international recognition depend upon the attitude of the African Union. David Shinn, a former US ambassador to Ethiopia and a close observer of Somaliland, has noted that:

> There is considerable sympathy for what Somaliland has achieved by way of internal stability, free elections, and the initiation of a democratic system of government. But the U.S. and Western countries tend to refer to the African Union when issues concerning boundary change or sovereignty arise in Africa. It is highly unlikely that the U.S. would move to recognize Somaliland before the African Union did so or, at a minimum, several key African states opted to do so.
>
> (ICG 2006: 13)

Prospects for attaining *de jure* recognition

As far as the issue of recognition is concerned, it is difficult to address it effectively because of the involvement of many issues and actors. However, some argue that, if Somaliland continues to manage to establish effective democratic governance while respecting human rights and democratic values, and leads the "state" along the path of democratization, it might attract good friends and allies (Nasir 2011). It is possible to argue that Somaliland's adoption of good governance, as well as reform of the state structure, might lead the international community to look again at the issue of Somaliland and offer *de jure* recognition.

In the same manner, some people argue that adopting a concrete foreign policy, such as involving the authorities in the Southern part of Somalia in discussion of the interests of the two sides (North and South), including Somaliland's right to secede from the rest of Somalia, remains one of the main factors which could help to resolve their problems amicably and could lead Somaliland to attain legal recognition from the international community.

Since charity begins at home, some scholars argue that Somaliland has to work hard in order to acquire *de jure* recognition by extending its authority over the Somaliland territory, particularly to the remote eastern regions. Concrete implementation of these approaches might end Somaliland's diplomatic isolation from the international community.

On the other hand, as some Somaliland scholars argue, it could be to the benefit of the international community to recognize Somaliland as an independent state, as Somaliland is strategically important in fighting terrorism, piracy and so on. Some security analysts argue that these are precisely the reasons why Somaliland merits international recognition and support (ICG 2006). ICG (2006) argues that Washington should take the lead not only in recognizing Somaliland but also in actively supporting it, a brave land whose people's quest for freedom and security mirrors America's values as well as its strategic interests. Moreover, as some experts on security and terrorism in Africa have noted, Somaliland is a fragile entity in a fragile region with a large Islamic population – all practically susceptible to terrorist and piracy activities.

However, there are Somaliland scholars who argue that Somaliland is hostage to its domestic actors and if it addresses its local loopholes it might attain international recognition.

Conclusion

In the final analysis, there are domestic, regional and international factors challenging Somaliland's quest for international recognition. Hence, since charity begins at home, Somaliland needs to address its domestic issues and implement the following steps to overcome these challenges before petitioning any country or organization for recognition.

First, both the elites and society at the grassroots level have to work hard and strengthen the established state institutions. Second, improving infrastructures and citizens' level of living standards will have a positive impact on the matter. Third, the lack of special consideration to the internal affairs of the state, including good governance, fighting corruption, institution building, and other internal issues that are important for the survival of the state and getting *de jure* recognition from other states rather than looking only for international recognition, also has its impact on the Somaliland quest for recognition. Fourth, since recognition cannot be easily acquired, the lack of effectiveness and dedication on the Somaliland side is another factor that could be addressed to reach the goal. Last but not least, the lack of international lobbyist groups is another challenge. Therefore, these factors remain the major challenges to Somaliland's quest to acquire *de jure* recognition.

The absence of international interests, such as military power or natural resources, has its own negative impact on Somaliland's quest for official recognition.

Although Somaliland has fulfilled the criteria of statehood, to attain *de jure* recognition there are many challenges to overcome. Even though there are international factors that challenge Somaliland's recognition, the major one is its parent state, which has been plunged in civil conflict and unrest for over 20 years.

Somalilanders' inability to lobby persistently for recognition is another challenge; therefore attaining *de jure* recognition is dependent on how Somaliland overcomes both the internal and the external factors that remain the major challenges crippling its quest for international recognition, and it remains to be seen how that will be achieved.

Notes

1 This was French Sudan in West Africa (the present Mali); it joined Senegal to form the Mali Federation.
2 Generally, abuse of democratic principles and values includes widely spread injustice, inequality, lack of a common good, rule of law violations, lack of accountability, absence of transparency, lack of political tolerance and power abuse.
3 Somaliland does not control the entire territory inherited from the British colony, which means that one of the elements required to become an independent state, as required by the Montevideo criteria, is missing.

References

Adam, M. Hussein. 1994. "Formation and Recognition of New States: Somaliland in Contrast to Eritrea," *Review of African Political Economy*, vol. 21, no. 59, pp. 21–38.
Chauhan, A. S. 2007. *Society and Environment*. New Delhi: Shri Sunil Kumar Jain.
Crawford, James. 2006. *The Creation of States in International Law*, 2nd edn. New York: Oxford University Press.
Hillier, Tim. 1999. *Principles of Public International Law*, 2nd edn. London: Cavendish Publishing.
HRW. 2009. *Somaliland: "Hostage to Peace" – Threats to Human Rights and Democracy in Somaliland*. New York: Human Rights Watch.
Ibrahim, Mohamed Hassan and Terlinden, Ulf. 2008. "Making Peace, Rebuilding Institutions: Somaliland – A Success Story?" in *Somalia: Current Conflicts and New Chances for State Building*, vol. 6, English edn. Berlin: Heinrich Böll Foundation.
ICG. 2006. *Somaliland: Time for African Union Leadership*, Africa Report no. 110. Addis Ababa: International Crisis Group.
Kaczorowska, Alina. 2002. *Public International Law*. London: Old Bailey Press.
Khadiagala, Gilbert M. 2008. *Eastern Africa: Security and the Legacy of Fragility*, Africa Program Working Paper Series. New York: International Peace Institute.
Kinfe, Abraham. 2002. *Somalia Calling*. Uppsala: NINA Press.
Kreuter, Aaron C. 2010. "Self-Determination, Sovereignty, and the Failure of States: Somaliland and the Case for Justified Secession," *Minnesota Journal of International Law*, vol. 19, no. 2 (23 April), p. 363, SSRN: http://ssrn.com/abstract=1938732.
Lewis, I. M. 2002. *A Modern History of the Somali*, 4th edn (rev., updated and expanded). United Kingdom: Long House Publishing Services.

Lowe, Vaughan. 2007. *International Law*. New York: Oxford University Press.

Maciver, R. M. 2006. *The Modern State*. New Delhi: Oxford University Press.

Müllerson, Rein. 2004. *International Law, Rights and Politics: Developments in Eastern Europe and the CIS*. London: Routledge.

Nasir, M. Ali. 2011. "Searching for Identity: Examining Somaliland's Quest for Recognition," Unpublished paper.

Schoiswohl, Michael. 2004. *Status and (Human Rights) Obligations of Non-Recognized De Facto Regimes in International Law: The Case of "Somaliland."* Leiden: Martinus Nijhoff.

Shaw, Malcolm N. 2004. *International Law*, 5th edn. New Delhi: Brijbasi Art Press.

Somaliland Ministry of Foreign Affairs. 2002. *Briefing Paper: The Case for Somaliland's International Recognition as an Independent State*. Hargeisa: State Printing Agency.

Tadesse, Medhane. 2002. *Al-Ittihad: Political Islam and Black Economy in Somalia*. Addis Ababa: Mega Printing Enterprise.

Tannock, Charles. 2009. "Stabilizing the Horn," *The Reporter*, 31 October, p. 14.

Walls, Michael and Kibble, Steve. 2010. "Beyond Polarity: Negotiating a Hybrid State in Somaliland," *Africa Spectrum*, vol. 45, no. 1, pp. 31–56.

10 The Zanzibar secessionist sentiments

Can regional integration theory provide insights into the phenomenon?

Francis A. S. T. Matambalya

Introduction

In a paradoxical turn of events, Africa is currently going through two apparently antagonistic processes related to nation building. On the one hand, Africa is striving to build greater economic and eventually political entities through regionalisation schemes. On the other hand, individual states face the threat of fragmentation manifested by the quest for secessionism.

Cognisant of the virtues of regional integration, the Lagos Plan of Action (LPA) of 1980 stipulated the resolve to fully integrate the then 53 African states (now numbering 54) into a single African Economic Community (AEC) by 2010.

Subsequently, the Abuja Treaty of 1991 – a direct derivative of the LPA and under implementation since 1994 – divided the African countries into five regional blocs: North Africa, West Africa, Southern Africa, East Africa and Central Africa. Further important provisions to strengthen the resolve for a systematic pan-African integration through regional integration were included in other frameworks, most notably the Constitutive Act of the African Union (AU) of July 2000, and the Accra Declaration of 2007 on the creation of the AU. The AU recognises eight major trade-driven economic integration blocs as being the key pillars of pan-African integration,[1] as well as several lesser integration blocs.[2]

Regional integration should spearhead pan-African integration in six phases, culminating in the establishment of the AEC. Under the AEC, there would be pan-African free trade, free factor mobility, and a common currency. Table 10.1 illustrates progress achieved in the integration process according to the targets set in the Abuja Treaty.

Nevertheless, secessionism is experiencing a boom in Africa. The last two states in the continent, Eritrea and South Sudan, emerged out of secessionist movements. In addition to the unresolved issue of the Sahrawi Arab Democratic Republic (SADR), part of which is currently occupied by Morocco, in recent years some serious secessionist sentiments have cropped up and simmer in several countries: Angola (Cabinda region), Kenya (Coast region), Senegal (Casamance region), and Tanzania (Zanzibar), to mention just a few.

Some of the interesting issues concerning secessionist movements in Africa are that:

Table 10.1 Evolution of Africa's integration vis-à-vis the Abuja Treaty

	Stages stipulated in the Abuja Treaty					
	Stage 1: 1994–99	Stage 2: 2000–07	Stage 3: 2008–17	Stage 4: 2018–19	Stage 5: 2020–23	Stage 6: 2024–34
Integration targets stipulated in the Abuja Treaty	Strengthen existing RECs. Creation of new RECs where they do not exist.	Coordination and harmonisation of intra-REC activities. Gradual elimination of tariffs and NTBs vis-à-vis intra-regional trade.	Launching of FTAs. Launching of CUs.	Creation of continental CU.	Establishment of the African CM.	Establishment of the African EMU.
Achievements by individual RECs	CEN-SAD COMESA EAC ECCAS ECOWAS IGAD SADC	In progress, with various RECs having attained different levels of achievement. In progress, with various RECs having attained different levels of achievement.	Not achieved. Achieved.* Achieved.* Achieved.* Achieved.* Not achieved. Achieved.* — Not yet. Not achieved. Achieved.* Not achieved. Not achieved. Not achieved. Not achieved.	Stage will be reached when all African RECs have achieved CU status, and can merge into a single continental CU.	Stage will be reached when all African RECs have achieved CM status, and can merge into a single continental CM.	Stage will be reached when all African RECs have achieved EMU status, and can merge into a single continental EMU.

Source: Author using various sources.

Notes: * Existing arrangement is being only partially implemented; CM: common market, CU: customs union; EMU: economic and monetary union; FTA: free trade area; NTB: non-tariff measure; REC: regional economic community.

1   They are happening, though through regional integration all African coun-
    tries aspire eventually to give up their national sovereignty in favour of
    larger territorial political entities. Zanzibar, for instance, belongs to the East
    African Community (EAC) – currently through the United Republic of
    Tanzania (URT). This second iteration of the EAC has a very ambitious
    integration agenda. While the first iteration took 73 years (i.e. from 1894 to
    1967) to reach a customs union (CU), Article 5(2) of the Treaty that cre-
    ated the current EAC chose to start with CU as the entry point and political
    federation as the ultimate goal.
        Importantly also for Zanzibar secessionist ambitions, this second iteration
    of the EAC resolved to expedite the integration process towards political
    federation as the destination stage. For some time, there was even talk about
    fast-tracking the process – and the political ruling class in Kenya, Rwanda,
    and Uganda still want to see this happen, though there is no common regional
    agreement on fast-tracking involving all five member states, that is, includ-
    ing Burundi and the URT.
2   There is a tacit understanding at the pan-African level that ultimately a sin-
    gle African political entity, the United States of Africa, should be formed.

This chapter is concerned with developing a better comprehension of the
secessionist sentiments in Zanzibar. To do so, it revisits the emergence of the
URT and assesses the state of the union and Zanzibar's position therein. In order
to understand the nature of Zanzibar's secessionism, it makes reference to and
reviews both the theoretical and the empirical literature on the fields of study
which help to shed light on the pertinent dynamics: regional integration theory and secession theory. On the basis of lessons from theory and empiricism, it
assesses the situation vis-à-vis Zanzibar's secessionist sentiments, and presents a
profile of the agitators. The chapter reflects also on a model for handling secessionist sentiments à la Zanzibar. Finally, it projects the future for Zanzibar and the
state of the union of the URT.

Theoretical frame of analysis of nation building and state disintegration in the United Republic of Tanzania

Nation-building dynamics from the perspective of regional integration theory

Most regional integration schemes in the world are trade-driven. Figure 10.1,
which derives from and builds on the classical Vinerian approach,[3] shows that
these schemes pass through four clearly defined phases, which pursue trade and
incrementally other 'policy convergence targets'. Each phase deals with a main
policy convergence issue. Accordingly, the main issues are logically sequenced in
order to facilitate smooth, systematic and (in terms of ambition) properly scaled
implementation schedules. The process is typical in the case of a regional economic community (REC)-based approach to state creation.

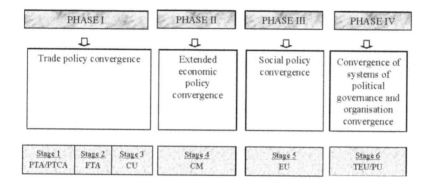

Figure 10.1 Main phases and stages of trade-driven regional integration schemes

Source: Based on Viner (1950) and lessons from the EU integration process.

Notes: CM: common market; CU: customs union; EU: economic union; FTA: free trade agreement; PTA: preferential trade agreement; PTCA: preferential trade and cooperation agreement; PU: political union; TEU: total economic union.

Table 10.2 elaborates further the various stages that entail creation of a single state through a regional integration process involving two or more countries. Thus, measured on the integration scale, theoretically URT presents the highest form of market-driven regional integration. In regional integration jargon, it is

Table 10.2 Clustering of the key policy convergence requirements at the various stages of integration

Stage of RTA	Focus of policy convergence	Specific policy areas
PTA/PTCA	Trade policy.	Intra-regional tariffs.
FTA	Trade policy.	Intra-regional tariffs.
CU	Trade policy.	Intra-regional tariffs, CETs.
CM and CMU	Broader coverage of economic policy (to facilitate the 'four freedoms': movements of goods, services, capital, and labour).	Intra-regional tariffs, CETP (i.e. CET with joint regime of NTBs), competition policy, employment policy, fiscal policy, growth policy, industrial policy, monetary policy, science and technology policy, sectoral policy, structural policies, regional policy.
EU	Social policy.	Rights to education, employment, shelter or housing, health, social security systems.
TEU or PU	System of political organisation and governance.	Civil liberties (life, speech, movement, association), political liberties (system of elections), rule of law, etc.

Source: Based on Matambalya (2011).

Notes: CET: common external tariff; CETP: common external trade policy; CM: common market; CMU: common market with monetary union; CU: customs union; EU: economic union; FTA: free trade area; NTB: non-tariff barrier; PTA: preferential trade area; PTCA: preferential trade and cooperation agreement; PU: political union; RTA: regional trade agreement; TEU: total economic union.

a total economic union (TEU), also referred to as a political union (PU). Other states which evolved into and give expedient examples of PUs are largely federal states, for example Austria, Canada, the Federative Republic of Brazil, Germany, the Republic of South Africa (RSA), and the United States of America (USA).

As in the case of the USA, Brazil and the RSA, the union between Tanganyika and Zanzibar did not follow a slow and systematic process of integration of formerly independent states. It did not go through one stage after another as depicted in Table 10.2, but instead it leapfrogged all the stages to create the URT as a PU.

Theoretically, a PU as the highest stage should embody all the dimensions of integration: trade integration, integration of other economic dimensions, social integration, and political integration. Expressed differently, besides full economic convergence, there should be a high degree of integration of the systems of political governance and organisation. Harmonised, though not necessarily identical, political governance standards would be used in the union, and joint political organs of the state, such as the presidency and Parliament, would be established.

In this context, as a form of regional integration, the URT is associated with an economic surplus, stemming from a full integration of the product markets, that is, the markets for goods (or tangible products) and services (or intangible products), as well as full integration of the factor markets, that is, markets for labour and capital.

The former (full integration of markets) is guaranteed through internally oriented trade policies, such as total elimination of tariffs, and harmonisation of internal business practices. Moreover, there is a single regime of externally oriented trade policy, the common external trade policy (CETP), whose key elements are a common external tariff (CET) regime as well as a common regime of non-tariff measures (NTBs).

The latter (full integration of factor markets) is guaranteed by the full mobility of capital through investments, and full mobility of labour. In addition, gains come through equalisation of prices and of wages (i.e. differences in wages and prices between geographical regions disappear or decrease).

If the PU triggers an equitable sharing of socio-economic benefits, the economic development indicators (e.g. investments in various areas of the economy, economic output triggered by investments, etc.) and social development indicators (e.g. diverse human development indicators) of the parties to the union will also tend to converge.

Moreover, integration theory is broadly conceived to take account of complementary development indicators, including achievements in cultural and political integration. Hence, in the assessment of the benefits of a PU, some of the questions of inquiry include whether the URT is developing a common national identity, and how the cultural tolerance and harmonious coexistence of cultures (i.e. cultural diversities) are managed, where the question is not so much to develop a mono-cultural society, but to achieve a society that believes in and practises tolerance of cultural diversity.

According to integration theory, we can tentatively conclude the following:

1   Dysfunctionality concerning any of the major aspects of the integration agenda (economic, social, political) will be a possible source of dissatisfaction with an integration mission, and the dissatisfaction can in turn trigger secessionist sentiments.
2   The shallower the level of integration, the less complicated it is for the parties to integration to separate.
3   From a legal perspective, the treaty establishing a regional integration scheme (which is in essence a constitution, in the case of PU) may have an 'exit clause', allowing a dissatisfied party to exit from the scheme. The Treaty of Lisbon, for instance, introduces an exit clause allowing members which want to withdraw from the European Union (EU) to do so. Likewise, the constitution of the URT of 1977 (which was in force as this chapter was written) permits the dissolution of the union, conditional upon support by two-thirds of all members of Parliament from mainland Tanzania and a two-thirds majority of all members of Parliament from Tanzania Zanzibar.

Forces underlying state disintegration from the perspective of secession theories

Secessionism has been addressed by many theories. The pertinent theories can be divided into two broad categories: remedial rights only theories and the primary rights theories. The following sub-sections highlight the content of each of these theories.

Remedial rights only theories

According to the remedial rights only theories, a group has:

1   general rights to secede if and only of it has suffered certain injustices, for which secession is the appropriate remedy of last resort (Buchanan 1997);[4]
2   special rights to secede if: i) the state grants the right to secede, such as in the case of the secession of Norway from Sweden in 1905; ii) the constitution includes the right to secede, as in the case of the 1977 constitution of the URT, which was the applicable constitution at the time this chapter was written; iii) the agreement by which the state was created permits secession, as was argued by the southern states of the USA in their (unsuccessful) attempt to secede (Buchanan 1997).[5]

So here the right to secessionism is tied to at least one of the four conditions: the right is a remedy to injustice (e.g. Zanzibar seeks secession from the URT to remedy an injustice); the unified state grants the right (e.g. the URT grants Zanzibar the right to secede); the constitution grants the right to secede (e.g. the constitution that created the URT grants Zanzibar the right to secede, in which case, as mentioned above, the constitution of the URT of 1977 permits the resolution of the union if such sentiments are supported by two-thirds of all members of Parliament from the mainland and a two-thirds majority of all members of Parliament from Zanzibar); or the agreement by which the state was created permits secession.

Primary rights theories

According to the primary rights theories, legitimate secession is not limited to being a means of remedying an injustice. Hence, certain groups can have a (general) right to secede, even in the absence of any injustice (Buchanan 1997).

There are two kinds of primary rights theories to secede: ascriptive rights theories and associative group theories. The ascriptive rights theories are based on the nationalist principle, according to which every 'nation' or 'people' is entitled to its own state. According to the associative group theories, if a majority group favour independence in a referendum[6] then they must be allowed to secede (Buchanan 1997).

Empirical assessment of nation building and state disintegration in the United Republic of Tanzania

Observations related to regional integration practices

In the area of regional integration, practice appears to diverge from theory in one critical aspect: there are not many cases of systematic regional integration progressions that have gone through the various stages as postulated in theory and ended up in PU (see Table 10.2). In fact, the most advanced scheme – and the only one to have advanced beyond the stage of a CM – and thus the most frequently cited is the EU.

However, if we consider the option of a PU formed by leapfrogging stages and creating single nation states, then we come up with several successful examples and a few unsuccessful ones. Such federal states as Canada, Brazil, Germany, South Africa, and the USA exemplify successful endeavours. Examples of failed cases include the Union of Soviet Socialist Republics (USSR), Yugoslavia, Senegambia, and the United Arab Republic (UAR).

Therefore, in attempting to practically relate nation building and secessionism to regional integration schemes, it is instructive to make a distinction between a PU on the one hand and shallower levels of integration (henceforth defined to refer to stages of integration below a TEU or PU) on the other hand. This gives a good base for comparisons.

Overall, the collapse of regional integration schemes can be attributed to diverse economic factors and political factors, which limit the benefits of the initiatives. However, these are not the sole triggers of collapse, as unbridgeable cultural differences can have the same effect.

Observations in relation to practical manifestations of secessionism

Practical experiences show that secessionism is triggered by two important rational justifications: social exclusion and poor governance. The discussion below elaborates further.

Social exclusion as a justification and trigger of secessionism

Social exclusion is a multi-dimensional phenomenon, which exists in many forms. It can manifest itself through unfavourable exclusion or unfavourable inclusion (i.e. it signifies unfavourable differential treatment through inclusion or exclusion). There have been and still are ample examples of access to state power being defined along the lines of age, caste, coalition of groups, ethnic group, gender, ideology, occupational hierarchy, race, religious group, regional origin, social position, and so on. Table 10.3 outlines some examples of social exclusion practices which possess the potential to trigger conflict, including feeding the sentiments for secession.

Moreover, social exclusion permeates all spheres of human interaction: cultural, economic, political, and social. Typically, the power-dominating group or coalition of groups exert domination over others politically, economically, and culturally. In practice, this translates into a denial of opportunities to the excluded individuals and communities:

Table 10.3 Examples of social exclusion practices

Dimension	Practical examples
Caste	In India this is also institutionalised through the Hindi religion. Africa's two most known cases are Burundi and Rwanda, both of which pit the tendentially dominant Tutsis against the Hutu (see Ziyauddin 2009; Thorat and Sadana 2010).
Ethnic group	In Turkey, the dominance of the Turks over the Kurds is a well-known case. Africa's two most known cases currently are probably the divide between the dominant Kikuyu and other groups in Kenya and the Shona–Ndebele divide in Zimbabwe, though the phenomenon is in fact widespread in the continent.
Race	This was common in the colonial states in Africa, Asia and the Americas. Race-based social exclusion has also been a major test in the many states which resulted from a colonisation of the 'New World', such as Brazil and the USA.
Religious group	Examples include India (marginalisation of Muslims) and Somalia (marginalisation of Christians) (see Ziyauddin 2009).
Region of origin	Nigeria's military dictatorships of the 1970s, 1980s, and 1990s provide good examples.
Coalition of groups	Nigeria is a good example. Coalitions of regional and religious groups have worked together to minimise social exclusion and bring about some stability.

Source: Based on a cross-section of literature, including: Ekeh (1975); Englebert (2000); Herbst (2000); Deng (2002); Abidi and Hussain (2009); Ziyauddin (2009); Thorat and Sadana (2010).

1   to exercise civil liberties, including the right to participation in the political process and the right of association;
2   to access social services, including the right to education and learning, the right to health care, and the right to decent housing;
3   to earn a livelihood, including the right to paid employment and the right to practise entrepreneurship;
4   to access and utilise natural resources, including the right to ownership and commercial exploitation of such natural resources as land.

Often social exclusion, which can be experienced by anyone, takes the form of persecuting the excluded, especially if they dare to demand their rights (see Deng 2002).

Thus, one of the main triggers of secessionism is that the state is often 'hijacked' by one group or by a coalition of groups. Owing to rampant social exclusion, the African state is usually perceived as being more culturally alien to its populations than most states in other regions of the world (Ekeh 1975; Englebert 2000; Herbst 2000). In this regard, one fact often goes unmentioned: though cultural colonialism by former colonial powers is usually blamed for this situation, in post-colonial Africa internal colonialism of one African group by another has emerged as an equally serious challenge.

Poor governance as a justification and trigger of secessionism

Poor governance is one of the major triggers of secessionism. Many African countries are vulnerable to this weakness. Though their institutions, rules and formalism make them nominally qualify as democratic, in reality they tend to fall far below the required threshold to the practice of democracy. Governments and their instruments of state power, such as security organs (police, army, and intelligence services), often act as instruments for profiling, discrimination, and exploitation. Examples include:

1   the monopoly of opportunities by an oligarch, typically with the members of the oligarchy exhibiting an insatiable desire to control and determine the lives of the citizens;
2   acting with impunity in grand and petty corruption;
3   suppressing civil liberties;
4   suppressing political freedoms and so on.

Overall, poor governance alienates part of the society (which can be a minority or majority group) and makes it believe that it is being targeted and marginalised in the running of the affairs of state. The ensuing dissatisfaction can feed secessionist sentiments.

There are many practical examples of this happening in the world. Nigeria's Biafra is a case in hand. Thus:

Founding Tanzanian president Julius Nyerere cited such exclusion as justification for his recognition of Biafra in its botched secession from Nigeria. He argued that 'Tanzania has recognised the state of Israel and will continue to do so because of its belief that every people must have some place in the world where they are not liable to be rejected by their fellow citizens.'

(Ndulo 2013)

Zanzibar and mainland Tanzania: decolonisation and union

As a modern nation state, Zanzibar was a product of Arab imperialism in Africa. It is estimated that the Arab merchants sailed to the area in the eighth century. They went there to look for 'human commodities' (i.e. slaves) and other commodities (e.g. ivory).

Zanzibar became popular as a base for traders plying the seas to Africa, the Arabian and Persian peninsulas, China, Europe, and India. Its strategic position made it suitable for re-supplying the explorers, and as a trading post and gateway to continental Africa, and it became a hotly contested post during the great seafaring and exploration era.

The Portuguese empire was the first European imperial power to gain control of Zanzibar, ruling it for nearly 200 years. The first Portuguese to reach the territory was the explorer Vasco da Gama, who arrived in 1498. At first the Portuguese coexisted peacefully with the Arab colonisers who were already there. This changed in 1503, when a ship commanded by Rui Lorenço Ravasco went to Unguja Island. The Portuguese subdued the Arab ruler of Zanzibar, the Mwinyi Mkuu, forcing him to grant the Portuguese access to Zanzibar, to provide Portuguese ships with food and water, and to pay tribute to Portugal. Mombasa and Pemba islands were captured in 1505 and 1506 respectively. During the sixteenth century the Portuguese took control of the coastal strip in present-day Tanzania and Kenya and built forts. They are also credited with founding Zanzibar Town in 1560.

The Omani Arabs and the Portuguese waged many wars for control of the territory. The Oman Arabs re-captured Unguja in 1652, while the last Portuguese were expelled from Pemba in 1695. Their last stronghold, Fort Jesus in Mombasa, was taken in 1698. In 1725 the Omani Arabs inflicted major defeats on the Portuguese, to remain the unchallenged rulers of Zanzibar (as well as the other important trading ports of that era, most notably Kilwa, which forms part of present-day mainland Tanzania or Tanganyika). Apart from the isles of Unguja and Pemba, the greater territory of Zanzibar of that time also embraced a ten-mile coastal strip of what is today mainland Tanzania and part of mainland Kenya.

Under the Omani Arabs' rule, Zanzibar became a key port and centre of the slave trade. In 1784 Zanzibar was annexed by and became part of Oman. To consolidate Arab power, in 1841 Sultan Seyyid Said moved his capital from Muscat to Zanzibar, bringing with him many Arab settlers. In 1856, the Sultanate of Zanzibar was separated from the Sultanate of Oman. Zanzibar became a British mandate.

The Zanzibar revolution was inspired by the conspiracy between the British and the Arabs to hoodwink the Africans. In utter disregard of the election results that gave victory to the Afro-Shiraz Party (ASP), the British granted 'independence' to the Arabs through the Zanzibar Nationalist Party (ZNP) on 12 December 1963. Together with an African-dominated but Arab puppet party, the Zanzibar and Pemba People's Party (ZPPP), the ZNP governed the island from 1961 to 1964. The actual power though was vested in the person of the Arab ruler, Sayyid Sir Jamshid bin Abdullah Al Said.

The deception by the British and the Arabs was to last for only 33 days. On 12 January 1964, the local African revolutionaries led by the ASP launched a successful revolution, overthrowing the sultan and his Arab government. The revolution's military commander was John Gideon Okello, an African revolutionary from the Lang'o community in Uganda. The ASP leader, Abeid Karume, became the chairman of the Revolutionary Council, president, and head of state, and Abdallah Kassim Hanga became the vice-president.

The region that eventually became Tanganyika and later mainland Tanzania attained the status of a distinct geographical and political entity following the partitioning and colonisation of Africa amongst European imperial powers. Indeed, the name Tanganyika only came into use after German East Africa was transferred to Britain as a mandate by the League of Nations in 1920. After the union with Zanzibar in 1964, Tanganyika has mainly been referred to as mainland Tanzania.

The process that ended in the colonisation of Tanganyika started with exploration of inland Africa by imperial European powers in the nineteenth century, which intensified in the aftermath of the Congo Basin Conference, also known as the Berlin Conference, of 1884.

Led by Karl Peters, who formed a company called Deutsch-Ostafrikanische Gesellschaft (German East Africa Company), the Germans began annexing the territories in 1885, with the approval of the imperial German government. A formal treaty, which created the official borders separating Tanganyika and Zanzibar, was signed between Germany and the United Kingdom in 1890. Eventually, in January 1891, the German government assumed direct control of the colony. After Germany lost the First World War, Tanzania was placed under the UK as a trustee territory of the League of Nations in 1918.

A peaceful struggle for independence was led by the Tanganyika African Association (TAA), which in 1954 was renamed the Tanzania African National Union (TANU). It participated in elections for the legislative council in 1958 and 1959, in which two-thirds of the seats were reserved for non-Africans. However, when in 1960 that restriction was removed, TANU overwhelmingly won the election, taking almost all the seats. Thus, Tanganyika attained its internal rule on 9 December 1960, with Mwalimu Julius Kambarage Nyerere as prime minister. It became a republic on 9 December 1961, and Nyerere the country's first president.

The union between Zanzibar and Tanganyika was concluded on 26 April 1964. The United Republic of Tanzania was thus born.

Economic development saliencies of the present-day United Republic of Tanzania

In order to support the analysis with empirical evidence, Table 10.4 depicts some figures which give invaluable clues about Tanzania's endowment with human and natural resources, and its performance in terms of socio-economic development.

Resource endowment

Tanzania is well endowed with diverse natural resources. Table 10.5 shows selected indicators of endowment with and access to natural resources of the URT in comparison to the other four member states of the EAC. Notably, the country dominates East Africa in terms of population, land mass, forests and woodland, inland water masses, permanent pasture, agricultural land, tourism attractions, and fishing grounds. With direct access to the Indian Ocean and a coastline of more than 1,400 kilometres, it also has ample marine resources.

The country also has several mineral belts where different commodities are produced, including tin, phosphates, iron ore, coal, gemstones (diamonds, tan-

Table 10.4 Comparable resource endowment and socio-economic development indicators

	Welfare indicator	Tanzania	Mainland	Zanzibar
1	Land area (square kilometres)	885,803	883,343	2,460
2	Inland water area (square kilometres)	123,000	123,000	0
3	Population (2012 census)	44,928,923	43,625,354	1,303,569
4	Population density (persons per square kilometre)	51	49	530
5	Total life expectancy (years)	56	56	60
6	GDP per capita (US$) (2010)		551	561
7	Electricity installed capacity (million kwH) (2009)	956	828	128
8	Households with access to electricity (%) (2010/11)	17	16.4	39.7
9	Households with access to safe drinking water – rainy season (%) (2010/11)	43	42	86
10	Households with access to safe drinking water – dry season (%) (2010/11)	50	49	84
11	Average literacy rate for overall household (%)	73	73	69
12	Households with roof of main building made of traditional roofing materials (grass, leaves, mud) (%) (2007, 2008)	49	49	35
13	Household using traditional pit latrines (%) (2007, 2008)	85	86	39
14	Households with three meals per day (%) (2007, 2008)	45	45	40

Sources: NBS (2010, 2013a, 2013b).

Table 10.5 Selected indicators of endowment with and access to natural resources

Total of the five EAC countries		Country's share of the regional resources (%)				
Variable	Sq. kms	Country	Landmass	Permanent pasture	Forests and woodland	Inland water masses
1 Permanent crops	37,392.44	Burundi	1.6	1.56	0.14	1.9
2 Arable land	138,758.94	Kenya	33.0	35.56	30.27	11.9
3 Permanent pasture	592,245.20	Rwanda	1.5	0.0	0.00	1.2
4 Forests and woodland	564,157.36	Tanzania	50.2	59.84	59.68	52.6
5 Other	372,791.58	Uganda	13.7	3.03	9.91	32.3
Total	1,705,345.52					

Source: Author, using data from various sources.

zanite, green tourmaline, etc.), gold, and nickel. Natural gas is abundantly available and already being produced, while there are indications of the availability of oil (both on land and offshore) as well.

According to government estimates, about 90 per cent of Tanzania's minerals – including gold, diamonds, and gemstones – are yet to be exploited (see KPMG 2012).

Economic integration policies and real economic activities

By all measures, the economies of mainland Tanzania and Zanzibar are highly integrated through the entire value chain (from investments to production to trade) and function as one. There is a largely free flow of goods, services, and investments between the two parts of the union. Zanzibar has particularly benefited from this integration. Many small business owners, particularly in Dar es Salaam, come from Zanzibar's Pemba Island. The owner of Bakhresa Group, one of the biggest companies in Africa, also hails from Zanzibar. The entrepreneur used mainland Tanzania as a launch pad for his now regional businesses, extending as far as Burundi, DR Congo, Malawi, and Rwanda (http://bakhresa.com/).

This situation is promoted both by natural factors (the two parts of the union are neighbours) and by the integration or harmonisation of policies that was made possible by the articles of the union. Though the process does not always run smoothly, experts from both sides of the union tend to work together in drafting those policies that concern union matters. They also exchange notes on policies concerning non-union matters, to ensure that they are highly harmonised. In addition, the union ministries employ people from both sides of the union.

Economic performance

Generally, the country's economic performance has not matched its resource potential. This can be proved with the assistance of many economic performance indicators. For instance, the country is still listed by the United Nations as a least developed country (LDC), with a GDP per capita that remains below the average for Sub-Saharan African (SSA) countries (see Figure 10.2), many of which are far less resource endowed.

Furthermore, empirical studies show that, though in recent decades the country's economic growth has accelerated, it did not translate into inclusive economic and sustainable development. Neither did the experienced growth create enough jobs, nor lay down the foundations for the structural change in the economy essential for sustainable and meaningful growth (see Research and Analysis Working Group 2009; Skarstein 2010).

Thus, the headcount poverty declined by only 2.4 percentage points between 1991 and 2007, compared to over 20 percentage points in Ghana and Uganda (Treichel 2005: 17; Hoogeveen and Ruhinduka 2009: 2). Hoogeveen and Ruhinduka (2009: 64) also show that the actual number of poor people has been increasing yearly, in spite of improvements in other aspects of people's lives (e.g. education and health care).

This is generally because, in addition to being driven by the wrong factors, the growth is partly not organic. The former is proven by reliance on the commodity boom. The latter is confirmed by the significant role of both foreign direct investment (FDI) and aid injections.

Another area where the union has not been successful is in significant movements of labour. This is because generally the URT has a very high unemployment rate.

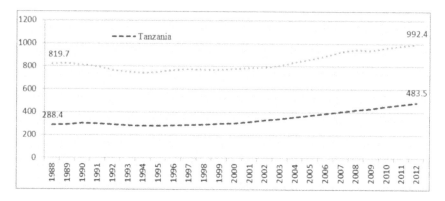

Figure 10.2 Evolution of GDP per capita: Tanzania versus Sub-Saharan Africa

Source: Author, based on WB (2013).

Note: In US $ (at constant 2005 prices).

Moreover, greater integration of the economies of the two parts of the union is hindered by underdevelopment of key productive capacities, such as entrepreneurial, knowledge and skills, organisational and institutional, physical infrastructural, technological, and financial resource capacities.

Overall, from an economic development perspective, the URT exhibits many factors that would seem to fuel dissatisfaction: extremely low GDP (see Figure 10.3), unequal access to opportunities, high unemployment, and so on. These malaises are exacerbated by such malpractices as emergent oligarchic tendencies that intensify unequal access to opportunities, mismanagement of the economic heritage, and embezzlement of public resources through rampant corruption. In short, it is a country where endemic and pervasive poverty exists in the midst of wealth, owing to bad management of the economic development agenda. That the country has remained remarkably stable and relatively peaceful has little to do with the economic performance. Presumably stability can be attributed to trust in a state system, the foundation of which was laid down by the country's founding fathers, Mwalimu Julius Nyerere and Sheikh Abeid Aman Karume. The current generation of the political elite have continued to benefit from the legacy left behind by the founding fathers and the goodwill associated with it.

Unfinished business of the economic management agenda

The URT has come a long way and posted a number of achievements. However, there are cracks and gaps in the system that indicate the venture's unfinished business. Obvious gaps in the economic management agenda include the lack of constitutional safeguards for the economic interests of indigenous and local

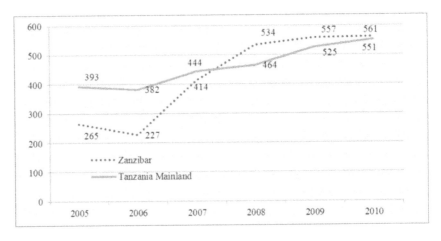

Figure 10.3 Comparable evolutions of GDP per capita

Source: Author, based on NBS (2011).

Note: In US $.

communities, gross mismanagement of the economic reform and transformation process, territorial fragmentation of economic policies, the disconnection of economic management institutions, and territorial fragmentation of the real economies.

Constitutional omissions on the safeguarding of the economic interests of indigenous and local communities

Owing to the lack of relevant constitutional safeguards, the naively conceived economic reforms that were carried out by the post-Nyerere governments grossly encroached on the economic rights of indigenous and local communities. Ironically, acts like the expropriation of land from indigenous and local communities, in favour of foreign investments, and the corrupted process of divestiture represent repetitions of the evils of colonialism.

Moreover, the resultant non-inclusive economic growth has compounded the problem. With a GDP growth rate of more than 6 per cent consecutively from 2005 to 2013, the URT is one of the fastest-growing economies in the world (AfDB 2014). However, while a small class of oligarchs from the ranks of the civil service, politics, and business are emerging, socio-economic and abject poverty is growing to unprecedented levels for large parts of the population, both on the mainland and in Zanzibar. These trends provide ideal political ammunition, not only for Zanzibar secessionists, but also for opposition political parties on both sides of the union.

Mismanaging the economic reform and transformation process

Another feature which is associated with the mismanagement of the economic reform and transformation process is the conspicuous emergent 'internal colonialism'. In this connection the corrupt elite, either acting on their own or colluding with international interests, have tended to behave like 'internal colonialists' to drain off their country's strategic resources, such as minerals, agricultural land, and state-owned enterprises, through dubious deals. Examples abound where such valuable assets as mines, state-owned enterprises, and land are sold at spot prices. Concrete scandals include the Buzwagi mine deal and the radar purchase scandal (see http://www.ippmedia.com/frontend/index.php?l=44677). In some but not all cases, they have led to the resignation of political leaders.

Noteworthy also is the fact that, although these types of misconduct have polluted the politics of the URT since the second-phase government, they generally went unpunished. President Jakaya Mrisho Kikwete – the fourth-phase government's president – has finally followed in the path of leaders from Malawi, Nigeria, South Africa, and Zambia by bringing to justice individuals alleged to have been involved in corrupt deals (http://seratz.blogspot.se/2008/12/who-is-next.html).

Assessed in the context of mainland Tanzania–Zanzibar relations, these events, which are almost exceptionally perpetrated by mainlanders, have alarmed the Zanzibaris and served well the interests of secessionists. The debate on autonomous ownership of potential oil resources for Zanzibar has, at least in part, been impelled by these facts.

Assessed from the perspective of Tanzania as a whole, these events have also had an impact. The corrupt elite involved in the scandals usually do not come from the affected communities, and this has enhanced the sense of 'internal colonialism', where Tanzanians from one part of the territory misuse their offices and positions in government and the civil service to steal resources from another part of the territory.

Unfinished business in the integration of economic policies, economic management institutions, and real economic activities

One of the characteristics of the URT is that it is a union of two countries, and there are union matters and non-union matters. Typically, policies dealing with non-union matters are not integrated and may additionally not be adequately harmonised. A good example here is that of intellectual property (IP), where there exist two parallel and interdependent regimes for the management of the intellectual property system (IPS): one for mainland Tanzania and one for Tanzania Zanzibar. While neither part of the union has an IP policy, there are parallel processes to develop them. In many cases, lack of policy integration causes operational problems, and leads to dissatisfaction and well-founded as well as ill-perceived complaints in Zanzibar.

Institutional integration is one of the factors which in many cases lead to dissatisfaction. Here too there are institutions which deal with union matters and those which deal with non-union matters in both mainland Tanzania and Tanzania Zanzibar.

Again, let us use the example of IP. In mainland Tanzania, the administration of industrial property rights is largely done by the Industrial Property Division of the Business Registrations and Licensing Agency (BRELA). Complementary administration services, such as those related to counterfeit and fair competition, are provided by the Fair Competition Committee (FCC). Zanzibar has its system of IP administration and other elements of the IPS. Hence the Office of the Registrar of Industrial Properties is anchored in the Ministry of Legal and Constitutional Affairs.

Nominally, institutions dealing with mainland Tanzania and Zanzibar matters are expected to maintain close working relations and, where necessary, coordinate their actions. However, turning intention into practice can be a challenge. For instance, since the particularities of the union are not known to the international community, there are visible uncertainties over the participation of Tanzania Zanzibar in international organisations dealing with IP. In many instances, invitations are sent to only the URT institution, which has jurisdiction on mainland but not Zanzibar matters, thus excluding Zanzibar from the process.

By and large, the economy of the URT functions as one, save for fractionalisation due to inadequate degrees of domestic market integration and domestic market development. The major existing challenge is that it is a lot more difficult for mainlanders to open up businesses in Zanzibar than the other way round. There are complaints that usually FDI has easier access to Zanzibar than to the mainland.

Social development saliencies of the present-day United Republic of Tanzania

Social development indicators

Table 10.4 also presents several comparative social development indicators: total life expectancy, labour force participation, households with access to electricity, households with access to safe drinking water, the average literacy rate for overall households, percentage of households with the roof of the main building made of traditional roofing materials, percentage of households using traditional pit latrines, and percentage of households with three meals per day. These figures contain no evidence of a clear trend of advantage of the mainland or Zanzibar over the other.

The prevailing situation disqualifies discrepancies in social benefits between the mainland and Zanzibar as a justifiable trigger of Zanzibar's secessionist sentiments.

Social cohesion

Social cohesion and stability are among the biggest achievements of the URT which have led to political stability. In this regard, the country is conspicuously an exception to the patterns of violence and instability in Africa (see Kessler 2006; BTI 2012). Given the presence of numerous destabilising factors, such as high poverty and unemployment, a large youth population, and regional insecurity, the URT's exceptionalism merits an explanation. What are the correct explanations? There is a broad consensus that the social, political, and economic policies adopted by the post-colonial government have created a political culture that is largely responsible for peace and security. As hypothesised by Kessler (2006), a 'self-perpetuating set of norms, values, and institutions has fostered widespread acceptance of national identity and rejection of political violence as being "un-Tanzanian"'.

Nevertheless, one of the areas where the integration between the mainland and Zanzibar appears to lag behind is in terms of social cohesion and identity. Though generally mainland Tanzania does not have a problem with state identity, the situation in Zanzibar is still a sensitive one. In Zanzibar, defining citizenship and who qualifies to be a citizen has remained a politically relevant and sensitive issue since the revolution of 1964. The situation is partly so because of the diaspora population residing in Oman and other parts of the world after running away following the revolution.

Cultural saliencies of the present-day United Republic of Tanzania

The ethnicity dimension

With more than 100 indigenous tribes as well as diaspora populations from all corners of the world, culturally Tanzania is a country of great ethnic diversity. The multi-ethnic identity is more pronounced in mainland Tanzania, where most of the population reside.

Zanzibar's ethnicity situation is slightly different, in the sense that, as proportions of the total population, there are stronger representations from the Asian diaspora, in the form of Persians (from Shiraz), Arabs (largely from Oman), and Indians.

However, one of the URT's hallmarks is that its multi-ethnic nature has so far not been a serious problem. Overall, the country appears to have a critical mass of anti-ethnocracy tendencies. Hence, ethnicity does not seem to be strong negative force influencing the interactions between parties to the union which could lead to its disintegration.

The religious dimension

Tanzania's multi-culturality in terms of religion is also more pronounced in mainland Tanzania. Here, the overwhelming majority of the population fall into one of the three big religious blocs: Christians, Muslims, and believers in traditional African religions. Minority religions such as Hinduism and Bahai also flourish.

In stark contrast (where most estimates put the population of Muslims in mainland Tanzania and Tanzania as a whole at around a third of the total population), in the case of Zanzibar about 97 per cent of the population is Islamic, a situation that makes it almost mono-religious.

Ostensibly, the one cultural factor which might prove to be Tanzania's Achilles heel, if not properly handled, is alien religions. Like most other African countries which were conquered and colonised by outsiders, the URT is also a country where alien religious culture has a strong influence on indigenous cultures, to the extent of influencing relationships not only among local communities (within both parts of the union), but also between the two parts of the union. For example, any religious scuffles that have been recorded in the past have been between the two major religions exported by outsiders to the region: Christianity and Islam. There are no cases of conflicts between the believers of these two religions and, for instance, the believers in traditional African religions (these constitute a large bloc, by various estimates accounting for about one-third of the population). Neither has the country experienced conflicts involving the Hindu, Bahai, and other minorities.

Traditionally, in Zanzibar, as in most Islamic countries, political issues have in recent years tended to be linked to religious issues. This is probably to be expected, considering its strong Islamic identity. Religious sentiments seem to have systematically intensified in the aftermath of the liberalisation of the policy space to allow multi-party democracy. For instance:

1   It is believed that both government and opposition leaders from Zanzibar want to join the Organisation of Islamic Cooperation (OIC). As long as Zanzibar is part of the union, such a move would make a country, the URT, with a minority Muslim population a member of an Islamic community of countries. The union government, which since the union was created some 50 years ago has been handling the matters of mainland Tanzania, is secular-oriented. The mainlanders oppose joining the OIC, and the union government has consistently refused to allow Zanzibar to join.

2   Some circles in Zanzibar would like to introduce laws based on the Islamic religion – the *sharia* – into the legal system of the URT. This stance too is alarming for most mainlanders. Despite the fact that only a small, radicalised minority of Muslim fundamentalists want an Islamic theocratic 'sharia' Zanzibar state, the precedent could trigger a domino effect and lead to unforeseeable complications.

3   Some of the radicalised minority of Muslim fundamentalist groups in Zanzibar have resorted to sporadic violent actions to drive their point home, by targeting attacks (e.g. bombing and setting on fire) on churches, institutions associated with the mainland, tourist centres, and Zanzibar state installations. Scores of Christians and their leaders have been assaulted and killed. Several such incidents have been carried out in recent years, particularly 2012 and 2013.

Mainland Tanzania has not been 100 per cent free of religious conflicts. In what seemed unthinkable events in the country of Nyerere and Kawawa, some religious conflicts did emerge, and even claimed people's lives, though they remained small in terms of scale. Some critics attribute these developments to the 'Zanzibar religious ripple effect on mainland'.

Therefore the country faces some real challenges in safeguarding the process of transformation to a culturally harmonious society, which started in the pre-independence era (e.g. as demonstrated through the solidarity during the Maji Maji rebellion against the German colonising power) and has since been progressing successfully. The question though is not so much to develop a mono-cultural society as to achieve a society that believes in and practises tolerance of cultural diversity.

Political saliencies of the present-day United Republic of Tanzania

From single-party to multi-party politics

In February 1990, Julius Nyerere, the architect of one-party rule, made an acrobatic U-turn and proclaimed that it was no longer treasonable to discuss the introduction of multi-party politics. He was quoted advising his party and government to get ready for changes: 'When you see your neighbour being shaved, wet your head to avoid a dry shave. The one party is not Tanzania's ideology and having one party is not God's will. One-party has its own limitations' (*Daily News*, 22 February 1990).

Subsequently, multi-party politics was re-introduced in Tanzania in 1992 through the Political Parties Bill, after being banned for decades. This change necessitated major constitutional amendments, which were contained in Act no. 34 of 1994. The amendments had significant implications for Zanzibar's influence in the union:

1   They introduced major changes to the position of vice-president. A system of running mate was introduced that paired a presidential and a vice-presidential candidate. Article 47(2) of the amended constitution of the URT stipulates that the vice-president shall be elected in the same general election as the president after being nominated by his/her political party. Furthermore, Article 47(3) provides that the president and vice-president shall come from different sides of the union. Thus, if the presidential candidate hails from mainland Tanzania, then the vice-president shall be appointed from Tanzania Zanzibar, and vice versa. The post of second vice-president of the URT was dropped altogether.
2   The president of Zanzibar ceased being automatically a vice-president of the URT and instead became a member of the union cabinet. This also meant that the president of Zanzibar and the vice-president of the union had to be two different people.

Discrepancies between the mainland and Zanzibar in the political reform process

Exercising political liberties in a culturally fractionalised society brings many challenges with it. The country has been going through the labour pains of the challenging process of democratic evolution. The following include some of the most notable issues:

1   Both parts of the union had to learn to deal with a mosaic of political associations, with different directions and ideologies – from those of the extreme left to those of the extreme right, from fundamentalists to moderates, from theocracists to secularists, from tribalists to integrationists, from regionalists to unionists, and even from racists to cosmopolites.
2   The responses to the challenges have not been identical, and instead the political developments have unfolded quite differently in the two parts of the URT. On the mainland, the transformation has been relatively more inclusive, peaceful, and smooth. The one-party system gave way quite peacefully to a multi-party system. In contrast, hitches marked the transformation in Zanzibar, which on several occasions translated into active violent clashes

and what many observers regard as sustained repression of opposition parties, especially the Civic United Front (CUF). As a result, political liberties have been relatively more restricted in Zanzibar (BTI 2012: 3).

Unfinished business of the political integration agenda: disputation of the constitution

The secessionist forces in Zanzibar disassociate themselves from the constitution of the URT, which they see as the constitution of mainland Tanzania. They emphasise that the discussion of the union constitution was never accomplished in 1965, a year after the creation of the union, as was originally intended, and rather that the Tanganyika constitution was amended to become the union constitution. The union constitution was subsequently amended several times.

Several real-life incidents are connected with the disputation of the union constitution: the assassination of Abeid Aman Karume in 1972, the replacement of Aboud Jumbe Mwinyi in 1984, and the replacement of Seif Shariff Hamad (chief minister of Zanzibar, 6 February 1984 to 22 January 1988) in 1988, ostensibly for his clandestine links with the Gulf states. Also notable was the insistence by Salmin Amour to be sworn in by the chief justice of the URT and not by the union president as required by the 11th Amendment of 1994 to the union constitution, as he did not consider himself subordinate to the union president.

Conclusions

From the perspective of integration theory, the dysfunctionality concerning any of the major aspects of the integration agenda (economic, social, political) would be a possible trigger of secessionist sentiments. To realise this, usually, a party wishing to secede can have recourse to the exit clause of the treaty establishing the regional integration scheme (which is in essence a constitution, in the case of PU).

From the standpoint of secession theory the right to secessionism arises from at least one of the four conditions: the right is a remedy to injustice; the unified state grants the right; the constitution grants the right to secede; or the agreement by which the state was created permits secession.

Consequently, the analysis in this chapter suggests that the collapse of regional integration schemes can be attributed to diverse economic factors that limit the benefits of the initiatives, and that such factors act in complementarity with political factors.

Applied to the case at hand, overall the URT exhibits many factors that would seem to fuel dissatisfaction: extremely low GDP, high unemployment, corruption, mismanagement of the economic heritage, embezzlement of public resources, and so on. The dissatisfactions are exacerbated by emergent oligarchic tendencies that intensify unequal access to opportunities.

The social development indicators show that the URT still has a long way to go to offer quality of life to its people. However, a comparison of the indicators for Zanzibar and the mainland disqualify discrepancies in social benefits between the mainland and Zanzibar as a justifiable trigger of Zanzibar's secessionist sentiments.

However, most of the elaborated economic and social development deficits do not afflict only a single party to the union, but bite equally on both sides of the union (Zanzibar and mainland). Indeed, they demonstrate the challenges facing the management of the economic and political development agenda in the multi-party era of the URT's politics, an issue that has become a major test to the union. Therefore, economic factors per se do not directly explain and cannot be the primary rationale for Zanzibar's secessionism.

One social aspect however stands out as potential ammunition for disintegration: presumably the diaspora community who left the country following the revolution of 1964 are among the *demandeurs* of change, and have been instigating a negative debate against the union.

Concerning the question of culture, the URT's multi-ethnic nature has so far not been a divisive issue, and the country appears to have a solid critical mass of anti-ethnocracy and anti-tribalism tendencies. Hence, ethnicity does not seem to pose one of the strong negative forces threatening unity between the parties to the union.

However, the religious dimension of culture is a more problematic issue. Religion is one of the most conspicuous traits which very categorically define the differences between the mainland and Zanzibar. The mainland is multi-religious, while Zanzibar is de facto mono-religious. This fact can be politicised and exploited by anti-unionists from both sides of the divide to steer the URT on to a disintegration course.

Finally, concerning the question of political integration, the evolution of political changes has effected a more telling polarisation of the political situation in Zanzibar than it did in the mainland. This made the Zanzibar opposition parties more prone to the agitation for a break-up of the union than their mainland counterparts. Imperatively, the modalities of managing the political competition process are among the forces that reinforce secessionist sentiments. Hence, as democratic economic and political governance takes root in Africa, a major factor for secessionist sentiments will be eliminated.

Likewise, the disputation of the union constitution, seen by many Zanzibaris as being a constitution of the mainland rather than the URT, has provided ever available ammunition for secessionists. The current process of drafting a new constitution could go a long way towards resolving the generations-old impasse.

Notes

1 The eight major integration blocs recognised by the AU are: the Community of Sahel-Saharan States (CEN-SAD), the Common Market for Eastern and Southern Africa (COMESA), the East African Community (EAC), the Economic Community of Central African States (ECCAS), the Intergovernmental Authority on Development (IGAD), the Economic Community of West African States (ECOWAS), the Southern African Development Community (SADC), and L'Union du Maghreb arabe (UMA).

2 The lesser regional blocs include: the Economic Community of Great Lakes Countries (CEPGL), the Southern African Customs Union (SACU), the Mano River Union (MRU), the West African Economic and Monetary Union (UEMOA), the Central African Economic and Monetary Community (CEMAC), and the Indian Ocean Commission (IOC).

3 These stages are derived from Jacob Viner's arguments of the 1950s, which were based on the vent for surplus. These arguments were later complemented by Béla Balassa's scholarly work in the 1960s.

4 Remedial rights only theories are seen as a supplement to Locke's theory of revolution and similar theories. However, there is a difference between the 'right to secede' and the 'right to revolution': a) The right to secede accrues to a portion of the citizenry concentrated in a part of a territory of a state. The object of the exercise is not to overthrow the government, but rather to serve the government's control of the seceding territory. b) The right to a revolution accrues when the government perpetrates injustices to the citizenry throughout, not just to a particular group of the citizenry concentrated in a given part of the territory.

5 The term 'right' in this case refers to one generated through promising, contract, or some special relationship.

6 This would apply in the case of Zanzibar.

Bibliography

Abidi, A. 2009. 'Dalits and Social Exclusion: Understanding the Conceptualisation', in K. Ziyauddin and E. Kasi (eds), *Dimensions of Social Exclusion: Ethnographic Explorations*. Newcastle upon Tyne: Cambridge Scholars Publishing.

Abidi, A. and Hussain, E. 2009. 'Social Exclusion and Marginalization of Muslims of Delhi: A Sociological Study', in K. Ziyauddin and K. Eswarappa (eds), *Dimensions of Social Exclusion: Ethnographic Explorations*. Newcastle upon Tyne: Cambridge Scholars Publishing.

AfDB. 2014. *African Economic Outlook 2014*. Abidjan: African Development Bank Statistics Department.

Ayres, R. 1998. 'Strategies and Outcomes in Post-Soviet Nationalist Secession Conflicts', *International Politics*, vol. 35, no. 2, pp. 135–63.

Bamfo, N. 2012. 'The Menace of Secession in Africa and Why Governments Should Care: The Disparate Cases of Katanga, Biafra, South Sudan, and Azawad', *Global Journal of Human Social Science: Sociology, Economics and Political Science*, vol. 12, no. 10, version 1.0.

Bideleux, R. 2013. 'The COMECON Experiment', in R. Bideleux and R. Taylor (eds), *European Integration and Disintegration: East and West* (pp. 174–204). London: Routledge.

BTI. 2012. *Tanzania Country Report*, Bertelsmann Stiftung's Transformation Index. Gütersloh: Bertelsmann Stiftung.

Buchanan, A. 1997. 'Theories of Secession', *Philosophy and Public Affairs*, vol. 26, no. 1, January, pp. 31–61.

Coggins, B. 2006. 'Secession, Recognition and the International Politics of Statehood', Ph.D. dissertation, Ohio State University, Columbus.

Deng, F. 2002. 'Beyond Cultural Domination: Institutionalizing Equity in the African State', in Mark R. Beissinger and Crawford Young (eds), *Beyond State Crisis? Postcolonial Africa and Post-Soviet Eurasia in Comparative Perspective* (pp. 359–84). Washington, DC: Woodrow Wilson Center Press.

Eerola, E., Määtanen, N. and Panu, P. 2004. 'Citizens Should Vote on Secession', *Topics in Economic Analysis and Policy*, vol. 4, no. 1, article 23.

Ekeh, P. 1975. 'Colonialism and the Two Publics in Africa: A Theoretical Statement', *Comparative Studies in Society and History*, vol. 17, no. 1, pp. 91–112.

Englebert, P. 2000. *State Legitimacy and Development in Africa*. Boulder, CO: Lynne Rienner.

Englebert, P. and Hummel, R. 2003. 'Let's Stick Together: Understanding Africa's Secessionist Deficit', Paper prepared for the African Studies Association 46th Annual Meeting, Boston, MA, 30 October – 2 November.

Gellner, E. 1983. *Nations and Nationalism*. Ithaca, NY: Cornell University Press.

Gwiazda, A. 1991. 'Disintegration of COMECON: New Perspectives for the Central European Countries', *Journal of East and West Studies*, vol. 20, no. 2, pp. 77–91.

Hannum, H. 1990. *Autonomy, Sovereignty and Self-Determination: The Accommodation of Conflicting Rights*. Philadelphia: University of Pennsylvania Press.

Herbst, J. 2000. *States and Power in Africa: Comparative Lessons in Authority and Control*. Princeton, NJ: Princeton University Press.

Hobsbawm, E. 1977. 'Some Reflections on the "Break-Up of Britain"', *New Left Review*, no. 105, pp. 3–23.

Hoogeveen, J. and Ruhinduka, R. 2009. 'Lost in Transition? Income Poverty Reduction in Tanzania since 2001', Unpublished background paper to Tanzania Population and Human Development Report 2009.

Huntington, S. 1993. 'The Clash of Civilizations?', *Foreign Affairs*, vol. 72, no. 3, pp. 22–49.

Kaplan, R. 1994. 'The Coming Anarchy', *Atlantic Monthly*, vol. 273, no. 2, February.

Kessler, I. 2006. 'What Went Right in Tanzania: How Nation Building and Political Culture Have Produced Forty-Four Years of Peace', Thesis submitted in partial fulfilment of the requirements for the award of Honours in International Politics and the African Studies Certificate in the Edmund A. Walsh School of Foreign Service of Georgetown University, May.

KPMG. 2012. *Mining in Africa towards 2020*. Johannesburg: KPMG Africa.

Lanyi, K. 1993. 'The Collapse of the COMECON Market', *Russian and East European Finance and Trade*, vol. 29, no. 1, Spring, pp. 68–86.

Lehning, Percy B. (ed.). 1998. *Theories of Secession*. London: Routledge.

Matambalya, F. (2011). 'Building the East African Common Market: Opportunities, Concerns, and Options', CSAE Conference Discussion Paper 468.

Muresan, M. 2008. 'Romania's Integration in COMECON: The Analysis of a Failure', *Romanian Economic Journal*, vol. 11, no. 30, pp. 27–58.

NBS. 2010. *Tanzania in Figures 2009*. Dar es Salaam: National Bureau of Statistics, Ministry of Finance.

NBS. 2011. *Tanzania in Figures 2010*. Dar es Salaam: National Bureau of Statistics, Ministry of Finance.

NBS. 2013a. *Population Distribution by Administrative Units: Key Findings*, 2012 Population and Housing Census. Dar es Salaam: National Bureau of Statistics.

NBS. 2013b. *Tanzania in Figures 2012*, June. Dar es Salaam: National Bureau of Statistics, Ministry of Finance.

Ndulo, M. 2013. 'Secession Bids in Africa are a Result of Poor Governance', *Business Day*, 16 January, http://www.bdlive.co.za/indepth/AfricanPerspective/2013/01/16/secession-bids-in-africa-are-a-result-of-poor-governance;jsessionid=C9D730AE9B2447917C5D 43D83062EE89.present1.bdfm.

Oloka-Onyango, J. and Nassali, M. 2003. 'Constitutionalism and Political Stability in Zanzibar: The Search for a New Vision', Unpublished report by Kituo cha Katiba.

Pomfret, R. 1997. *The Economics of Regional Trade Arrangements*. Oxford: Oxford University Press.

Research and Analysis Working Group. 2009. *Poverty and Human Development Report 2009*. Dar es Salaam: Research and Analysis Working Group of the MKUKUTA Monitoring System, Ministry of Finance and Economic Affairs.

Skarstein, R. 2010. 'Smallholder Agriculture in Tanzania: Can Economic Liberalisation Keep Its Promises?', in K. Havnevnik and A. Isinika (eds), *Tanzania in Transition: From Nyerere to Mkapa*. Dar es Salaam: Mkuki na Nyota Publishers.

Thorat, S. and Sadana, N. 2010. *Caste and Social Exclusion: Issues Related to Concept, Indicators and Measurement*, Working Paper Series, vol. 02, no. 01. New Delhi: Indian Institute of Dalit Studies and UNICEF.

Treichel, V. 2005. *Tanzania's Growth Process and Success in Reducing Poverty*, IMF Working Paper WP/05/35. Washington, DC: International Monetary Fund.

Viner, J. 1950. *The Customs Union Issues*. New York: Carnegie Endowment for International Peace.

WB. 2013. *World Development Indicators*. Washington, DC: World Bank.

Wong, Y. 1994. 'Impotence and Intransigence: State Behavior in the Throes of Deepening Global Crisis', *Politics and the Life Sciences*, vol. 13, no. 1, pp. 3–14.

Ziyauddin, K. 2009. 'Dimensions of Social Exclusion: An Introduction', in K. Ziyauddin and E. Kasi (eds), *Dimensions of Social Exclusion: Ethnographic Explorations*. Newcastle upon Tyne: Cambridge Scholars Publishing.

Part IV

Identity groups claiming secession that failed

11 Why Katanga's quest for self-determination and secession failed

Tukumbi Lumumba-Kasongo

General introduction: objectives and general issues

In this chapter, I examine the origins, causes, and implications of the process of post-colonial state formation and failure. The chapter is divided into five main sections. This introduction deals with the general issues about my objectives, general elements of the approaches and problematic developed, and the general concerns about secessionism; the second section is a brief political history of the nature of Belgian colonialism; the third section is a commentary on the form of the Congolese government; the fourth section deals with the nature of the Katangese secession; and the last section contains concluding remarks.

The post-colonial state formation in the Democratic Republic of Congo (DRC) has been constantly challenged by various forces of contestation and protest internally and externally with different social and ideological origins and agendas. However, the failures of the decolonization process and also of political transition can partially explain the Congolese crisis. The contestations and protests have created a high level of political violence, which has characterized Congolese politics since the 1960s. By and large, these movements can be divided between the claims of nationalists to create a united government, those of secessionists to advance separatism and those of federalists to create a weak, decentralized state.

In the middle of Cold War politics, which started around 1947, these movements were either supported and/or organized by the agencies of world capitalism and of international socialism. The intensity of the international ideological struggles in the Congo was due mainly to massive efforts of appropriation or control of the so-called perceived accidental geological 'scandal' by international capitalist forces. The country is so well endowed with natural richness that the capitalist European and American powers saw the cancer of Congolese destruction as being implanted in the heart of darkness of its land. However, for the Congolese, these possessions are not in any way a curse. The natural resources are the assets upon which progress has to be politically envisioned and economically constructed.

Thus, within these movements, there were expressions of predatory kinds of self-definitions or self-reconfigurations, and some demands for self-determination.

Most works on secessionism are based on the assumption that every secession can be explained by a single theory of suffering, a single theory of distance, a single remedy theory or a combination of either two or three of these theories. There must be grievances and allegations upon which the discourses or the movements of secessionism can be built. We have to identify the actors involved, discuss their goals, explain their functioning systems and project the outcomes of their intent.

In Katanga in the Democratic Republic of Congo, the secessionist tendencies and claims have been manifesting themselves almost quasi-permanently since 1960s post-colonial Congolese politics when Katanga was declared a sovereign independent nation-state on 11 July 1960. Since then, the secessionist discourse in Katanga has taken different forms, such as the political opposition of the so-called natives to the national government in Kinshasa, the ethnic protest against the people who are considered to be originally from the two Kasais (there are two Kasai provinces, namely Oriental Kasai and Occidental Kasai), or a power struggle instrument among some members of the Katangese political elite.

Regardless of the length of time that people have been under the management and imperatives of the contemporary African state and its apparatuses, some ethnic groups, individuals or clans still resist their functioning incorporation into the state or the nation-state for different reasons. Some scholars refer to the methodologies or approaches of the artificial or forced incorporation of the subjects as a part of the problematic related to the resistance. While the ways various groups were forced to coexist in Africa can be considered the causes of the demand or the struggle for separatism, the intensity of the African nation-state's works to create social cohesion – or something resembling it – has not eliminated the desires or the views of some groups to argue for separatism. Generally, these groups or individuals perceive themselves as being either culturally or historically different from other groups as defined by the state or as the victims of the state's operations and functions. Some of these differences may be considered to be perceptions rather than realities. How have these perceptions been created? Who created them, and to what end?

At the heart of secessionism in Africa lie issues about how a given group of people, based on their common history, sociology, physical looks, ethnicity, language, religion, or imagined social values and territoriality, may make favourable interpretations of self-determination and human rights in order to declare themselves as being unique or different and 'eligible' to separate themselves from their assigned or forced locations by the state. These people see different groups as 'others' or various groups may perceive them as 'others'. It is the dichotomy between 'we' and 'they' that has led to the propositions of separatism.

It is necessary to examine the topic of 'why Katanga's quest for self-determination and secession failed' within a broad analytical context of the nature of the Congolese colonial political structure, the conceptualization of the state and the post-colonial Congolese political crisis as reflected in the first Congolese Constitution (Fundamental Law). Who are those members of the Katangese elite who created this political formula? What are the political conditions that favoured it?

In this chapter I argue that the aim of 'self-determination' in Katanga was essentially originated from, and motivated by, the interests of the private corporations (multinationals) in Katanga, their managers and their associates. It is in the structure of the colonial economy that a small association of Belgian colons planned in the 1930s to make Katanga a special province of Belgium, autonomous from the Belgian Congo and associated directly with Belgium as a special province *d'outremer*. The idea was cultivated even earlier with the establishment of the giant mining company Union Minière du Haut Katanga (UMHK) on 18 October 1906 under Leopold II's Congo Free State. Furthermore, the idea of secessionism was strongly supported by the risk of balkanization of the Congo, the threat of which the prime minister Patrice Lumumba warned the Congolese in 1960.

As alluded to earlier, some political and economic forces and the predators of international capital perceived the size of the Congo and its natural riches as a problem for nation-state building and also an opportunity for the global market. Some members of the United States Congress, for instance, in various periods have looked into balkanization as a possible option that would create population and resources equilibrium in the region. Four decades later, this option was strongly supported through the war of invasion when Rwanda and Uganda coalesced, with their accomplice Burundi, against President Laurent-Désiré Kabila between 1998 and 2002. However, this time it was explored more in the East of Congo, another naturally endowed region with resources, than in Katanga. However, though the actors are not necessarily the same, the main reasons for supporting the balkanization are similar to those advocated for Katanga. The new and old actors belong to the same school of thought.

On 30 June 1960, the Belgian Congo, now the Democratic Republic of Congo, gained its political independence from Belgium, which started with the rioting in Léopoldville (now Kinshasa) in January 1959. Within a few weeks of independence, the government was confronted with a military mutiny and political struggles between the prime minister, Patrice Emery Lumumba, and the president, Joseph Kasavubu, regarding the nature of their respective constitutional responsibilities. This was the beginning of what was known as the Congo saga or crisis, the cornerstone of Cold War politics in Africa.

It should be noted that the resource-rich Katanga region (Shaba province) played a major role in establishing colonialism and a post-colonial Congolese political economy and state formation. Despite the fact that secessionism in Katanga institutionally failed in the 1960s and is not likely to succeed soon, it left scars on Congolese politics, which ethnic tensions and the sentiments of the Katangese elite to the Kasaians continue to fuel, leading to violent expulsions, pillage and the frequent killings of the people from Kasai since the 1960s.

On 11 July 1960, Moïse Kapenda Tshombe, the leader of the CONAKAT (Confédération des Associations Tribales du Katanga/Confederation of Tribal Associations of Katanga) political party, declared Katanga, then one of the six provinces of the Belgian Congo, an independent state. This was not simply the result of hatred between the Lunda ethnic group and other ethnic groups, notably the Baluba of Katanga, known as the BALUBAKAT in the new power configuration. The processes and intrigues of creating a separatist state with the status of a 'sovereign state', though highly combated, led to a civil war that lasted until 15 January 1963. As previously indicated, the evolution, origins and sponsorship of this secessionism, its agencies and its agents are strongly localized in the dynamics of the international political economy, the type of colonial machine built to create a Congolese federal state, and the instrumentalization of ethnicity by the newly emerging national political elite to seat its new power base.

Using a historical-structural approach and a critique of neo-liberal approaches and their assumptions, I study the following propositions, which are formulated in the form of hypotheses as to the reasons for the failure of this experience: firstly, the rise of a relatively strong nationalist consciousness in the need to build a model of a unitary political system among the new Congolese political elite; secondly, the internal constraints, especially the ethnic strife in Katanga, which weakened the common 'vision' among the Katangese elites, with the Congolese constituencies divided on the issue; thirdly, the cost for maintaining this new state, which should be linked to the Southern African economy and Western Europe, factored into failures; and, fourthly, the effect of Cold War bloc politics, which was part of the calculation of how power should be distributed in Katanga – for instance, although the United States had mineral interests in the Katanga–Rhodesia Copperbelt, it could not replace Belgium in the business and economic arenas in Katanga at large. It is within a weak and decentralized federal government that free market and free trade principles would be expanded better. Finally, what kind of self-determination are we talking about here? Could it advance the causes of the Congolese in building a strong, developmental, democratic state?

The issues raised about the case of Katanga are broadly and intellectually articulated. We ask what lessons we can learn from this specific case. Do the cases of South Sudan and Somaliland vary from the case of Katanga? What might they have in common in terms of the arguments and conditions that support secessionism?

On 2 August 2012, Dr Goodluck Diigbo, president and spokesman of the Movement for the Survival of the Ogoni People (MOSOP), declared the political autonomy of Ogoniland in Nigeria as he vowed: 'By this declaration of political autonomy, we, the Ogoni people, are determined to enforce the United Nations Declaration on Rights of Indigenous Peoples, without fear or retreat.' Jubilations continued throughout Ogoniland in southern Nigeria on this day. Although many nations and people in Africa probably did not take this declaration seriously, its content reflects an existing permanent problem in Nigeria. In Katanga (or, today, the Shaba province) in the Democratic Republic of Congo, there are some members of the Katangese elite who still continue to believe in secessionism. Although their arguments and propositions are weak and not supported by any major groups, they should be examined and understood in the context of the process and nature of a given state formation.

It should be noted that secessionism and the variables within nation-states have been coexisting since the Westphalian Peace Accords in Prussia in 1648, which is considered the foundation of the modern nation-state in Europe. These accords, which ended 30 years of religious war between the Catholics and Protestants, did not stop various European social groups and ethnicities from seceding from larger political configurations. It should be noted that not only small groups secede – there are cases of large social groups initiating separatism. Despite the fact that African politics had produced its own different forms of nations and states in the forms of kingdoms, autonomous political formations, and empires before the coming of the West, Africa at large inherited the current structures and political philosophy of the model of governance from the West through slavery, colonialism and the expansion of global capitalism.

Since most African countries gained their political independence, there have been many cases of claims of political separatism and secessionism. These claims have taken different forms: while some are essentially political, others are culturally based; some have been quasi-permanent, while others have been spontaneous and temporary; some have origins in the colonial states, while others have their origins in post-colonial politics. However, within the existing boundaries of the nation-state, its sovereignty and its territoriality, it is difficult to know exactly why a given group of people decide to be different and separate themselves from the majority of other groups in the assemblage of what we call the state or nation-state.

The search for self-determination as a universal principle and its utilization have led to power struggles even within civil society. Political parties as well as individual citizens have claimed self-determination. They feel free to interpret self-determination as they wish. However, it is important to contextualize how the claims have been made and where the political forces are located within the parameters of the nation-state and within the dynamics of the international political economy. Self-determination is not an absolute concept or dogma; it is a philosophical concept used by contemporary states, individuals and societies to acquire autonomy or independence. Thus, in order to understand its meaning, the context in which it is being used is as important as the concept itself.

A brief geo-politics and colonial political history of the Congo

The Democratic Republic of Congo is a vast country located in Central Africa, which occupies an area of 905,063 square miles (2,500,000 square kilometres). Its population is estimated at 63,660,551 people as of 2007. This population is divided into about 250 to 400 ethnic groups, which in addition to the contemporary system of governance – the state itself – are governed by various political systems, traditions and customs, which in many cases are not similar or identical to one another.

It is the most populous country in Central Africa and the fourth most populous on the continent. Not only does the Congo have an African geo-political importance in which the South and North, and East and West sub-regions meet, but it is slightly under a quarter the size of the United States of America or the size of the whole of Western Europe.

DRC is bordered by the Republic of Congo (Congo-Brazzaville) in the west, the Central African Republic in the north, South Sudan in the north-east, Uganda, Rwanda and Burundi in the north-east to east, Tanzania in the east to south-east, Zambia in the south, and Angola in the south to south-west. Lake Tanganyika forms most of the border with Tanzania.

The Democratic Republic of Congo, known during the colonial period as the Belgian Congo or Congo Free State, was not officially or formally a settlement colony, as compared to Algeria, Kenya, Zimbabwe or other countries in Southern Africa. This was essentially a colony of exploitation. As Jewsiewicki confirmed: 'Il n'y a pas de place au Congo pour une colonisation agricole européenne massive. Pour des raisons propres au mode d'exploitation économique, le Congo ne pouvait pas devenir une colonie de peuplement' (1979: 559).

Because of the tropical climate, the complex local and regional political structures, the local resistance to the imperial systems, and the weak financial enterprises of the colonial operations, among many other factors, a strategic decision was not implemented equally in all regions of the Congo. Many regions of the Congo had their islands or pockets of European settlers, such as in Katanga, Kasai, Kivu, Manièma and Oriental Province. These regions or provinces had amassed a relatively large population of Belgian settlers because of the climate and the availability of resources. Resources from the colony were intended to support the colonial enterprises.

The Congolese state formation was different from that of other colonies. During the Berlin Conference of 1884–85, which was organized by Bismarck of Germany, Africa was formally divided among the participating European monarchs. With his astute diplomatic skills, Leopold II managed to win international recognition from the European powers and the USA to obtain the whole country as a personal property. The conference lasted from 15 November 1884 to 26 February 1885. The major focus of the conference was on the question of the Congo and the freedom of navigation and commerce in the Congo Basin. By creating the Etat independent du Congo (EIC) – or Congo Free State (CFS) – Leopold II was recognized as its sovereign (Nzongola-Ntalaja 2002: 13–20). The first step in the state formation was establishing institutions which should make his enterprise profitable.

It should be noted that the Congo Free State was 80 times the size of the Belgian kingdom. Given the unpreparedness of the productive forces in Congo and lack of any serious training of labour, the king and his agents had to resort to primitive accumulation. Primitive accumulation refers to the use of excessive coercive techniques – such as torture, murder, terror and other inhumane methods – to compel the Congolese to produce or do whatever the colonial state required of them. Colonial or primitive accumulation is based on forced labour and free labour. It is a form of slavery in which the colonial state prioritized economically exploiting and competing for the control of natural resources, such as rubber, ivory and rich mineral resources, over state building and humanitarianism (Nzongola-Ntalaja 2002: 20–26).

The degree of atrocities was so high that other Western colonial powers in Africa felt that it was in their interests to intervene and that their so-called humanitarian mission in the Congo should be maintained, as the subjects reacting to these extreme abuses could challenge the system violently. Thus, France, Great Britain and the United States agreed to force King Leopold II to maintain the same rules, but strategically gave the control and management of the Congo to the Belgian state. The second step in the state formation was establishing the Belgian Congo in 1908. Managing the property and the colony was fused into a hybrid system in which the Belgian fundamental laws were used to make the colony commercially international but politically a firm subject of Belgium.

The colony was governed by a trinity complex of church, private companies and the state on the dogma of God, Good and Glory, with the motto of '*pas d'élite, pas de problème*' (no elite, no problem) governing the colony. As compared to other Western European colonial powers, Belgium did not provide any solid higher education to prepare the Congolese for the top responsibilities, except in the clergy. This is why, at the time of independence, there were fewer than ten university graduates in the whole country. Under a special contract between the king and the Catholic Church, the Catholic Church provided a pacifist but limited formal education to institute a specific form of Christianity (obedience and subordination) and its value system through which the Africans were asked to respect the colonial authority (Lumumba-Kasongo 1999: 82). This mass primary education was intended to enable the Congolese to read the Bible and, thus, respect the authority as described by the Bible.

Economically, the colony developed rich agricultural products (animals and plants) through semi-private corporations. It also had a wide array of minerals, including copper, diamonds and gold, strategic minerals such as uranium (for nuclear technology) and rare minerals such as niobium and tantalum (for space aeronautics) (Nzongola-Ntalaja 2002: 28–9).

The most important company was the UMHK's Shinolobwe mine, a giant mining company and the most important business enterprise in the Congo's economy. It was established on 18 October 1906 under Leopold II and with direct ties to foreign interests. The UMHK is a modern capitalist corporation formed by a group of interlocking partners. Prior to the formal establishment of the UMHK, the partnership had already created the Compagnie du Congo pour le commerce et l'industrie (CCCI), which constructed the Lower Congo railway in 1898 and other major public works in Katanga, the most economically important region of the Belgian Congo.

Another major corporation established shortly before the transfer of power from the Belgian king was the Compagnie du chemin de fer du Bas-Congo au Katanga (BCK), which built the rail networks that connected the international ports in Congo and the Portuguese-controlled Angola and Mozambique. These transportation systems brought commercial and administrative development to Congo (Nzongola-Ntalaja 2002: 30). The threat by the British South African Company (BSAC) and the ambitions of Cecil Rhodes, founder of the global diamond company De Beers (Meredith 2007: 162), which extended their commercial empire northward into the resource-rich Katanga region, as well as the Congolese resistance, mutinies and revolts prior to and after the assassination of

King Msiri of Katanga in 1891, resulted in a corporate venture called the Comité spécial du Katanga (CSK) which was formally established in 1900.

The CSK was the de facto landlord and government of Katanga province. However, with the blessing of Leopold II, Rhodes's partners succeeded in negotiating and collaborating with the CSK for mineral prospecting in Katanga, where the South African British managed to penetrate later (Nzongola-Ntalaja 2002: 31, 77–89). Situated in the complex networks of immense Western interests, the Katanga region was gradually incorporated into the larger global capitalistic system.

Thus, at the time of political independence, troubled by prolonged local resistance and nationalist revolts, and having partially lost control of the situation in Congo, the Belgians militarily intervened on 10 July 1960. The next day, Katanga province declared independence from Congo. In this event, Katanga's interior minister and a descendant of the Nyamwezi king Msiri, Godefroid Munongo, collaborated with the Belgians to expel all or most of the non-Katangese soldiers from the province, while retaining natives for military service. In actuality, the new native Katangese lords such as Tshombe and Munongo served as the African security front for the joint interests of foreign mining companies and white settlers (Nzongola-Ntalaja 2002: 98).

A comment on the Congolese post-colonial form of government

Since the Belgian Congo gained its nominal political independence and became, successively, the Republic of Congo, then the Democratic Republic of Congo, then Zaire and then the Democratic Republic of Congo again under the Third Republic, it has had among the most violent politics in Africa. The sources of the violence can be located in two major areas: 1) the nature of the Congolese political economy and its role in global capitalism; and 2) the nature of the Congolese state as a unitary state with federalist dysfunctional features. These two interrelated sources have caused uninterrupted clashes, manifesting themselves in various forms of Congolese maladies and occasionally full-fledged wars.

Some forms of government may be considered more conducive to the demands or struggles for secessionism than others. Thus, it is necessary to contextualize my arguments and propositions within the framework of the Congolese government's form in the early 1960s to understand its reactions to the secessionist movements, especially the Katangese one.

In the post-colonial politics of the Congo in the early 1960s, one of the major characteristics of the Congolese crisis was the ambiguity of its basic laws and their inability to articulate clearly the division of powers and the general rules that should govern society at large (Lumumba-Kasongo 2005: 55).

The first generation of the Congolese political elite (*les évolués*, or 'evolved' people) in the 1960s who debated the question of the nature of the Congolese state did not produce any consensus on this issue about federalism or a unitary system. They had common grievances against colonialism. However, as the prospects for independence quickly improved, the competition among members of the political elite increased, and their solidarity on the national question became secondary. They were deeply divided on the question of what kind of state the Congo should be. However, this issue has often been raised at moments of political transitions. From a generalized perspective, Lumumba's view of a unitary system has become more consolidated today among intellectuals than ever. However, practically, the Congolese constitutions are still ambiguous on the issue.

As indicated earlier, the DRC, then the Belgian Congo, gained its nominal political independence abruptly on 30 June 1960, after the violent uprising of 1959 by the Congolese masses in Léopoldville followed by a series of unplanned roundtable conferences between 20 January and 20 February 1960 and an economic conference between 16 April and 16 May 1960 in Brussels between the Belgian colonial authorities and the major Congolese political leaders. Patrice Emery Lumumba of the Congolese National Party (Parti National Congolais), who attended this conference straight from prison, emerged as the nationalist spokesperson. The Congo won independence with a deep institutional crisis, which led to military mutiny on 5 July 1960. This revolt had a great political impact on the formation and functioning of the First Republic. The first feature of the Congo crisis was the failure of the Fundamental Law to define adequately the division of powers within the executive branch. For instance, both the president and the prime minister could dismiss one another with a majority vote in the parliament. In fact, this is exactly what they did. The president was elected directly by universal suffrage, while the prime minister was elected in the parliament by the elected representatives.

DRC is not a federal state like Nigeria, Ethiopia, India, the United States of America or Canada. Since the 1960s, all of its constitutions, produced by three republics, have generally defined the forms of the Congolese state and government as a unitary system. Yet the DRC has always had federalist principles embodied in its constitutions. The Constitution of 2006, for instance, is more implicit on the specific division of powers between the national government and that of the provinces. Depending on the nature of the republic and its political regimes, these federalist principles and features have not been clearly actualized in a manner that could lead to political and policy consistency, accountability, predictability, and trust in the apparatuses of governance. The hybridity and eclecticism of the Congolese constitutions on the question of federalism or its national identity have contributed to political instability and political violence in the country.

Furthermore, it should be noted that the discussion on the principles and practices of federalism within the process of state formation in the DRC as defined through the constitutions is tragically an unfinished story and process. The debates on this issue have been limited, random, top-down and essentially partisan. That is to say, they have not been systematic at the national level. The assumption here is that the debates should deal with the question of whether federalism or a type of regionalism would be able to solve the crisis of both state and citizenry identities. This author thinks that the discourse should be a way of exploring the possibility of inventing alternative development models.

In general, the Congolese, especially ordinary people, do have low expectations for what the national government can or should do for them. Even without any survey on this issue, most people do not believe that the government has any prescribed commitment to fulfil its obligations and its constitutional duties to protect its citizens. Because of the Congo's large territorial size, the diversity of its ethnicities, and the nature of its state formation, the issue of the nature of the relationship between the sub-regional, provincial and national politics and development schemes is central in a study of state formation in the DRC. In some indigenous songs, folk cultural stories, professional organizations, urban clubs, wedding ceremonies or funerals, for instance, the issues of development are discussed within the centrality of local impetus or commitment. Loyalty to localism tends to be stronger than loyalty to the national government. In most cases, ethnic instinct prevails over civil citizenship duty, class interest or any national vision. All social movements have had some ethnic characteristics and claims.

The Congolese national political forces and the former colonial powers – King Leopold II, the Belgian state, the Catholic Church and the multinationals – also had historically substantive disagreements on how to construct the so-called Congolese nation-state and what its nature should be. These disagreements and their political and policy implications have permanently produced ambiguous articles of constitutions regarding the political identity of the country and that of its people – issues which have partially contributed to the violence associated with Congolese politics. No political figures and regimes within the three republics since 1960 have been able to solve definitively this ambiguity, despite some efforts, about the nature of the Congolese state as examined in this chapter.

Political unity has mostly characterized the dominant national discourse, despite the fact that separatist or secessionist movements have also challenged the concept of a unitary state, though not on the scale of Biafra in Nigeria. However, these movements in Africa are part of the forces that have permanently created political violence and instability since the 1960s. Thus, various interpretations by political elites of the Congolese constitutions have, as mentioned earlier, also favoured federalism. With this ambiguity, the dysfunctionality of the central government, and the manipulation of some politicians, some ethnic groups have been attempting to function as autonomous from the national government. This ambiguity of the Congolese constitutions on the issue of federalism has raised serious issues about the governance of Congolese society and some lapses in defining the question of civil citizenry (or nation-state citizenry versus sociological citizenry).

In sum, this study is contextualized within the framework of the Congolese crisis that has been manifesting itself by a deep political instability, civil wars, secessionisms, violent power struggles, foreign invasions, extreme economic underdevelopment, the collapse of the state, and currently a partial restoration of a peripheral state. All these dimensions are part of the crisis of the state and society.

The nature of the causes of the secession in Katanga and its failures

On 11 July 1960, Katanga was declared an independent country separated from the newly declared independent Democratic Republic of Congo of 30 June 1960. Despite the consolidated efforts by its supporters, this new state did not develop its own infrastructures and lasted only until 14 January 1963. Although the feelings about Katanga were mixed in international bodies, especially within Western powers and their allies, it was not officially recognized by the General Assembly of the United Nations, the United Nations Security Council or any international intergovernmental organizations. However, it had strong sympathetic forces and real supporters among the business groups and officials in Belgium, France, the United States and Great Britain.

In this section, I examine further and broadly the main causes that led to the secession in Katanga, the expectations of the leadership in Katanga and Belgium for the secession, and the consequences of such an enterprise in both the short and the long term in a nation-building process for a new country the majority of whose people were ill prepared for political independence as compared to those in the British and French colonies. I am not examining statistically causal analytical relations; rather, I am discussing the nature of the correlations between the internal and external factors that supported a political phenomenon, which is the secession. The context is part of this correlative analysis. Cold War politics influenced the perceptions of the political actors about the secession.

The general political context in the Congo toward the end of the 1950s was that of nationalism and the struggles for independence or general demands for social equality in major urban areas among the working class and the rising middle class. The *évolués* or *ayants droits* wanted to share with the Belgians or the *colons* the social advantages and privileges associated with their status.

Despite some gradual reforms and openness, the system did not incorporate their demands fast enough in terms of salary structure, medical entitlement and considerations related to the living standards of these new elites. In short, although the majority of the new elites were generally pacifist, many members of the Congolese elite were not satisfied with what was given to them and what was allowed by the system of governance. Many wanted to become like Belgians.

As indicated earlier, the causes of the secessionist movement in Katanga are not localized in one single event or factor, one single individual or one single ethnic group. Although its ideas might originate from one group or one individual, its realization was not done monolithically. Various interests were combined and organized, and thus were taken into account. However, it is necessary to identify and distinguish the major factors from the secondary or instrumental factors and balance the power of the actors within these factors. Thus, it is through the dynamics of the relations between the structures of the Katangese political economy, the structures of inter-ethnic relations within that economy and the overall structures of the Congolese state that this phenomenon was actualized.

It was not by accident that, less than two weeks after the declaration of independence on 30 June 1960, the mineral-rich province of Katanga seceded under the leadership of Moïse Tshombe. After his private businesses began to fail, Tshombe turned to politics from 1951 to 1953, and he became one of the few Congolese to serve on the Katanga Provincial Council. In 1959, he became president of CONAKAT, a political party that was supported by Tshombe's ethnic group, the powerful Lunda, and by the Belgian mining monopoly. As expanded below, while the Belgian state withheld formal recognition of the new state, substantial support for the secession originated in Belgium. For instance, the recruitment agencies of the mercenaries and other security forces were set up in Brussels to defend Katanga. Professor René Clemens of the University of Liège was invited to draft the Katangese Constitution, and Belgian advisers helped to establish new structures of administration.

Katanga was one of the richest and most developed of the six provinces of the Belgian Congo. However, this province was also special and had a special status both during the Congo Free State as a property of Leopold II and as a colony of Belgium. As indicated earlier, during the Congo Free State a committee called Special Committee of Katanga (Comité Spécial du Katanga) was established in Katanga to run the business of the UMHK until 1910. As René Lemarchand, citing *La situation économique du Congo Belge et du Ruanda-Urundi en 1958* (Ministère du Congo Belge et du Ruanda-Urundi 1959: 22), stated:

> With a population of 1,709,659 – approximately 13 per cent of the total population of the country – the Katanga was in 1960 one of the most sparsely populated of all the Congo provinces, but one where European settlers were the most numerous. The Katanga claimed in 1956 a non-African population of 34,047 – about 34 per cent of the total European population of the Congo – and a ratio of Europeans to Africans approximating 20.8 per thousand, as against 10.3 for the Leopoldville Province.
>
> (Lemarchand 1964: 233)

Under the colony, Katanga had a vice-governor general. It was only after the reforms of 1933 that Katanga became an effective administrative unit of the Belgian Congo in line with the other provinces. However, this province was endowed with minerals and a mild climate, and inhabited by many Bantu ethnic groups, some of which have a strong attachment outside the colonial boundaries, especially in Zambia.

According to Moïse Tshombe, the leader of CONAKAT, when he declared this independence, Katanga had to secede to avoid the chaotic situation of generalized instability created by the central government in Kinshasa, and another important factor was that he accused Patrice Lumumba, prime minister of the Congo, of being a communist. It should be noted that 50 per cent of the revenues of the Congo then came from the mining-related industrial activities in Katanga.

CONAKAT was one of the three main political parties in 1958–60 in the Belgian Congo. CONAKAT included several ethnic associations with different interests and cultures. These groups were: 1) Group of Mutual Association of Lunda Empire; 2) Association of Baluba of Katanga; 3) Association of Basonge; 4) Federation of the Tribes of Haut Katanga; 5) Association of Bena Maruga; 6) Association of Bahemba's People; and 7) Association of Minugu (Lumumba-Kasongo 1988: 103). The pro-Western regionalist Moïse Tshombe and his interior minister Godefroid Munongo led the enterprise of convincing the new political leaders of each group about the need for building a coalition against the unitary system. The party strongly believed that the mineral riches of Katanga should be kept for the 'genuine' people of Katanga. Tshombe was elected president of Katanga in 1960, as his party gained the majority in the provincial legislative elections. He was Christian, anti-communist, pro-West and a businessman.

Who were considered the authentic Katangese? According to Sauvy, cited by Tukumbi Lumumba-Kasongo: 'Authentic Katangese are natives of Katanga or inhabitants who have been settled in Katanga territory for at least two generations. These groups that are often considered to be the Katangese are Lunda, Baluba of Katanga, Bayeke, Basanga, Tshokwe, Batabwa, and Babenda' (1988: 103).

The Lunda, who have fairly strong traditional political and social structures, live in Southern Katanga, which is very rich in copper and other minerals. They also are in Zambia (Northern Rhodesia), with an economy that was dominated by the white settlers in Southern Africa.

CONAKAT was a reactionary party, which advocated a loose federation and Belgo-Congolese Community. For the purpose of this work, the nature and the goals of this party can be summarized in what Georges Nzongola-Ntalaja stated as follows:

> CONAKAT was founded on the premise that the wealth of the mineral-rich Katanga province should benefit mainly the 'authentic' Katangese or those native to the province. It was ironic that a person such as CONAKAT leader Godefroid Munongo, a descendant of the Nyamwezi ruler Msiri, could consider himself more authentic as a Katangese than the Luba-Kasai, whose ancestral homeland is in Katanga. In reality, the major theoreticians and financial backers of the party worked behind the scenes and were to be found among the white settlers. The settlers saw and used the party as a vehicle for their long-held dream of a separate political entity likely to close ranks with the white redoubt in Southern Africa.
>
> (2002: 100)

A few months before the independence of the Congo, CONAKAT was organized as the Rassemblement Katangais (Katangese Rally). In February 1958, white settlers created the Union Katangaise (the Katangese Union). The main objectives of this union included:

> Dividing the Congo into large autonomous regions, the promotion of the federation of these territories with Belgium as partners, and the

encouragement of immigration from Belgium as partners and other Western nations. This Western political association was the true engine behind the Katangese secessionism. It defended: (a) decentralization; (b) the re-establishment of the vice-governorship in Katanga; and (3) giving of the real autonomy to the provinces.

(Lumumba-Kasongo 1988: 103)

This secession was militarily protected for its short period by the Belgian military and mercenaries. It was viewed during the Cold War era as the work of private mining corporations in Katanga and their Katangese associates. The big problem is that the Katangese people did not have any public debates on this issue. Thus, it was an imposition from the top Belgian business and corporate elite down to the Katangese party elite.

It should be noted that the BALUBAKAT, which means mainly the Luba people of Katanga or people of Luba ancestry who mostly migrated from Kasai either by force or voluntarily in the nineteenth century, were divided concerning their support to the CONAKAT party. Some supported this party as others supported the unity system. However, at large BALUBAKAT in Northern Katanga also protested by declaring its small secession in January 1961, while the central government of Patrice Lumumba had collapsed, as Joseph Kasavubu had dismissed him. He also dismissed the president according to the then Congolese Constitution. Finally, it was Joseph Mobutu, the new military leader in Kinshasa, who made his first military coup d'état and arrested Lumumba on 14 September 1960. This is the beginning of the major manifestation of political disorder in the country.

However, the position of the central government in Kinshasa was clear even before Lumumba's assassination in Katanga on 17 January 1961 and also after he was eliminated from the political scene. Before he was dismissed, Lumumba was determined to crush the secessionist movements in both South Kasai and Katanga for the sake of the national unity of the Congo. The intervention of the United Nations peacekeeping forces was tempered with the internal domestic politics. Lumumba succeeded in bringing in Soviet military assistance, with which he intervened in Kasai. Without any success, he also travelled to the United States and Canada to request bilateral military assistance.

Thus, the responses to these secessionist movements, constitutional crisis and international ideological struggles created the proxy situation of war in the Congo between the Soviet Union and the United States. The Congo remained in this situation, whose contradictions led to the collapse of the state until the coming to power of Laurent-Désiré Kabila on 17 May 1997 and the flight of Joseph-Désiré Mobutu, who died in Rabat, Morocco, recognized as a villain.

Why did this secession fail?

This question is a very complex one in view of a multitude of issues involved during the time of Cold War politics. However, a few sets of suggested answers are possible in light of the interpretations of political events as articulated in this chapter. It is clear, based on facts, that the Katangese secession was philosophically and ideologically engineered in the structures of the Congolese political economy. The members of the special committee and their associates in Katanga and Belgium wanted to keep Katanga as a unique province in order to advance their particular interests and those of the mining industries. However, because of its foreign base, it did not succeed in transcending sufficiently its colonial roots. CONAKAT's alliance was not strong enough vis-à-vis the nationalist imperatives in the country at large.

Massive negotiations between the central government after Lumumba and that of Tshombe and the forceful role of the United Nations peacekeeping operation led to the final resolution of the dismantling of the secession. Thus, as a result of all these processes, in July 1964 Moïse Tshombe replaced Cyrille Adoula as prime minister of a new national government in Léopoldville with a mandate to end the regional revolts.

Among his first moves, Tshombe recalled the exiled Katangese gendarmerie and recruited white mercenaries, integrating them with the Congolese National Army (ANC). Many of these mercenaries had fought for Katanga when Tshombe was leader of the breakaway province.

Throughout 1961–62, Tshombe maintained the independence of Katanga. In December 1962 the UN launched Operation Grand Slam on Katanga's political and military infrastructure. This proved to be a decisive attack, and by January 1963 Elizabethville was under full UN control. This ended the secession of Katanga. However, the operation and negotiations would not have succeeded if there had been strong local alliances and organizations, and a committed political will among its leaders.

Furthermore, despite the weak and ideologically divided political leadership at the national level after the elimination of Patrice Lumumba, the consciousness of nationalism was strong among the new political elite and people. Even the reactionary Mobutu, under whom the secession was terminated, adopted the language of nationalism and unity of the Congo. He used the military support from the United States, France and other friendly states to stop any further attempts at secessionism.

The secession failed partially because the Western belligerents in the Congo started to understand that the secession was going to create a permanent or quasi-permanent war in the middle of a central Africa country with a lot of resources. All the interest groups and political forces could be the losers if a major war occurred, although later this war did happen in the East of the Congo.

There were no unified purposes in Katanga itself. BALUBAKAT and other small groups did not entirely support this initiative. Even members of CONAKAT themselves did not sell their cause well in the whole province. There was no referendum or large conference on the issue, only some propaganda against communism in urban and semi-urban areas.

Conclusion

The principle of self-determination as used by the secessionists in Katanga did not express the full rights of the Katangese for self-governing with the same benefits and citizens' rights for all as articulated in the Charter of the United Nations and that of the Organisation of African Unity. It was interpreted as rights of a segment of society and its white settlers to protect their privileges within the corporate world. It was instrumentalized to consolidate the goals and the means of a specific social class and not those of citizens at large. This is to say that the principle was not in itself a universal absolute principle that included unconditional rights, social justice, equality and freedom.

Rights of the white settlers and those of the Katangese elite did not mean rights of the ordinary people and those of workers and peasants. For instance, white South Africans claimed their rights for self-determination through the implementation of the apartheid laws and policies. Thus, the usage of the principle of self-determination has to be critically contextualized.

Secession in Katanga was essentially an externally designed phenomenon based on the imperatives of contemporary capitalism: it was initiated and supported by the corporate world. As such, this secessionist movement was not about creating political autonomy in Katanga. It was attempting to create a peripheral state or a client state of the Belgian state and global capitalism. Although inter-ethnic tensions did allow this secession to expand and to be heard internationally, these tensions were not about the superiority complex of the groups involved. They reflect issues related to the division of labour and labour migration, human resource allocations, and power relations within the colonial administration rather than the values of ethnicities within the Bantu way of life and traditional societies.

This secession ended partly because the masses of Katangese did not believe in it and partly because the strength of the views and claims of the unitary state supporters were stronger than those of the supporters of separatism. Furthermore, the supporters realized that they could lose more if permanent political instability or fear was going to be installed in Katanga. The scenario of the consolidation of a neo-colonial Congolese state in the control of the central government in Léopoldville without the radicalism of nationalists like Lumumba, with Katanga as a full member, was considered a better option than advancing with a secessionist agenda that could have a negative impact on the functioning of capitalism in the long run.

Bibliography

Chomé, J. 1966. *Moïse Tshombe et l'Escroquerie Katangaise*. Brussels: Editions de la Fondation Joseph Jacquemotte.

Debauw, A. 1920. *The Katanga*. Brussels: Veuve Ford, Lacier.

Gérard-Libois, J. 1966. *Katanga Secession*. Madison: University of Wisconsin.

Gérard-Libois, J. and Verhaegen, B. 1961. *Le Dossier de CRISP, Congo*, vol. 1. Brussels: CRISP.

Jewsiewicki, B. 1979. 'Le colonat agricole européen au Congo-Belge, 1910–1960: Questions politiques et economiques', *Journal of African History*, vol. 20, no. 4, pp. 559–71.

Lemarchand, René. 1964. *Political Awakening in the Belgian Congo*. Berkeley: University of California Press.

Lumumba-Kasongo, Tukumbi. 1988. 'Katanga Secession: Creation of the West or Manifestation of Congolese Internal Power Struggles?', *Journal of African Studies*, vol. 15, nos 3–4, Fall/Winter, pp. 101–09.

Lumumba-Kasongo, Tukumbi. 1991. *Nationalistic Ideologies, Their Policy Implications and the Struggle for Democracy in African Politics*. Lewiston, NY: Edwin Mellen Press.

Lumumba-Kasongo, Tukumbi. 1992. 'Zaire's Ties to Belgium: Persistence and Future Prospects in Political Economy', *Africa Today*, vol. 39, no. 3, pp. 23–48.

Lumumba-Kasongo, Tukumbi. 1994. *Political Re-Mapping of Africa: Transnational Ideology and the Re-Definition of Africa in World Politics*. New York: University Press of America.

Lumumba-Kasongo, Tukumbi. 1999. *The Dynamics of Economic and Political Relations between Africa and Foreign Powers: A Study in International Relations*. Westport, CT: Praeger.

Lumumba-Kasongo, Tukumbi. 2002. 'Reconceptualizing the State as the Leading Agent of Development in the Context of Globalization in Africa', *African Journal of Political Science*, vol. 7, no. 1, pp. 79–108.

Lumumba-Kasongo, Tukumbi. 2005. *Who and What Govern in the World of the States? A Comparative Study of Constitutions, Citizenry, Power, and Ideology in Contemporary Politics*. New York: University Press of America.

Meredith, Martin. 2007. *Diamonds, Gold, and War: The British, the Boers, and the Making of South Africa*. New York: Public Affairs.

Ministère du Congo Belge et du Ruanda-Urundi. 1959. *La situation économique du Congo Belge et du Ruanda-Urundi en 1958*. Brussels: Ministère des Colonies.

Nzongola-Ntalaja, Georges. 2002. *The Congo from Leopold to Kabila: A People's History*. London: Zed Books.

Nzongola-Ntalaja, Georges. 2004. 'The International Dimensions of the Congo Crisis', *Global Dialogue*, vol. 6, nos 3–4, pp. 116–26.

Peemans, J. P. 1973. 'Le rôle de l'Etat dans la mobilisation de la force du travail au Congo', *Contradiction*, no. 4, December, Brussels.

Reno, William. 1998. *Warlord Politics and African States*. Boulder, CO: Lynne Rienner.

Richards, Paul. 1996. *Fighting for the Rain Forest: War, Youth and Resources in Sierra Leone*. Oxford: International African Institute in association with James Currey.

Sauvy, J. 1961. *Le Katanga: 50 Ans Décisifs*. Paris: Connaissance de l'Afrique.

Verhulpen, E. 1936. *Baluba and Balubalisés du Katanga*. Anvers: Avenir Belge.

Young, C. 1965. *Politics in the Congo*. Princeton, NJ: Princeton University Press.

12 Nigeria and the Biafran war of secession

When national unity triumphs over self-determination?

Godwin Onuoha and Cyril Obi

Introduction

This chapter is based on a retrospective exploration of the failed attempt at secession from Nigeria by the Igbo ethnic group-dominated Eastern region, which in
May 1967 declared its territory the Republic of Biafra, fought a three-year war
for self-determination, but suffered defeat by federal forces in 1970. It also provides some explanations regarding the evolution of the concept of self-determination and its relevance to the understanding of certain political struggles in post-
colonial contexts. This provides a context for addressing the nature of the failure
of the Biafran secessionist attempt. It also analyses the role of the Nigerian government and the implications of the secessionist attempt for stability, peace security
and national unity in a post-civil war federal Nigeria, including drawing some
lessons from the encounter that may be relevant to an understanding of more
recent struggles for self-determination in Nigeria and other parts of Africa. This
assumes more significance in the context of the post-Cold War paradigm shifts
in the concepts of self-determination, sovereignty, territoriality and international
law.

The attempt at secession by the Eastern region of Nigeria (Biafra) marked the
climax in a series of events that had to do with the country's turbulent political history, particularly the ethnic coloration given to the coup and counter-
coup of January and July 1966, and the pogroms against ethnic Igbo living in
Northern Nigeria. These events partly demonstrated the failure of the Nigerian
state to forge cohesive inter-ethnic relations, its use of violence as a tool of governance, and the 'failure of the Nigerian security agencies to stop the pogroms
of 1966–67 in which thousands of Eastern Nigerians were killed in several
Northern Nigerian cities' (Ukiwo 2009: 12). Biafra's secessionist attempt was
based in self-determination, which implied that, having suffered persecution (in
the North) without any form of protection or redress, the Igbo of the Eastern
region felt that they would be better off leaving Nigeria to form another sovereign
nation.

The Nigeria–Biafra war emerged as one of the earliest post-independence
conflicts in Africa where the claim for self-determination gained attention,
both locally and globally (Johnson 1967). As Mayall (1999: 482) notes, 'of the
three Cold War secessionist crises which spilled onto the world stage (Katanga,

Biafra and Bangladesh), only the Biafran case was debated seriously in terms of the substantive meaning of self-determination'. The main issue in the war had to do with the Eastern region's right to self-determination by seceding from the Nigerian federation and declaring its independence as the Republic of Biafra. Writing shortly after the war, Nixon (1972: 473) argued that the Biafran case constituted, 'in its starkest form, the question of whether the concept of self-determination can have meaning in post-colonial Africa'. Although the collapse and defeat of Biafra in 1970 marked the end of the war, it also reopened the debate about the meaning, application and implementation of the principle of self-determination in post-colonial Africa.

Biafra's secessionist attempt presented the most critical challenge to the conventional understanding and interpretation of self-determination, which had earlier been widely perceived as being synonymous with decolonization or freedom from colonial domination. In that regard, self-determination was strictly interpreted as being limited to processes of decolonization and not relevant to intra-state or internal nation-building processes within post-colonial (multi-ethnic) African states. Some African states were of the view that Biafra's quest was incompatible with the goal of African unity, and the policy of the Organisation of African Unity (OAU) regarding the sanctity of European-delineated boundaries inherited at independence.

Many decades later, the Biafran case still assumes some significance in the context of the post-Cold War paradigm shifts in the concepts of self-determination, sovereignty, territoriality and international law. These include, but are not limited to, developments linked to globalization and global change (including the emergence of new states in the former Soviet Union, Eastern Europe and Africa), and the evolution of new norms (particularly the norms on non-indifference and non-recognition of unconstitutional changes in government) in the African Union (AU), which underline the reality that the struggle for self-determination will remain on the international agenda for some time to come. By drawing upon lessons from the Biafran case and its implications for the post-civil war Nigerian national unity project, this chapter contributes to the understanding of contemporary struggles for self-determination across Africa.

In setting about its task, this chapter is divided into six sections. The introduction provides a concise description of its objectives. The second is an analysis of the concept of self-determination, particularly the form it assumed in multi-ethnic post-colonial African states. The third section provides an in-depth analysis of Biafran claims to self-determination and the dynamics of secession in Nigeria. The fourth section explores the challenge to Biafra's claim to self-determination in three phases: internal dynamics and responses in Nigeria; intra-African responses and positions on self-determination; and the role and responses of the international community to Biafra's secession. The fifth section draws lessons from the Biafran attempt at secession for current struggles for self-determination in Africa, not least the resurgence of Biafran nationalism three decades after a victorious federal government had celebrated the triumph of the national unity project over the forces of separatist rebellion in Africa's most populous country.

The conclusion sums up the arguments and highlights what these developments portend for multi-ethnic states on the African continent.

Self-determination: understanding its evolution

Self-determination movements seeking to secede from states witnessed some complex and uneven developments in the course of the twentieth century. These have been linked to the evolution of the principle of self-determination during the eras of colonialism, decolonization, the Cold War and more recently the post-Cold War and the post-September 11 global order. The literature suggests that there have been three distinct phases in the evolution of the principle of self-determination (Lata 2004; Venugopal 2006). The first phase consists of the emergence of self-determination after the First World War, when the principle was associated with non-self-governing peoples under different empires and multi-national states. The collapse of the Habsburg, Hohenzollern, Romanov and Ottoman empires, the enduring implications of the outbreak of the Bolshevik Revolution, and the emergence of the Wilsonian democratic ideology based on self-determination of under-represented minorities of post-First World War Europe were all factors that combined to accord the principle of self-determination greater universal relevance. But it was the second phase of the 'evolution' of the principle of self-determination that turned out to have lasting consequences for African states. The 1941 Atlantic Charter and the 1944 Dumbarton Oaks proposals as affirmed by both United States president Franklin Roosevelt and British prime minister Winston Churchill declared the desires of the signatories to see that all peoples had the right to self-determination and that territorial adjustments must be in accordance with the wishes of the people concerned (Brinkley and Facey-Crowther 1994). Following the end of the Second World War, self-determination was included in the United Nations Charter, and between 1945 and 1990 self-determination became almost synonymous with the process of decolonization, as the administrative borders of several colonial territories and colonial possessions were remodelled into those of sovereign independent states.

In practical terms, the implementation and application of the principle of self-determination to the decolonization process witnessed a major challenge owing to the conflicting interpretations to which it was subjected by the victorious powers. On the one hand, the United States adopted a 'maximalist' approach to the principle by extending it to European colonial possessions, while, on the other hand, Britain, France and other European powers preferred a 'minimalist' approach and were not prepared to give up their colonial possessions owing to the prevalent feeling that these rights did not apply to Africans and other peoples under colonial occupation in Asia, the Pacific, South America and the Caribbean (Porter and Stockwell 1987: 103). Britain's wartime prime minister, Winston Churchill, argued that 'he had not become the King's First Minister in order to preside over the liquidation of the British Empire' (Porter and Stockwell 1987: 25). The British colonial governor in Nigeria, Bernard Bourdillon, was equally unambiguous about demands for African independence, arguing that the British did not anticipate any change in their colonial policy towards Nigeria (Njoku 1987: 180). France, realizing that the security of its colonial possessions were at stake, was also contemptuous of granting independence to its African colonies, as well as those in Asia, the Pacific and the Americas. The French position that self-government for its colonies was not an immediate consideration, not even in the distant future, was emphatically reiterated at the 1944 Brazzaville Conference of exiled French colonial governors from across the world chaired by General Charles de Gaulle (Deschambs 1970: 249). This position proved to be costly, as France withheld the right to self-determination to many of its territories in Africa and other parts of the world even when other European countries were giving up their colonial possessions for independence.

Given the nature of revolutionary changes on the continent and opposition to colonial rule, the interpretation of indigenous African rule as an expression of self-determination was upheld, and the possibility of intra-African domination was perceived as implausible. The fate of ethnic groups within newly independent African states was subsequently sealed by the dismissive attitude towards diversity and pluralism, and the nation-building project adopted by post-colonial African states that drew extensively on the Westphalian model, which demanded that the plurality and diversity of African ethnic groups must be subdued in order for these (homogenized) nation-states to emerge (Keller 1995: 622). The Cold War era witnessed the emergence of ethno-nationalist claims in various parts of post-colonial Africa, but these were rendered inconspicuous by the East–West ideological face-off, and the repressive policies of one-party or military regimes that held sway in most African states. In spite of these, the quest for self-determination persisted, in extreme cases assuming insurgent or secessionist dimensions that were increasingly steeped in sub-nationalist/ethnic, socialist or liberal ideologies. It was often associated with the quest of marginalized identity groups for their own autonomy, particularly in cases where they had been forcibly included in multi-ethnic states or separated from their kith and kin by the imposition of colonial boundaries.

The quest for self-determination received new impetus following the end of the Cold War and the collapse of state socialism in Eastern Europe and the Soviet Union. These developments were marked by the disintegration of large federations and multi-ethnic states such as the Union of Soviet Socialist Republics (USSR), Yugoslavia and Czechoslovakia. This wave of nationalist resurgence drew heavily on the right to self-determination to justify the assertion of minority rights within large federations, and contributed to the resurgence of hitherto suppressed currents of nationalism on a global scale. Under this wave of nationalist resurgence, the unification of Germany was achieved, 22 successor states emerged out of the ruins of the former USSR and Yugoslavia, and the Czech and Slovak republics voted to go their different ways.

The lessons from the renewed struggles for self-determination at the global level were not lost on national and local forces in Africa that had for long struggled for self-determination under very difficult conditions. The de-legitimization of one-party rule and military regimes in the face of a virtual disappearance of super-power rivalry and support for client African states meant that such states under pressure from their own citizens had to open up the political space to accommodate hitherto suppressed identity, including minority groups and movements. The democratic struggles which had been waged for decades in Africa, but had hitherto been perceived by ruling elites as unpatriotic acts of subversive elements seeking to derail the project of nation building, were now perceived as emancipatory projects for democracy, human rights and self-determination by the West (Ake 2000: 98).

Thus, the principle of self-determination was invoked in support of Eritrean independence from Ethiopia in 1991, the struggles of the oppressed African racial majority in apartheid South Africa which eventually culminated in the first multi-party elections in the country in 1994, and the independence of South Sudan from Sudan in July 2011. It is also a feature of the struggles for self-determination by ethnic minorities in Nigeria's oil-rich Niger Delta, particularly by groups such as the Movement for the Survival of the Ogoni People (MOSOP). Since the end of the Cold War in the late 1980s, various separatist movements either emerging or re-emerging, such as those in Senegal's Casamance province and Angola's Cabinda province, and Tuaregs in Mali and Niger, have challenged the authority and sovereignty of the state in various countries based on the principle of self-determination.

Biafra's claim to self-determination and the road to secession

There have been attempts at secession by various groups in the course of Nigeria's political evolution (Tamuno 1970). These tendencies crystallized within the framework of colonial politics, went on to dominate the outlook of nationalist and party politics and, consequently, laid the foundations for post-independence politics in the Nigerian public space. After independence in 1960, Nigeria's inter-ethnic power struggle was given a much broader appeal when it became a zero-sum contest and ushered in a host of other destabilizing crises such as the emergency rule in the Western region in 1962, the census crisis of 1962–63, the election crisis of 1964–65 and, finally, the intervention of the military on 15 January 1966 (interpreted as an Igbo-led coup) and a counter-coup (interpreted as a reprisal Hausa–Fulani/Northern-led coup) which followed six months later on 29 July 1966 and effectively marked the end of Nigeria's First Republic and federal experiment. In the ensuing crisis the Igbo ethnic group paid a huge price in terms of the loss of lives and property they suffered in pogroms in Northern Nigeria (allegedly in retaliation for Northern leaders killed by Igbo soldiers in the January coup). Different accounts suggest that the May and September riots of 1966 carried out by the mobs in Northern Nigeria resulted in the massacre of thousands of Igbo, and the displacement of more than one million survivors who returned to the Eastern region maimed, mutilated or demented (Nixon 1972: 477; Unoke 2010: 159). Though instigated by the perception that the military coup of 15 January 1966 was essentially an Igbo coup, the massacres of Igbo people living in the North in 1966 were not isolated events. Prior to independence, the Igbo population of Northern Nigeria had been victims of earlier massacres at different times during Nigeria's decolonization process between 1945 and 1953 (Ekwe-Ekwe 2007: 8). After the 29 July 1966 counter-coup masterminded by military officers of Northern origin, there were strong separatist feelings in Northern Nigeria. The Western region, foreseeing the possibility of a break-up of the Nigerian federation, warned that, 'if any region secedes, the federation as we know it shall cease to exist and Western Nigeria shall automatically become independent and sovereign' (*Africa Research Bulletin*, vol. 4, 1967: 777, cited in Nixon 1972: 478).

At the Ad Hoc Constitutional Conference convened on 12 September 1966, the leader of the Western region, Chief Obafemi Awolowo, reiterated this position by stating that, 'if the Eastern Region were allowed by acts of omission or commission to secede from or opt out of Nigeria, then the Western Region and Lagos must also stay out of the Federation' (*Africa Research Bulletin*, vol. 4, 1967: 776, cited in Nixon 1972: 478). On the part of the Easterners, it was assumed that, given the situation of the country and broad-based public opinion from other sections of the country, secession was the only legitimate option to follow. There were suggestions pointing to a unified position between the Western and Eastern regions, and the need to 'stand firm' or risk the potential of Northern domination (Nixon 1972: 479). From August 1966, Lieutenant-Colonel Odumegwu Ojukwu, the military governor of the Eastern region, had started mobilizing the people of the region through the periodic meetings of the Consultative Assembly in Enugu, the capital of the region, and through a series of mass rallies in major cities across the region. By 26 May 1967, the assembly had finally passed a resolution requesting the proclamation of independence, and mandated the military governor of the Eastern region 'to declare at the earliest practicable date Eastern Nigeria a free, sovereign and independent state by the name and title of the Republic of Biafra' (*Proclamation of the Republic of Biafra* 1967).

After a series of negotiations, disagreements and differences between General Yakubu Gowon (Nigeria's military head of state) and Ojukwu over the future of Nigeria and the political structure to adopt, there was the suspension of an orderly process of engagement. By then, it had become obvious that the Eastern region was convinced that further negotiations with the federal government would not be capable of resolving the crisis. The FMG lost its effective authority over the Eastern region, and the region seceded from the main federation, declaring its independence as the Republic of Biafra on 30 May 1967. Nigeria's military head of state, General Yakubu Gowon, who had indicated on several occasions that he would resort to the use of force in keeping Nigeria together, opposed Biafra's secession. With significant military preparations and guaranteed military superiority, the FMG maintained that the Eastern region was still part of Nigeria. On 6 July 1967 it embarked on what it referred to as 'police action', then 'military action' and finally 'full military action and war', resulting in the Nigeria–Biafra civil war and the eventual collapse of Biafra on 15 January 1970 (Osaghae et al. 2002).

Challenges to Biafra's claim

Internal dynamics and developments in Nigeria

The challenge mounted against Biafran claims can be articulated at two levels: legal and political. While the former consisted of an outright rejection of Biafran rights to self-determination, the latter consisted of the mobilization of the entire country based on the vision of a united, strong and prosperous Nigeria with brighter prospects for all its major and minority ethnic nationalities as opposed to what an independent Biafra offered. Indeed, it was on this basis that General Gowon and the federal government mobilized Nigerians to oppose the Biafran quest for independence (Nixon 1972: 488). In considering the Biafran quest for independence, it is important to note that, based on the 1963 population census of Nigeria, the Eastern region had a population of 12 million to 15 million, out of which the Igbo majority constituted 64 per cent, Efik and Ibibio 17 per cent, Annang 5.5 per cent, Ijaw and Ogoni 7.5 per cent, Ekoi, Yalla and Ukelle 3.4 per cent and others 2.5 per cent (cited in Nixon 1972: 480). For the reason that Biafra's secession included a cross-section of minority ethnic groups in the former Eastern region of Nigeria, the secession was depicted more as an Igbo ethnic rebellion rather than a war for self-determination for the entire Eastern region. This perception held sway despite the fact that Biafra's proclamation of independence clearly indicated that Biafra would not assert any form of independent Igbo statehood but would have a multi-ethnic character reflecting its multi-ethnic constituencies (Nixon 1972: 480). A notable aspect of the politics deployed by the Nigerian state in winning the war entailed the deconstruction of the Biafran secessionist attempt not only morally and ethically as a rebellion, but also politically and territorially. The latter strategy combined the use of state violence and the imposition of a total blockade of Biafra by air, land and sea which proved to be very costly in terms of the complete isolation of Biafra as the war progressed.

In a swift move aimed at checkmating Biafra's secession, on 27 May 1967, three days before Biafra's declaration of independence, the federal government by decree replaced Nigeria's four regions with 12 states. It carved three states out of the Eastern region, of which two states were allocated to the ethnic minorities of the Niger Delta. This move mobilized most elites of such ethnic minorities to oppose Biafra's claim to the oil-rich Niger Delta region, and further severed the strategic ethnic minority groups on the Atlantic shoreline from the Biafran project.[1] This move provided autonomous space for these elites to operate in, and the balance of power in the erstwhile minorities' areas (of the Eastern region) tilted quickly in favour of the national unity project and centralizing position of the federal government, as opposed to Biafra's separatist and decentralizing tendencies (Obi 2001: 24). The federal government also moved to co-opt elites and minorities from other regions into the Federal Executive Council, and cemented the alliance between government at the centre with minority ethnic groups in other regions, thus also welding the West and the Mid-West into a solid opposition to Biafra's bid for independence.[2]

Between 15 January 1966 when the first coup occurred and 6 July 1967 when the Nigerian civil war broke out, Nigeria experienced many twists and turns, some of which undermined Biafra's quest for an independent statehood. Nixon (1972) argues that a certain conception of Nigeria emerged, based first on the creation of 12 states out of the large autonomous four regions which had previously existed, and second on the proposition that out of this would emerge a strong central government and weak states. These features had fundamental implications for Nigeria in that they were meant to reduce regional rivalries and interests by vesting enormous economic powers and resources in the central government, and forestall the possibility of any single region dominating either the centre or other regions in the federation. These propositions reflected and aligned with the interests of different groups in the Nigerian federation. The first reflected the demands of ethnic minority nationalities and key issues in Nigerian politics dating back to 1956 when the Minorities Commission was set up to address the needs of the minorities in the event of independence. The second aligned with the long-held conviction not only of top federal civil servants and economic planners in Nigeria, but also of the United Kingdom and the United States, which were both concerned about their economic interests in Nigeria.

Based on this, in the Middle Belt (Central Nigeria), there appeared to be some kind of consensus between the leadership of the army from the region and General Gowon that Biafra's secession should be halted. Also, the political elite of the Northern region soon realized that a united Nigeria was not detrimental to Northern interests in any way. As these developments unfolded, a strong consensus emerged among the public, minority group leaders, the army leadership and the central government in Lagos that federal power and authority should be asserted to bring Biafra back into the federation. This led to the deployment of economic pressures, such as denying Easterners payment of their federal salaries, refusing to allocate financial resources that would enable the East to cater for displaced persons and refugees, and imposing a complete blockade on the region when it resisted federal authority. Within the Nigerian context, Biafra's secession was not considered in isolation, but its complete ramifications were weighed against the backdrop of various economic, political and military options that would accompany it.

From a Northern perspective, the prospects for future development depended largely on its relations with the South, and any political arrangement that would completely separate the North from the South was considered a disaster. The landlocked North considered that, with the South's access to the sea, the region was a critical factor in the economic development of the North, which depended on Southern ports for its economic ties to the outside world.

In 1956, Nigeria struck oil, and ten years later in 1966 it had become clear that the country possessed the greatest known petroleum reserves in sub-Saharan Africa (Diallo 1969: 25), most of which were located in the Eastern region. Given the decline in international prices for the traditional cash crop exports of the four regions, alongside the growing significance of increased oil exports, interests in gaining access to and controlling the new source of national revenue intensified.

Thus, the ruling elite at the federal level also interpreted the secession as a ploy to deprive Nigeria of access to these oil resources, and were concerned about what would happen if an oil-rich Biafra was allowed to exit the federation. This also explains the oil dimensions to the struggle for self-determination in Nigeria, in terms of both the economic viability of a secessionist Biafra and the agitation of the oil-producing minorities of the Niger Delta.

It is therefore no coincidence that one of the earliest actions of the FMG was to recapture the oil fields in the Eastern Niger Delta and enact decrees affirming federal (rather than regional) control of oil revenues. Both actions denied Biafra access to a source of revenue that would have been critical to its war efforts at home, while it also contributed to the decision of the world's powers to side with the federal government against a Biafra that represented little strategic or economic value to their national interests.

Western Nigeria has had a difficult history with the North when one considers the imposition of emergency rule by the Northern People's Congress (NPC)-led federal government on the region, which was under the control of the opposition Action Group (AG) party in 1962. Tensions also arose when Chief Obafemi Awolowo (the AG leader) and his close associates were arrested and tried for treason and jailed by the NPC-controlled federal government, and boiled over in the form of widespread violent protests against the massively rigged regional elections of 1965, which imposed an NPC-backed premier on the West. It was therefore a master stroke that one of the earliest actions of the Gowon regime was to free Awolowo and his associates from prison, and later offered Awolowo the position of finance minister in the federal government.

Thus Yoruba leaders in Western Nigeria were divided over the future of the region and whether the Eastern region should be allowed to secede, but the dominant view was one which opposed the secession of the East, as this would lead to an even more overwhelming domination of the West by the North. The Mid-West region, Nigeria's newest region and the only region created after independence, preferred remaining in a larger federation and was opposed to any kind of fragmentation, as this could prompt its larger and more powerful neighbours in the South (the Igbo and Yoruba) to re-absorb it into their regions.

African responses to Biafra's claim to self-determination

After independence, post-colonial Africa was immediately confronted with the challenge of whether the principle of self-determination was strictly limited to the process of decolonization or applicable to the internal political contexts in independent African states. Emerson (1964: 31) points out that new African states were opposed to any challenge to their colonially defined boundaries for fear that existing political arrangements on the continent might be swept away by a process of endless partitions. In a bid to forestall claims and demands along this line, African states discouraged post-independence territorial quests for self-determination by incorporating definite provisions in the Charter of the OAU in 1963, followed by the adoption of a resolution on colonial boundaries in 1964 (Organisation of African Unity 1964).

Quite clearly, there was no explicit reference to self-determination in the OAU Charter, but Article II of the Charter was unambiguously opposed to post-independence territorial claims by stating that one of the objectives of the OAU was to 'defend the territorial integrity and independence of member states'. In pursuance of this objective, Article III states that 'member states solemnly affirm and declare their adherence to [*inter alia*] respect for the sovereignty and territorial integrity of each state and its inalienable right to independent existence'. The provisions of the Charter thus became a guiding principle for intra-state relations in post-independence Africa, and where this principle was being challenged by self-determination claims the provisions of the Charter were invoked to reiterate implicitly and explicitly a clear rejection for post-independence self-determination claims, although there were explanations regarding the provisions of the Charter limiting its application and relevance to inter-state relations in Africa[3] and not to territorial changes occurring as a result of intra-national conditions.[4] But the real interpretation of the provisions of the Charter was manifested in the refusal of the organization to support the breakaway attempts of Biafra, Southern Sudan and Eritrea (Blay 1985: 150–51). The resolutions of 1964 provided a strong basis for the rejection of post-independence self-determination claims on the continent, and the responses of African states were generally geared towards supporting this position (Blay 1985: 152).

While the position of the OAU remained that of opposition to any form of territorial claims, by 1969 four African states (Gabon, Ivory Coast, Tanzania and Zambia) had broken ranks with the organization and accorded recognition to the Biafran government. At the annual summit of the organization in that year, President Julius Nyerere of Tanzania, who prior to this time shared the views of the 1964 resolution of the OAU, reneged on his views and urged his fellow African heads of state to abandon the commitment. Nyerere argued that colonial borders were accepted as a matter of expediency to enhance and facilitate inter-state cooperation, reduce opportunities for conflict, and harness and release the energies of African peoples for development purposes, and that the right of any government depended largely on its ability to serve its people. But, in a situation when a government can no longer perform these duties or protect the lives of its citizens, or when a specific group of people believe they are threatened by genocide, then such a government relinquishes its legitimacy and authority. For him, the same political considerations that inspired his support for the sanctity of existing territorial arrangements invariably amounted to what had inspired his support for self-determination (Kirk-Greene 1971: 429–39).[5] Nyerere's argument was compelling, unequivocal and honest, but the conventional wisdom at the time, which was also ironically conceded by the government of Tanzania, was that the recognition of Biafra amounted to a setback to Africa's goal of continental unity (Government of the United Republic of Tanzania, 'Case for Recognition of Biafra: Statement of the Government of the United Republic of Tanzania', 13 April 1968, cited in Kamanu 1974: 362).

The role of the international community

As time went on, the Nigeria–Biafra (civil) war ceased being an 'internal affair' and became an 'African affair', and eventually metamorphosed into an 'international affair' when the United Kingdom, the USSR, France, Portugal and to some extent the US took different positions on the conflict.[6] But the fact that the major super-powers of the Cold War supported the same side in the conflict was quite uncanny. Reports emanating from the Western super-powers in alliance with Nigeria's propaganda machine were that a dissident band of renegades led by a weird colonel in the Nigerian army were trying to secede forcefully from the Nigerian federation. It was also alleged that they did not have the support of the local population and that the Nigerian army with its superior firepower would crush the rebellion and complete the entire operation within ten days or two weeks at most.[7] Britain spearheaded the foreign support for the Nigerian federal government for obvious reasons. For the British, Nigeria was the 'rudder of black Africa', the pride of the Colonial Office, and the largest and most profitable of its colonial possessions on the continent (Diamond 2007: 345). A series of events suggests that the British rigged the federation in favour of the North,[8] and British influence in post-independence developments was markedly clear. Following the counter-coup of 29 July 1966, the Nigerian head of state, General Gowon, had publicly declared that Nigeria was unworkable and preparations were being made by the coupists to pull the Northern region out of the federation, but the British insisted on a federation and convinced them that it was in their interests to retain the structure as it was (Diamond 2007: 350).

The British, despite nationwide opposition to the Nigerian–Biafran conflict, embarked on a robust international political and diplomatic campaign throughout the period of the war which ensured that there was no official disapproval of the Nigerian state's handling of the war (Ekwe-Ekwe 2007: 5–6). The British supplied Nigeria with arms, ammunition and the technical assistance it needed to prosecute the war. Such was the situation that, as the war progressed with the massacre of the Igbo, the British prime minister, Harold Wilson, remained calm and informed Clyde Ferguson, the US State Department special coordinator for relief to Biafra, that he 'would accept a half million dead Biafrans if that was what it took to resist the secession' (Morris 1977: 122). Although no one expected the British to stay out of the conflict, some were surprised that it would be actively and directly involved in the 'acts of genocide carried out against the seceding Eastern Region' (Ekwe-Ekwe 2007: 8). British support helped Nigeria to pursue the war to its very bitter end, leading to the death of about three million people (Ekwe-Ekwe 2007: 12).

At the onset of the conflict, apart from the stocks left behind by the departing Nigerian army, almost half of Biafran arms were locally manufactured in Awka in the Eastern region. But this figure varied considerably as the war intensified and Biafra resorted to whatever means were possible to purchase arms in a desperate bid to survive (Diamond 2007: 343–4). The intensification of hostilities, the displacement of men and materials, and the sacking of the capital, first in Enugu and then in Umuahia, made local weapons production virtually impossible. As Diamond (2007: 343) points out, Biafra had mines, armour plates, short-range mortars, ammunition and dynamite, and it manufactured explosives from local stores of dynamite, all based on local resources or supplemented by ingredients purchased in Europe, and it also purchased or copied (where possible) electronic components from Europe and assembled them locally. The untold stories of the Nigerian–Biafran war are of the local ingenuity and intellect that underpinned the Biafran war efforts, and how the Biafrans initiated, built, operated and maintained these weapons in one of the most extraordinary war efforts in the history of modern warfare.

France had issues with Nigeria,[9] and it capitalized on the situation to support the Biafran secession and break-up of Nigeria. But the French government made no official arms sales and did not extend any grants directly to Biafra, and for the first 18 months of the war it was responsible for the supply of about 10 per cent of Biafra's foreign arms. Most of these came in through black market operations with the knowledge of the French government, but in the last year of the war the amount of French arms rose to about half of the total foreign arms supplied to Biafra (Diamond 2007: 343). Charles de Gaulle and Félix Houphouët-Boigny (the president of Ivory Coast) had both expressed their sympathy for the Biafran cause and were both stimulated by the prospects of a possible deterioration of British influence in Nigeria and the chance of opening up its vast oil fields to French and French-allied oil interests. French support for the Biafran cause proved to be very unpredictable, and it did not come as a surprise when it failed to recognize Biafra and subsequently reduced its arms supply drastically. Portugal supplied arms, ammunition and automatic weapons to both warring parties strictly based on commercial cash transactions. Supplies were made to Biafra directly from Lisbon, while supplies were made to Nigeria through commercially registered flights from Madrid through Las Palmas to Lagos (Diamond 2007: 344).

Unlike those of other external actors in the war, Soviet interests and support for Nigeria during the war were difficult to understand. Expectations were rife that the Soviets would throw their support behind the Biafran secession, not only for the purposes of exporting a revolution but also to gain a foothold on one of the continent's most strategic oil-rich territories. As Diamond (2007: 353–5) argues, the Soviets had to recalibrate their interests in the region based on realpolitik, and two key issues explain the Soviet support for Nigeria: religion and oil. Though overly simplistic, one of the main narratives of the war was that it was a conflict between the Muslim North and the Christian South. With the largest population bloc in Nigeria capable of subjecting millions of peasants to its authority the Soviets understood that the defeat of Biafra would guarantee Northern dominance, which it could profit from in the long run. The support for the Muslim North appeared to present the Soviets as champions of Islam and helped to solidify their relations with North Africa and the Middle East.

With regard to oil, there appeared to be a more straightforward and strategic calculation based on the fact that Nigeria had been an oil producer before the war, and its full potential was yet to be realized. The Soviets felt that keeping Nigeria intact and preserving their geopolitical influence in the country would serve their long-term interests. The Soviet position over the war inevitably extended the Soviet Union's confrontation with China, sparking off a confrontation between the former's geopolitical and strategic interests in the war and the latter's ideological commitment to the global proletariat and peasantry. At the end, Biafra did not gain any form of recognition from European states.[10] Diamond (2007: 344) points out that, apart from a group of non-political church charities (Joint Church Aid Group), the Czech and Chinese sources of arms, and half a dozen planes purchased through private Swedish sympathizers, Biafra was left entirely on its own. The United States under the Nixon administration regarded the war as falling within the British sphere of influence and supported the position of its closest ally.

Lessons from the Biafran experience

The Biafran experience underscores the relevance of self-determination to the quest for political autonomy by groups seeking to exit the territorial confines of post-colonial African states. Such agitation for a transition from perceived sub-national subordination to full nationhood has since Biafran times led to a mixture of success and failure in other African cases. Eritrea fought a successful war of liberation from Ethiopia, and South Sudan gained independence in 2011 following the holding of a referendum as laid down by an internationally recognized Comprehensive Peace Agreement that signalled the end of decades of war between the North and South Sudan.

Perhaps the most enduring lesson of the Biafran case was that an oppressed people in a post-colonial setting could legitimately use the principle of self-determination to claim nationhood. Beyond this, however, it laid bare the hard reality that a combination of local and international factors or actors is critical to the success or failure of secessionist attempts. Thus, the Biafran bid for independence not only posed a challenge to the Nigerian state, but also had implications for the quest for self-determination in other African countries, many of which learnt important lessons from the failure of the Biafran secessionist bid. Apart from the fact that the civil war took place at the height of the Cold War, with global powers supporting the federal side, the lesson was not lost on other groups fighting for self-determination in other parts of the continent. Subsequent struggles for self-determination in Africa worked assiduously at a higher level of sophistication to win local and international support from state and non-state actors.

A changed post-Cold War global context has not rendered the Biafran experience completely irrelevant to current struggles. The principle of self-determination remains relevant to the contemporary realities of post-Cold War Africa, although requiring new tactics, strategies and alliances. However, the international recognition of minority rights and the legitimization of international humanitarian intervention to save the lives of people whose rights were being violated or threatened by their own states have opened up the political space for both democratization and the quest for self-determination.

Even then, it has not resulted in the opening of the floodgates of new nations in Africa.

It is therefore not surprising that post-Cold War struggles for self-determination have resulted in a few success stories in the form of new states in Africa, such as Eritrea and South Sudan, even though cases like the Saharawi Democratic Republic and the secessionist attempts in Senegal's Casamance, Angola's Cabinda, the Tuareg area of Northern Mali and Niger, and Ethiopia's Oromo provinces have either stagnated or recorded no success. In the same vein, the two new states created following the collapse of central authority in Somalia – Somaliland and Puntland – have not been accorded any international recognition. What remains clear is that, in a post-Cold War world, the quest for self-determination continues to inform the nation-state project by seeking liberation for groups marginalized and oppressed within existing territorial boundaries. However, it remains a contested terrain on legal and political grounds.

Conclusion

Given that crises of citizenship and nation building continue to plague many multi-ethnic African states, the struggles for self-determination by oppressed groups remain at a crossroads. In a rapidly globalizing Africa where peoples, information and arms easily move across borders, the struggles for self-determination have assumed complex and transnational forms. Secession by groups is not only defined territorially but in part fuelled by non-state and trans-state actors. It also plays out in different parts of the world, particularly among diasporic communities, even if it means connecting with the 'homeland' from a long distance.

Two opposing views are at the heart of the debate on self-determination and statehood. While one school of thought advocates giving recognition and primacy to people's rights, the other supports upholding the state's territorial integrity. More paradoxical is the fact that recognition of people's right to secede has not solved internal problems within those states, and the sanctity of inherited colonial borders still remains a sticking point in continental conflicts. These developments should give pause for thought, particularly in the context of ongoing efforts at integration in all the regions of the continent, including the grand vision of a united Africa.

Forty-two years after Biafra, the Nigerian political space is littered with self-determination movements from different sections of the country, some seeking autonomy and other seeking outright secession from the Nigerian state. Of note is the agitation of the ethnic minorities of the oil-rich but impoverished Niger Delta for self-determination in the form of local autonomy and control over the oil producing in the region. Given the legacy of decades of military misrule – corruption, oppression of minorities and the circulation of power within a narrow elite since the country's return to civil rule in 1999 – several movements are pushing for the restructuring of the Nigerian nation-state project based on social justice, local autonomy, and the decentralization of power and resource control.

A major flashpoint of current self-determination struggles against the Nigerian state is the challenge posed by an assortment of neo-Biafran groups, the most prominent being the Movement for the Actualization of the Sovereign State of Biafra (MASSOB). Drawing on a prior idea of statehood and the failed Biafran secessionist attempt of 1967, the advent of MASSOB marks a shift in the tenor of ethnic nationalism by virtue of the fact that the movement entirely rejects a state-led process and demands the creation of an independent state of Biafra. The fact that the neo-Biafran project is currently floundering does not in any way detract from the validity of its claims that the issues which led to Biafra's secession in the 1960s are yet to be fully addressed, as the Igbo have remained marginalized at the federal level (Ukiwo 2009: 24).

The manner in which the non-violent neo-Biafran project has evolved since its inception in 1999, in spite of intense state repression and the ambivalent attitude of the Igbo elite aligned to the federal government, points to a change in the tempo of popular struggles for self-determination. MASSOB has so far shunned the use of violence, while emphasizing the 'acquisition of most of the appurtenances of a sovereign state, except for a national army' (Ukiwo 2009: 25), and preferring to mobilize Igbo youth both within Nigeria and abroad. Although the Nigerian state still endures, its legitimacy is severely eroded by the alienation of diverse groups within the polity, some of which continue to demand self-determination on the basis of a renegotiation of the basis of the Nigerian federation or its restructuring in ways that grant more autonomy to its constituent parts. Thus, while the national unity project 'won' at the end of the Nigerian civil war, it remains clear that, until the conditions that led to the Biafran rebellion are fundamentally addressed in ways that fully include the Igbo in the mainstream of federal governance and ensure the protection of their lives and property in all parts of the country, their quest for self-determination will persist, albeit in new forms. This also suggests that, unless similar conditions that marginalize or alienate certain groups are radically addressed, the quest for self-determination by groups in other African countries will continue to take on diverse and complex forms in a post-Cold War and post-9/11 world.

Notes

1 The two states are Rivers state and Southeastern state.
2 Some of these elites included Chief Obafemi Awolowo of the West, Chief Anthony Enahoro of the Mid-West and Joseph Tarka of the Middle Belt of Nigeria.
3 For example, the Somali support for the secession of the Ogaden region in Ethiopia.
4 This includes cases of self-determination motivated by the desire of an ethnic group in a state to seek independent statehood, as in the case of Biafra in Nigeria.
5 A full text of 'Tanzania's Memorandum on Biafra's Case' is available in Kirk-Greene (1971).
6 Some have argued that, from the very beginning of the crisis, there was international involvement on a formal and informal basis (see Nixon 1972: 495).
7 These views according to Frederick Forsyth emanated from the British Foreign Office (see BBC 1995).

8 For example, there were widespread feelings that the census exercise was rigged to give the North a numerical advantage over the Western and Eastern regions put together. This had serious implications for power sharing in Nigeria's First Republic owing to the fact that Nigeria opted for the majoritarian principle of the Westminster parliamentary system, a system which ensured that the numerical majority can make decisions that will be binding on other groups.

9 Some of these issues include Nigeria's opposition to the testing of the atomic bomb in the Sahara, and the perception that it would be good for Nigeria to break up since it constituted a threat to French colonies and interests on the continent.

10 France and Portugal remained staunch supporters of Biafra, but they did not accord it formal recognition.

References

Ake, C. 2000. *The Feasibility of Democracy in Africa*. Dakar: CODESRIA Books.

BBC. 1995. 'Biafra: Fighting a War without Guns', 30 July, http://www.bbc.co.uk/programmes/p00frgy2 (accessed 10 January 2013).

Blay, K. N. 1985. 'Changing African Perspectives on the Right of Self-Determination in the Wake of the Banjul Charter on Human and People's Rights', *Journal of African Law*, vol. 29, no. 2, pp. 147–59.

Brinkley, D. and Facey-Crowther, D. R. (eds). 1994. *The Atlantic Charter*. New York: St. Martin's Press.

Deschambs, H. 1970. 'France in Black Africa and Madagascar between 1920 and 1945', in L. H. Gann and P. Duignan (eds), *Colonialism in Africa, 1870–1960*. Cambridge: Cambridge University Press.

Diallo, M. M. 1969. *The Power and Energy Resources and Utilization of Nigeria*. Ibadan: Nigerian Institute of Social and Economic Research.

Diamond, S. 2007. 'Who Killed Biafra?', *Dialectical Anthropology*, vol. 31, pp. 339–62.

Ekwe-Ekwe, H. 2007. *Biafra Revisited*. Dakar: African Renaissance.

Emerson, R. (1964), 'Self-Determination Revisited in the Era of Decolonization', Occasional Paper No. 9, December, Centre for International Affairs, Harvard University.

Johnson, H. S. 1967. *Self-Determination within the Community of Nations*. Leyden: A. W. Sijthoff.

Kamanu, O. S. 1974. 'Secession and the Right to Self-Determination: An OAU Dilemma', *Journal of Modern African Studies*, vol. 12, no. 3, pp. 355–76.

Keller, E. J. 1995. 'The Ethno-Genesis of the Oromo Nation and Its Implications for Politics in Ethiopia', *Journal of Modern African Studies*, vol. 33, no. 4, pp. 621–34.

Kirk-Greene, A. H. M. (ed.). 1971. *Crisis and Conflict in Nigeria: A Documentary Sourcebook*, vol. 2: *July 1967 – January 1970*. Oxford: Oxford University Press.

Lata, L. 2004. *The Horn of Africa as Common Homeland: The State and Self-Determination in the Era of Heightened Globalization*. Waterloo, Ontario: Wilfred Laurier University Press.

Mayall, J. 1999. 'Sovereignty, Nationalism and Self-Determination', *Political Studies*, vol. 47, 474–502.

Morris, R. 1977. *Uncertain Greatness: Henry Kissinger and American Foreign Policy*. London: Quartet Books.

Nixon, C. R. 1972. 'Self-Determination: The Nigeria/Biafra Case', *World Politics*, vol. 24, no. 4, pp. 473–97.

Njoku, O. N. 1987. 'Nigeria's Contributions to War Efforts', in Toyin Falola (ed.), *Britain and Nigeria: Exploitation or Underdevelopment?* (pp. 164–81). London: Zed Books.

Obi, C. 2001. *The Changing Forms of Identity Politics under Economic Adjustment: The Case of the Oil Minorities of the Niger Delta*, Research Report no. 119. Uppsala: Nordiska Afrikainstitutet.

Organisation of African Unity. 1964. 'Border Disputes among African States', Assembly of Heads of Government Resolution 16 (I), Cairo, 17–21 July, http://www.au.int/en/sites/default/files/ASSEMBLY_EN_17_21_JULY_1964_ASSEMBLY_HEADS_STATE_GOVERNMENT_FIRST_ORDINARY_SESSION.pdf (accessed 6 February 2013).

Osaghae, E. E., Onwudiwe, E. and Suberu, R. T. (eds). 2002. *The Nigerian Civil War and Its Aftermath*. Ibadan: John Archers Publishers.

Porter, A. N. and Stockwell, A. A. 1987. *British Imperial Policy and Decolonization, 1938–1951*. Basingstoke: Macmillan.

Proclamation of the Republic of Biafra. 1967. Enugu: Government Printer, http://groups.yahoo.com/group/TalkNigeria/message/42862?var=1 (accessed 6 February 2013).

Tamuno, T. 1970. 'Separatist Agitations in Nigeria since 1914', *Journal of Modern African Studies*, vol. 8, no. 4, pp. 563–84.

Ukiwo, U. 2009. 'Violence, Identity Mobilization and the Reimagining of Biafra', *Africa Development*, vol. XXXIV, no. 1, pp. 9–30.

Unoke, E. 2010. 'Biafra, Human Rights and Memory', in C. J. Korieh and I. Ezeonu (eds), *Remembering Biafra: Narrative, History, and Memory of the Nigeria–Biafra War*. Glassboro, NJ: Goldline & Jacobs Publishing.

Venugopal, R. 2006. 'Self-Determination in the Global Context', in V. Fitzgerald, F. Stewart and R. Venugopal (eds), *Globalization, Violent Conflict and Self-Determination* (pp. 95–118). Basingstoke: Palgrave Macmillan.

13 The paradoxes of secessionism amongst the Tuareg in Northern Mali[1]

Ole Martin Gaasholt

Introduction

After several rebellions against both the colonial and the post-colonial regimes, Tuareg rebels from Northern Mali belonging to the Mouvement National pour la Libération de l'Azawad (MNLA) declared the independence of the state of Azawad on 6 April 2012, soon after acquiring military control of the three northern regions of Mali. At first glance, the Tuareg would appear to be a clear-cut example of a group seeking independence, not least considering their minority situation in Mali. The MNLA, like others who have promoted the cause of the Tuareg, refer to their minority situation as well as their long struggle against the colonial and post-colonial regimes. Yet the struggle is about more than the Tuareg and independence. The MNLA casts itself as the champion of all ethnic groups of Azawad, who are equally concerned as part of an oppressed and marginalised minority.

Even so, secessionist projects, and indeed all armed conflicts since independence, have been dominated by Tuareg, with participation from the Arabs in Mali, while other ethnic groups have even been opposed to these undertakings. MNLA members are predominantly Tuareg and Arab. Still, the degree of involvement of different Tuareg groups and the political aims, including secession itself, have varied from one conflict to another.

In a comparative perspective, secessionism amongst the Northern Malian Tuareg is interesting for the following reason. Because it is a *seemingly* clear-cut example, it reveals many of the limits to secessionism in the relevant geographical area. By the same token, it hopefully also provides a useful contrast to examples of secessionism elsewhere in Africa.

To return to Northern Mali and the composite nature of the conflicts occurring there, one must look at its history, taking due note of its peripheral location and the minority situation of its population. Undeniably, the area is a part of Mali because of the colonial legacy. The manner in which it was included in the colony of French Sudan, rather than neighbouring colonies, also with Tuareg populations, and how it was ruled compared to other parts of the colony may account for later differences in treatment and position. Since the colonial conquest rarely entirely undermined the previous socio-political organisation, the degree of continuity with pre-colonial times should be considered.

I shall thus undertake a historical examination of Northern Mali's changing socio-political organisation in relation to encompassing polities and their regimes. This history is related in different ways depending on the degree to which it is employed for a political agenda. Such use does not automatically disqualify the resulting claims. My presentation will begin with an account close to the one put forward by the MNLA, and accompanied by observations from researchers expressing a high degree of sympathy with the predicament of the Tuareg. This will enable me to show the main points of the history of the area, as there is little controversy as concerns the main events. But their interpretation depends on concurrent accounts. Drawing on other sources, including competing claims, I shall advance an alternative interpretation. Its aim will be to situate all relevant accounts with regard to the foremost historical and socio-political characteristics of the area under study.[2]

Through a comparison and contrasting of the accounts of the history and politics of Northern Mali, it will transpire that people championing the cause of the Tuareg of Northern Mali have frequently also framed the issue in a different register. Alleging marginalisation and discrimination, they have sought improved representation in the state and increased state investments in the northern regions. As the problem then takes on a regional cloak as much as an ethnic one, the ethnic component has been diverse, in actual practice including Arabs and in discourse including all Northern Malians. But the actual participation of either Tuareg or Northern Malians varies geographically. The limited degree of cooperation between Tuareg inhabiting different countries brings additional nuances to the ethnic dimension. As they nevertheless retain a Tuareg emphasis, the territorial notions of movements fighting for Northern Mali must be examined. Yet conflicts have been directed against the state, producing negotiations concerned with the shortcomings of the manner of incorporation of Northern Mali into the state.

Northern Mali's value as an example for a discussion of secessionism stems exactly from the multi-faceted nature of movements issuing from the area. They have never been exclusively about the self-rule of a people or a territory, but also about the relationship to the state of an admittedly marginal and peripheral geographical area. As their struggle stems from and is addressed in terms of such a relationship, it explains why independence has only been attained during extraordinary circumstances, as in 2012, a success that it proved difficult to secure moreover. Buoyed by weapons from Tuareg who had served in the Libyan army until the demise of Gaddafi, the MNLA was later overcome by Islamists who drove its members from most parts of Northern Mali.

Tuareg resistance and rebellion

The Tuareg have been considered as having been in strong opposition to the colonial conquest and the colonial regime in the anthropological and historical literature. Similarly, the MNLA emphasise battles with advancing French troops from 1880 onwards. Such resistance, exemplified by the revolt of 1916 in Mali, formed part of local and regional history. In my fieldwork location, fights with the French figured in the history of the once dominant local group of Tuareg. More generally, the leader of the revolt of 1916, Firhoun, was commonly known, although the details were not. Such history nevertheless presented Tuareg as leaders in Northern Mali, with significant exploits before foreign rule was firmly established.

The MNLA employs such history in a similar vein, to emphasise the Tuareg's presence, political influence, and willingness to fight to defend their lands against foreign intrusion. MNLA members, and other advocates of the Tuareg before them, see these events as part of a continual process. In it, the Tuareg appear as uniform and essentially identical (see Gaasholt 2011) throughout a historical process which leads towards the uprising in the Kidal region[3] shortly after the independence of Mali. All conflicts are thus considered acts of resistance which form part of the same impetus to shake off foreign domination.

At independence, Malian government representatives replaced those of the colonial regime, but they retained their authoritarian way of dealing with the Tuareg population. Moreover, the Tuareg had not been given the opportunity to participate in the government structures of either the colonial regime or the post-colonial state.

This harsh mode of rule and exclusion of the Tuareg made itself felt most acutely in the remote north-eastern region of Kidal, which like the rest of Northern Mali suffered from limited involvement from the authorities, resulting in a lack of development and public services (Boilley 1999). This was accentuated as the Malian authorities were mostly represented by the politically dominant Bambara from Southern Mali. Tensions between the authorities and groups of Tuareg produced clashes. An uprising broke out in 1963 in protest against a form of rule which was experienced as another foreign imposition. It was savagely quashed by the Malian authorities. The surviving rebels and their leaders retreated to Algeria and particularly to Libya. Meanwhile, the Kidal region was placed under military control, which lasted until 1990. The single-party socialist regime of the time tried to impose a nationalist culture, partly denying the Tuareg the use of their own language, Tamashaq. These efforts were concentrated in Kidal, and lasted only until the overthrow of the regime of Modibo Keita in 1968 (Boilley 1999). But the new regime of Moussa Traoré continued the practice of limiting the access of Tuareg to high offices in the Malian state, including the military academy and senior officer posts (Poulton and Ag Youssouf 1998).

The Tuareg were now excluded from proper participation in the Malian state, in which they had been forcibly included. According to the MNLA, and also some researchers, the Tuareg of Northern Mali had expressed a desire not to become part of Mali at independence. Instead, they had wished to join a structure contemplated by the French at the time, the Organisation Commune des Régions Sahariennes (OCRS). A means for France to retain control of the Saharan parts of its West and North African territories (Boilley 1993; Bourgeot 2000), it was abandoned at the approach of independence of the West African colonies, as the elites of the future independent countries dismissed it. The Tuareg, however, petitioned General de Gaulle, expressing their desire to remain attached to France and not to become part of the successor to the French Sudan (Claudot-Hawad 1993a). Even if this request did not receive a favourable response, the Tuareg had thus demonstrated in yet another way that they sought a destiny separate from the one of Mali.

Having become attached to Mali, however, they suffered from discrimination and indifference. This became clear during the droughts of the 1970s and 1980s. Food aid for Northern Mali was scarce, and aid arriving from international organisations was to a large extent diverted by the Malian authorities. Enriching themselves with the proceeds, Malian officials built the infamous '*villas de la faim*' (villas of hunger) (see Claudot-Hawad 1993a) in Bamako. The crisis, which left many pastoralists destitute, losing their entire herds, drove people into exile, once more towards Algeria and Libya (see Bellil and Dida 1995).

The people already in exile in Libya organised for the purpose of promoting self-rule for the Tuareg, founding an organisation to promote this aim in 1978 (Boilley 1999). They were joined in this by Nigerien Tuareg. They too had suffered oppressive rule, if not harsh repression as in Kidal. Not least, many had fallen victim to the same neglect as in Mali during the droughts. The ethnic element and similar experiences thus played a role in federating Tuareg from different areas.

Gaddafi supported this Tuareg organisation for a few years (Boilley 1999). It fitted his own designs on his Sahelian neighbours. After a rapprochement with Niger in the early 1980s, Gaddafi withdrew support from the Tuareg secessionists, but still managed to recruit many Tuareg into his Islamic Legion. They were dispatched to theatres like Lebanon and Chad in the 1980s. Serving Gaddafi's political aims, these Tuareg, accompanied by numerous Malian Arabs, nevertheless gained valuable combat experience (Bourgeot 1990).

Meanwhile, the Tuareg in exile, particularly the ones in Algeria, were increasingly pushed out. A repatriation scheme with only limited support for the returnees targeted thousands of Nigerien and Malian Tuareg, who were assembled in large camps in desert areas in Northern Mali and Northern Niger. The cramped and unsatisfactory living conditions produced clashes between camp dwellers and Nigerien armed forces, culminating in a massacre of tens or hundreds of people, or, according to Tuareg activists, as many as 1,500 in the locality of Tchin Tabaraden (Dayak 1992; Salifou 1993).

Nigerien Tuareg were still wanted by the Nigerien authorities for their role in the clashes. Some fled to Mali, where they were arrested and jailed by the Malian authorities. Shortly afterwards, Malian Tuareg attacked the prison in Menaka where they were held, killed the soldiers present and left with a cache of arms (Poulton and Ag Youssouf 1998; Boilley 1999). Other attacks followed not long after, targeting army posts for weapons, and NGOs for cars and money. Rebellion against the Malian state was officially declared, the rebels claiming to belong to the Mouvement Populaire de l'Azawad (MPA), an organisation promoting the cause of the Tuareg (Boilley 1999), long neglected by the Malian state (Poulton and Ag Youssouf 1998).

The thrust of the rebels' argument was the consistent discrimination of the Tuareg and the marginalisation of Northern Mali, an area that they called Azawad. The significance of this appellation is exceedingly complex. In the rebels' version, this area corresponded to territories controlled in the pre-colonial period by groups of Tuareg. Beyond that, there was scarcely any detailed account of the political organisation of the area, or the relations between the Tuareg and other ethnic groups, although Arabs participated in the rebellion. Thus the Arabs were considered part of the population of Azawad, and they formed their own movement, the Front Islamique et Arabe de l'Azawad (FIAA). They participated in negotiations between the rebels and the Malian state (Poulton and Ag Youssouf 1998).

As regards the basis of and justification for the rebels' struggle, ideas had circulated regarding a pre-colonial Tuareg empire. During my fieldwork from 1999 to 2001, these notions were aired on occasion, but with scarcely any detail. No one could furnish me with any information regarding its alleged political organisation. The rebel movements did not employ these ideas in their negotiations with the Malian state, but supporters and sympathisers of the Tuareg rebels developed these notions at some length.

One source of propagation of such ideas was a Tuareg lobby in France, which was influenced by Nigerien Tuareg. From 1991 until 1998, there was a parallel Tuareg rebellion in Niger (Deschamps 2000), but there was very little in the way of cooperation between the rebellions in the two neighbouring countries despite not just the commonalities of ethnicity and language but also the instigators' common experience of exile in Libya. The rebels in both Mali and Niger as well as the Tuareg lobby in France put forward a common sense of belonging because of a shared, unique culture, in which Tamashaq, the Tuareg language, played an important part, but this lobby went further to emphasise the political unity of all the Tuareg until the coming of the French. Once more, however, details were lacking, save for their thus laying claim to the Tuareg lands.

This only left researchers arguing for the existence of a pre-colonial Tuareg polity. Arguing for a pre-colonial Tuareg nation with a flexible, federated political organisation, Claudot-Hawad (1993b) and her husband, the Tuareg poet Hawad, claimed that the post-colonial states had dismembered the Tuareg nation (Dupraz and Decoudras 1993), and undermined Tuareg culture by artificial boundaries creating obstacles to the free movement of nomads, an essential ingredient of their culture (Claudot-Hawad 1993a). Movement and flexibility were necessary to sustain their socio-political organisation and their world-view. Still, the threats against Tuareg culture had not yet made people forget this previous form of organisation. The Tuareg rebellions must therefore be understood as responses to the oppression and neglect that the Tuareg had suffered (Claudot-Hawad 1992), but also as an initiation reviving the essential movement and dynamism that characterised Tuareg society (Hawad 1990).

While these notions were challenged by other researchers (Bourgeot 1994; Casajus 1995), the Tuareg themselves opted for different solutions that rapidly downplayed the importance of secession, until the MNLA's use of the history of the Tuareg and also of Northern Mali. It should be noted, however, that ideas of a common Tuareg identity and territory were put forward in the context of the rebellion taking place in Northern Mali from 2006 to 2009. Once more there was a parallel rebellion in Northern Niger, from 2007 to 2009. A little more contact took place between the rebels from the two countries, and a joint organisation for the Tuareg of both Mali and Niger was created. Yet there was extremely limited cooperation for military or political purposes. In Mali, the rebels' claims were concerned with bringing an end to the perceived marginalisation of Northern Mali rather than with independence, except for a fringe of hard-liners, who would later feed into the MNLA. In fact, only with the emergence of the MNLA would independence be insisted upon as the primary aim. Until then, rebels engaged in negotiations in which alternative demands were put forward. These must be understood in the context of Northern Mali's relationship with the central state. I shall now investigate this relationship. To understand why it has been so fraught with tension, it must be examined over time, giving me the opportunity to bring out other aspects of the history of Northern Mali which the secessionist perspective obscures.

Administering nomads

It is indisputable that Northern Mali was placed in an unprofitable relationship with the rest of the country. In fact, such had been the case since the colonial conquest. The northernmost parts of the colony of French Sudan were not administered in quite the same way as the rest of the colony. This was primarily because the Tuareg and Arabs were defined as belonging to nomad groups, whilst all other ethnic groups, even the Fulani, were defined as sedentary people.

The Kidal region, however, was more strongly set apart. Only submitting to the French in 1909 (Boilley 1999), it ended up as a remote area that was administered in a very superficial manner. The French scarcely invested there and did little to promote schooling, leaving the area at independence with few educated people (Boilley 1999). By ruling through privileged local chiefs, including the paramount chief of the area (Klute 1995), the French could nevertheless maintain a minimum of order at a low cost, but by the same token they effectively separated the Kidal region from the rest of the colony (Boilley 1999).

The common arrangement in Northern French Sudan was rule through local chiefs. This applied both to sedentary people and to nomads. The nomads had often maintained chiefs from pre-colonial times, creating a de facto indirect rule in which the point of contact with the nomadic population was their own chiefs and the colonial administrator. The latter was frequently a French officer (Bernus et al. 1993). Depending on a group's willingness to comply, it was either kept intact under its original chief or broken up. Subordinate chiefs were then promoted to chiefs of entire groups, answering directly to the colonial administrator.

In Northern Mali before the French, smaller and larger groups of Tuareg and Arabs had dominated the territory. There was no one large single polity, but there were some big groups dominating extensive territories, such as the Iwellemeddan (see Richer 1924). The Songhay and Fulani were under their dominance, in addition to people of slave status. The colonialists only partly meddled with the latter, but removed the Songhay from the Tuareg. In the process, grazing land along the Niger River was partly transferred to the Songhay (Marty 1999).

There was a certain preferential treatment of the sedentary population. This probably stemmed from misgivings about the previous dominance of the Tuareg, which was based on military might (see Gallais 1975), but many nomad groups enjoyed privileged relations with the colonial authorities. The larger Tuareg groups remained essentially similar, except that previous processes of power struggles within and between groups were halted by the French. Dominance was no longer extended by arms, and processes of sub-division of groups and movement of people between them ceased. However, this maintained and even increased the autonomy of several groups, allowing them to prosper (Gallais 1975).

The nomads were nevertheless assigned territories that were more strictly delineated than in pre-colonial times, yet the authorities were not truly capable of controlling all nomad movements, for which they needed authorisation, as intersecting trajectories of transhumance across the territories of neighbouring groups continued (Gallais 1975).

Even today, Malian law distinguishes between the Tuareg and Arabs as nomads, administratively organised in 'fractions' with their 'chiefs', while the sedentary population inhabit 'villages' also with 'chiefs' (Mission de Décentralisation 1999). Interaction with the authorities is still very much through chiefs. If this applies more strongly to the nomads, it appears as a result of their remoteness from urban centres and their mobility.

More than an administrative system per se, actual practice aimed at administering the nomads separately kept many of them at a distance from the evolving political life of the colony. Even so, some Tuareg groups were politically astute, and had occupied important positions in Mali since independence. A certain nostalgia amongst French colonial officers for the days of glory of the Tuareg (Bernus et al. 1993), despite the sedentary bias noted above, may have been responsible for their not involving the Tuareg more extensively in the life of the colony. Whether for reasons of conservatism or to avoid upsetting the nomads, schooling was introduced and made available much later and more half-heartedly than elsewhere in French Sudan, or even amongst the Songhay.

At independence, 'traditional' chiefs were retained, because the Malian state had to rely on them for local administration as had the colonialists before them. Larger groups were split up, however, and numerous smaller 'fractions' consisting of previous constituent sub-groups of the erstwhile larger groups were created. They were each given their own 'chief', and, in some cases of sub-division of local groups, people with no previous claim to a position of 'chief' were made so by the administration (see Gaasholt 2011), for in fact the entire organisation was considered an extension of the state administrative system, as it still is in Malian law (Mission de Décentralisation 1999).

Considering the similarity with the sedentary population, whose 'villages' and 'chiefs' also still form part of the state administrative system, the relationship to the state of the nomads resulting from the administrative regime is of less significance than the peculiar situation and experience of areas such as the Kidal region. By the same token, marginalisation may be considered to have affected all of Northern Mali rather than one ethnic group.

Northern Mali and the state

Rebels themselves have argued for their projects based on different groups of reference and sets of causes. The Tuareg have been mentioned, but also all of Northern Mali. This invokes the discrimination of particular ethnic groups, but also the marginalisation of a geographical area, Northern Mali, called Azawad by the rebels.

The name Azawad provides a good point of departure to discuss these paradoxes. It was not employed during the uprising in the Kidal region in 1963. Despite its consequences for the Tuareg in Mali, it primarily affected this area. No political project emerged which explicitly involved the population as Tuareg or Northern Mali as a distinct territory. In the late 1980s, such ideas had matured, however, and an organisation was created with Azawad in its name. As the rebellion developed, more rebel movements were formed, including an Arab one, and all of them had Azawad in their names. Strictly speaking, Azawad refers to a depression north of Timbuktu, in the lands of the Berabich Arabs. No full account of the reasons for choosing this name to denote all of Northern Mali has ever emerged. The presence and participation of a contingent of Malian Arabs among the rebels promoting self-rule in exile in Libya might explain why a name was chosen which included a territory inhabited not only by Tuareg but also by Arabs. When I discussed this issue in Northern Mali, people admitted that Azawad was originally only the smaller area, but the name had been extended to all of Northern Mali, making it take on a new meaning.

The name of Azawad thus reveals the ambiguity of the ethnic component of the rebellion of the 1990s. Although it is often presented as a Tuareg rebellion, the Arab participation was important. While the presence of the Arab organisation, FIAA, is commonly acknowledged, its political and military role has not been fully appreciated. It only became evident as the rebellion developed, when both the rebels' demands changed, making the rebellion address other issues than those of self-rule, and the ethnic dimension became far more complex, both between the rebel groups and vis-à-vis the remaining population of Northern Mali and even the rest of Mali.

While observers and sympathisers put forward interpretations and expressions of support with reference to the Tuareg's minority situation and alleged discrimination (Rosenberg 1992; Prasse 1995), the rebels themselves soon engaged in negotiations with the authoritarian regime of Moussa Traoré. As the rebels dominated the Kidal region outside the towns, they could not be defeated, and they inflicted instead severe casualties on the Malian army (Boilley 1999). Faced with pro-democracy protests in the capital Bamako, the Malian authorities accepted negotiations with the rebels (Diarrah 1991; Poulton and Ag Youssouf 1998).

They left any claim to independence to one side and demanded instead positions in and transfers from the state. Their initial demands included all the most important ministerial posts, among them foreign affairs and defence (Poulton and Ag Youssouf 1998). Demands were soon reduced to an increased presence in the state apparatus, including the administration and the armed forces. The rebels were also granted that nearly half the state's development budget should be allotted to Northern Mali (Klute and von Trotha 2000). But autonomy was not completely abandoned. The rebels obtained a promise of a 'special status' for Northern Mali (Seely 2001), allowing for independent agreements of cooperation with foreign agencies and countries.

The 'special status' created negative reactions amongst other Malians, but in any case the Treaty of Tamanrasset of January 1991 soon became obsolete, as Moussa Traoré's regime was overthrown in a coup in March of the same year following demonstrations and violent state repression. In the interim government, the rebels held two ministerial posts, one by the Tuareg movement, the MPA, and one by the FIAA, the Arab movement (Diarrah 1991). Meanwhile, negotiations began between the rebel movements and the government, which produced the National Pact of 1992. In essence, demands and what was offered resembled the previous treaty. The rebels retained one ministerial post, and that was maintained until 1997 (Poulton and Ag Youssouf 1998). In addition, they obtained positions in the administration for the rebel leaders, and integration into the armed forces of the rank and file. Northern Mali was to have a separate assembly and great autonomy in dealings with foreign agencies and countries. Increased investments in Northern Mali were also promised (Poulton and Ag Youssouf 1998).

A quest for access to the state was thus undeniably taking place. Yet, looking at the basis for the rebels' claims, they had argued in terms of exclusion from the state. Secession was thus not the only option provided their situation of marginalisation could be remedied. For this to happen, people from Northern Mali had to be integrated into the state apparatus, and this part of the country had to receive preferential treatment. Considering a degree of discrimination against ethnic groups characterised by a distinctive culture, a measure of autonomy was nevertheless required. But such an interpretation should not make one blind to a manifest attempt at gaining access to the resources of the state.

Thus, as the integration of ex-rebels into the armed forces gained pace, the rebels increased their demands regarding the number of positions that they should receive. Two more rebel movements had come into existence since the signing of the National Pact in 1992. Initially rejecting the peace agreement, they had eventually accepted it (Poulton and Ag Youssouf 1998). Beyond ideological orientations, there was a struggle for influence and leadership (see Klute 1995), which was in turn linked to attempts to gain access to the state and its resources. But with more rebel movements the demands for positions were quite substantial. In addition, the positions were distributed by each rebel movement to its members (Poulton and Ag Youssouf 1998).

This was the situation in early 1994, after integration had begun in 1993. Tensions started growing between ex-rebels and army members who had sometimes been bypassed for promotion by the new arrivals. Simultaneously, there was widespread insecurity in Northern Mali because of attacks and looting by people connected to the rebels (Poulton and Ag Youssouf 1998). Rebel attacks had largely consisted in attacks on government and NGO structures (see Boilley 1999), but there had also been numerous cases of the looting of civilians. Such acts persisted on a very much larger scale than before the rebellion (see Gaasholt 2011). Dissatisfaction with this state of affairs, and the integration which benefited the Tuareg and the Arabs, led to the creation of a Songhay vigilante group, the Ganda Koy. Its leaders were known to be army officers who had deserted, but the army did little to stop them. Tensions within the army between ex-rebels and the other soldiers led to clashes, and then large-scale desertion by ex-rebels, who took their service weapons with them (Poulton and Ag Youssouf 1998).

As early as 1991 and 1992, there had been a tendency to associate all Tuareg and Arabs, the 'Red' population, with the rebels, seeing them as permanently opposed to the rest of the people, the 'Black' population. Persecution had occurred in the larger cities in Northern Mali in particular, but also in Bamako (Gaasholt 2011). There were numerous refugees in Algeria, Mauritania and Burkina Faso who were scheduled for repatriation (Poulton and Ag Youssouf 1998). The emergence of the Ganda Koy led instead to clashes between Tuareg and Arab rebel movements and this group and, increasingly, persecution of all 'Red' people by the army and also by 'Black' civilians (Gaasholt 2011).

A rapprochement between one Tuareg rebel movement and the Ganda Koy, a peace process which included the latter and offered certain positions in the armed forces, the dissolution of the rebel movements and the burning of their weapons in a peace ceremony, brought the rebellion to an end in 1996 (Poulton and Ag Youssouf 1998). Most refugees had returned by 1998, but many Tuareg felt that they were not part of 'Mali'. Their usage of this name cast the Malian state and its armed forces as an alien, intrusive body (see Klute and von Trotha 2000). Furthermore, as related to me during fieldwork, the integrated rebels were accused of having sought only positions and of thus having betrayed the cause. However, this had resulted in an increased representation of people from Northern Mali in the Malian state, not least the armed forces, and this was considered an improvement.

Just as ordinary people expressed ambiguous attitudes towards the state and the outcome of the rebellion, the rebels pursued various agendas. Because of the ethnic tensions created during the rebellion, the autonomy for Northern Mali was never granted in the form of a separate assembly. In fact, the entire issue ceased to be discussed, while autonomy was supposedly offered to all of Mali through a process of decentralisation (Mission de Décentralisation 1998; Poulton and Ag Youssouf 1998; see Seely 2001). Breaking with the excessive centralisation of previous regimes, it allowed for the first ever elections to municipal councils in 1999, with elections planned for county and regional assemblies as well. In addition, the decentralisation purported to enable rule in tune with local and indigenous practices. By removing earlier authoritarian tendencies and promoting local and regional autonomy, the marginalisation and discrimination to which Northern

Mali and the Tuareg had fallen prey should end (Poulton and Ag Youssouf 1998; see Mission de Décentralisation 1998).

More rebellions

Subsequent developments, including two more rebellions, force one to question such grandiose aspirations. Yet the Tuareg and Northern Mali did at first appear to become more closely incorporated into the state and to improve their participation in it. This was in contrast to the misgivings about 'Mali' just mentioned and the severity of the ethnic conflict. In fact, in 2003, a Tuareg was made prime minister of Mali, a first for both Northern Mali and the Tuareg. In the following years, yet more people rose to high offices in the state, a Tuareg being appointed vice-president of the National Assembly.

However, the rebellions had not ended. In 2006, integrated ex-rebels revolted in Kidal, taking hold of the military arsenal and launching a new rebellion. They alleged that the government had not fulfilled its promises of increased investments in Northern Mali. Initially, autonomy, let alone independence, was not on the agenda, and arguments were scarcely in terms of ethnic group membership, but rather in terms of what was considered to be owed to Northern Mali. A negotiated agreement was soon reached, but it took another year before implementation began. Even then, the process was slow, with several setbacks. The military presence in the town of Kidal was reinforced, resulting in the maltreatment of civilians.

A hard-line fringe continued the fight, insisting on a reduced military presence in the Kidal region. At the time, smuggling, already an important part of the regional economy, had become very widespread, and one can speculate that a reduced military presence would facilitate smuggling. It was assumed that many rebels, and also soldiers, and not only from Northern Mali, entertained links to smugglers.

Nevertheless, this rebellion did retain an element of secessionism. As noted earlier, a joint movement was formed linking the rebellion in Mali to the parallel one in Niger, although it never appeared to have much operational relevance. The hard-liners, who never completely abandoned the idea of self-rule, were defeated by the Malian army, however. It contained large contingents of Tuareg and Arabs, many of them ex-rebels from the 1990s. As the peace agreement referred to the National Pact of 1992 and otherwise imposed similar measures, increased investments in Northern Mali and integration of ex-rebels into the army, those people who did not seek self-rule became more closely linked to Mali. This is less surprising when considering that Tuareg politicians in high offices in Mali consistently urged the rebels and the Malian authorities to find a negotiated solution. Opposition political parties also pressed the government to limit the military option.

The hard-liners' refusal to abandon their struggle still made the government step up its fight, culminating in the army's victory in 2009. Those still opposed to the peace agreement withdrew to Libya. Their leader died there in 2011, under not fully elucidated circumstances. With the developments in Libya in the same year, these people, joined by soldiers of Tuareg extraction who had served in the Libyan army of Gaddafi, and reinforced by their weapons, entered on the path to yet another rebellion. Meanwhile, in Mali, an integration of ex-rebels was intended to result in the creation of mixed forces to improve the security in Northern Mali, and particularly the Kidal region.

Wider problems had existed since before the rebellion of 2006, and would feed into the one of 2012. Not only smugglers but also Algerian Islamists were present in Northern Mali. The latter were involved in smuggling in Algeria and increasingly in Mali, in addition to the kidnapping of Europeans for ransom. The rebels of 2006 opposed them, however, and drove them further into the desert. They even used this as proof of their being Malian patriots, whose part of the country should thus receive proper treatment from the Malian state. Once more, the rebels played in several registers, ranging from self-rule to improved access to the state.

After the most intransigent rebels left for Libya, problems of insecurity because of smuggling and the Islamist presence continued. The mixed forces were never created, and the Malian authorities were accused in some quarters of connivance with the Islamists and involvement in the smuggling networks. The existence of systematic rather than individual links is yet to be proven. The Algerian Islamists changed their name from GSPC to Al-Qaida of the Islamic Maghreb (AQIM) in 2007, and implanted themselves more firmly.

A higher degree of incorporation into the state had not resolved many of the problems underlying the previous complaints of marginalisation. The high incidence of smuggling in the Kidal region is evidence of its limited degree of economic diversification. The economy is based on pastoralism and trade, as in all of Northern Mali, but the two other regions (the region of Timbuktu and the region of Gao) also have some agriculture, and more varied exchanges with the rest of the country. Smuggling occurs there too, though, as all of Northern Mali depends on external outputs. Ultimately, this accounts for the importance of resources from the state. However, as long as these do not lead to economic diversification, and access to the state passes through membership in national elites or is reserved for those local notables and chiefs who entertained the closest relations to the state both before and after decentralisation, criticism of the state's inequitable character should not surprise. To this was added a searing indictment of the state's handling of the security situation in Northern Mali, particularly the presence of Islamists groups. Opposition parties decried this situation. Interestingly, the MNLA employed much of the same reasoning to argue for the failure of the Malian state and in favour of their proposed independent state, Azawad.

The independent state of Azawad

A detailed exposé of the rebellion of 2012 belongs elsewhere. Suffice to say that the MNLA launched a rebellion with reference to their arguments, as set out above, in support of secession for Northern Mali, or Azawad. Joined by Tuareg soldiers fleeing the dissolution of the Libyan army, and greatly supported by heavy armaments acquired from the same source, the MNLA made considerable headway, but until mid-March the MNLA did not manage to take control of the larger towns. They did capture an important military camp, and were engaged in a drawn-out battle for another. In both these cases, rumours emerged of the MNLA cooperating with the Islamists. A tactical cooperation was later confirmed, despite the MNLA's insistence on their opposition to the Islamists and even their purporting to constitute the best safeguard against them.

Demonstrations erupted in January 2012 with complaints of too little support for the army, followed by attacks on Tuareg in and around Bamako. As in the 1990s, this made a large proportion of the 'Red' population leave the country. In late March, discontent among army personnel had reached such a level as to usher in a coup d'état by junior officers. Ironically, as the president was deposed and all governing institutions suspended, the lines of command within the army evaporated. This allowed for a very swift advance by the rebels, who rapidly conquered the regional capitals of Northern Mali. For the most part, the army offered no resistance, as soldiers simply fled, while some Tuareg and Arab soldiers temporarily changed sides. Later, many of them withdrew to Burkina Faso and were poised to join the Malian army in the event of a campaign to reconquer Northern Mali.

The MNLA declared the independent state of Azawad after having taken military control of all of Northern Mali. Gradually, they appointed administrators and began organising a preliminary government of Azawad, but they were faced by three Islamist groups. In addition to AQIM, there was a Tuareg Islamist group, the Ansar Dine, whose aim was sharia in all of Mali, not independence for Northern Mali. A splinter group from AQIM, the Mouvement pour l'Unicité et le Jihad en Afrique de l'Ouest (MUJAO) emerged. Consisting of a mix of North and West Africans, various Northern Malians, Tuareg, Arabs and Songhay have since swelled its ranks, giving it control of one regional capital, Gao.

The MNLA tried to establish a common platform with Ansar Dine, but the attempt fell through because of different political aims. The MNLA's effective control of territory was limited. Somewhat schematically, AQIM controlled Timbuktu and Ansar Dine retained Kidal, although there were overlapping presences, yet the MNLA were sole masters only in marginal areas. Then, in late June 2012, they were driven from Gao by the MUJAO and, for all practical purposes, out of Northern Mali altogether.

Prospects for Northern Mali

The unilateral declaration of independence of Azawad was condemned in unison by the international community. The UN, the EU, ECOWAS and the African Union all rejected the claim and emphasised the territorial integrity of Mali. In previous conflicts, secession was never considered seriously by any major power or institution. Even in this case of de facto independence, it was never thought of as an alternative.

Negotiations between rebels and ECOWAS have taken place since April 2012 with the MNLA, and in June 2012 Ansar Dine joined in. It is too early still to predict the outcome, but at the time of writing the MNLA had recently relinquished independence. Ansar Dine have exhibited an ambiguous attitude, while MUJAO and AQIM are not involved in any negotiations. A formal request from the Malian transitional government to ECOWAS for military support was passed on to the UN, where on 12 October 2012 a resolution was adopted authorising support for the Malian army to restore its national integrity, but also encouraging continuing negotiations with all the rebels not compromised by connections to 'terrorists'.

There is thus little likelihood that Northern Mali will secede permanently as Azawad. A negotiated solution with some of the rebel groups remains an option, but it is hard to discount an attempt by the Malian state to re-establish control over Northern Mali through its army. Despite potentially devastating consequences for the civilian population, Mali will seek to restore its sovereignty in the face of Islamist groups who are unwilling to negotiate and who pursue their goal of sharia, already imposed by meting out harsh punishments. Negotiations with the less intransigent rebels will have to address the security and the economic situation of Northern Mali.

In a longer perspective, Northern Mali requires economic diversification, lessening its dependence on external inputs, from state resources to smuggling. The security situation, characterised by the problems of controlling a vast desert territory and having allowed the presence of Islamists, can only be appropriately addressed by improved regional cooperation, not least with neighbouring Algeria.

Conclusion: the simultaneous embrace and rejection of the state

Tuareg rebellions and uprisings in Northern Mali have been about identity and the quest for autonomy, but they have rarely and not always even predominantly been about such issues. The Tuareg identity itself remains underspecified in all the conflicts and statements from their supporters. Besides, it is not necessarily an exclusive Tuareg identity that is being put forward. Any territorial notion is informed by the people present in the area where the rebels originate, but, as concerns the precise historical trajectory, the characteristics of this territory and its population vis-à-vis surrounding polities also remain imprecise.

The superiority of Azawad for the most recent secessionists has resided in its contrast to the shortcomings of the Malian state. It has been presented as offering the promise of an equitable distribution of resources, contrary to the Malian situation of unequal access to the state. And yet, until the events of 2012, the only remedy to such inequality was to try to improve access to the state. In the process, such improvement partly rectifies exclusion stemming from a history that has served to accentuate a peripheral position that was even amplified by colonisation. It temporarily reduces the import of identity both as a basis for exclusion and as a source of mobilisation in response to marginalisation.

But notions of autonomy and secession resurface as a form of political protest against the limitations of the existing mechanism of incorporation and as the best alternative to it.

Previously, negotiated agreements have gone some way towards reducing the distance, in terms of lack of participation in the state, of Northern Mali and the Tuareg. Yet the agreements soon became regarded as incomplete, setting in motion a new cycle of rebellion, where once again the combined claims of increased access to the state and, its apparent opposite, autonomy or secession are voiced. Despite the misgivings of the rebels of the last conflict, the insti-gators have already given up on independence and are once more involved in negotiations.

The on-going cycle of rebellions testifies to an incomplete incorporation into the Malian state. Improving it slightly each time through peace agreements can never remedy the failings produced by partial integration. Yet there is a measure of incorporation, however imperfect. The distance vis-à-vis the central state does not preclude a degree of contact, which in turn enables incorporation to progress a little further, albeit through a mechanism that can never resolve the more per-ennial problems.

The cycles of rebellion affecting a people, the Tuareg, and a part of the country, Northern Mali, that appear removed from the central state because of their history of limited incorporation produce an impression of a clear-cut case of opposition between the two parties, where secession would offer the only long-time solution. I have tried to show that this impression is only part of the picture. The relevance of a case such as the one in question is thus that it provides an example of factors, distance from the central state and incomplete incorporation, that can produce a demand for secession, but which are not sufficiently pronounced to shut out other factors militating against it. The contact with the state, however limited, and the multi-faceted nature of any identity constructs in the area have so far ensured that alternative demands and solutions never entirely lose their pertinence. In other situations of secessionist struggles in Africa, the conflicts have been permanent, and secession has seemed the only remedy to otherwise interminable struggles. By contrast, the Tuareg of Northern Mali have been caught in a self-reproducing cycle which brings conflicts to an end, but never provides a sufficient solution to avoid a renewed outbreak at a later date.

Notes

1 Part of the research for this chapter was funded by a grant from the Central Research Fund, University of London, and an Additional Fieldwork Award from the School of Oriental and African Studies. The material for this chapter stems from extensive field-work in the Gourma area of Northern Mali and sustained contact with informants ever since, coupled with detailed study of media sources regarding Mali.
2 For reasons of simplicity, I shall refer to this area as Northern Mali, even employing this usage anachronistically, except when more precision is called for.
3 The intermediate administrative entity (*cercle*) of Kidal only became a separate region during the rebellion of the 1990s.

References

Bellil, Rachid and Dida, Bida. 1995. 'Les migrations actuelles des Touaregs du Mali vers le Sud de l'Algérie (1963–1990)', *Études et documents berbères*, no. 13, pp. 79–98.

Bernus, Edmond, Boilley, Pierre, Clauzel, Jean and Triaud, Jean-Louis (eds). 1993. *Nomades et commandants: Administration et sociétés nomades dans l'ancienne A.O.F.* Paris: Karthala.

Boilley, Pierre. 1993. L'Organisation Commune des Régions Sahariennes (OCRS)', in Edmond Bernus, Pierre Boilley, Jean Clauzel and Jean-Louis Triaud (eds), *Nomades et commandants: Administration et sociétés nomades dans l'ancienne A.O.F.* Paris: Karthala.

Boilley, Pierre. 1999. *Les Touareg Kel Adagh*. Paris: Karthala.

Bourgeot, André. 1990. 'Identité touarègue: De l'aristocratie à la révolution', *Études rurales*, no. 20, pp. 129–62.

Bourgeot, André. 1994. 'Le corps touareg désarticulé ou l'impensé politique', *Cahiers d'Études africaines*, vol. 34, no. 136, pp. 659–71.

Bourgeot, André. 2000. 'Sahara: Espace géostratégique et enjeux politiques (Niger)', *Autrepart*, no. 16, pp. 21–48.

Casajus, Dominique. 1995. 'Les amis français de la "cause touarègue"', *Cahiers d'Études africaines*, vol. 35, no. 137, pp. 237–50.

Claudot-Hawad, Hélène. 1992. 'Bandits, rebelles et partisans: Vision plurielle des événements touaregs, 1990–1992', *Politique africaine*, 46, 143–9.

Claudot-Hawad, Hélène. 1993a. *Les Touaregs: Portrait en fragments*. Aix-en-Provence: Édisud.

Claudot-Hawad, Hélène. 1993b. 'Le politique chez les Touaregs: Un ordre absent, insoupçonné ou occulté?', in Hélène Claudot-Hawad (ed.), *Le politique dans l'histoire touarègue*. Aix-en-Provence: Édisud.

Dayak, Mano. 1992. *Touareg, la tragédie*. Paris: J.-C. Lattès.

Deschamps, Alain. 2000. *Niger 1995: Révolte touarègue: Du cessez-le-feu provisoire à la 'paix définitive'*. Paris: L'Harmattan.

Diarrah, Cheick Oumar. 1991. *Vers la IIIe République du Mali*. Paris: Harmattan.

Dupraz, Paule and Decoudras, Pierre-Marie. 1993. 'Hawad: L'utopie des marges et la quête d'une autre vérité', *Politique africaine*, no. 51, pp. 110–20.

Gaasholt, Ole Martin. 2011. 'Associating with an Overstretched State: Politics in Tuareg-Dominated Malian Gourma', Ph.D. thesis, University of London.

Gallais, Jean. 1975. *Pasteurs et paysans du Gourma: La condition sahélienne*. Paris: CNRS.

Hawad. 1990. 'La *teshumera*, antidote de l'État', in Hélène Claudot-Hawad (ed.), *Touaregs: Exil et résistance*, *Revue des mondes musulmans et de la Méditerranée*, vol. 57, no. 3 (Édisud, Aix-en-Provence).

Klute, Georg. 1995. 'Hostilités et alliances: L'aspect historique de la dissidence dans le mouvement rebelle des Touaregs du Mali', *Cahiers d'Études africaines*, vol. 35, no. 137, pp. 55–72.

Klute, Georg and Trotha, Trutz von. 2000. 'Wege zum Frieden: Vom Kleinkrieg zum parastaatlichen Frieden im Norden von Mali', *Sociologus*, no. 1, pp. 1–36.

Marty, André. 1999. 'La division sédentaires–nomades: La Boucle du Niger au début de la période coloniale', in Lisbet Holtedahl, Siri Gerrard, Martin Z. Njeuma and Jean Boutrais (eds), *Le pouvoir du savoir de l'Arctique aux Tropiques*. Paris: Karthala.

Mission de Décentralisation. 1998. *Le cadre d'une nouvelle dynamique de démocratisation et de développement*. Bamako: Mission de Décentralisation et des Réformes Institutionnelles.

Mission de Décentralisation. 1999. *Lois et décrets de la décentralisation*. Bamako: Mission de Décentralisation et des Réformes Institutionnelles.

Poulton, Robin-Edward and Ag Youssouf, Ibrahim. 1998. *A Peace of Timbuktu: Democratic Governance, Development and African Peacemaking*. Geneva: UNIDIR.

Prasse, Karl-G. 1995. *The Tuaregs: The Blue People*. Copenhagen: Museum Tusculanum Press.

Richer, Ange-Marie-Joseph. 1924. *Les Touareg du Niger (region de Tombouctou-Gao): Les Oulliminden*. Paris: Larose.

Rosenberg, Dominique. 1992. 'Le peuple touareg du silence à l'autodétermination', *Revue belge de droit international*, no. 1, pp. 5–39.

Salifou, André. 1993. *La question touarègue au Niger*. Paris: Karthala.

Seely, Jennifer C. 2001. 'A Political Analysis of Decentralisation: Coopting the Tuareg Threat in Mali', *Journal of Modern African Studies*, vol. 39, no. 3, pp. 499–524.

Part V

Colonially created, annexed by neighbouring countries cases

14 Namibia's negotiated transition to independence

Henning Melber

Introduction

This chapter analyses the negotiated transformation within the process of Namibian decolonisation towards a sovereign state. Notably, the Namibian case is located in a different context in so far as it relates to factors of international policy and diplomacy more so than in most other decolonisation processes. The stakeholders and main actors in the Namibian independence process were mainly rooted and operating externally in the course of the negotiations. The direct parties were a colonial power occupying the territory and a liberation movement representing the colonised majority. The mediating agencies based their mandate and legitimacy either on the United Nations system or on the degree of direct involvement in the local (Namibian) and regional (Southern African) dimension of the conflict.

Namibian decolonisation gained relative importance as a genuine case of United Nations intervention on the basis of the special status of the territory both in historical perspective and from the point of view of international law. There consequently exists a wide range of literature on the Namibian decolonisation process in general and the negotiated settlement process in particular.[1] A short historical background to Namibian decolonisation will be followed by a summary of some relevant factors and determinants for the role of the United Nations in the negotiating process. Next, a few of the relevant steps in the negotiated decolonisation will be highlighted, and finally some of the results in the final stages of implementation are considered.

The case: a trust betrayed

Most parts of the territory known today as the Republic of Namibia were declared a protectorate of imperial Germany in 1884. German South-West Africa lasted for 30 years. It was shaped by violent means into a settler-dominated society under foreign rule, which established strict racial segregation with lasting effects far beyond the actual period of German rule (see Melber 2000). After the First World War the territory was declared a C mandate, and the trusteeship was executed on behalf of the British crown by the geographically neighbouring Union of South Africa. With the end of the League of Nations as the supervisory power to the trusteeships and the establishment of the United Nations, a long-lasting dispute emerged with South Africa over the fate of the country, the administrative and legal responsibilities, and its future course in terms of international law and self-determination. The 'winds of change' resulted in the decolonisation of most African countries until the late 1960s. They contributed towards a diversified composition of the family of sovereign states within the United Nations. This in turn had an impact on the discourse in international policy as discussed in this arena. The emergence of independent African states and the establishment of both an Organisation of African Unity and a Non-Aligned Movement contributed markedly towards shifts in policy issues, including the perception of such unsolved conflicts over control of territory and the right to self-determination. The changes of the 1960s therefore finally contributed towards an end to tolerating a continued occupation of the territory by South Africa in the absence of any legitimacy by the United Nations. Namibian independence became a global responsibility (see Singham and Hune 1986), which for most of the more than two decades between the mid-1960s and the late 1980s could be classified as 'war without victory, negotiations without resolution' (Green 1995: 207).

The dispute over the mandated territory escalated into an open conflict, which demanded continued recognition also in terms of international law.[2] The United Nations assumed full responsibility to remain seized with the matter in both the General Assembly and the Security Council. Namibia turned into a singular case of United Nations concern, manifested also by the creation of the United Nations Council for Namibia[3] and the United Nations Institute for Namibia. The liberation movement established in the late 1950s and acting since 1960 as the South West African People's Organization (SWAPO of Namibia) was acknowledged by the General Assembly as the only legitimate agency of the Namibian people[4] and obtained observer status to the United Nations bodies. But the transition process to Namibian independence was deeply affected by a polarised situation of superpower rivalry. Hence any meaningful decolonisation was blocked until the late 1980s, when UN Security Council Resolution 435(1978) was finally implemented by the stakeholders – more than a decade after its adoption.[5]

Since its inception until Namibian independence, as proclaimed on 21 March 1990, the United Nations played a crucial if not decisive role, culminating in the establishment of the United Nations Transitional Assistance Group (UNTAG) with supervisory powers for the transition of Namibia towards internationally accepted independence as a sovereign state under UN Security Council Resolution 435(1978).[6] The UN system can hence be considered by all standards as a midwife to the independent Namibian state. The United Nations agencies, however, were in themselves by no means homogeneous or uniform. United Nations positions and policies on Namibia were represented in different ways, be it through the most radical support to SWAPO as expressed in the General Assembly resolutions, the role assumed by the United Nations Council for Namibia as an institution acting on behalf of a generally assumed Namibian interest otherwise not represented, or the far more compromising positions taken by the Security Council resolutions. The existing differences on how to approach a lasting and acceptable solution to the problem gave birth to the Western Contact Group. It was composed of the then five Western member countries of the Council, seeking to negotiate a peaceful settlement of the Namibian dispute. Its first major success was the adoption of the United Nations Security Council Resolution 435(1978). Instead of its implementation, however, a stalemate dominated the following decade.

Subsequent policies through most of the 1980s were a reflection of negotiated compromise between the different power blocs and global policy interests. Critics classified the stagnation as the result of an evasive approach, seeking to protect foremost South African and Western interests in the Southern African region instead of confronting the continued illegal occupation of Namibia as a breach of international law with all the consequences at hand. Hence, it would be errone-ous to assume that there has been one binding position on the Namibia conflict since it emerged as a topic on the agenda of the United Nations bodies. Instead, the United Nations created different fora to negotiate the decolonisation proc-ess and ultimately to secure its implementation. This process lasted more than two decades after declaring South Africa's presence in the territory as illegal and finally brought to an end more than a hundred years of foreign occupation. In its course, it was accompanied by the articulation of different and at times conflict-ing political approaches from several social forces operating in a local Namibian, regional Southern African and global context.

In the light of this complexity the United Nations was more than a conflict mediator and power broker seeking to reconcile the various interests operating even within its own structures with the overall goal of correcting the existing anachronism of 'a trust betrayed'.[7] This chapter is mainly focused on the negotia-tions initiated and conducted by the Western Contact Group. After all, despite all the setbacks and scepticism during the course of the long interaction, they resulted in the guiding framework for Namibia's transition to independence. The initiative by the Western Contact Group therefore ultimately paved the way towards a settlement of the dispute.

Negotiated decolonisation: framework and result

SWAPO's armed liberation struggle, launched in the mid-1960s, had a major impact on the further course of decolonisation (see Brown 1995; Lamb 1998).[8] But Namibian independence was as much the achievement of an international community, which finally after the end of the Cold War period managed to end lengthy and complicated diplomatic negotiations first and foremost dominated by the strategic interests of the two power blocs. The internationally negotiated settlement ultimately resulted, after far too many delays and sacrifices, at least in a by and large peaceful transition towards independence with a decisive degree of United Nations involvement. It paved the way for a legitimate government led by the previous liberation movement SWAPO.

The goal of the struggle was national liberation defined as political independ-ence in a sovereign state under a government representing the majority of the previously colonised people, who were excluded from full participation in society through the imposed apartheid system. The power of definition concerning the post-colonial system of political governance was exercised during this process mainly by the national liberation movement in interaction with the international system represented by a variety of competing actors under the polarised conditions of superpower rivalry during the 1970s and 1980s. This also implies that the emphasis of the struggle was clearly on the exile politics and in terms of international diplomacy. In her comprehensive analysis, Dobell (1998: 23) proposes that:

> Namibia provides a particularly fascinating case study of the gradual dismantling of a century of colonial rule, and its ultimate replacement – through democratic means, and monitored by external powers – by a movement which, some would argue, had in certain respects come to resemble the forces against which it had originally struggled.

With reference to some of the contributions to the four-volume study on *Transitions from Authoritarian Rule*,[9] she suggests that there are three especially pertinent paths to democracy applicable to the Namibian case, namely 'a) externally monitored installation; b) redemocratization initiated from within an authoritarian regime; and c) elements of the "party pact" model' (Dobell 1998: 77). While the term 'redemocratization' is misleading to the extent that it suggests that there was a political system of democracy in Namibia previously (which was certainly not the case), the different components indeed offer a partly valid framework for analysis. The 'externally monitored installation' model suggested by Stepan describes, as Dobell (1998: 77) summarises further, 'cases in which an authoritarian regime is defeated by foreign democratic powers, which then "play a major role in the formulation and installation of the democratic regime"'.

Dobell's study has the merit of showing the relevance of translating these general theoretical reflections into the socio-political reality of the Namibian case, but a word of caution seems justified too. The all too often assumed equation that liberation from the illegal occupation of Namibia by a colonial minority regime would imply more or less automatically the installation of a truly democratic society seems to be misleading. This applies to perceptions and discourses among not only the activists of the liberation movement (see the contributions to Melber 2003 and 2007), but to some extent also the other stakeholders and parties in the negotiated settlement, including the representatives of the United Nations agencies (Melber 2004). The agenda was first and foremost shaped by the goal of establishing a formally legitimate and internationally recognised sovereign Namibian state. By implication the expectation among many of the forces involved might have been that this required the establishment and consolidation of democracy as a lasting political system. Explicit evidence for this, however, remains scarce and scattered. Throughout the 1970s and 1980s the liberation struggle was understood and perceived foremost as the right to self-determination of the Namibian population on the basis of free and fair general elections. Once achieved, the task of formulating and adopting further specifications were left to those policy makers who emerged as representatives of the Namibian electorate as a result of such elections. It was therefore not democratisation which was the priority on the agenda for Namibia, but decolonisation. From a logical point of view this is an understandable approach, since there is no democracy under colonialism.

The mandate implemented by UNTAG under UN Security Council Resolution 435(1978) provided the supervision of free and fair general elections for a Constituent Assembly among all parties registered under the transitional authority, composed jointly by the South African administrator general and the United Nations special representative. Those in competition for political power, however, were not operating on a level playing field. The South African allies under the previous interim government coalition led by the Democratic Turnhalle Alliance (DTA) could operate with the massive material support from the de facto still existing colonial authorities. The liberation movement SWAPO had in contrast the privilege and strategic advantage of being the only recognised representative of the Namibian people internationally. The possibility of any meaningful support to other forces not aligned with the two sides was basically eliminated by the factual constraints imposed upon these since the increased polarisation emerging from the 1970s. Martti Ahtisaari, who on behalf of the United Nations Council for Namibia was the main negotiator and official in charge of the United Nations-supervised transition, summarised later the intrinsic contradiction of this constellation: 'I don't think it was the most democratic way of going about it but I think the justification for that was to concentrate the efforts vis-à-vis the occupying power.' As a result, he continued to argue, the political forces not affiliated to SWAPO 'were eliminated from that political opportunity and that of course diminished plurality and complicated matters' (Soiri and Peltola 1999: 185).

The United Nations was hence more a power broker than a promoter of lasting democracy. That the transition took place under conditions of free and fair general elections following democratic rules offered a necessary legitimacy to the outcome and contributed decisively to the general acceptance. To that extent, democracy in practice offered some essential ingredients to the success of the decolonisation process. But the Namibian independence process was first and foremost an internationally supervised and legitimated transfer of political power. That the political power exercised met by and large the definitions and expectations of a democratic political system was a desired result but not the main goal. After all, rather logically, the democratically elected representatives of the Namibian population should have the discretion and power to decide themselves upon the character of the political system. On the other hand, as a study based on several fact-finding missions to Namibia during March to November 1989 concluded, the United Nations did succeed in redirecting a profound (also military) conflict into electoral competition and provided a democratically oriented solution: 'The Settlement Plan was not just a device for instituting independence; it also helped Namibians develop a democratic system of government, where meaningful elections are held periodically and where human rights are generally respected' (National Democratic Institute for International Affairs 1990: 84).

The following section explores in more detail the background, effects and results of the negotiated settlement as initiated by the Western Contact Group. United Nations Security Council Resolution 435(1978) is considered as the crucial point of reference in this endeavour.

Western Contact Group, Resolution 435(1978) and Namibian independence

Between January 1977 and December 1978 the Federal Republic of Germany (FRG) assumed for the first time a temporary (elected) seat in the United Nations Security Council.[10] The permanent Western member states (the United States of America, the United Kingdom and France) were joined by Canada as another elected member. The five consulted informally as a matter of routine among each other concerning the positions on relevant issues. It happened to be that owing to an initiative by the group of African states the first Security Council debate of the year to come was facing a confrontation over South Africa. Four draft resolutions were in circulation, demanding among other matters that sanctions should be imposed on the apartheid regime. They were considered unacceptable to the Western countries. In early March 1977, strategic meetings between the representatives of the five Western countries therefore contemplated the option of convincing the African states not to pursue the confrontational line but instead to agree on a joint declaration of principles. In this context the idea was brought up of mobilising the Security Council for a debate with South Africa over Namibia. This was in line with a previous reassessment of the positions on Namibia[11] and an earlier policy concession: afraid of being isolated on the Namibia issue, the Western powers backed United Nations Security Council Resolution 385 in January 1976. It demanded the withdrawal of South Africa from the occupied territory and UN-supervised and -controlled elections.[12] For the first time the notion of a 'contact group' initiated by and centred around the five Western states (without any fixed or defined members yet) was presented but remained undecided. After further consultations the group met again on 16 March 1977 in the Canadian United Nations mission. According to Vergau (2002a: 229) this could be considered the date of birth for the Western Contact Group (WCG).[13]

Its original main message was to threaten South Africa with support for 'stern action' (meaning sanctions) in the Security Council if South Africa did not soon agree to an internationally acceptable arrangement for Namibia. A démarche was conveyed on 7 April 1977 to the South African prime minister Vorster. According to Vergau (2002a: 229), an obviously worried Vorster agreed in principle to enter negotiations with the five governments. This was followed by a series of intensive rounds of meetings and negotiations in the 'Gang of Five' – as the Group was soon termed by the more suspicious witnesses to the initiative – during 1977–78.[14]

The WCG operated from a New York basis at the United Nations missions, but originally as a purely Western initiative to seek an acceptable compromise solution among the stakeholders. This included South Africa, SWAPO, the

Frontline States (FLS) (Tanzania, Botswana, Mozambique, Zambia, Angola and from 1980 also Zimbabwe), Nigeria and the United Nations secretary-general. Most of the consultations took place either in New York or in Africa in separate meetings. The contact group furthermore continuously though less officially kept the local groups in Namibia informed. The most critical issue was to avoid the implementation of a South African-manipulated and -orchestrated 'internal solution' without SWAPO. Another sensitive issue was the administration of the territory during the preparations for United Nations-supervised elections, and the United Nations competence. The size of the United Nations personnel and of the remaining South African troops, the timing of their withdrawal, the bases allocated to SWAPO and the control thereof were other critical questions that required agreement and an accepted modus operandi. Four rounds of discussions each between the WCG and South Africa and SWAPO respectively were conducted until early 1978 and complemented by an intensive shuttle diplomacy with the neighbouring countries in Southern Africa and Nigeria. This might in retrospect be considered as the most crucial time of confidence building, especially with regard to the group of African countries, which turned out to play an essential role in ultimately bringing a reluctant SWAPO on board.[15] The liberation movement did not originally want to compromise on its achieved status as 'sole and authentic representative' through direct negotiations with the occupying colonial power, whose presence was in the same spirit as the exclusivity attached to SWAPO considered to be illegitimate. The African allies ultimately managed to convince the SWAPO leadership (and in particular its president) of a more pragmatic approach.

While progress was made, no decisive breakthrough was achieved. This provoked the first round of 'proximity talks' in February 1978 in New York with the aim of bringing about the necessary concessions in separate mediations between the foreign ministers of the WCG and the different parties. Vergau (2002a: 231–2) suggests that the abrupt ending of the talks by South Africa was based on the information that SWAPO seemed finally willing to consider the acceptance of a compromise as a result of peer pressure from the African states. The South African position was guided by the calculation that the negotiations would ultimately fail because of SWAPO's refusal to accept the compromise, which in its eyes the entering of direct negotiations with the occupying power in itself would be. Notwithstanding the lack of a common denominator among the stakeholders, the WCG proceeded by pushing for a platform. In April 1978 it tabled a proposal for the solution of the Namibian situation to the chairman of the Security Council.[16] South Africa agreed to this proposal before the end of April, expecting that SWAPO would not consent. This was initially indeed the case and resulted in further attempts to convince the FLS to persuade SWAPO. Owing to their influence the SWAPO president agreed ultimately to announce in July 1978 the organisation's agreement to the proposed plan submitted by the WCG.[17] This was the point of departure for firstly clarifying by unanimous adoption of Security Council Resolution 432(1978) on 27 July 1978 the territorial integrity of Namibia.[18] On 29 September 1978, Security Council Resolution 435 ultimately introduced the plan submitted by the WCG as the official United Nations position for the solution of the Namibia issue.[19] The WCG had achieved a plan for the settlement of the Namibia dispute, serving as an agreed framework for the United Nations policy to come.

South Africa reacted with obstruction. Confronted with the unwanted acceptance of the plan by SWAPO,[20] Pretoria announced internal elections for a Constituent Assembly to be held in Namibia in December 1978. What seemed to have been achieved through Resolution 435(1978) as a starting point for a solution in the near future became a blueprint, pending for another decade until its implementation. The results of the internal elections in December 1978 were recognised only by South Africa itself, but served as the basis for creating a platform for the internal forces allied to South Africa, constituting themselves as a Constituent Assembly and subsequently National Assembly. While the international pressure remained on both parties (South Africa and SWAPO) to seek a negotiated settlement in line with Resolution 435,

> both Pretoria and SWAPO sought to appear reasonable and accommodating, and to place on the other the onus for any breakdown in the negotiations. Yet both sides seemed, in fact, to have written off serious negotiations, Pretoria in favour of its internal settlement, and SWAPO in favour of intensified guerrilla warfare. An internationally acceptable solution seemed no closer than it had been a year before.
>
> (du Pisani 1986: 426)

Notwithstanding this setback, several achievements could be recorded as common ground between the parties, as du Pisani (1986: 426) hastens to add: South Africa was prepared to accept the notion of a unitary independent Namibian state on the basis of general democratic elections with universal suffrage and an involvement of the United Nations in the transitional phase. SWAPO accepted elections as a necessary step to confirm the legitimacy of its claim to being the representative of the people, and the role of both the United Nations and a South African (even military) presence in the transitional process. It also accepted that the controversy over Walvis Bay should be treated as a separate issue and excluded from the terms of settlement.

This provided the basis and framework for more negotiations aiming to reach agreement on several issues not yet solved within the general guiding framework of Resolution 435. Both SWAPO and South Africa, however, deployed more than ever a dual-track strategy of negotiating on the one hand and continuing to pursue confrontation on the other hand. Negotiations around the establishment of a de-militarised zone in Southern Angola and Northern Namibia culminated in a United Nations conference in Geneva during November 1979 but finally failed to achieve sustainable results. While by 1980 there was no concrete evidence for any major achievements or even results on the issue of implementing Resolution 435, mainly because of other factors (not least the successful transition under the Lancaster House Agreement towards independence in Zimbabwe) and the emerging mindset among United Nations officials that the outstanding issues should without any further delay be settled among the various stakeholders in direct interaction and communication, a 'pre-implementation multi-party meeting' was scheduled during October 1980 for January 1981 in Geneva.

The Pre-Implementation Conference (by its title misleadingly suggesting that Resolution 435 was about to become reality after the solving of some outstanding technicalities) for the first time offered and provided an opportunity for the internal Namibian parties operating in alliance with South Africa to present their case internationally. They exploited this opportunity to the fullest, and the result was disastrous. By the time of the conference, South Africa had obviously made up its mind not to offer any compromises which would allow for a settlement. The 'dirty work' was left by the South African officials to the members of their delegation representing the internal parties who attended as part of the South African contingent. The eye-witness report by one of these delegates offers sufficient testimony to this.[21]

For many observers, Geneva represented 'the collapse of the Western Plan' (du Pisani 1986: 443) or 'the breakdown of the UN settlement plan' (Dreyer 1994: 145).

In a differing and different insider perspective, Vergau (2002a: 237) refers to the continued negotiations of the WCG during 1981 and 1982 as a 'proved method' of intensive diplomacy (including frequent visits to Southern Africa and Nigeria). He qualifies the results thereof, achieved in July 1982 in consultation with the FLS, Nigeria and SWAPO in New York (and later receiving South Africa's approval) on agreed constitutional principles and a United Nations 'impartiality package',[22] as closest to a turning point if concentrated political pressure by the Western Five had been applied. Instead, the emerging US American–South African common understanding, resulting in the 'linkage' issue, replaced the concept advocated so far by the WCG through what was perceived as common security interests in the Southern African region by the two countries.

Most of the 1980s were subsequently influenced by the South African-backed US demand that only a withdrawal of Cuban forces from neighbouring Angola would allow for a transition to independence in Namibia. 'Linkage' effectively translated under the given circumstances into 'blockage', and the notion of 'constructive engagement' as advocated by the Reagan administration turned out to be very destructive for years to come.[23] In a nutshell, 'the United States became the defender of South African interests' (Sparks and Green 1992: 45). As a result of its disagreement with the imposition of the 'linkage' on the Namibia issue, France announced in December 1983 its suspension of membership in the WCG and emphasised its continued support for implementation of Resolution 435.[24]

Despite being dormant, the relevance of the blueprint, including the constitutional guidelines and the impartiality package as defined during 1982, became obvious when as a consequence of the international situation – largely owing to emerging new global policy factors complementing the changing regional policy aspects – by the end of 1988 the ultimate implementation of the plan between April 1989 and March 1990 was decided upon.[25] In none of the cases was SWAPO directly involved as a signatory to the documents. Negotiations and ultimate agreements were officially confined to the Angolan, Cuban and South African governments. This reflected in terms of 'ownership' the selective composition of the signatories on the basis of those countries considered to be relevant for a regionally oriented conflict solution at that time – and interestingly enough SWAPO was no direct party in this. This underscores that Namibia's ultimate decolonisation was brought about by a combination of local, regional and global factors. The military aspect, though certainly far from being decisive, was one of them.

The Republic of Namibia

The Constitution of the Republic of Namibia represents the end of an era of colonial oppression and resistance against foreign rule, drafted and adopted by consensus of the members of Namibia's Constituent Assembly. The 66 men and six women represented seven parties. They were elected under the United Nations-supervised general elections in November 1989. Since the constitutional document had to be adopted by a two-thirds majority, none of the parties involved in the process of negotiations had the power to impose a unilateral decision upon the other groups represented. SWAPO, with 41 seats (57 per cent of the votes), had missed the two-thirds majority. The DTA with its 21 seats (28 per cent of the votes) failed to emerge as a really powerful opposition. The emerging process has been qualified as 'an impressive example of successful bargaining by opposing political elites in a transitional democratic context' (Forrest 1998: 43).

For Dobell (1998) the negotiated settlement in Namibia resembles aspects of an 'elite pact' as defined by O'Donnell and Schmitter (1986: 38). The constitutional negotiations were the final chapter of a decolonisation process 'closely supervised by international forces, and facilitated by a "transitional pact"' (Bauer 2001: 36). As Erasmus (2000: 80) points out in retrospective, the international settlement plan as designed in Security Council Resolution 435(1978) 'gained an important additional element when it was decided to determine the basic content of Namibia's Constitution in advance. Constitution-making became part of the international peace-making operation.' He further points out that the adoption of these principles implied 'that Namibians actually did not enjoy a completely free hand in writing their own constitution' (Erasmus 2000: 81).

SWAPO offered from the outset full recognition of the 1982 Constitutional Principles, which:

> laid down ground rules for a multiparty democracy with regular elections by secret ballot, an independent judiciary, and a declaration of fundamental human rights, including recognition of property rights. The reassertion of these principles laid to rest the spectre of a one-party state that had worried some of SWAPO's opponents.
>
> (Cliffe et al. 1994: 199f.)

In other words, the negotiated settlement started under United Nations supervision continued to acknowledge the externally defined rules of the game, and the parties involved were eager to document their constructive approach. As a result, 'the constitution was rushed through by all parties, eager to seize the reins of power' (Cliffe et al. 1994: 213). 'The 80-Day Miracle' (Diescho 1994: 29–38), which marked the beginning of the sovereign Namibian state, consequently received rather mixed appraisals.

Concluding remarks

Most observers agree that the internal will to close the chapter of colonial rule was very much supported by external factors shaping the particular type of Namibian independence. The Namibian transition 'was the product of a complex political compromise between a right wing, racist South African government and a leftist, nationalist SWAPO government in exile, brokered by the United Nations' (Harring 1995: 31).

It was a unique decolonisation process in several ways: the occupying colonial power was a neighbouring state, which had pursued for decades and against international law a policy of integration of the adjacent territory into its own state (Namibia was always considered as 'the fifth province'). Only the change in global governance institutions forced South Africa to concede that the country needed to be governed by its own people. The constellation also brought several external actors into the picture: the Western Contact Group as an effort to find a solution also in the interest of the Western states; the FLS as the local players in the sub-region; the Liberation Committee of the Organisation of African Unity; the Soviet Union and Cuba as allies of Angola and supporters of the anticolonial liberation movement; and SWAPO, recognised as the representative of the Namibian people. This blend provided sequences of negotiations and a diplomacy which was often not at hand in other cases. Last but not least, the change in the global bi-polar world of the Cold War era, which was brought about with the collapse of Soviet hegemony, provided a window of opportunity to finally implement the transition negotiated (and formally agreed upon) earlier.

Despite a wide range of secondary studies on the Namibian decolonisation process, there is however still insufficient evidence based on primary sources, which themselves are far from consistent.[26] The question remains whether, without the military-regional aspect, the change in international policy and the increasing loss of internal legitimacy, the South African regime would have compromised in the late 1980s and what the difference would have been if such a compromise had been enforced during the early 1980s by means of credibly threatening or even imposing sanctions in the case of non-compliance.

Ironically, in retrospect, the decolonisation of Namibia can to a considerable extent be qualified as a successful confidence-building measure with far-reaching implications beyond its own borders: Namibia was, under the specific constellation of the late 1980s and early 1990s, the laboratory and experimental blueprint for controlled change in South Africa itself (Saunders 2001: 7). It is only that this came at too high a cost for too many of the people of Namibia, who otherwise might still be alive and would certainly have benefited from independence at an earlier stage.

Notes

1 See for an earlier summary Melber and Saunders (2007), parts of which are also reproduced in this chapter. It also draws on an interview with Hans-Joachim Vergau on 22 March 2002, conducted within the framework of a research project by the Centre for Conflict Resolution at the University of Cape Town. Nicknamed 'Mr Namibia' among his colleagues, Vergau was based at the diplomatic mission of the Federal Republic of Germany to the United Nations in New York between 1976 and 1980 and was from 1980 to 1985 head of the Southern Africa Department in the Foreign Ministry in Bonn. Between 1977 and 1983 he was the German member of the Western Contact Group and was until 1990 an active participant in almost every stage of Western involvement. He has since then published his experiences in a very personal monograph (Vergau 2006).
2 By Resolution 2145 the United Nations General Assembly on 27 October 1966 terminated South Africa's mandate over South-West Africa and subsequently qualified its continued presence as illegal occupation.
3 This was subsequent to Resolution 2145(XXI), decided upon by the General Assembly on 19 May 1967, to create an entity representing the interests of the Namibian people within the United Nations agencies.
4 United Nations General Assembly Resolution 3111 of 12 December 1973 recognised SWAPO as 'the authentic representative of the Namibian people'. This was amended in United Nations General Assembly Resolution 31/146 of 20 December 1976 to 'sole and authentic', endorsing an exclusive status and political monopoly of SWAPO in the negotiations on behalf of the Namibian population.
5 There is an abundance of literature that has been produced on the Namibian case over the years, much of it characterised by a preference for one or more of the parties involved in the conflict and reflecting the bias of the Cold War period. Informative though not necessarily non-partisan overviews for the period under review are offered by Rocha (1984), Dore (1985), Nyangoni (1985: 40–93), du Pisani (1986: 272–460), Singham and Hune (1986), United Nations Institute for Namibia (1987), Manning and Green (1989), Kössler and Melber (1990), Sparks and Green (1992: 39–62), Dreyer (1994) and Kaela (1996), to mention just a few, as well as – of course – by a wide range of United Nations publications. Many of the above sources offer access to the relevant United Nations documents.
6 See for details on the last stages to Namibian independence in particular Herbstein and Evenson (1989), Harneit-Sievers (1990), Melber (1990, 1991), M'Passou (1990), National Democratic Institute for International Affairs (1990), Ansprenger (1991), Lush (1993), Cliffe et al. (1994) and Hearn (1999).
7 A popular phrase coined by a United Nations publication with reference to the violation of the trust South Africa was asked to administer on behalf of the League of Nations in good faith as a mandatory power.
8 Even Dirk Mudge, who during the 1970s until independence represented the option for an 'internal solution' as the chairman of the Democratic Turnhalle Alliance, conceded in an interview in 1995: 'if there were no armed struggle, maybe nothing would have happened' (Sellström 1999: 81).
9 See in particular the chapters by Adam Przeworski ('Some Problems in the Study of the Transition to Democracy') and Alfred Stepan ('Paths towards Redemocratization: Theoretical and Comparative Considerations') in O'Donnell et al. (1986), as well as O'Donnell and Schmitter (1986).

10 The FRG was admitted together with the German Democratic Republic (GDR) to membership status of the United Nations in 1973. Both countries shared a special affinity to Namibia for the same historical but very different contemporary political reasons: the FRG (and in particular members of its conservative parties) still had a strong emotional and ideological affinity to the former colony and personal ties to the German-speaking minority there. This relationship was not entirely free from economic influence and interest. The GDR, in its attempts to strengthen its profile, was pursuing an opposite political and practical international solidarity through direct support to the liberation struggle by SWAPO. See for a comparison Engel and Schleicher (1998: 259–336).

11 Du Pisani (1986: 280–81) maintains that as early as 1974 'the West made the decolonization of Namibia under UN auspices one of its preconditions for continued cordial external relations with South Africa'.

12 As already mentioned, the FRG had a specific interest in contributing to a solution of the Namibian issue. Although for different reasons more related to the ongoing negotiations concerning Rhodesia/Zimbabwe, so had the British Foreign Office, 'in its search for a middle course between outright identification with white settler power in the sub-continent and alignment with radical black nationalism' (Rich 1993: 76). With David Owen as the Labour government's foreign secretary, the initiative had a strong personal advocate and supporter – similar to the West German foreign minister Genscher (see Jabri 1993: 62).

13 Vergau (2002a, 2002b and personal interview) motivates his account (also in his comments in Weiland and Braham 1994) with the explicit reason of counteracting the 'strange legends' that have since then been constructed around the origin of the WCG. In contrast to his view, Vivienne Jabri (1993: 61, 63) represents the dominant perception that Andrew Young was the initiator of the contact group.

14 Vergau criticises notions suggesting an almost exclusive role of US policy under the Carter administration by Cyrus Vance (1983: 272–313) for 1977 to 1980.

15 The Africa policy under the US president Jimmy Carter might have been a contributing factor towards a relatively favourable environment. There were also deliberate efforts by the West German foreign minister Genscher. According to Vergau (2002a: 230–31), Genscher's meetings with President Nyerere of Tanzania (May and August 1977, February 1978), with President Kaunda from Zambia (June 1977) and later with President Mugabe from Zimbabwe – immediately after he came to office (April 1980) – played a supportive role. More important even was the decision of the West German cabinet upon the initiative of Genscher – in spite of furious protests by his opponents in the conservative parties (see Brenke 1989: 119–23) – to close the consular mission in Windhoek by the end of October 1977. This was due to the refusal of SWAPO to attend the second round of discussions with the WCG scheduled for mid-October 1977 in the West German diplomatic United Nations mission with reference to the continued existence of diplomatic representation in the illegally occupied territory.

16 Proposal for a Settlement of the Namibian Situation, UN Doc. S/12636, 10 April 1978 (documented in Dreyer 1994: 270–73).

17 Vergau (2002a: 232, 2002b: 49 and personal interview) is convinced that, without the role of the FLS and Nigeria, SWAPO would not have agreed to the proposed plan by the Western initiative. He qualifies the influence of the African states, and in particular of President Julius Nyerere and even more so of Nigerian president Olusegun Obasanjo, as decisive. The constructive role of the (Southern) African states is well documented for the whole period of decolonisation by Khadiagala (1994) and for the earlier stages in Nyangoni (1985).

18 With the Council's decision 'to lend its full support to the initiation of steps necessary to ensure early reintegration of Walvis Bay into Namibia' it took a clear and uniform stand denying South Africa the right to continued occupation of the enclave Walvis Bay as an integral part of South Africa. While the dispute over Walvis Bay was only

settled in 1993 with its formal reintegration into Namibian territory, it clarified in terms of the legal dispute a relevant issue in favour of the position held by SWAPO and the African states.

19 Documented *inter alia* in Dreyer (1994: 275–6). The People's Republic of China did not attend, and the USSR (and Czechoslovakia) abstained from the vote. Owing to the explicit consensus of SWAPO, documented also by a letter of its president to the secretary-general of 8 September 1978 (UN Doc. S/12841), the two permanent members uneasy with the Western initiative felt unable to actively oppose the resolution by a veto. Vergau (2002b: 49) points out an almost ironical parallel in the approaches by South Africa and the Soviet Union. South Africa had decided not to turn down the Western proposal up front, assuming that SWAPO would find it impossible to accept the compromises and hence would be blamed for obstruction. The Soviet Union had not objected to the Western initiative, assuming that SWAPO would not accept a compromise offered by the imperialist camp. After SWAPO announced its approval of the plan, South Africa was trapped and the Soviet Union could not object.

20 To make it impossible for SWAPO to accept a negotiated settlement, South Africa increased direct military aggression parallel to the negotiations. This culminated in the killing of several hundred Namibian refugees living at the SWAPO camp at Kassinga in Southern Angola. The attack cynically took place on Ascension Day (4 May) 1978, and made use of bombardments, chemical weapons and the deployment of ground forces. After the genocide in the early twentieth century, Kassinga was the biggest single massacre recorded in the history of the Namibian liberation struggle.

21 Report-back from the 1981 Geneva Conference by J. S. Kirkpatrick, who attended as chairman and representative of the Federal Party of Namibia, who attended the talks in the South African delegation (Namibia Peace Plan 1987: 65–71). If there was a positive side effect to this abortive conference, then it was that it contributed towards a critical sensibility of some of the smaller internal parties towards the destructive aims of South Africa and its local allies in preventing instead of seeking a United Nations solution. To that extent the Geneva Conference offered an opportunity gradually to convince members among the liberal elements of the white (and in particular English- and German-speaking) communities of the necessity to seek Namibian independence by implementation of Resolution 435 – as the publication by the initiative formed later on under the name Namibia Peace Plan (1987) documents (see also O'Linn 1987). A particular case in point was the consultations initiated by SWAPO (supported financially by the Swedish government) in June 1988 with more progressive white Namibians in Stockholm (see Dobell 1998: 84–7; Sellström 2002: 380). This initiated a series of confidence-building meetings and was followed by a similar encounter in October 1989 in Kabwe, Zambia.

22 As documented in Security Council documents S/15287 and S/20635 respectively.

23 For analyses with a particular focus on the emerging role of the United States, see Price (1982), Cooper (1988), Rotberg (1988), Chakaodza (1990), Rich (1993) and Hampson (1996).

24 See Marchand (1988) for the French policy on Namibia during the early 1980s. For overviews on the developments during the 1980s see *inter alia* Dreyer (1994: 145–93) and Jaster (1985, 1988, 1990).

25 Relevant steps to this are the Protocol of Geneva of 5 August 1988, the Protocol of Brazzaville of 13 December 1988 and the Agreement between Angola, Cuba and South Africa (New York Accords) of 22 December 1988 (all reproduced in Dreyer 1994: 277–83).

26 Jabri (1990: 181) identified access to decision makers involved in the process as a 'primary research problem', increased by 'the reluctance of decision-makers to reveal important aspects of the negotiations', as well as 'that different decision-makers at times gave different responses to particular questions'. A similar diagnosis was made

in a comparative analysis of the Namibia policy of the two German states (Engel and Schleicher 1998: 263). The scarce 'memory literature' (see Vance 1983; Crocker 1992; Nujoma 2001; Vergau 2006) reflects certain ambivalences and contradictions. So does the recollection of events in Weiland and Braham (1994). As so often, there is no singular or absolute 'truth'.

References

Ansprenger, Franz. 1991. *Freie Wahlen in Namibia: Der Übergang zur staatlichen Unabhängigkeit.* Frankfurt am Main: Peter Lang.

Bauer, Gretchen. 2001. 'Namibia in the First Decade of Independence: How Democratic?', *Journal of Southern African Studies*, vol. 27, no. 1, pp. 33–55.

Brenke, Gabriele. 1989. *Die Bundesrepublik Deutschland und der Namibia-Konflikt.* München: Oldenbourg.

Brown, Susan. 1995. 'Diplomacy by Other Means: SWAPO's Liberation War', in Colin Leys and John Saul, *Namibia's Liberation Struggle: The Two-Edged Sword* (pp. 19–39). London: James Currey and Athens: Ohio University Press.

Chakaodza, Austin M. 1990. *International Diplomacy in Southern Africa from Reagan to Mandela.* London: Third World Publishing.

Cliffe, Lionel with Bush, Ray, Lindsay, Jenny, Mokopakgosi, Brian, Pankhurst, Donna and Tsie, Balefi. 1994. *The Transition to Independence in Namibia.* Boulder, CO: Lynne Rienner.

Cooper, D. (ed.). 1988. *Allies in Apartheid: Western Capitalism in Occupied Namibia* (pp. 175–92). London: Macmillan.

Crocker, Chester A. 1992. *High Noon in Southern Africa.* New York: Norton.

Diescho, Joseph. 1994. *The Namibian Constitution in Perspective.* Windhoek: Gamsberg Macmillan.

Dobell, Lauren. 1998. *Swapo's Struggle for Namibia, 1960–1991: War by Other Means.* Basel: P. Schlettwein Publishing.

Dore, Isaak I. 1985. *The International Mandate System and Namibia.* Boulder, CO: Westview Press.

Dreyer, Ronald. 1994. *Namibia and Southern Africa: Regional Dynamics of Decolonization 1945–90.* London: Kegan Paul.

Engel, Ulf and Schleicher, Hans-Georg. 1998. *Die beiden deutschen Staaten in Afrika: Zwischen Konkurrenz und Koexistenz 1949–1990.* Hamburg: Institut für Afrika-Kunde.

Erasmus, Gerhard. 2000. 'The Constitution: Its Impact on Namibian Statehood and Politics', in Christiaan Keulder (ed.), *State, Society and Democracy: A Reader in Namibian Politics* (pp. 77–104). Windhoek: Gamsberg Macmillan.

Forrest, Joshua Bernard. 1998. *Namibia's Post-Apartheid Regional Institutions: The Founding Year.* Rochester, NY: Rochester University Press.

Green, Reginald Herbold. 1995. 'Namibia: From Blood and Iron to Reconciliation', in Oliver Furley (ed.), *Conflict in Africa* (pp. 199–222). London: I. B. Tauris.

Hampson, Fen Osler. 1996. *Nurturing Peace: Why Peace Settlements Succeed or Fail.* Washington, DC: United States Institute of Peace Press.

Harneit-Sievers, Axel. 1990. *Namibia: Wahlen zur Verfassungsgebenden Versammlung 1989: Analyse und Dokumentation.* Hamburg: Institut für Afrika-Kunde.

Harring, Sidney L. 1995. 'The Constitution of Namibia and the Land Question: The Inconsistency of Schedule 5 and Article 100 as Applied to Communal Lands with the "Rights and Freedoms" Guaranteed Communal Land Holders', Paper presented to a workshop on 'Traditional Authorities in the Nineties – Democratic Aspects of

Traditional Government in Southern Africa', Centre for Applied Social Sciences/ Faculty of Law at the University of Namibia, 15–16 November.

Hearn, Roger. 1999. *UN Peacekeeping in Action: The Namibian Experience*. Commack, NY: Nova Science Publishers.

Herbstein, Denis and Evenson, John. 1989. *The Devils Are among Us: The War for Namibia*. London: Zed Books.

Jabri, Vivienne. 1990. *Mediating Conflict: Decision-Making and Western Intervention in Namibia*. Manchester: Manchester University Press.

Jabri, Vivienne. 1993. 'European Involvement in the Western Contact Group: The Stress and Convenience of Coalition Mediation', in Stephen Chan and Vivienne Jabri (eds), *Mediation in Southern Africa* (pp. 60–72). Basingstoke: Macmillan.

Jaster, Robert S. 1985. *South Africa in Namibia: The Botha Strategy*. Lanham, MD: University Press of America and Centre for International Affairs, Harvard University.

Jaster, Robert S. 1988. *The Defence of White Power: South African Foreign Policy under Pressure*. Basingstoke: Macmillan and London: International Institute for Strategic Studies.

Jaster, Robert S. 1990. *The 1988 Peace Accords and the Future of South Western Africa*, Adelphi Papers 53. London: International Institute for Strategic Studies.

Kaela, Laurent C. W. 1996. *The Question of Namibia*. Houndmills: Macmillan and New York: St. Martin's Press.

Khadiagala, Gilbert M. 1994. *Allies in Adversity: The Frontline States in Southern African Security 1975–1993*. Athens: Ohio University Press.

Kössler, Reinhart and Melber, Henning. 1990. 'Namibia 1978 bis 1988/89 . . . 1990? Hintergründe der aktuellen Lage Mitte 1989', in Vezera Kandetu, Gerhard Tötemeyer and Wolfgang Werner (eds), *Perspektiven für Namibia* (pp. 12–27). Bonn: Informationsstelle Südliches Afrika.

Lamb, Guy. 1998. 'Civil Supremacy of the Military in Namibia: An Evolutionary Perspective', Master of Social Science thesis, University of Cape Town.

Lush, David. 1993. *Last Steps to Uhuru: An Eye-Witness Account of Namibia's Transition to Independence*. Windhoek: New Namibia Books.

Manning, Peter and Green, Reginald H. 1989. 'Namibia: Preparations for Destabilization', in Phyllis Johnson and David Martin (eds), *Frontline Southern Africa* (pp. 153–89). Peterborough: Ryan Publishing.

Marchand, Jacques. 1988. 'French Foreign Policy towards Namibia 1981–1985', in Allan D. Cooper (ed.), *Allies in Apartheid: Western Capitalism in Occupied Namibia* (pp. 79–90). London: Macmillan.

Melber, Henning. 1990. 'Ein Modell mit Schönheitsfehlern: Die Umsetzung des Lösungsplans für Namibia durch die Vereinten Nationen', *Vereinte Nationen*, vol. 38, no. 3, pp. 89–94.

Melber, Henning. 1991. 'Der UNO-Lösungsplan für Namibia: Sicherheitsratresolution 435(1978)', in Frank T. Gatter and Manfred O. Hinz (eds), *Krisen – Entwicklungen – Konfliktlösungen: Sektionsbericht III/Jahrestagung der Vereinigung von Afrikanisten in Deutschland e.V. 1989* (pp. 165–80). Frankfurt am Main: IKO.

Melber, Henning. 2000. 'Economic and Social Transformation in the Process of Colonisation: Society and State before and during German Rule', in Christiaan Keulder (ed.), *State, Society and Democracy: A Reader in Namibian Politics* (pp. 16–48). Windhoek: Gamsberg Macmillan.

Melber, Henning (ed.). 2003. *Re-Examining Liberation in Namibia: Political Culture since Independence*. Uppsala: Nordic Africa Institute.

Melber, Henning. 2004. 'Decolonization and Democratisation: The United Nations and Namibia's Transition to Democracy', in Edward Newman and Roland Rich (eds), *The UN Role in Promoting Democracy: Between Ideals and Reality*. Tokyo: United Nations University Press.

Melber, Henning (ed.). 2007. *Transitions in Namibia: Which Changes for Whom?* Uppsala: Nordic Africa Institute.

Melber, Henning and Saunders, Christopher. 2007. 'Conflict Mediation in Decolonisation: Namibia's Transition to Independence', *Africa Spectrum*, vol. 42, no. 1, pp. 73–94.

M'Passou, Denis B. (ed.). 1990. *'We Saw It All'*. Katutura: Churches Information and Monitoring Service.

Namibia Peace Plan. 1987. *The Choice! Namibia Peace Plan 435 or Society under Siege!* Windhoek: Namibia Peace Plan Study and Contact Group (NPP 435).

National Democratic Institute for International Affairs. 1990. *Nation Building: The U.N. and Namibia*. Washington, DC: National Democratic Institute for International Affairs.

Nujoma, Sam. 2001. *Where Others Wavered: The Autobiography of Sam Nujoma*. London: PANAF.

Nyangoni, Wellington W. 1985. *Africa in the United Nations System*. London: Associated University Presses.

O'Donnell, Guillermo and Schmitter, Philippe C. (eds). 1986. *Transitions from Authoritarian Rule*, vol. 4: *Tentative Conclusions about Uncertain Democracies*. Baltimore, MD: Johns Hopkins University Press.

O'Donnell, Guillermo, Schmitter, Philippe C. and Whitehead, Laurence (eds). 1986. *Transitions from Authoritarian Rule*, vol. 3: *Comparative Perspectives*. Baltimore, MD: Johns Hopkins University Press.

O'Linn, Bryan. 1987. 'UN Resolution 435 (1978) and the Future of Namibia', in Gerhard Tötemeyer, Vezera Kandetu and Wolfgang Werner (eds), *Namibia in Perspective* (pp. 36–53). Windhoek: Council of Churches in Namibia.

Pisani, André du. 1986. *SWA/Namibia: The Politics of Continuity and Change*. Johannesburg: Jonathan Ball.

Price, Robert M. 1982. 'U.S. Policy toward Southern Africa: Interests, Choices, and Constraints', in Gwendolen M. Carter and Patrick O'Meara (eds), *International Politics in Southern Africa* (pp. 45–88). Bloomington: Indiana University Press.

Rich, Paul. 1993. 'The United States, Its History of Mediation and the Chester Crocker Round of Negotiations over Namibia in 1988', in Stephen Chan and Vivienne Jabri (eds), *Mediation in Southern Africa* (pp. 75–99). Basingstoke: Macmillan.

Rocha, Geisa Maria. 1984. *In Search of Namibian Independence: The Limitations of the United Nations*. Boulder, CO: Westview Press.

Rotberg, Robert I. 1988. 'U.S. Policy toward South and Southern Africa', in Robert I. Rotberg (ed.), *Africa in the 1990s and Beyond: U.S. Policy Opportunities and Choices* (pp. 220–41). Algonac, MI: Reference Publications.

Saunders, Christopher. 2001. 'From Apartheid to Democracy in Namibia and South Africa: Some Comparisons', in Henning Melber and Christopher Saunders, *Transition in Southern Africa: Comparative Aspects – Two Lectures*, Discussion Paper no. 10 (pp. 5–16). Uppsala: Nordic Africa Institute.

Sellström, Tor (ed.). 1999. *Liberation in Southern Africa: Regional and Swedish Voices*. Uppsala: Nordic Africa Institute.

Sellström, Tor. 2002. *Sweden and National Liberation in Southern Africa*, vol. II: *Solidarity and Assistance 1970–1994*. Uppsala: Nordic Africa Institute.

Singham, A. W. and Hune, Shirley. 1986. *Namibian Independence: A Global Responsibility*. Westport, CT: Lawrence Hill.

Soiri, Iina and Peltola, Pekka. 1999. *Finland and National Liberation in Southern Africa*. Uppsala: Nordic Africa Institute.

Sparks, Donald L. and Green, December. 1992. *Namibia: The Nation after Independence*. Boulder, CO: Westview Press.

United Nations Institute for Namibia. 1987. *Namibia: A Direct United Nations Responsibility*. Lusaka: United Nations Institute for Namibia.

Vance, Cyrus. 1983. *Hard Choices*. New York: Simon & Schuster.

Vergau, Hans-Joachim. 2002a. 'Genscher, Europa und das südliche Afrika', in Hans-Dieter Lucas (ed.), *Genscher, Deutschland und Europa* (pp. 223–39). Baden-Baden: Nomos.

Vergau, Hans-Joachim. 2002b. 'Namibia-Kontaktgruppe: Katalysator des Interessenausgleichs', *Vereinte Nationen*, vol. 50, no. 2, pp. 48–9.

Vergau, Hans-Joachim. 2006. *Verhandeln um die Freiheit Namibias: Das diplomatische Werk der westlichen Kontaktgruppe*. Baden-Baden: Nomos.

Weiland, Heribert and Braham, Matthew (eds). 1994. *The Namibian Peace Process: Implications and Lessons for the Future*. Freiburg: Arnold Bergstraesser Institut.

15 Eritrea, a colonial creation

A case of aborted decolonisation

Redie Bereketeab

Introduction

The current African states were produced as a result of the infamous European strategy of a scramble for Africa designed and executed in the Berlin Conference of 1884–85. The roots of the multifaceted predicament Africa grapples with therefore originate in the Berlin Conference. Some seven decades later the people of Africa began to unsaddle the yoke of imperial domination. The people who were subjected to European colonial rule were consequently given the right to consummate independence. Yet there were exceptions who were denied that right. The borders that were inherited from colonialism and assumed an international legal personality following independence and the decolonisation process were declared sacrosanct. International law also conferred upon a people who had been subjected to European colonisation and domination the right to constitute their own sovereign state. Any quest for a separate statehood by identity groups from the colonially created state was however perceived as a breach of the sacrosanctity of the colonial borders and thus fiercely opposed.

Eritrea, like other colonial states in Africa, was tailored by colonialism into its present form and content. Therefore according to the decolonisation principle it should have achieved sovereignty as a consequence of the demise of colonial rule during the Second World War in 1941. In violation of the principle of decolonisation and through the operations of the emergent United Nations, Eritrea was federated with Ethiopia, which was put into force in 1952. Ten years later the federation was violated by Emperor Haile Selassie of Ethiopia with implicit UN endorsement in abrogation of its obligations. The annexation of Eritrea in 1962 led to 30 years of bloody war of independence (Pool 1979, 2001), which ended in 1991 with the defeat of the occupation forces.

Quite often the Eritrea struggle for sovereignty was presented erroneously as a separatist struggle, in breach of the sacrosanctity of colonial borders, seeking to dismantle an old and celebrated state. Ethiopia was one of the two countries in the continent that evaded colonial subjugation, while Eritrea was under colonial rule for nearly six decades. Nonetheless, ignoring colonial experience, Eritrea was seen as an integral part of the Ethiopian empire and was denied the right of self-determination. This was in violation of the sacrosanctity of colonially inherited international borders. The way the Organisation of African Unity (OAU), UN and international bodies treated Eritrea has been a puzzle to Eritreans (Yohannes 1991). So far as Eritreans were concerned the liberation struggle was to achieve the unconsummated decolonisation process.

The chapter seeks to explore the process of the formation of Eritrea as a result of colonial political economy and nationalist struggle. It provides a succinct account of how interplay between foreign colonial domination and nationalist resistance spawned the formation of a colonial state, and the final emergence of the sovereign Eritrean state. Six analytical dimensions are provided that depict the processes and mechanisms of the formation of Eritrea as a multi-ethnic nation. The chapter also advances the argument that Eritrean national identity, which was the foundation of the quest for self-determination, was consolidated in four consecutive periods, notably Italian colonialism, British rule, federation and national liberation. This chapter analyses the four periods. The main argument of the chapter is that the case of Eritrea is a case of decolonisation, since Eritrea was the creation of colonialism, like any current African state that was entitled to self-determination and statehood pursuant to decolonisation.

Analytical dimensions

The six analytical dimensions to be discussed below explain the processes, mechanisms and dynamism through which the foundations of the Eritrean nation were laid down successively. The six dimensions serve as analytical tools to explicate the emergence of Eritrean statehood and common national identity. The interplay between external occupying forces and nationalist forces for over a hundred years resulted in the emergence of Eritrea.

The first of these analytical dimensions contributing to the fostering of the colonial territoriality of Eritrea related to bringing together the distinctive regions, that is, the creation of *territorial integration*. The presumption here is that the first stepping stone in the creation of states is territorial integration. Delimitation and delineation of borderlines that visibly and concretely separate a territory from its neighbours, defining its international political and legal borders while simultaneously consolidating its internal cohesiveness, represent the requisites for the emergence of territoriality (Rokkan 1975; Seton-Watson 1977; Smith 1983; Väyrynen 1993). This is the presupposed infrastructure for the realisation of the other dimensions.

The delineation of Eritrea's territoriality through the delimitation of the political and legal borders of the territory occurred through conventions that were signed between three powers. Concerning the southern borderlines an agreement was signed between the Italian colonial power and Ethiopia; the south-eastern border was delineated through agreement between the Italians and the French; and the western borders were defined as a result of an agreement between Italy and the British (Habte Selassie 1989). Therefore, through laying down the first presupposition of regional integration, Italian colonial rule firmly laid down the foundation for the emergence of colonial Eritrean statehood. Nonetheless, territorial integration needed to be supplemented by the second analytical dimension.

The second analytical dimension pertains to *socio-economic integration*. Socio-economic integration pertains to the emergence of a socio-economic system, pursuant to territorial integration, wherein the presumption is that the various ethno-linguistic groups will interact and react within the encompassing social and economic realms confined to the perimeters of the common territoriality. Here it is argued that social and economic common centres where the various ethno-linguistic groups have accessibility to social spaces to intermingle and interact ultimately foster familiarity, and a sense of solidarity among them is developed. This in turn creates socially and economically interdependent and cohesive societies (Bendix 1964; Gellner 1983; Hobsbawm 1990; Anderson 1991). From this we can safely infer that the political economy of European colonialism generated socio-economic integration that further laid down a building block in the formation of Eritrean identity that was to be enhanced by the third dimension.

The third is *politico-legal integration*. In terms of politico-legal integration arguably centralisation and standardisation of polity and jurisprudence took place (Smith 1983, 1991; Renan [1882] 1991). The emergence of a centralised and standardised politico-legal system cross-cutting geographic, ethnic, linguistic, religious, gender and class borders is presumed to engender the gradual development of the civic nation. This effects a state wherein the various ethno-linguistic groups are compelled to cohabit a common space under the same legal and political roof. Moreover, politico-legal integration is presumed to lead to the emergence of political and legal institutions that unite society and foster a common national identity. In the general literature a nation is perceived as a 'group of people inhabiting a given territory and obeying the same laws and government' (Smith 1986: 135):

> consolidation and maintenance of a centralised political and legal order, penetrating and encompassing the entire society from centre to periphery, creates the necessary milieu for the evolution of a nation. Common values and norms, founded upon the legitimate legal and political institutions and structures accepted and revered by all members, furnish the needed requirement for the development of the nation. When the rule of law and legal bureaucratic domination in the administration of societies triumphs, then, and only then, is the formation of nations possible.
>
> (Bereketeab 2007: 43)

The contribution of Italian colonial rule in the politico-legal dimension is thus to be seen in terms of the above comments. Colonial bureaucratic rule imposed on indigenous communities thus tried to enforce standardised and formalised rules and regulations (Trevaskis 1960).

The fourth analytical dimension is *common historical experience*. This dimension constitutes a repertoire of the other dimensions accumulated along the historical trajectories in the process of formation of Eritrea. Common history in this sense serves as an aggregation of all the things the ethno-linguistic communities went through, which were fermented in order to create an edifice that defined and characterised their collectivities. Historical experience plays the role of cement-ing the dimensions into an integrated body of shared experiences. Shared his-tory constitutes an accumulated depository of past deeds that generate collective social memory, and serves as a guide for the future. The awareness of common history, actual or imagined, is indispensable to the formation of national identity. In the dialectics of historiographical understanding and interpretation, a nation bears a common historical heritage of the past as well as cognisance of a common destiny for the future (Emerson 1960; Rustow 1967; Renan [1882] 1991).

The fifth analytical dimension is *common culture*. The presumption here is that common culture develops as a result of cumulative conflation of the other dimen-sions. Presumably common culture serves as the bricks and mortar gluing commu-nities together. National common culture is by definition and necessity political. The nation as a political organisation is expressed in political culture (Deutsch 1966; Smith 1986; Geertz 1993). Identity-wise, sub-national groups coalesce at a national level, in a political culture, to conform into nationhood. Lobban (1976: 339) notes: 'It is my argument this common tradition of colonial oppression has brought a variety of Eritrean language groups into a common national culture.' This by no means negates the prevalence of sub-national communal culture and identity. Indeed, Eritrea is characterised by duality of identity where the ethnic (sub-national) and civic (supra-ethnic or national) coexist (Bereketeab 2002).

The last, sixth, analytical dimension, the *will to live together*, is produced as an outcome of all the other five dimensions. A collectivity, a nation, develops the will to live together as a result of various integrative measures and a concomi-tant binding common national political culture. The growth of the will to live together is an illustration of the development of a sense of commonality and feeling of difference (Slowe 1990; Renan [1882] 1991). At this stage two distinct phenomena, notably internal inclusivity and external exclusivity, could be said to have developed. In terms of internal inclusivity, members of the imagined community are embraced as members, while those living beyond the perimeters of the internal imagined community are excluded as alien. Nonetheless there are always paradoxes that present and express contradictions, inconsistencies, nega-tions and discontinuities in the process of nation formation, a testimonial to the non-linearity of the process of the construction of nations. This fact was to be manifested in Eritrea following the demise of Italian colonial rule and disposal of the ex-colony of Eritrea in 1941–50.

We have analysed the various integrative dimensions, processes and mecha-nisms that generated the formation of Eritrea. Below we will examine, empiri-cally, the various periods through which the formation process took place, and what factors and actors operated against a peaceful realisation of self-determina-tion that necessitated an armed struggle.

Italian colonialism

The first foothold that was to pave the way for the creation of the colony of Eritrea was established in 1869, when the Rubattino Shipping Company purchased a piece of land in Assab (Almedom 2006: 106), the south-eastern tip of today's Eritrea, from a local sultan. Assab was declared an Italian colony in 1882. Subsequently, in expanding its colonial grip, Italy occupied the port of Massawa in 1885. The colonial expansion scheme further took the Italians to Asmara in 1889. Finally, on 1 January 1890, Italy formally declared the birth of its first colony of Eritrea (Machida 1987; Negash 1987; Mesghenna 1988; Gebre-Medhin 1989; Iyob 1995; Bereketeab 2007).

In this manner the successive formation of Eritrean territoriality took place. Prior to the territorial formation of Eritrea there were three distinct regions: the southern plateau connected with Abyssinia; the western lowland under Egyptian influence; and the south-eastern lowland of the Afar homeland governed by autonomous sultanates (Bereketeab 2007). The three distinct regions, through colonial artefact and engineering, were brought together to constitute the emergent colonial territory of Eritrea. Arguing in terms of the theory of colonialism as the creator of territorial nations in Africa it could then be purported that the prime Italian contribution to the formation of Eritrea as a colonial state was putting in place the foundation for the six serially interrelated dimensions.

After ensuring territorial integration the Italians proceeded with socio-economic integration. Of course the socio-economic integration was not intended to serve the interests and wellbeing of local people. Indeed the investments, economic activities and projects were directed to home consumption back in Italy, yet the unintended consequences to the local people were very visible. The main constructs and mechanisms that generated socio-economic integration included construction of cottage industries, transportation and telecommunications (railways, roads, telegraph lines, ports) projects, infrastructures, mining, agricultural concessions, establishing urban centres, emergence of bureaucratic offices that provided job opportunities for junior clerks, translators, cleaners and so on (Johnson and Johnson 1981: 182–3). The economic and construction activities were intensified in the second half of 1930 in conjunction with the invasion of Ethiopia in 1936.

These developments in material dimensions generated the emergence of urban-based modern classes and social groups (Houtart 1982; Leonard 1982; Killion 1985; Mesghenna 1988). The emergence of these work places also played a significant role in bringing together people of different ethnic, religious, linguistic and social backgrounds. The socio-economic integration was also further boosted by politico-legal integration as the various ethno-linguistic groups were brought under a common political and legal system. Administratively, the territory was parcelled into provinces while simultaneously being centralised and integrated into encompassing state structures. The division into administrative provinces, on one hand, and centralising in a territorial state, on the other, gave Eritrea its modern politico-legal form.

Italian colonialism through the various integrative measures along the colonial trajectory from territorial integration (the creation of Eritrean territoriality) to the politico-legal, socio-economic integrations (Pool 1980: 34; Leonard 1982) that engendered the development of a binding common political culture, which in turn spawned the will to live together which was to be expressed in the 30-year liberation struggle, contributed to the creation of Eritrean nationhood and identity (Bereketeab 2007). It was this development of the Eritrean national identity that underpinned the quest for self-determination. Italian political economy consolidated Eritrean identity and nationalism primarily through fostering three analytical dimensions, notably territorial integration, socio-economic integration and politico-legal integration. The remaining three analytical dimensions of the formation of Eritrea were primarily consolidated under British rule, federation and the national liberation struggle.

British protectorate

Ethiopia claimed Eritrea and Italian Somaliland following the defeat of Italy in 1941 (Greenfield 1986: 11). The claims were made with reference to past historical connections where according to the imperial regime the territories were part of the empire but were forcibly severed by Italy from the mother country (Habte Selassie 1980). The logic behind the claim was that, since the colonial power that had separated the territories had lost the war, the territories should be returned to the original owner (Cervenka 1977).

Following the outbreak of the Second World War and the defeat of Italy in East Africa in 1941, Italian colonial rule in Eritrea was brought to an end. Eritrea therefore was placed under a British protectorate until the destiny of the ex-Italian territories was determined by the United Nations. The British military administration (BMA) that took over the administration of Eritrea oversaw the transition of the territory. At the Paris Peace Conference in June 1946, Italy formally renounced its rights to Eritrea, Italian Somaliland and Libya. The treaty also stipulated that the victorious 'Big Four' would take on the responsibility of disposal of the territories within a year. Upon failure of the Big Four to find a settlement, the case was to be referred to the UN (Habte Selassie 1980: 36–7). The Big Four dispatched a commission of investigation to find out the wish of the Eritrean people. The commission came back with an inconclusive report; consequently the Big Four could not resolve the matter, and it was therefore placed before the UN in 1949 (Cumming 1953: 128).

According to the Vienna Convention the BMA assumed merely a caretaker administrative role. Therefore, technically the BMA was constrained by the Vienna Convention guiding the administering state as to what measures it should take. Nonetheless the BMA was involved in taking measures that had far-reaching implications for the territory. These measures were particularly in the economic and political spheres. In the economic sphere the role of the BMA was of a negative nature. Initially, for the duration of the war, the BMA continued the economic boom that the Italians had started. This was primarily because the British used Eritrea as a military base for their war efforts to boost military-related industries. Once the war was over, however, they began dismantling large amounts of plant and equipment. Equipment worth £86 million was removed from Eritrea, which included port facilities, a cement factory, a potash factory, a salt-processing plant and railway equipment. A few days after they surrendered the territory, in September 1952, for instance, it was disclosed that the British took out of Eritrea stores worth over USD$900,000 (Firebrace 1986: 48). This was hardly helpful to the declared British position of the non-viability of Eritrea as an independent state. Indeed it was dishonest to claim that Eritrea was economically incapable of standing on its own while simultaneously destroying its economic assets.

On a positive note the British introduced liberalisation of the political and social system. The first measure they took was to lift the colour ban introduced by the Italian Fascist regime. In the area of political liberalisation they allowed the formation of political parties and trade unions. Beginning in 1946 several parties were formed. This political liberalisation however produced a divided national-ism that was actively encouraged by the British. One category of nationalism was based on Islamic identity, which produced the Muslim League. Countering this sectarian nationalism, another sectarian nationalism based on Christian identity was in operation. The Muslims in the Muslim League, induced by the fear of dom-ination by a Christian empire, opted for independence. A section of the Muslim League, the Muslim League of the Western Province, even advocated a split and for the Muslims of the western lowland to join Sudan, a Muslim country. Chris-tians represented by the Unionist Party, referring to history, culture, religion and other similarities, sought union with Ethiopia. External forces, the BMA, Italian residents and Ethiopia, played a significant role in provoking and aggravating the sectarian division in Eritrean society. Indeed Eritrean nationalists later placed the responsibility for the division squarely on foreign forces that were presumably against the independence of Eritrea and fomented sectarian division in order to deny Eritrea the right to self-determination (Tesfai 2001; Almedom 2006).

By 1949 the parties were parcelled into two blocs, the independence bloc and the unionist bloc, who pursued their separate convictions until the UN resolved to federate the territory with Ethiopia. The formation of political parties was intended to influence the disposal of Eritrea. The influence, nonetheless, was not in unison. Probably encouraged by a lack of unity of purpose among Eritreans, the British came up with a partition plan known as the Bevin–Sforza plan, a scheme that had no support among the political parties. According to the plan, the Muslim lowland was to be ceded to Sudan and the Christian highland was to be joined to Ethiopia. Although the political parties were divided as regards the final solution between those advocating union and those backing independence, partition was not on their agenda. Owing to differences of opinion in the UN General Assembly (UNGA) the partition plan was defeated.

The failure of the Bevin–Sforza plan compelled the UN to take up the issue of disposal of Eritrea. Within the UNGA a serious division occurred as to how to dispose of the territory. While the Soviet bloc supported the independence of Eritrea, the West led by the United States wanted to unite it with Ethiopia. The UNGA decided to send a commission of investigation consisting of representa-tives of Burma, Norway, Guatemala, South Africa and Pakistan to ascertain the wish of the Eritrean people. The commission submitted a divided report as to how the territory should be dealt with. South Africa and Burma recommended the federation of Eritrea with Ethiopia; Guatemala and Pakistan recommended UN trusteeship that would lead to independence; and Norway recommended complete union with Ethiopia (Cumming 1953: 128).

Finally the UNGA passed a compromise resolution wherein Eritrea was to be federated with Ethiopia in spite of the fact that the overwhelming majority of Eritreans expressed the wish to be independent. It was in recognition of this wish that the then US secretary of state, John Foster Dulles, when addressing the UN Security Council in 1952, had this to say:

> From the point of view of justice, the opinion of the Eritrean people must receive consideration. Nevertheless, the strategic interest of the United States in the Red Sea basin and consideration of security and world peace make it necessary that the country had to be linked with our ally, Ethiopia.
>
> (Quoted in Habte Selassie 1980: 39)

As is still the case today, therefore, Eritrean rights were sacrificed for geostrategic interests. It was a time when the Cold War was intensifying, so rivalry for domination and controlling strategic areas was spreading, not least in the Red Sea region. The strategic location of the Red Sea induced the US government to build a communication installation in Asmara, Eritrea in 1953 (Wrong 2005). The Kagnew intelligence centre in Asmara, the largest communication base in the world connected with NATO, was then used as a bargaining piece between Ethiopia and the US, where the former would allow the latter to establish the communication base and the latter would support the former's claim on Eritrea (Cervenka 1977). This quid pro quo exchange had been set in motion before the future of the territory was sealed, when it was placed before the UN. Emperor Haile Selassie could not even wait until the federation came into operation; he signed a secret defence agreement that was to last for 25 years by which the US was granted a lease of the Kagnew base in Eritrea and Ethiopia received substantial military aid.

The British handed over Eritrea in 1952, following the approval of the Constitution by the Eritrean National Assembly and Emperor Haile Selassie. British rule was replaced by the federation.

The significance of the British rule in the context of national identity formation and the quest for self-determination, particularly seen from the perspective of the six analytical dimensions, was in consolidating a common historical experience and common culture. Political liberalisation and expansion of education played an important role in raising national consciousness and mobilisation of the population. In its cognitive dimension Eritrean identity was thrust to a higher level.

The UN-sponsored federation

The UN endorsed a resolution on 2 December 1950 known as Resolution 390A (V) to bind the territory of Eritrea, until 1941 an Italian territory and after the defeat of the latter a British protectorate, with Ethiopia. The federation was enforced on 11 September 1952 (Becker 1952; Gebre-Medhin 1989; Iyob 1995; Fessehatzion 1998; Tesfai 2005; Bereketeab 2007). This followed its approval by the Eritrean National Assembly on 10 July 1952, and its endorsement by Emperor Haile Selassie on 6 August 1952 (Medhanie 1986: 21). The federal arrangement lasted for ten years (1952–62), until it was arbitrarily abrogated by the emperor (Medhanie 1986; Habte Selassie 1989; Fessehatzion 1998). The provisions of the federation consisted of a range of liberal principles and institutions by which the autonomous Eritrean state was to be governed (Scholler 1994). Once the federal dispensations were enforced, Eritreans from both camps (nationalists and union-ists) welcomed the unsolicited federation, convinced that it represented and sym-bolised a separate Eritrean political identity.

The UN decision in favour of federation provided a general frame, the details of which were left to be worked out by the UN special commissioner (Negash 1997). Generally, the UN resolution stipulated that the Constitution would be based on democratic principles, human rights and fundamental liberties (Cumming 1953: 130). The main provisions of the resolution were laid down by the UNGA. The profound distinction of discretionary powers between the autonomous state of Eritrea and the Ethiopian state was arranged in such a manner that 'domestic affairs were left for the government of Eritrea to deal with; while foreign relations, currency and finance, foreign and inter-state commerce, external and inter-state communications, and so forth, were all the responsibility of the Federal Govern-ment, which is synonymous with the Ethiopian Government' (Cumming 1953: 134). It was clearly stated in the resolution that Eritrea would exercise consider-able autonomy, and there would be clearly delineated power divisions allotted to the Eritrean government and the federal government. Nonetheless, in the draft-ing of the Eritrean Constitution, the provisions were weakened and truncated, which seriously undermined Eritrea's autonomy. However, more was to come in the undermining of the autonomy provisions pursuant to enforcement.

Between 1950 and 1952 the UN commissioner and his team set out to draft a constitution for the autonomous Eritrean state. Nonetheless, even during the drafting process, the UN special commissioner, Dr Eduardo Anze Matienzo, from Bolivia, who was tasked by the UNGA to draft the Constitution, met stiff resistance from the Ethiopian imperial regime (Cervenka 1977: 40). Ethio-pia strongly opposed many of the provisions of the federal arrangements. The prime provisions of the federation as articulated by General Assembly Resolu-tion 390A (A) were:

(1) recognition of the national identity of the Eritrean people and the ter-ritorial integrity of Eritrea within its colonially established boundaries; (2) an autonomous Eritrean government with its own legislative, executive and judicial bodies; (3) assurance to the inhabitants of Eritrea 'the fullest respect and safeguard' of their traditions, religions and languages as well as the widest possible measure of self-government; (4) guarantee the enjoyment of human rights and fundamental freedoms by the Eritrean people.[1]

All the points mentioned here were anathema to the Ethiopian political system, which was grounded in divine personality powers. The very principles and institutions were abhorred by the Ethiopian state, since they counterpoised the archaic feudal governance systems through which Ethiopia was governed, as well as represented a danger to the unity and integrity of the empire, because other regions might be tempted to demand similar autonomy and devolution of power. The significance of the federal structures and institutions with regard to Eritrean statehood and identity rested on the fact that they upheld and preserved the colonial creation and entity of Eritrea. Therefore the imperial authorities, particularly foreign minister Aklilu Habte Wold, worked relentlessly to frustrate the efforts of the UN special commissioner in his drafting of the Eritrean Constitution. Some of the provisions the Ethiopian authorities wanted to include in the Constitution were that: the emperor should appoint the chief executive for Eritrea; Tigrinya and Amharic should be official languages in Eritrea; and the flag of Ethiopia should also be the flag of Eritrea. This would have severely undermined the autonomy of Eritrea.

The federation was doomed to fail for various reasons. Certainly affecting its functionality and sustainability was that neither part solicited it. One bloc of the political parties requested immediate independence, while another wanted union. The idea of federation was alien to the political parties. When it was decided, however, all parts agreed to preserve it. Its worst enemy was that it had a serious structural defect. Instead of the originally stipulated situation, there was no distinction between the Ethiopian state and the federal state; the Ethiopian state became the federal state. This gave Ethiopia an unfettered ability to intervene in Eritrean internal affairs. Ethiopia was adamant that, once the case was removed from UN oversight, it would make sure that all the stipulated provisions were eroded (Medhanie 1986; Fessehatzion 1998). The process of erosion had already begun during the drafting of the Constitution. A bitter struggle took place between the special commissioner of the UN to Eritrea, who was entrusted with the task of drafting the Constitution, and the foreign minister of Ethiopia, Aklilu Habte Wold.

The UN special commissioner to Eritrea wrote in his final report:

> It is true that once the Federal Act and the Eritrean Constitution have come into force the mission entrusted to the General Assembly under the Peace Treaty with Italy will have been fulfilled and the future of Eritrea must be regarded as settled, but it does not follow that the United Nations will no longer have any right to deal with the question of Eritrea. The Federal Act and the Eritrean Constitution will still be based on the resolution of the U.N. and that international instrument will retain its full force. That being so, if it were necessary either to amend or to interpret the Federal Act, only the General Assembly, as author of that instrument, would be competent to take a decision. Similarly if the Federal Act were violated, the General Assembly could be seized of the matter.
>
> (Quoted in Greenfield 1986: 14–15)

In spite of all the deficiencies, but also trusting that the UN would act if there were any breaches once it was endorsed, the Eritreans demonstrated every effort to make it successful. The federation was endorsed by the two blocs at the Wa'ala Selam held at the Cinema Impero in Asmara on 31 December 1950 (Killion 1997: 12). Both the unionists, who were for union with Ethiopia, and the independence bloc, who championed independence, convened the reconciliation conference, which they designated as a peace conference, reconciled their bitter differences and pledged to work together for the success of the federation (Gebre-Medhin 1989; Killion 1997: 12; Tesfai 2005: 105). Ethiopia, on the other hand, from day one worked hard to foil it. For Eritreans the federation embodying Eritrean autonomy represented Eritrean separate identity and nationhood (Fessehatzion 1998; Bereketeab 2007). As the saying goes, however, one cannot clap with one hand, because Ethiopia reneged from its commitment; thus the arrangement began to founder from the very outset. From 1953 to 1962 when the federation was formally abrogated, the main pillars were systematically dismantled.

In 1955, Tedla Bairu, the chief executive of the Eritrean government, was dismissed and replaced by an ardent unionist, Asfaha Woldemichael. The Eritrean press and trade unions were banned. The Eritrean flag was replaced by the Ethiopian one. The following year the Ethiopian Penal Code replaced the Eritrean Penal Code, the chief executive was changed to an Eritrean administrator, and the Eritrean government became the Eritrean administration. Eritrean languages were banished from the public realm and replaced by Amharic (the Ethiopian official language). At last, on 14 November 1962, Asfaha Woldemichael read a statement to the Eritrean National Assembly in Amharic in which it was declared that the federation had been dissolved and Eritrean had joined its mother country, Ethiopia (Cervenka 1977; Sherman 1980; Erlich 1983; Medhanie 1986; Markakis 1987; Araya 1990).

Although the provisions were dismantled one by one and finally the federation abrogated, the decade represented an important stage in the process of formation of Eritrean identity and nationhood. It not only provided Eritreans with the experience and taste of self-governance but also gave them the opportunity to develop national political institutions and symbols that further consolidated the six analytical dimensions, particularly politico-legal integration, common historical experience and common culture.

Annexation: special colony

Abrogation of the federation led to annexation that transformed Eritrea into an administrative province within the Ethiopian empire. The case of Eritrea was erroneously analogised with the cases of secession such as Katanga, Biafra and South Sudan (Medhanie 1986: 278). The analogical incompatibility derives from the fact that Eritrea, unlike the mentioned cases, was a creation of colonialism that should be governed by the decolonisation regime. For Eritrean nationalists the annexation of Eritrea in November 1962 converted the territory into a special colony. The Eritrean Liberation Front (ELF) in its First National Congress, in

1971, defined the Eritrean case as a special colony (ELF 1971: 6–7). In contrast to the theory of a classical colony, the theory of a special colony postulates a case wherein a third world underdeveloped state colonises a territory on behalf of an imperial power. In this case Ethiopia, virtually a feudal country, colonised Eritrea on behalf of American imperialism and political economy.

The Marxist and materialist conception of colonialism explicated that when an advanced capitalist state in search of cheap raw materials, labour and markets for its processed industrial products forcibly occupies a territory and people that are at a lower level of the socio-economic development scale it is called colonialism. This dogma thus excluded any form of occupation by a backward, feudalist or feudo-capitalist state from the category of colonialism. It was this understanding that induced scholars as well as politicians to label the Eritrean struggle an ethnic secessionist movement, though it was a multi-ethnic society.

Ethiopia as a feudo-capitalist state was therefore perceived to be incapable of carrying out an act of colonialism. It was perceived to be lacking the necessary economic, political, military and technological capacity to engage in acts of colonisation. The Eritrean nationalists, who were under the influence of this dogma, adopted this notion and devised the notion of special colony. The notion of special colony was intended to engage two important interlocutors in the quest for self-determination. The first group was the Marxist internationals and the Eastern bloc whose support and recognition of the Eritrean struggle as a national colonial struggle were seen as decisive. The second group related to Ethiopian leftists who, influenced by the Marxist and materialist conception of colonialism, rejected the independence of Eritrea on the grounds that Eritrea could not be a colony of Ethiopia (EPRP-D 2008), since the latter was not a capitalist state. This ideological and theoretical engagement or rather disengagement between progressive Ethiopian forces, such as the Ethiopian People's Revolutionary Party (EPRP) and the All-Ethiopia Socialist Movement (in Amharic, MEISON), and Eritrean nationalists constituted a considerable political hindrance to finding a peaceful political solution to the Eritrean problem.

Following the proclamation of socialism by the self-professed Marxist group of the military junta that deposed the monarchy, the socialist bloc inclined to supporting the Ethiopian claim against the Eritrean invocation of the right of self-determination. To win the support of the Socialist International, the special colony, which according to Eritreans was indeed a continuation of the imperialist-hatched federation that in turn was in fact an abrogation of self-determination expressed in the principle of decolonisation, was perceived as a vital instrument to appeal to forces of a similar ideological persuasion.

The appeal to Ethiopian progressive forces through innovative theoretical and ideological argument failed to bear fruit. Deep down the leftist socialist forces in Ethiopia were nationalists. Therefore they perceived the Eritrean quest for self-determination as a secessionist movement that intended to break up the Ethiopian state. The OAU's 'bible' of sacrosanctity of the colonially inherited borders was deployed as a reference for their position of not acceding to the right to self-determination of Eritreans. The right of the state preceded the right of the people.

Nonetheless Eritrea was entitled to the right of self-determination in accordance with the provisions of the UN Charter, which confers the right of self-determination to: 1) colonial people and 2) people subjected to foreign domination. Eritrea fulfils both criteria. It was a creation of Italian colonialism and thus fulfils the first criterion. Since the abrogation of the federation and annexation, it has also fulfilled the second criterion, because it fell under the provisions for people subjected to foreign domination (Tesfagiorgis 1987). The failure to resolve the Eritrean problem through peaceful means, by addressing the quest of Eritreans for self-determination, then led to armed struggle.

War of decolonisation or secession?

The conception of decolonisation and secession constituted the conceptual and ideological point of dispute until the end between Ethiopian leftists who wished to retain Eritrea within Ethiopia and Eritrean nationalists who wanted independence. Even the military junta, the Dergue, a self-professed Marxist council that ascended to power after deposing the *ancien régime*, rejected the Eritrean view of decolonisation and independence. Therefore it opted to continue the military option. The idea of territorial integrity and access to the sea still lingers in the minds of the majority of Ethiopians. Indeed, the Ethiopian claim on Eritrea could be boiled down to the aspiration of access to the sea. There were many attempts to sever the port of Assab from the territory of Eritrea in order to satisfy this lingering aspiration, yet it was embedded in the argument of precluding the evils of secession. The Tigray People's Liberation Front (TPLF), perhaps motivated by the ambivalent aspiration of the struggle in Tigray, accepted the colonial nature of the Eritrean struggle (TPLF 1986). The acceptance of the thesis of colonial origin obligated recognition of the right of decolonisation. Thus the TPLF became the only Ethiopian organisation to accept Eritrean independence.

By coining the notion of special colony, Eritrean nationalists challenged the Ethiopian perception of secessionism. The principle of self-determination as an expression of decolonisation that benefits two groups of people, 1) colonial people and 2) people subjected to foreign domination (Tesfagiorgis 1987: 92), was invoked by Eritreans to confer political, moral and legal legitimacy on their claim in accordance with the UN Charter's Resolution 1514 (XV) and Resolution 2625 (XXV). For Ethiopia the secessionism argument, by glossing over the colonial construction of Eritrea and referring to the UN Charter that upholds the territorial integrity of a state, served as logical and instrumental tool to deny Eritreans statehood. By defining the Eritrean struggle for self-determination as a secessionist movement Ethiopia labelled it as a criminal act that violated its sacrosanct territorial integrity.

Both Eritrea and Ethiopia invoked the contradictions incorporated in the UN Charter. While Eritrea's claim was based on the UN Charter upholding the principle of self-determination, Ethiopia invoked the UN Charter upholding the principle of the territorial integrity of states. Invoking the two principles of rights of self-determination (colonial people, and people subjected to foreign domination), Eritreans claimed that their armed struggle (1961–91) was a war for decolonisation that was aborted on two occasions. The first occasion was when the UNGA resolved to join Eritrea with Ethiopia in federation against the wishes of its people. The second occasion was when Ethiopia annulled the federation and annexed Eritrea, whereby the territory was converted to a simple province.

The OAU's colonial border sacrosanctity and Eritrea

The OAU passed a resolution at its summit conference in Cairo in 1964 where territorial integration of the post-colonial African states was declared sacrosanct (Farley 2010: 802). Thereby colonial boundaries were transformed to international borders. It was further declared that any attempt at secession from existing states was to be treated as a criminal act.

Ethiopian officials who were involved in devising the territorial integrity clause in the OAU Charter in 1964 made sure that Eritrea was annexed before the adoption of the clause. By the time the clause was endorsed Eritrea was a province of the empire; therefore, when the federation was terminated through Proclamation Order no. 27 (Greenfield 1986: 14), the matter was to be conceived as one relating to the sanctity of the colonial borders, since by then the Eritrean case was seen as an internal Ethiopian question. The paradox however was that Ethiopia, as a country that had escaped colonisation, was permitted to play a considerable role in the shaping of the colonial borders regime in the OAU.

In the treatment by the OAU, Eritrea came out as a victim on two counts. First, unfortunately for Eritrea the federation was abrogated and concomitantly Eritrea was annexed and converted to the 14th province in the imperial state of Ethiopia. Therefore for the OAU the case of Eritrea was a closed chapter; it was an internal Ethiopian affair in which the continental organisation was prohibited from interfering. Second, in what is known in the theoretical discourse as distance theory, notably the cultural distance between the contesting units as a source of legitimisation of the exercise of self-determination and decolonisation, Eritreans were seen to be the same as the Ethiopian people. Therefore their quest for independence was met by the rhetoric 'You are the same people. Why do you want to destroy a respected and old state?' The underpinning rationale in the OAU for not heeding the Eritrean quest for self-determination was that people of identical or similar cultural pedigree could not be divided. The Eritrean quest was also seen from a pan-African vantage point where Africans were supposed to aim at unity rather than disintegration.

The OAU, as an aggregate body, as well as the majority of its member states thus simply accepted the Ethiopian propaganda that the Eritrean movement was a secessionist movement led by few misguided individuals who wanted to sell Eritrea to the Arabs for petrodollars. This representation placed the Eritrean struggle at the heart of the Arab–Israeli conflict, further complicating the matter for Eritreans, as they were unable to get sympathy and support from the OAU and many African states.

Conclusion

Modern Eritrea is the creation of Italian colonialism. In the last hundred years it has experienced three consecutive foreign rules, Italian followed by British and Ethiopian rule. These foreign rules have shaped and reshaped Eritrean national identity and nationhood. Indeed the interplay between two sets of actors, colonial and nationalist, propelled the gradual gestation of Eritrean nationalism that in parity with all colonial territories sought statehood. Unlike the overwhelming majority of colonial territories that emerged as independent states as a consequence of the decolonisation process, Eritrea was denied that right and was joined with Ethiopia through a UN-sponsored federal arrangement. US geo-strategic interests necessitated that Eritrea was joined with an ally.

With the abrogation of the federation and annexation of Eritrea by Ethiopia, Eritrean nationalists were compelled to launch a liberation struggle in 1961 in search of the right to self-determination. The inception of the liberation struggle heralded the highest form of Eritrean agency in the formation and transformation of Eritrean national identity and nationhood that eventually made the consummation of the right of self-determination inevitable.

In terms of consolidation of Eritrean national identity and nationhood, it could be argued that the three consecutive regimes – Italian, British and federation – also clearly contributed. In this process of formation and transformation six identifiable mechanisms have been in play. These were: 1) territorial integration; 2) socio-economic integration; 3) politico-legal integration; 4) common historical experience; 5) common culture; and 6) the will to live together. The first of these, territorial integration, was the very foundation upon which the others were built. Eritrean nationalists through strengthening these six dimensions tried to consolidate their national identity and nationhood, which they saw as the prerequisite to achieving their objective, self-determination.

The annexation and 30-year occupation, on the other hand, represented an attempt by Ethiopia to wipe out Eritrean national identity and statehood. Nationalist symbols such as the flag, languages, holidays and institutions were replaced by Ethiopian ones. Eritrean nationalists, therefore, attempted to reinforce and preserve those symbols and institutions by creating an alternative space in the body of the national liberation movement. It could be argued that the annexation, occupation and subsequent war against suppression galvanised Eritrean nationhood and statehood in fulfilling the subjective conditions of nationhood. Italian colonialism, British administration and the federation on the other hand helped in laying down the objective requisite factors of nationhood and statehood that finally provided the necessary prerequisite for the will to live together. In a nutshell, the 30-year armed struggle was seen as between forces of destruction and construction of national identity and nationhood, between forces for self-determination on the one hand and territorial integration on the other.

Note

1 General Assembly Resolution 390, 5 UN GAOR Supp. (no. 20) at 20–22, UN Doc. A/1775(1950).

References

Almedom, Astier M. 2006. 'Re-Reading the Short and Long-Rigged History of Eritrea 1941–1952: Back to the Future?', *Nordic Journal of African Studies*, vol. 15, no. 2, pp. 103–42.

Anderson, Benedict. 1991. *Imagined Communities: Reflection on the Origin and Spread of Nationalism*. London: Verso.

Araya, Mesfin. 1990. 'The Eritrean Question: An Alternative Explanation', *Journal of Modern African Studies*, vol. 28, no. 1, pp. 79–100.

Becker, George Henry. 1952. *The Disposition of the Italian Colonies 1941–1951*, Ph.D. thesis, University of Geneva. Annemasse: Imprimerie Granchamp.

Bendix, Reinhard. 1964. *Nation-Building and Citizenship: Studies of Our Changing Social Order*. New York: John Wiley & Sons.

Bereketeab, Redie. 2002. 'Supra-Ethnic Nationalism', *African Sociological Review*, vol. 6, no. 2, pp. 137–52.

Bereketeab, Redie. 2007. *Eritrea: The Making of a Nation, 1890–1991*. Trenton, NJ: Red Sea Press.

Cervenka, Zdenek. 1977. 'Eritrea: Struggle for Self-Determination or Secession?', *Africa Spectrum*, vol. 12, no. 1, pp. 37–48.

Cumming, Duncan. 1953. 'The U.N. Disposal of Eritrea', *African Affairs*, vol. 52, no. 207, pp. 127–36.

Deutsch, Karl W. 1966. *Nationalism and Social Communication: An Inquiry into the Foundation of Nationality*. Cambridge, MA: MIT Press.

ELF (Eritrean Liberation Front). 1971. The First Eritrean National Congress of the ELF: The Programme of the Eritrean Revolution, Approved by the First National Congress Held Inside the Liberated Area, 14 October – 12 November.

Emerson, Rupert. 1960. *From Empire to Nation: The Rise to Self-Assertion of Asian and African Peoples*. Cambridge, MA: Harvard University Press.

EPRP (D) (Ethiopian People's Revolutionary Party (D)). 2008. Political Program, January.

Erlich, Haggai. 1983. *The Struggle over Eritrea, 1962–1978: War and Revolution in the Horn of Africa*. Stanford, CA: Hoover Institution Press.

Farley, Benjamin R. 2010. 'Calling a State a State: Somaliland and International Recognition', *Emory International Law Review*, vol. 24, no. 2, pp. 777–820.

Fessehatzion, Tekie. 1998. 'A Brief Encounter with Democracy: From Acquiescence to Resistance during Eritrea's Early Federation Years', *Eritrean Studies Review*, vol. 2, no. 2.

Firebrace, James. 1986. 'The British Responsibility towards Eritrea and the Moral Responsibility of the International Community', in *Eritrea: The Way Forward*, Proceedings of a conference on Eritrea organised by the United Nations Association, 9 November 1985, United Nations Association – United Kingdom (UNA-UK). Nottingham: Bertrand Russell House.

Gebre-Medhin, Jordan. 1989. *Peasants and Nationalism in Eritrea: A Critique of Ethiopian Studies*. Trenton, NJ: Red Sea Press.

Geertz, Clifford. 1993. *The Interpretation of Cultures: Selected Essays*. London: Fontana Press.

Gellner, Ernest. 1983. *Nations and Nationalism*. Oxford: Blackwell.

Greenfield, Richard. 1986. 'The Historical and Legal Background of Eritrea and the Role of the United Nations', in *Eritrea: The Way Forward*, Proceedings of a conference on Eritrea organised by the United Nations Association, 9 November 1985, United Nations Association – United Kingdom (UNA-UK). Nottingham: Bertrand Russell House.

Habte Selassie, Bereket. 1980. 'From British Rule to Federation and Annexation', in Basil Davidson, Lionel Cliffe and Bereket Habte Selassie (eds), *Behind the War in Eritrea*. Nottingham: Spokesman.

Habte Selassie, Bereket. 1989. *Eritrea and the United Nations and Other Essays*. Trenton, NJ: Red Sea Press.

Hobsbawm, Eric J. 1990. *Nations and Nationalism since 1780: Programme, Myth, Reality*. New York: Cambridge University Press.

Houtart, François. 1982. 'Social Aspects of the Eritrean Revolution', in *Proceedings of the Permanent People's Tribunal of the International League for the Rights and Liberation of People: The Eritrean Case*. Rome: Research Information Centre on Eritrea.

Iyob, Ruth, 1995. *The Eritrean Struggle for Independence: Domination, Resistance, Nationalism 1941–1993*. Cambridge: Cambridge University Press.

Johnson, Michael and Johnson, Trish. 1981. 'Eritrea: The National Question and the Logic of Protracted Struggle', *African Affairs*, vol. 80, no. 319, pp. 181–95.

Killion, Tom. 1985. 'Workers, Capital and the State in the Ethiopian Region, 1919–1974', Ph.D. thesis, Stanford University.

Killion, Tom. 1997. 'Eritrean Workers' Organization and Early Nationalist Mobilization, 1948–1958', *Eritrean Studies Review*, vol. 2, no. 1.

Leonard, Richard. 1982. 'European Colonization and the Socio-Economic Integration of Eritrea', in *Proceedings of the Permanent People's Tribunal of the International League for the Rights and Liberation of People: The Eritrean Case*. Rome: Research Information Centre on Eritrea.

Lobban, Richard. 1976. 'The Eritrean War: Issues and Implications', *Canadian Journal of African Studies*, vol. 10, no. 2, pp. 335–46.

Machida, R. 1987. *Eritrea: The Struggle for Independence*. Trenton, NJ: Red Sea Press.

Markakis, John. 1987. *National and Class Conflict in the Horn of Africa*. Cambridge: Cambridge University Press.

Medhanie, Tesfatzion. 1986. *Eritrea: Dynamics of a National Question*. Amsterdam: B. R. Gruner.

Mesghenna, Yemane. 1988. *Italian Colonialism: A Case Study of Eritrea, 1869–1934*, Ph.D. thesis. Lund, Sweden: Studenlitteratur.

Negash, Tekeste. 1987. *Italian Colonialism in Eritrea, 1882–1941: Policies, Praxis and Impact*. Uppsala: Almqvist & Wiksell International.

Negash, Tekeste. 1997. *Eritrea and Ethiopia: The Federal Experience*. Uppsala: Nordic Africa Institute.

Pool, David. 1979. *Eritrea: Africa's Longest War*. London: Anti-Slavery Society.

Pool, David. 1980. 'Revolutionary Crisis and Revolutionary Vanguard: The Emergence of the Eritrean People's Liberation Front', *Review of African Political Economy*, no. 19, pp. 33–47.

Pool, David. 2001. *From Guerrillas to Government: The Eritrean People's Liberation Front*. Oxford: James Currey and Athens: Ohio University Press.

Renan, Ernest. [1882] 1991. 'What Is a Nation?', in Homi K. Bhabha (ed.), *Nation and Narration*. London: Routledge.

Rokkan, Stein. 1975. 'Dimensions of State Formation and Nation-Building: A Possible Paradigm for Research or Variation within Europe', in Charles Tilly (ed.), *The Formation of National States in Western Europe*. Princeton, NJ: Princeton University Press.

Rustow, D. A.1967. *A World of Nations: Problems of Political Modernization*. Washington, DC: Brookings Institution.

Scholler, Heinrich. 1994. 'Future Relations between Ethiopia and Eritrea: Two Perspectives', in Peter Woodward and Murray Forsyth (eds), *Conflict and Peace in the Horn of Africa: Federalism and Its Alternatives*. Aldershot: Dartmouth Publishing.

Seton-Watson, Hugh. 1977. *Nations and States: An Enquiry into the Origins of Nations and the Politics of Nationalism*. London: Methuen.

Sherman, Richard. 1980. *Eritrea: The Unfinished Revolution*. New York: Praeger.

Slowe, Peter M. 1990. *Geography and Political Power: The Geography of Nations and States*. London: Routledge.

Smith, Anthony D. 1983. *State and Nation in the Third World*. Brighton: Wheatsheaf Books.

Smith, Anthony D. 1986. *The Ethnic Origin of Nations*. Oxford: Blackwell.

Smith, Anthony D. 1991. *National Identity*. London: Penguin Books.

Tesfagiorgis, Gebre Hiwet. 1987. 'Self-Determination: Its Evolution and Practice by the United Nations and Its Application to the Case of Eritrea', *Wisconsin International Law Journal*, vol. 6, no. 1, pp. 75–128.

Tesfai, Alemseged. 2001. *Ainfelale, 1941–1950* [Let Us Not Split, 1941–1950]. Asmara: Hidri Publishers.

Tesfai, Alemseged. 2005. *Federashin Ertra M's Etiopia: Kab Matenso K'sab Tedla, 1951–1955* [The Federation of Eritrea with Ethiopia: From Matenzo to Tedla, 1951–1955]. Asmara: Hidri Publishers.

TPLF. 1986. 'Statement by the Central Committee of the Tigray People's Liberation Front (TPLF) on the Occasion of the 24th Anniversary of the Armed Struggle in Eritrea', *Review of African Political Economy*, no. 35, pp. 92–4.

Trevaskis, K. N. 1960. *Eritrea: A Colony in Transition: 1941–1952*. Oxford: Clarendon Press.

UN. 1950. General Assembly Resolution 390, 5, UN GAOR Supp. (no. 20) at 20–22, UN Doc. A/1775(1950).

Väyrynen, Raimo. 1993. 'Territory, Nation-State and Nationalism', in Jyrki Livonen (ed.), *The Future of the Nation-State in Europe*. Cheltenham: Edward Elgar.

Wrong, Michela. 2005. *I Didn't Do It for You: How the World Betrayed a Small African Country*. London: Fourth Estate.

Yohannes, Okbazghi. 1991. *Eritrea: A Pawn in World Politics*. Gainesville: University of Florida Press.

16 The Saharawi people's quest for self-determination

The complexities of unachieved decolonisation

Belkacem Iratni

Introduction

The Western Sahara is considered Africa's last colony and the 'longest, most protracted conflict in the history of the United Nations', to use the words of former US assistant secretary of state John Bolton (1998). According to many scholars, it is one of the 'forgotten' or 'frozen' disputes (Zoubir 2007).

Situated on the Atlantic shore of north-western Africa and stretching over 260,000 kilometres, the territory is disputed by Morocco and the Polisario Front, which claims to represent the Saharawi people. In 1975, Spain, the colonial power, withdrew without implementing its mandatory duties of carrying out a referendum over the right of the Saharawi people to self-determination. Morocco claims sovereignty on the basis of 'historical ties' with the territory, while the Polisario Front maintains that it is an occupied land and advocates its independence. The stalemate over the Western Sahara continues in spite of numerous resolutions taken by the United Nations to resolve the conflict.

The chapter seeks to provide a meaningful analysis of the Western Sahara quest for self-determination deriving from its historical roots and speculations over its future. It starts by reviewing briefly the historical background. It provides an account of the process of the foundation of Western Sahara under Spanish colonialism that began in 1884. Following this, claims by Morocco over the territory will be succinctly presented. This is followed by an account of the process of the annexation of the Western Sahara by Morocco. Further it presents the contradicting claims of both Morocco and the Polisario Front over the territory since the end of Spanish colonial rule in 1975. Finally, the chapter looks at the recent features of the stalemate the Western Saharan case has reached and reviews possible solutions to the conflict. It is concluded that neither a compromise solution nor a 'war of attrition' by the two belligerent parties is possible. The contention is that the status quo will persist. A continuation of the conflict however would have unpredictable implications for the Sahel–Saharan region, which has recently become a major hub for terrorist activities and drugs and arms trafficking.

The formation of the territory of Western Sahara: Spanish colonialism and Moroccan irredentism

The Western Sahara has an ancient history. However, for the purpose of the present analysis, it is sufficient to begin with the eighth century. This territory was inhabited by the Sanhadja, a Berber tribal confederation coming from North Africa. As a result of the Arab conquest the native population embraced Islam and came to speak mainly the Hassaniya language, an Arabic-based dialect. Throughout its history, the Western Sahara has been a crossroads for traditional routes used by caravans of Reguibat nomads and camels for the transport of salt and gold between North and West Africa. The present-day populations of the Saharawis are the descendants of tribes which came from Yemen during the fifteenth century. They succeeded in stabilising the country and in establishing Saguia Al Hamra, a renowned religious and educational centre.

Like the North African countries, Western Sahara was the object of a colonial scramble, while its population resisted repeated incursions of the Western powers and Moroccan expansion. In 1724, Sultan Moulay Ismail of Morocco for instance sent Black troops, the Abid al-Bukhari, to help the Emir of Trarza in the Western Sahara to attack the French post of Saint Joseph in Senegal (Pennell 2003: 105). These repeated incursions by Moroccan troops constituted the historical basis of Morocco's claims over the Western Sahara territory. After the death of Moulay Ismail, Moroccan control of the territory became more uncertain. Thus, on 28 May 1767, Sultan Mohammed III signed the treaty of Marrakesh with King Charles III of Spain, through which he recognised that:

> His Imperial Majesty has reservations to deliberate on the colonial trade spot His Catholic Majesty intends to set up to the south of river Noun because he cannot take the responsibility of accidents and sorrows, his domination does not extend to that limit. . . . From Santa Cruz to the North, his Imperial Majesty allows people from the Canary Islands and Spain to fish but not any other nation.
>
> (Mercer 1976a: 96)

In the Treaty of Meknes signed with Spain in 1799, Morocco indicated that the Oued Noun itself was not under its sovereignty. However, at the end of the eighteenth century, the enthronisation of the emir of the Trarza confederation depended on the sultan of Morocco (Mercer 1976a). Without the support of Morocco the Trarza confederation would not have survived.

In 1859, Spain launched its African war against Morocco and was able to impose its conditions through the Treaty of Tetouan, which was signed a year later. Spain obtained a possession around the site where the fort of Santa Cruz de Mar Pequeña was situated, but without indicating its precise localisation.

At the end of the nineteenth century, the southern part of Morocco was still a *bilad Al-Siba* or a land which the throne did not control. While the Moroccan sultan tried to retain trade links with the Western Sahara, the Spanish authorities attempted to stop a Scottish merchant company from setting up a colonial trade post in the region of Rio de Oro. In 1895, a treaty was signed between the Moroccan and British authorities stipulating that 'no power will make claims on the territories extending from Oued Draa to Cape Bojador called Tarfaya . . . because these territories belong to Morocco' (Wikipedia 2012).

This treaty was one of the documents Morocco displayed before the International Court of Justice (ICJ) in 1975 in order to prove its claims over these territories. However, the ICJ confirmed that the British diplomatic correspondence of that time indicated that the region of Cape Juby did not belong to Morocco, whose limits ended at Oued Draa. The Court stated that, by signing this treaty, the British authorities had only admitted the pretensions of the Moroccan sultan's claim over the southern parts and had not recognised Morocco's sovereignty over these territories.

Some writings however confirm the recognition by foreign powers of Moroccan sovereignty over Rio de Oro, such as the letter sent by the French ambassador to Tangiers. In contrast, the convention signed by France and Spain in 1904 indicated that the government of the French Republic recognised that Spain had, from that day, all the freedom of action over the territories situated between 26 degrees and 27 degrees 40 minutes north and from the 11th meridian west of Paris, which are outside the limits of Morocco. Furthermore, there was no official document from that period which clearly shows the sovereignty of Morocco over the Western Sahara (Wikipedia 2012).

Fishermen from Spain and the Canary Islands operated near the coast of the Western Sahara, which was renowned for its fish wealth. Thus, many fishing companies were created at the end of the nineteenth century in order to exploit the sea wealth of this territory. Spain was the first Western power to claim rights over the territory, as attested by treaties concluded between Spanish fishing companies and some of the chiefs of the Saharawi tribes and by the construction of landing platforms and colonial trading posts. On 26 December 1884, Spain proclaimed the formation of a protectorate called Rio de Oro stretching from the coast of Bojador to White Cape (Bahia del Este). Villa Cisneros was chosen as the administrative city of this protectorate. This move, which was facilitated by the indigenous population, helped to put an end to the efforts of a Scottish merchant company that aimed at setting up colonial trading posts along this part of the Atlantic coast. On 6 April 1887 the Spanish protectorate was extended to Saguia al Hamra, which was placed under the indirect authority of the general governor of the Canary Islands.

The first stages of the Spanish protectorate were confronted with unrest from the local tribes (Ouled Delim) in 1887, March 1892 and November 1894. Furthermore, bloody attacks were committed against employees of the Compañía Mercantíl Hispano-Africana in Villa Cisneros in March 1898, despite the existence of an agreement signed on 2 March 1895 between the representatives of Ouled Delim and the Spanish authorities (Wikipedia 2012).

On 27 June 1900, France and Spain signed the Paris Treaty, which delimited the frontier between Rio de Oro (then under Spanish domination) and Mauritania, which was a French colony at that time (Jensen 2005: 41). The Paris Convention fixed the borders of Saguia Al Hamra and Cape Juby (southern Spanish Morocco) on 4 October 1904, and the Madrid Convention confirmed these borders and fixed the frontiers of the enclave of Ifni in November 1912, following the establishment of the French protectorate over Morocco (Wikipedia 2012).

Resistance against Spanish occupation of the Western Sahara began to emerge with the appeal by a religious chief, Ma al-Ainin, after he had succeeded in setting up a powerful *ribat* (urban and military centre) in Smara for a holy war launched in 1895 (Mercer 1976a). The sultan of Morocco provided this tribal leader with arms and financial aid, hoping to obtain from him the recognition of Moroccan sovereignty over the Western Sahara and Mauritania. Instead, Ma al-Ainin came to occupy the colonial trading post established by the Scottish merchant company in Cape Juby and organised a fierce resistance against the French in the Mauritanian Adrar in 1905. Repeated clashes with the French army occurred in 1908–09, but the resistance of Ma al-Ainin ended with the defeat of his troops in June 1910. One of his sons, Ahmed al-Hiba, extended his power over the Western Sahara and, with his other brothers, he managed to attack garrisons inside the French-dominated Moroccan protectorate. However, the resistance of the Saharawis began to fade away as the French succeeded in beating the Reguibat tribes in 1934. The Spanish colonial authorities completed their control of the Western Sahara with the support of auxiliary forces which were recruited from among the nomads.

Under Spanish rule

Gradually Spain succeeded in creating the colonial territory of Western Sahara, and with that began the formation of the Saharawi nation. The way of life of the Saharawi people did not change considerably under the Spanish occupation. Colonial political economy barely touched their lifestyle. They lived as nomad pastoralists and maintained ancient traditions such as tribal assemblies (*jemaa*) and specific Islamic justice and customs (*orf*). The Spanish presence was confined to a few cities where the colonisers traded with nomad merchants. During the Second World War, the Spanish authorities started to improve the social and economic conditions of the Western Sahara. Thus they founded Spanish Western Africa in 1947, which included Ifni, the Tarfaya band, Saguia Al Hamra and Rio de Oro.

Since the 1950s, successive droughts have pushed a large portion of the nomad population into settling down in urbanised areas and coming into contact with the Spanish authorities. However, these relations did not fail to create tensions between the two communities over the colonial status of the Western Sahara territory.

After it gained independence in 1956, Morocco attempted to complete the project of 'Greater Morocco', following the design of Allal Al Fassi, the leader of the nationalist party, Istiqlal. He disclosed a map that claimed a geographic configuration which enclosed territories from Mauritania down to the Senegal River as well as large swathes of the Algerian territory. In the Moroccan discourse, 'historic rights' went back to ancient times and continued throughout the rule of the Alawite dynasties, which started in 1645. This official rhetoric asserted that Morocco was divided in 1912 into three administrative zones: French, Spanish protectorate, and Tangiers, which was granted an international status. It claimed also that Morocco had lost to Spain the towns of Ceuta, Melilla and Ifni situated on its northern coast, as well as the Western Sahara and the cities of Al Huceimas, Valez and Chaffarina, which were located in the southern flank of its territory.

Therefore, Morocco opposed the independence of Mauritania from France in 1960. Mauritania in turn claimed Western Sahara as an integral part of a territorial entity called 'Greater Mauritania', as expressed by its president, Mokhtar Ould Daddah, in 1957. There was no doubt that the discovery of large phosphate deposits in 1947 explained the real motivations of both Morocco and Mauritania for their claim over Western Sahara. In parallel, Saharawi nationalism was consolidated against the territorial claims of the two countries.

In order to get rid of Spanish domination over Ifni and the Western Saharan territory, Morocco set up the national liberation army of Southern Morocco in 1956. Meanwhile, Spain announced the creation of Spanish Sahara on 1 January 1958 through the regrouping of Rio de Oro and Saguia Al Hamra. In the same year, Spain restored Tarfaya to Morocco and dissolved Spanish Western Africa. The two regions of Rio de Oro and Saguia Al Hamra became Spanish provinces and were represented in the Spanish parliament, the Cortes. The city of Laayoune was elevated to the status of the capital of Spanish Sahara. Furthermore, measures to develop the territory were accompanied by the convening of local elections, which were conducted every two years from 1963. Finally, the Spanish colonial authorities set up a territorial assembly (the *Jemaa*) in 1967, but with no real powers.

Resistance to the Spanish colonial grip was sporadic but never ceased, as highlighted by the rebellions that occurred in 1957 and 1958. The first movement claiming the independence of the territory was El Frente de Liberacíon Bajo La Dominacíon Española (Front for the Liberation of the Sahara from Spanish Domination), which was created in 1966. As this movement failed to reach its objectives, another movement, called Harakat Tahrir Saguia Al Hamra wa Wadi Adhab (Liberation Movement of Saguia Al Hamra and Rio de Oro), was created under the leadership of Mohammed Bassiri a year later. This leader died in jail after he was arrested by Spanish colonial forces during a bloody conflict organised by Saharawi militants in June 1970 (Pennell 2003: 335). Another party, the Movement of Blue Men (Le Mouvement des Hommes Bleus, or Morehob), was created by Eduard Moha in 1969 which challenged the trend that advocated independence. Moha instead advocated the rejoining of the Western Sahara territory with Morocco.

To hasten the decolonisation process of the territory and to undermine the idea of the reunion with Morocco, El Frente Popular de Liberacíon de Saguia El Hamra y Rio de Oro (Popular Front of Liberation of Saguia Al Hamra and Rio de Oro, or

Polisario) was founded in 1973 by a group of Saharawis attending universities in Morocco led by El-Ouali Mustapha Sayed. This front quickly engaged in an armed struggle against Spanish colonial rule and carried out concerted attacks on Spanish military targets inside the Western Sahara territory. Both Morocco and Spain reacted by setting up allied movements, which however proved too weak to contest Polisario's ascendancy and political credo among the Saharawi population.

The process of annexation of Western Sahara and contradicting claims

This section examines the process of annexation of the territory of Western Sahara following the jettisoning of the territory by Spain in 1975. It also examines the contradictory claims over the territory made by Morocco and the Polisario. When the winds of decolonisation were sweeping the world, the General Assembly of the United Nations enacted the renowned Declaration on the Granting of Independence to Colonial Countries and Peoples on 14 December 1960 (UN Resolution 1514(XV)).

This declaration stemmed from the principle of safeguarding the territorial integrity and the inviolability of the frontiers of existing states. It stemmed also from the determination to permit peoples and territories under colonial rule to gain independence. The achievement of the decolonisation process and the crumbling of colonial empires became the *leitmotiv* of the United Nations in the early 1960s under the impulse of the two superpowers of that time. These efforts allowed the emergence of the Third World, which gathered the newly formed states as the result of independence gained from Great Britain and France through a more or less violent process. Other territories still under colonial domination or mandates, such as the Western Sahara, were expected to follow suit.

On Morocco's request, the Western Sahara question was inscribed by the United Nations in the list of non-autonomous territories in 1963, probably because King Hassan was convinced that the Saharawi population would overwhelmingly opt for the integration of the territory with his country. Morocco also expressed strong reservations to the principle of the inviolability of frontiers inherited from colonialism that was adopted by the Organisation of African Unity (OAU), which was created in 1963.The implicit objective of Morocco was to contest the delimitation of its own borders, which the Moroccan rulers believed were drawn arbitrarily during the colonial era. In doing so, they intended to regain the land they assumed they had lost. Thus, they did not recognise the independence of Mauritania and waged a war against Algeria in October 1963, which lasted a few days only. The conflict between the two countries was finally settled through the good offices of Haile Selassie, the emperor of Ethiopia, under the OAU's guidance in conformity with the charter of the organisation, which had established the sacrosanct principle of the inviolability of frontiers inherited from the colonial era. The OAU's objective was to avoid a scramble on the subject of borders, which would have resulted in violent conflicts and the redrawing of the African map. Political realism prevailed over ethics, despite the claims of tribal groups for self-rule. Many of these groups considered themselves to be the victims of the arbitrary division of African peoples which was made on the basis of the geo-strategic and economic interests of the colonial powers.[1]

While respect for the sovereignty of states and the inviolability of borders inherited from the colonial era remained unquestioned for the OAU, the desire to achieve decolonisation was also gaining ground. Thus, on 17 December 1965 the United Nations General Assembly adopted Resolution 2072 (XX) recommending that Spain immediately take measures to lead to and engage in negotiations over the independence of Ifni and the Western Sahara. Until 1974, Morocco complied with these recommendations, being perhaps convinced that the outcome of the referendum would confirm its sovereignty over the Western Sahara. However, when news of an eventual withdrawal of Spain (Operation Swallow) was disclosed (Miguel 2003), King Hassan decided to take over this territory by initiating multifarious strategies. Such a decision seemed to have been motivated by other urgent objectives, rather than the argument of 'achieving national territorial integrity'.

It was argued, for instance, that the strategy initiated by the Moroccan ruler to take over the Western Sahara was intended to consolidate the legitimacy of the throne. It would rally the nation around an issue that would cement national unity and divert the army's attention away from domestic policies. Indeed, King Hassan escaped two attempted military coups in 1972 and 1973. It was also assumed that this strategy would help Morocco alter the balance of power in the Maghreb, which was largely in favour of Algeria. King Hassan's belief was that a takeover of the Western Sahara would boost the economic capabilities of his country. Indeed, Morocco became the world's first country to export phosphates, started to exploit the fish resources of the Western Sahara and was expected to benefit from the hydrocarbon wealth in which the territory was believed to be rich.

To achieve his objectives, King Hassan asked the ICJ to answer this question: 'Was the territory really subject to no state (*terra nullius*) when the Spaniards colonised it and, if not, what legal ties linked its inhabitants to those of Morocco and Mauritania?'

King Hassan believed the Court would confirm the legal links existing between the Saharawi population and the Moroccan rulers. Contrary to Moroccan claims however the Court found that, while there were indeed links between the Moroccan sultan and the inhabitants of parts of the Western Sahara and similar ties with Mauritania, there were no ties of sovereignty.[2]

Believing that 'it only remains to reintegrate our Sahara whose doors have been opened to us', King Hassan launched the 'green march' through sending 350,000 marchers and more than 25,000 soldiers to the Western Sahara on 31 October 1975. Morocco and Mauritania obtained a partition of the territory from Spain through the Madrid Agreements concluded on 14 November 1975 thanks to the manoeuvres of the pro-Moroccan members of the Spanish government during the brutal rule of President Franco.[3] The Moroccan king also managed to obtain approval for his move from a so-called Saharawi *jemaa* (people's assembly), which the Polisario Front did not consider legitimate.

The United Nations Security Council took a resolution (no. 380) on 6 November 1975 through which it 'deplored the holding of the march' and called upon Morocco 'to withdraw immediately from the territory of the Western Sahara all the participants in the march' (Zoubir 2007).

The Polisario Front rejected 'the fait accompli' and so did Algeria, which has ever since lobbied for the holding of a referendum under United Nations auspices and provided the Polisario Front with staunch support (Boukhari 2004). In Moroccan discourse, Algeria was inevitably depicted as advocating the independence of the Saharawi people and was accused of fuelling the tensions between the two countries.[4] Algeria has repeatedly stated that its support for the Saharawi cause stems from its own colonial past and complies with the resolutions taken by the United Nations on the Western Sahara. This issue has poisoned relations between the two Maghreb states. The difference was also generated by different ideological conceptions and security strategies.

Under pressure from the Polisario Front, Mauritania gave up its claims over the Western Sahara after the downfall of President Mokhtar Ould Daddah in July 1978. The next step was to pull out of the portion of the territory (Tiris Al-Gharbiya) it had received from Spain. Morocco then occupied the land from which the Mauritanians had withdrawn. Such a move was 'vigorously condemned' by the United Nations.[5]

In order to preserve 'the useful Sahara' it had conquered, Morocco went on to build a 1,200-kilometre sand and stone wall (*berm*, or *rabotu* as the Saharawis call it), 2 to 3 metres high and heavily protected by barbed wire, landmines and sophisticated surveillance devices. Meanwhile, thousands of Saharawi refugees were moved to remote desert camps situated about 180 kilometres from the southwestern Algerian city of Tindouf. They have since then been totally dependent on humanitarian aid.

In the early 1980s, the Polisario Front responded by using desert-adapted guerrilla tactics to harass the Moroccan troops in the disputed territory. The OAU adopted Resolution AHG 104 in 1984, which reaffirmed the right of the Saharawi people to self-determination. It also called on Morocco and the Polisario Front to engage in direct negotiations, to accept a cease-fire and to organise a referendum. In September of the same year, King Hassan declared his commitment to the holding of the referendum when addressing the UN General Assembly. From 1986, Javier Perez de Cuellar, the UN secretary-general, became personally involved in trying to find a solution to the pending conflict, but Morocco refused to accept direct negotiations with the Polisario Front prior to the UN mediation. The Polisario Front on its part requested direct administration of Western Sahara by the United Nations. It also requested the deployment of a joint UN–OAU force and the withdrawal of Moroccan troops from the territory as well as of non-Saharawi residents. These conditions were regarded by the Polisario Front as a priority before convening any referendum. In August 1988, the United Nations presented the joint settlement proposal to the two belligerent parties. This proposal, drafted by a top-level joint task force set up by the UN and OAU, received acceptance in principle by both Morocco and the Polisario Front in 1988.

These new developments were the result of the end of the Cold War, the easing of political frictions between Algeria and Morocco and the conviction reached by the Polisario Front that the solution to the conflict would not come from a military confrontation only. Therefore, the Polisario Front declared a truce unilaterally, and King Hassan met a Saharawi delegation in Marrakesh in January 1989. Both parties continued a dialogue in February and September of the same year.

In June 1990, the United Nations secretary-general presented the settlement plan to implement the UN–OAU proposals. This plan received the approval of the UN Security Council, and a mission known as MINURSO was dispatched to the Western Sahara in April 1991. It was tasked with monitoring a cease-fire and organising the long-postponed referendum on self-determination.

The referendum was due to be held no later than February 1992, but its implementation faced hurdles owing to disagreements over the size of the voting population (Saharawis residing in the disputed territory, the refugees living in camps near the Algerian border, and Moroccans posing as Saharawis as the Polisario Front suspected).[6] However, the real reasons behind Morocco's blockade of the countdown could be explained by the uncertainty of the referendum outcome, the political instability of Algeria, which went on throughout the 1990s, and the positions of the United Nations and France, which favoured the Moroccan stand (Zoubir 2007).

Therefore, an alternative to the referendum was proposed by the then United Nations secretary-general, Kofi Annan, but was rebuffed by the Security Council. Thus, the former US secretary of state James Baker was named as United Nations envoy to the Western Sahara in order to find a solution to the problem. He drafted a peace plan after he had succeeded in bringing Moroccans and Saharawis face to face in June 2002 for the first time. The plan proposed a period of autonomy for the Western Sahara under provisional Moroccan sovereignty, followed by a referendum through which Saharawi settlers would vote for either integration with Morocco or independence. The plan was accepted by Morocco but was rejected by the Polisario Front on the basis that it favoured the Moroccan standpoint. The former's position was further enhanced by a UN document issued in 2002 which considered Morocco as an administrative authority over the Western Sahara for the first time.[7] A revised plan (known as Baker Plan II) was issued in 2003, but this time Morocco did not accept it. It appears that the 'winner-takes-all' approach has prevailed in both cases.

Various resolutions of the United Nations calling for a referendum to determine the fate of the Western Sahara irremediably failed because of Morocco's refusal and the veto applied by both France and the USA.[8] In these conditions, the UN Security Council opted for direct negotiations between the two belligerent parties at its October 2005 meeting. In April 2006, Kofi Annan shifted the responsibility on to the two belligerent parties to find a solution to their conflicting claims and appointed Peter van Walsum as his special envoy to the Western Sahara. However, this solution should be 'just and durable, mutually accepted and permit the self-determination of the Western Sahara', as stated by the resolution adopted by the Security Council at its April 2007 meeting.[9]

Various informal meetings between the Moroccan and Saharawi delegations were held in Manhasset, New York from July 2007. All these meetings proved to be in vain, as the Moroccan 'large autonomy plan' clashed with Polisario's wish for independence.

Persistent stalemate in Western Sahara and evolving dangers

In a thorough and highly pertinent study, William Zartman, a distinguished US scholar, has reviewed four options that would help to resolve the Western Sahara issue. The first two options involve a compromise, either territorial or functional. These concern partition of the territory with its own government but under Moroccan sovereignty. The result would avoid the zero-sum, winner-takes-all characteristics. The third option relates to affording the region a transnational status, for instance placing it in the Union of the Arab Maghreb (UMA).[10] The fourth option relates to compensation, in which some external value would 'buy' the support of one of the two interested parties (Zartman 2007).

The first option (partition of the territory) was never accepted by the two sides. The second type (functional), which duplicated the 'autonomy plan' proposed by Morocco, was also categorically rejected by the Polisario Front. The 'autonomy plan' provides domestic prerogatives for the Saharawi people with regard to local administration, police forces, jurisdictions, economic planning, investment, trade, budget, taxation, social welfare and cultural heritage. However, the Moroccan state 'will keep its powers in the legal royal domain, especially with defence, external relations and the constitutional prerogatives of his Majesty the King'.[11] For Morocco everything may be negotiable, except 'the stamp and the flag', as King Hassan once declared. For the Polisario Front, everything may be negotiable except the right to self-determination.

On many occasions, the Polisario Front has expressed commitment to accept the results of the referendum whatever they are. It has also declared that it would negotiate with Morocco concerning giving guarantees to Moroccans who have resided in the Western Sahara for more than ten years in the event that the referendum leads to independence. In addition, the Polisario Front has promised to provide Morocco with guarantees with regard to political, economic and security concerns.

If the entrenched 'zero-sum' attitude continues (Morocco rejecting the referendum and the Polisario Front opposing the 'autonomy plan') it could lead to indefinite stalemate. The consequences of this stalemate will be the endangering of peace and stability in the region. In the light of new developments and of what has taken place so far, it is difficult to envisage a quick resolution of the Saharawi problem.

It seems unlikely that Morocco will abandon its 'autonomy plan', as the Saharan question is driven by the logics of internal politics. Equally unlikely is that the Polisario Front will reverse its advocacy for self-determination. The Polisario has grown out of an anti-colonial movement, involving nearly 40 years of militant activism. It has unwaveringly adhered to its self-proclaimed Democratic

Republic, which also succeeded in getting membership in the OAU and later the African Union (AU).

It is in addition hard to see Algeria turning its back on the Saharan cause after all the efforts it has made in support of the self-determination principle. To abandon 'a just cause' and 'a genuine' liberation movement, thereby depriving it of the right to achieve independence, as the Algerian official discourse proclaims, may be seen as a betrayal of Algeria's sacrosanct foreign policy principles.

Given these facts the Western Sahara problem may continue to be a destabilising factor in the region. This could be witnessed by the growing resistance of the Saharawis living in the areas occupied by Morocco, where frequent protests, riots, hunger strikes and clashes with the security forces have been taking place since May 2005. According to the Polisario Front's secretary-general, Mohamed Abdelaziz, this unrest seemed to have extended to cities situated in South Morocco, such as Zak, as was seen in September 2007.[12] More violent protests also occurred in November 2010, which led to the dismantling of a camp set up by Saharawi rioters in the suburbs of the city of Laayoune. These clashes were regarded as constituting the first flame of what came to be known as the 'Arab spring'. Apparently these disparate demonstrations were conducted by Saharawi youngsters and have endogenous roots. It is not clear that an autonomy status for the Western Sahara would attenuate the claims of the Saharawi youth to distinctive identity and national aspirations. Therefore, political and social unrest might remain a continuous feature of the region. Saharawi and international organisations have recently reported increased abuses of human rights and repressive policies carried out by Moroccan troops in the occupied Saharan territory.

Even if 'a third-way autonomy' is put in motion, the future of the Saharawi refugees living in camps near the Algerian border will not be easy to foresee. Despair would incite some prominent refugees to defect to Morocco and would alter the legitimacy of the Polisario Front.[13] For the leaders of the movement, these defections are a part of their strategy to infiltrate the Saharawis residing in the territory occupied by Morocco and consolidate support for the right to self-determination. In any case, the 'integration' of exogenous elements would prove hard for the Moroccan authorities because of the difficulties of adaptation, pressing social and economic demands and possible tensions between the local population and these repatriates.

The attempt to urge the Saharawi refugees living near the Algerian border to move to a third country, as the Moroccan authorities have recently requested, may further complicate the case of refugees, as observed in Pakistan, and the Great Lakes in Sub-Saharan Africa. If the Saharawi refugees are prevented from returning to their homeland because of Moroccan occupation, how would they opt to live elsewhere? Moreover, mass defections expected from the exchange of family visits recently organised by the United Nations high commissioner for refugees have failed to happen. The relations between indigenous Western Saharawis and settlers of Moroccan origin (referred to as *Dakhilis*, or non-Saharawis) are reported to be tense and may lead to violent confrontation in the future. Granting greater autonomy to the Saharawi population might have serious political consequences for the Moroccan state. It could have a domino effect, with other regions demanding similar rights. For this reason the Moroccan government was very cautious about opening the system and creating a democratic society; instead it is sticking to a highly centralised state system that preserves the prerogatives of the ruling class.

Moroccan media and scholars have reported the existence of links between the Polisario Front and some terrorists groups of Al-Qai'dah in the Islamic Maghreb (AQIM) operating in the Sahel–Sahara region. Some of these reports have also accused the Polisario guerrillas of being implicated in terrorist-affiliated networks of drug smuggling.[14] Attempts to tarnish the Saharawi movement with either terrorism or drug trafficking may lead only to the strengthening of the stature of AQIM and its affiliated smuggling networks. They would also complicate the efforts to fight the propagation of *jihad* (holy war) and the expansion of religious extremism in the Sahel–Sahara region, as was observed in North Mali. In an attempt to deny the allegations made against his movement, Mohamed Abdelaziz, the secretary-general of the Polisario Front, asserted that 'the Moroccan drug traffic is at the origin of insecurity in the Sahel'.[15]

Amid these intricate risks and threats, what is the way forward in the near future? On the basis of the concerns recounted above, two sets of questions can be raised. One set relates to Morocco, while the other relates to Polisario. With regard to Morocco pertinent questions are: Can Morocco still keep investing a large part of its diplomatic efforts on the Western Sahara? Will it be able to sustain increasing military expenditures and the arms race it has engaged in with Algeria?[16] Do the advantages it draws from the Western Sahara compensate for these efforts? With regard to Polisario we could raise pertinent questions such as: Is the Polisario Front able to contain the impatience of its population, especially young people? It was assumed that the general feeling among Saharawi refugees is that 'We have lost patience, but not the war'. Can war be a possible answer? Can the Polisario Front force resolution of the issue militarily?[17] A further pertinent question, with regard to Algeria, is: Would Algeria be drawn into this conflict?

All these intricate questions are testimony to the complexity and difficulty of the Western Sahara quest for self-determination. The difficulties of finding adequate and relevant answers to these questions stem not only from the lack of data and absence of empirical studies, but also the unpredictability of the evolution of the Western Sahara quest for self-determination, except perhaps the 'attrition' dimension that has applied since the early 1980s.

An all-out war seems, however, perilous to the whole region. Equally, foreign powers would not encourage it, because the Maghreb is relatively important for the security of the southern flank of Europe, especially in the light of the political upheavals generated by the so-called Arab spring in some parts of North Africa. Stability in this region would attenuate threats perceived by Europe such as illegal migration, weapons of mass destruction (WMD) and drug trafficking, but most of all it would prevent what the Europeans and Americans are terrified of, the global expansion of terrorism.

Both Morocco and Algeria are important partners of the US and France, though old alliances may have lost some of their importance. Morocco is still regarded by the US as a reliable friend,[18] and the EU has granted it an 'advanced status' partnership.

Algeria is an important market for the products of the southern European countries and a reliable source of energy supplies for the EU. It had become a 'pivotal state' in the US fight against terrorism in the Sahel–Saharan confines, following the drive by Al-Qai'dah to establish a new operational base in the region from which to infiltrate West Africa. In addition, the rebellion of the Tuareg in North Mali has seriously threatened the territorial integrity of this country and the stability of its neighbours.[19] The threat became more tangible as the Sahel–Saharan region, which stretches from the Horn of Africa to the western Atlantic shores (Gulf of Guinea) and is considered to be of great importance to US interests (notably oil supplies), was subjected to serious dangers.

Many have stressed the need for the parties to come to some kind of understanding. In the end it is the parties themselves that should find a solution to their problems. The French president Jacques Chirac, for instance, stated that the 'autonomy plan' supported by France required 'the agreement of the principal parties' (Jensen 2005).

The US tried to adopt a 'positive neutrality' policy in order to avoid hurting or alienating either Algeria or Morocco. In July 2009, President Obama sent a letter to the Moroccan king in which he expressed the wish that the United Nations special envoy to the Western Sahara, Christopher Ross, should 'reach the promotion of a constructive dialogue between the parties'.[20] He also insisted on a solution to be worked out by the belligerents. The US position remains confused, as it indicates that the autonomy plan proposed by Morocco is a serious option, while referring at the same time to the necessity of respecting the will of the Saharawi people. The joint statement issued at the end of the visit of the Moroccan king to Washington in November 2013 asserted that:

> the President pledged to continue to support efforts to find a peaceful, sustainable, mutually agreed upon solution to the Western Sahara question. . . . The US has made clear that Morocco's autonomy plan is serious, realistic and credible, and that it represents a potential approach that could satisfy the aspirations of the people of the Western Sahara to run their own affairs in peace and dignity. We continue to support the negotiations carried out by the United Nations, including the work of the UN Secretary-General's personal envoy Ambassador Christopher Ross, and urge the parties to work toward a resolution.
>
> (White House sources, http://m.allafrica.com/stories/
201311251371.html/, accessed 25 November 2013)

However, the declaration did not constitute a clear indication of the recognition by Washington of Morocco's sovereignty over the Western Sahara. Both the UN Security Council and the US State Department have repeatedly deplored the abuse of human rights by the Moroccan authorities in the occupied parts of Western Sahara.[21] The Polisario Front has declared that these criticisms cannot be effective as long as MINURSO does not fulfil its initial mission assigned by the UN Security Council, which consists of organising a referendum for self-determination in the Western Sahara as soon as possible.[22]

Until now, the United Nations has not officially departed from its position of holding a referendum on the fate of the Western Sahara, and the proposals of its envoy are still awaited. The confirmation of Christopher Ross in his role as the special envoy to the Western Sahara by the UN Secretary-General, Ban Ki-moon (with the tacit support of the USA), may demonstrate the fact that Morocco's sovereignty over the Western Sahara territory has not yet been acknowledged by the UN.[23]

It is noteworthy that no major power has officially acknowledged the Moroccan hold over this territory. On the other hand, the Polisario self-declared Saharawi Arab Democratic Republic (RASD) is still a full member of the AU, which replaced the OAU in 2002. Although the RASD is a member of the AU, Morocco is not a member of this continental gathering (it withdrew from the OAU in protest at RASD's admission in 1985). The AU maintains that the Western Sahara question can be resolved only by the United Nations.

Ideally, a referendum could be convened after some kind of understanding has been reached that, whatever the outcome, the involved parties would resolutely engage in the process of strengthening the UMA, for instance. This could be a major move, especially because this organisation ultimately aims at ensuring the political unity and economic integration of the region.

Such a deal would remove the border obstacles and nationalistic interests that have been among the factors impairing the process of creating a united Maghreb. Thus, trade exchanges, common development projects and security arrangements would be possible. It is in this direction that foreign powers and the international community should push forward. And, equally, no party will benefit from either the status quo or an armed conflict.

Conclusion

Appraising a conflict that has lasted for so long and whose outcome seems quite remote may not be an easy task. This is due to the complexities of the decolonisation process of the Western Sahara territory. Indeed, the Saharawi quest for self-determination was badly handled by Spain through its failure to complete its decolonisation mandate by setting up a referendum that would guarantee the right of the Saharawi people to self-determination in conformity with United Nations resolutions. The case also proved hard to settle because of two irreconcilable nationalisms that make two diametrically opposed claims over a territory and over the fate of a people. While one side tends to believe that it has a de facto right to its claims (Morocco), the other (the Polisario Front) thinks that it has a legal and *moral* right (international legality) to recover its national claims.

The Western Sahara quest for self-determination constitutes an embarrassment to the United Nations. It miserably failed to resolve the situation under the decolonisation regime that saw the great bulk of colonies all over the world and especially in Africa attain political independence. Unlike many former African colonies in the past, the Western Sahara is not currently under the domination of powerful Western empires (Britain and France). It did not represent an important stake in East–West rivalry such as the Lusitanian African territories, for instance, and failed to arouse the interest of the superpowers. The result was that the decolonisation process of the Western Sahara was put in suspension indefinitely. On the contrary, Western powers, France and the USA in particular, driven by their geo-strategic interests, have been reluctant to put pressure on Morocco. Hence the stalemate may continue as long as France and the USA persist in favouring Morocco's stand. Such a stalemate could also go on indefinitely if other members of the Security Council (China and Russia) continue to show reluctance in pushing for the implementation of the UN resolutions.

It seems that the United Nations current disposition is tending towards catching up with the spirit of the Arab spring and the rise of the will of the people in the conduct of world affairs. Humanitarian bodies, relief agencies, independent personalities and civil societies may, in the future, have a stronger say over issues linked to the respect of human rights, the protection of civil populations and minorities, and the right of peoples to self-determination. The return of Christopher Ross, the special envoy to the Western Sahara, in October 2013 may be a good indication of this new mood that could be sweeping the United Nations.

The Western Sahara is a question of decolonisation that has yet to see its consummation. Like Eritrea and Namibia, it is a case of Western colonisation that in the era of decolonisation was transformed into a case of annexation a by neighbouring African state. Governed by the principle of decolonisation, Western Sahara represents one of the few cases that awaits the consummation of decolonisation. The AU, UN and international community are duty bound to put an end to this festering conflict.

Notes

1 The issue of peoples' rights for self-determination as against respect for state sovereignty still remains critical in African politics. The secession of Eritrea from Ethiopia, the division of Sudan into two states, the de facto existence of Somaliland and the current separatist attempts of the Tuareg nomads in Mali stand as real examples of attempts to redraw the geo-political map of Africa. Risks of the dislocation of Nigeria and Libya on the basis of religious tensions and economic interests in the future may not be simply theoretical.
2 A political scientist gave this testimony when he appeared as an expert in this case before the ICJ. See Benchenane (2002).
3 Notably prime minister Carrero Blanco.
4 For instance, Khalid Naciri, the minister of communication and government spokesman, stated that Polisario 'had no freedom of movement in its negotiations with Morocco due to Algerian domination' (*Moroccan Associated Press*, 28 April 2012).
5 Resolutions 3437/1979 and 3518/1980.

6 The Spanish 1974 census established the Saharawi population at 74,000 persons. With the Moroccan occupation, Moroccan residents and their descendants were estimated between 300,000 and 400,000 against 160,000 Saharawis (see Mundy 2006). The Polisario Front disclosed other figures, fixing the number of refugees living near Tindouf at 150,000. For a contradictory point of view, see Ammour (2006: 1–7).

7 Such a qualification, which would permit Morocco to exploit the natural resources of the Western Sahara, was not however mentioned on the UN's list of non-autonomous territories. Morocco effectively went on exploiting the riches of the Western Sahara, granted Western firms permits for mining and oil exploration in the territory and concluded agreements with the European Union (EU) concerning fishing facilities. The Polisario Front denounced these exploration permits as well as the conventions signed with the EU on the basis that: i) it was the Saharawi people who had the right of control over the natural resources; and ii) the signing of such agreements meant an implicit recognition of Morocco's domination over the Western Sahara. Under United Nations pressures and Polisario lobbying, the EU suspended in July 2011 the fishing agreement it has previously signed with Morocco.

8 In an interview to French-language, privately owned Algerian daily newspaper *El Watan*, Baba Mustapha Sayed, president of the Saguia Al Hamra and Rio de Oro Centre for Strategic and Political Studies, blamed France for blocking the execution of the resolutions adopted by the UN Security Council in favour of the right of the Saharawi people for self-determination (*El Watan*, 26 May 2012).

9 In *Liberté* (Algiers), 18 September 2007.

10 The Union of the Arab Maghreb was set up by the Treaty of Marrakesh signed by Morocco, Algeria, Libya, Tunisia and Mauritania in September 1999.

11 http://www.maec.gov.ma/initiative/En/default.asp.

12 *El Watan*, 20 October 2007.

13 One of the founders of the Polisario Front, Ould Souilem Souilem, defected to Morocco in July 2009 and was appointed ambassador to Spain. Similar discontent was voiced by the then police inspector-general of the Polisario, Mustapha Salma Ould Sidi Mouloud, who publicly endorsed Morocco's proposal to grant autonomy to Western Sahara in August 2010. That statement led to his imprisonment and then expulsion from the Saharawi refugee camps situated near the Algerian city of Tindouf (Murphy 2009).

14 Two young Saharawis were assumed to have kidnapped two Frenchmen in Hambori in north-eastern Mali at the end of October 2011 under the influence of 'the legend of Hakim Ould Mohamed M'Barek, alias Houdeifa, a major figure in Polisario AQIM' (see Boukhars 2012).

15 Interview to *El Watan*, 22 December 2011.

16 According to a Saharawi source based in Algiers, in 2014 there were in the territory under Moroccan control about 200,000 Moroccan armed forces, 130,000–159,000 Moroccan settlers and 350,000 Saharawi indigenous elements.

17 Sources set the troops of the Polisario Front at 3,000–6,000, but these figures were believed to be underestimated.

18 In June 2004, President George W. Bush hailed Morocco as 'a major non-NATO ally' a month before the visit made by King Mohammed VI to Washington.

19 At the beginning of 2012, the National Movement for the Liberation of Azawad (MNLA), which was formed by militias of Targui origin (a portion of a nomad people living in a huge Saharan space which transcends the frontiers of Mali, Niger and Burkina Faso), announced the setting up of an independent state from Mali, after decades of rebellions against the central authorities of the country. However, the MNLA's control of northern Mali has been strongly challenged by a dissident group called Ansar Eddine (the supporters of Islam) and by another pro-AQIM movement, the Movement for Unity and Jihad (MUJAO). Both parties have been engaged in terrorist activities and call for the establishment of a theocratic state and the rejection of Western as well as indigenous cultures.

20 *Le Quotidien d'Oran*, 4 November 2009.
21 See Resolution 2204 adopted by the Security Council on 24 April 2012. Further-more, in October 2012, Hillary Clinton's department sent a report severely criticising Moroccan policies towards the Saharawi population (*El Watan*, 6 October 2012).
22 Baba Mustapha Sayed interview to *Liberté*, Algiers, 26 October 2012.
23 Ross was rebuffed by Morocco on the basis of his favouring Polisario's stand. He resumed his mission by paying a visit to Rabat in late October 2012 as the first step of a new tour in the Maghreb and Sahara regions.

Bibliography

Addi, Lahouari. 2000. 'Claims on Western Sahara Hamper Maghreb Unity', *Le Monde Diplomatique*, June.

Aggad, Fatten. 2004. 'Western Sahara: Understanding the Conflict and Its Deadlock', Annual Conference, African Studies Association of Australia and the Pacific.

Ammour, Laurence. 2006. *A qui profite le gel du conflit du Sahara Occidental?*, Research Paper no. 30, November. Rome: Research Division Branch, NATO Defense College.

Ammour, Laurence. 2009. *An Assessment of Crime Related Risks in the Sahel*, Research Paper no. 63 (pp. 1–7). Rome: Research Division Branch, NATO Defense College.

Barbier, Maurice. 1982. *Le Conflit du Sahara Occidental*. Paris: L'Harmattan.

Benchenane, Mustapha. 2002. 'La situation géopolitique en Méditerranée', Conference of the Third Mediterranean Session of High Strategic Studies, Marseilles, 16 November.

Bodansky, Y. 2008. 'POLISARIO and the Algerian Power Struggle, with Itself and the West', *Defense and Foreign Affairs Strategic Policy*, vol. 1, no. 36.

Boilley, Pierre et al. 2012. 'La résistance Sahraouie à Gdaim Izig', *Cahiers des Etudes Multidisciplinaires*, vol. 8.

Bolton, John. 1998. *Resolving the Western Sahara Conflict*, Washington, DC: Congressional Defense and Foreign Policy Forum, Defense Forum Foundation.

Boukhari, Ahmed. 2004. *The International Dimension of the Conflict over the Western Sahara and Its Repercussions for a Moroccan Alternative*, Working Paper no. 6, April. Madrid: Elcano Royal Institute for International and Strategic Studies.

Boukhars, A. 2012. *Simmering Discontent in the Western Sahara*. Washington, DC: Carnegie Endowment for International Peace.

Daymani, Najib. 2011. 'Sahrawis Hope for Conflict Resolution', *Magharebia*, 6 September.

Fisher, Humphrey. 1970. 'The Western Sahara and Central Sudan', in P. M. Holt, A. K. S. Lambton and B. Lewis (eds), *The Cambridge History of Islam*, vol. 2. Cambridge: Cambridge University Press.

Gaudio, Attilio. 1978. *Le dossier du Sahara Occidental*. Paris: Nouvelles Editions Latines.

Goodman, David and Mekhennet, Souad. 2011. 'Morocco Says It Foiled Terror Cell in Sahara', *New York Times*, 5 January, www.nytimes.com/2011/01/06/world/africa/06morocco.html.

Hodges, Tony. 1983. *Western Sahara: The Roots of a Desert War*. Westport, CT: Lawrence Hill.

Hodges, Tony, 'La stratégie américaine et le conflit du Sahara Occidental', http//www.cesd.orgntonotes/notes51htm.

Husson, Philippe. 1960. *La question des frontières terrestres du Maroc*. Paris: Nouvelles Editions Latines.

Iratni, Belkacem. 2008. *Strategic Interests of the Maghreb States*, Forum paper, November. Rome: Research Division, NATO Defense College.

Iratni, Belkacem. 2010. 'The Western Sahara Conflict: Political Reverberations, Incidences on the Maghreb Union and Future Prospects', Conference, NRCC, NATO Defense College, Rome, 14 November.

Jensen, Erik. 2005. *Western Sahara: Anatomy of a Stalemate*, International Peace Academy Occasional Paper series. London: Lynne Rienner.

Junqua, Daniel. 1977. 'Au Sahara Occidental, la France a choisi son camp', *Croissance des Jeunes Nations*, no. 190, December.

Lagarde, Dominique and Larhdaf, Eddah Mohamed. 2001. 'Sahara: Le conflit ensablé', *L'Express*, 18 October.

Lugan, Bernard. 1996. *Histoire du Maroc: Des origines à nos jours*. Paris: Critérium.

Maclean, William. 2012. 'Analysis: Africa's Sahel Scrambles to Avert Slide into Hell', *Reuters*, 23 January, http://af.reuters.com/article/maliNews/idAFL5E8CN13M20120123?sp=true.

Mercer, John. 1976a. *Spanish Sahara*. London: George Allen & Unwin.

Mercer, John. 1976b. 'The Cycle of Invasion and Unification in the Western Sahara', *African Affairs*, vol. 75, no. 301, October.

Miguel, Carlo Ruiz. 2003. *El Largo camino Jurídico y Politico hacía el Plan Baker II: Estacíon de Termino?*, Working Paper 2003/19, 13 October. Madrid: Elcano Royal Institute for International and Strategic Studies.

Miské, Ahmed-Baba. 1978. *Le Front Polisario: L'Ame d'un people*. Paris: Editions Rupture.

Mundy, J. 2006. 'Autonomy and Intifada: New Horizons in the Western Sahara', *Review of African Political Economy*, no. 108, January.

Murphy, Colin. 2005. 'Thirty Years of Conflict: How the US and Morocco Seized the Spanish Sahara', *Le Monde Diplomatique*, November.

Murphy, Colin. 2009. 'Western Sahara Conflict Goes On', *Le Monde Diplomatique*, English edn, November.

Pennell, C. R. 2000. *Morocco since 1830*. New York: New York University Press.

Pennell, C. R. 2003. *Morocco: From Empire to Independence*. Oxford: Oneworld.

Perez de Cuellar, Javier. 2006. *Pilgrimage for Peace: A Secretary-General's Memoirs*. New York: Palgrave Macmillan.

Pham, J. Peter. 2010. 'Not Another Failed State: Toward a Realistic Solution in the Western Sahara', *Journal of the Middle East and Africa*, vol. 1, no. 1, pp. 1–24.

Saidy, B. 2011. 'American Interests in the Western Sahara Conflict', *American Foreign Policy Interests*, vol. 33, pp. 89–92.

Shelley, Toby. 2004. *Endgame in the Western Sahara: What Future for Africa's Last Colony?* London: Zed Books.

Simanovitz, Stephan. 2012. 'Western Sahara: Revolution or War?', *Think Africa Press*, 16 March.

Soudan, François. 2010. 'La longue marche d'Ahmedou Ould Souilem', *Jeune Afrique*, 9 June, www.jeuneafrique.com/Articles/Dossier/ARTJAJA2577p022-030.xml11/algerie-maroc-ambassadeur-mohammed-vila-longue-marche-d-ahmedou-ould-souilem.html.

Theofilopoulos, Anna. 2006. *The United Nations and Western Sahara: A Never-Ending Affair*, Special Report 166, July. Washington, DC: United States Institute of Peace.

Thobhani, Akbarali. *Western Sahara since 1075 under Moroccan Administration: Social, Economic and Political Transformation*. Lewiston, NY: Edwin Mellen Press.

Thompson, Virginia and Adloff, Richard. 1980. *The Western Sahara*. London: Croom Helm.

UN Resolution 1514(XV), http://www.unorg/fr/decolonisation:declaration:shtml.

Wikipedia. 2012. 'Histoire du Sahara occidental', http://fr.wikipedia.org/wiki/histoire_du_sahara_occidental (accessed 3 November 2012).

Zartman, William. 2007. 'Time for a Solution in the Western Sahara Conflict', *Middle East Policy*, vol. 14, no. 4, Winter, pp. 178–83.

Zoubir, H. Yahia. 2007. 'Stalemate in Western Sahara, Ending International Legality', *Middle East Policy*, vol. 14, no. 4, pp. 158–77.

Zoubir, H. Yahia and Gambier, Karima-Benabdellah. 2005. 'The United States and the North African Imbroglio: Balancing Interests in Algeria, Morocco and the Western Sahara', *Mediterranean Politics*, vol. 10, no. 2, July.

Zunes, S. 1987. 'Nationalism and Non-Alignment: The Non-Ideology of the Polisario', *Africa Today*, vol. 34, no. 3, pp. 33–46.

Index

For Product Safety Concerns and Information please contact our EU
representative GPSR@taylorandfrancis.com
Taylor & Francis Verlag GmbH, Kaufingerstraße 24, 80331 München, Germany

www.ingramcontent.com/pod-product-compliance
Ingram Content Group UK Ltd.
Pitfield, Milton Keynes, MK11 3LW, UK
UKHW021619240425
457818UK00018B/646